THE TRAN

P
SOULS
SPEAK

THROUGH ROBERT SHAPIRO

OTHER BOOKS BY ROBERT SHAPIRO

EXPLORER RACE SERIES

1 The Explorer Race

2 ETs and the Explorer Race

3 The Explorer Race: Origins and the Next 50 Years

4 The Explorer Race: Creators and Friends

5 The Explorer Race: Particle Personalities

6 The Explorer Race and Beyond

7 The Explorer Race: The Council of Creators

8 The Explorer Race and Isis

9 The Explorer Race and Jesus

10 The Explorer Race: Earth History and Lost Civilizations

11 The Explorer Race: ET Visitors Speak Vol. 1

12 The Explorer Race: Techniques for Generating Safety

13 The Explorer Race: Animal Souls Speak

14 The Explorer Race: Astrology: Planet Personalities and Signs Speak

15 The Explorer Race: ET Visitors Speak Vol. 2

16 The Explorer Race: Plant Souls Speak

17 The Explorer Race: Time and Beyond

MATERIAL MASTERY SERIES

A Shamanic Secrets for Material Mastery

B Shamanic Secrets for Physical Mastery

C Shamanic Secrets for Spiritual Mastery

SHINING THE LIGHT SERIES

Shining the Light: The Battle Begins!

Shining the Light II: The Battle Continues

Shining the Light III: Humanity Gets a Second Chance

Shining the Light IV: Humanity's Greatest Challenge

Shining the Light V: Humanity Is Going to Make It!

Shining the Light VI: The End of What Was

Shining the Light VII: The First Alignment—World Peace

ULTIMATE UFO SERIES

Andromeda: UFO Contact from Andromeda

Zetas, Hybrids and Human Contacts

SECRETS OF FEMININE SCIENCE SERIES

Book 1: Benevolent Magic & Living Prayer

Book 2: Disentanglement & Deep Disentanglement

Book 3: Disengagement, Engagement & Connections

SHIRT POCKET BOOKS SERIES

Touching Sedona

Feeling Sedona's ET Energies

HEALING ENERGIES OF LIVE PLANTS

PLANT
SOULS
SPEAK

THROUGH ROBERT SHAPIRO

3 LIGHT
Technology
PUBLISHING

* * *

ISBN-13: 978-1891824-74-6
ISBN-10: 1-891824-74-0

Light Technology Publishing, LLC
Phone: 800-450-0985
Fax: 928-714-1132
PO Box 3540
Flagstaff, AZ 86003
www.lighttechnology.com

Contents

ℰℭ

Herbs

Trees

Grasses

Grains

Beans

Ornamentals

INTRODUCTION

The Transformative Energies of Live Plants

ZOOSH, ISIS, AND GRANDFATHER SPEAKING AS A JOINED ENERGY

JULY 13, 2011

৪৩

GREETINGS. Learning to live on Earth is all about paying attention to life around you. The life around you is often quite vigorous, even shockingly so in the plant world. Sometimes those of you who have nice green lawns or perhaps green pastures are alarmed at the plants that will volunteer and grow vigorously. Others will welcome these plants without condemning them into the category of this or that weed and trying to eliminate them. Please know that all the plants you condemn as weeds are, in one way or another, intended to be supporting of you on a physical basis to cure all of your ills, physical and otherwise, and that even though they may not always be safe to consume in whole or in part, they are always safe to interact with on a living basis. For instance, as you might read in this book, you would just look at the plant from a short distance and breathe in and out; just breathe in and out, looking at the plant and absorbing the life and light-filled gifts the plant has to offer you.

You will read more about that when you get into the pages of the book itself, but I wish to speak to you very simply in this: All life on the Earth is alive. All has been created by the Creator of All Things—you have many names for this being. Since all has been created by the Creator of All Things, all is a portion of that being. I know there's a popular belief that evil or evil ones somehow have inflicted themselves on this creation, but this is not so—much as that can be, not exactly enjoyed or liked, but it can say in its own way that this or that horrible act has been caused because of evil ones (you know; you have many names for these beings). Creator of All Things has—and this is written in many books—given you, as you say, free will, but it is not will. Will has come to be known as something associated with the mind and, to a degree, with the physical actions of the body. But in fact, Creator has given you freedom, not just free will: freedom to interact with all life.

You Have Lost Much Ancient Wisdom
While Seeking to Gain Knowledge

In the beginning, you interacted with all life in a way that was perhaps too intimate (I'm talking about the beginning of human beings on Earth, you understand), and sometimes you touched things or ate things or came too close to things that weren't safe for you, and people were harmed or worse. But then, as always happens in situations where the beings on a given planet are meant to *do something as* well as meant to survive and thrive, there were other humans who said, "Wait! Don't touch. Maybe this is about something else." So then some of you began to observe: What are the plants doing? What are the animals doing? Why do they do that? In short, you learned by observation. Then came the time, eventually, of not only imitation of what the animals were doing and what the plants were doing but of the application of that knowledge and wisdom in your lives.

Over time, quite naturally, a body of knowledge and wisdom was built up, not as a myth, but as a practical application of how to live in the best possible way, whether times are hard or times are good. Much of this was brought about by observing the plants and the animals: What do they do? Well, you know very often that the animals will either gather more food or they will move; they will do something because they instinctually feel that they must. They do not question it, they do not argue about it; they do it. And thus they are more likely to survive and thrive.

Through observation, human beings learned how to do this as well, but then over time, human beings became more interested in the mind and the gathering of knowledge, and what was wisdom beforehand—knowing how to survive and thrive in times that were hard and times that were good—was transformed into being knowledge instead of wisdom. There's a difference: Wisdom is the experience—the application, you might say, of experience—that you use in your life on a regular, daily basis because it works, you see. That's wisdom, and it's not always the same for everyone. Some people will develop wisdom or even knowledge because of this or that desire by their soul. You understand these things.

So certain knowledge and wisdom came to be noted within the plant worlds as well. Sometimes it would be seen, for instance, that seeding plants would start to seed greatly—much more so than at any other time. And those who were observers of plant activity took note and said, "Hard times may be coming" or "There is something that is going to happen," and "Look at the tree! Look at the plants, how they seed this year much more so than ever before" (though they wouldn't say "this year"; they would say "this season" in their own language). And so the peoples would be ready to migrate at a moment's notice because they knew that if the trees and the plants were seeding so much that something was going to happen. So they were always ready to move, and that's how not only peoples began to be more nomadic but how they also began to be more quickly nomadic. [Chuckles.]

Now, I don't want to go into too much because you learn more in the book, but just to go on a little more: In time then, this wisdom accumulated through centuries and was passed on to this group and that group and reconfirmed by observing the animals and by observing the plants and what they do, and then noting—if not immediately, then in time—"Ah, this is why they did that!" You see, in this way, a body of wisdom was built up. Why? Because wisdom is the knowledge in your life that you apply because it works, and when wisdom works, one does it without question—without the questions that are in the mind. The mind can accept that because the mind understands that one thing leads to another. However, remember what the animals have: instinct. Creator of All Things has given you this as well, and I referred to it before as freedom.

Knowing that, you can then follow along a little more easily, because you can see where I'm going. Once wisdom, as it was known and understood all over the world, began to be converted in the minds of people into knowledge, it became equal with other knowledge, but it lost its value as wisdom. Then it was necessary for humankind to begin to transform the world in ways that involved, yes, initially tools and then also the shaping of the world, which involved parts of the world being converted into things that served the human being. And before long, you had the Age of Technology.

Thus there was the transformation of what was initially the old wisdom: Instead of interacting with the living plants, instead of interacting with the living animals, the old wisdom was transformed into knowledge, and humans began interacting with the animals only when they were dead and using their parts to consume, or only interacting with the plants when they were dead and using their parts to heal and support and also to consume. Do you see? Then what is cherished as wisdom because it works simply falls into words, which is knowledge. Knowledge can be helpful, but wisdom brings about survival and often the opportunity to thrive and to be well for yourself and others.

In this book you will learn some of the old wisdom again. It will not be taught as a philosophy, as something you must learn. It will not be thrust upon you as if to say you must abandon your beliefs, your understanding of the world—none of that. The old wisdom will be shared so that you can discover how to interact with the plants while they are alive, while they are a portion of the Creator of All Things. And with this, you will learn the beginnings, the reminders—and for many of you, the fulfillment—of the transformation of that which does not work in your body, in your life, in your community, and in your world: the transformation of what you call dis-ease or disharmony into harmony and ease.

✳   ✳   ✳

Bamboo Spirit

MAY 5, 2009

ℭ

The purpose of this book is primarily to help you to ease your life and the lives of others. By creating a system of specific details, you will be able to intersect with that moment of life between yourself and plants that will help you avail yourself of the opportunity to become healthier, acquire greater wisdom and capacities, and most importantly, cure or prevent a great many diseases, some of which are profoundly interfering with your well-being

What more can we go into about interacting with the live plant? Is there more beyond what is being said by the plant beings?

There may be more for the advanced practitioner of the kind of study this book is suggesting, but I feel it's first important to get people started. You'll notice that no particular plant goes into very elaborate detail about long-term interactions with the plant. That's because all plants are attempting to serve the most immediate needs, in their perception, for the human being. Once you establish better health through this type of interaction with the living plant, then we'll see.

HERBS

CHAPTER ONE

Dandelion

DECEMBER 18, 2007

GREETINGS, THIS IS DANDELION.

Greetings, Dandelion. Okay. Welcome!

Now, this book is going to follow a different process. Many uses of plants are known by herbalists and shamanic healers in your time, as well as people with knowledge of medicine. So as a representative of the plants, what we intend to speak about—if I may speak in general for everyone—is how you can interact with plants in a more benevolent way for you as the human species.

For a long time, you have been clear on medicinal uses of leaves, stems, seeds, flower petals, and so on, but you are only getting about one-tenth of the healing energy available for you that way. It is always better to interact with the plant in its live form, but you need to know how. Ancient peoples knew how, and that is why, contrary to a great deal of theories, ancient peoples lived long lives without disease. They had been taught how to interact with all species around them in the most benevolent ways for themselves, the plants, and the animals. The intention with this book is to reveal that formula, so that you as a human race can stop searching for the magical cures to diseases by exhausting the supply of life forms around you when a much simpler process is available. So

3

I believe this book will be another valuable contribution in the long line of books that you have been treading on that path to produce.

You Must Form a Personal Relationship with the Seeds You Plant

I want to begin in the case of speaking for myself. I am but a single dandelion. Generally speaking, you will find in this book that individual plants will speak because we are always connected to the full range of knowledge and wisdom of who we are, who we've been, where we're from—everything. No secrets on the basis of species wisdom are withheld from us. Also, we have connections to other wisdom that may help you.

Now, without further ado, let me simply say how to interact with plants. For those of you who have gardens that are struggling: As you know, sometimes it's the soil and sometimes it's little beings who are causing problems, yes? But before you even plant anything—seeds too—if you expect to have the best results, you must form a personal relationship with the seeds. If they come in a packet, take them out of the packet. You don't have to wash your hands, as you understand it, but if you've been using your hands for other things and you're uncomfortable, you may wash your hands with perfume-free soap.

After you do that, set the seed packet aside and find some good planting soil, the kind you would use for bedding plants. When you have that, make sure there are no worms in there so that they are not disturbed. As you know, they are most valuable creatures to have in your garden, because they produce the best possible soil. Make certain that this is the case. Once you just have the soil, then thrust your hands into it. Grab the soil around the back and front of your hands to about two to three inches above where your hands meet your wrists. After you brush all the excess soil away, there'll still be a little bit in the lines of your skin and under your fingernails—you know this if you are a gardener.

Then take the seeds out of the packet. If it is a small packet, you might be able to do the whole thing at once, but if it is a large packet, then take as many seeds out as you can lay in the palm of your right or left hand, whichever one feels good to you. Don't make a pile of the seeds. Put them in your palm so that each one has contact with the skin of your hand. Then take the other hand and, while gently holding it over the one that has the seeds in it, simply talk to the seeds. Introduce yourself; say your name and who you are. Try to relax before you put the seeds into your palm so that they're not startled or frightened. They are alive. Say your name and who you are. It's best you say who you are in the most benevolent terms. Say what you hope for the seeds and how you will use the plants, and promise you will not abuse the plants. We will get more into what abuse is later.

After you do that with that group of seeds, put them into a separate container. I would recommend a container that is made of paper—natural paper, not something that has been bleached, just natural paper, something open to the air. Or you can put them in a piece of natural wood also—not painted, not treated in any way, but perhaps something you've carved out yourself and allowed to become air-dried. Continue on until you've brought out enough seeds for your project. After that, you can sprout the seeds in your greenhouse if you like, or you can take them out and plant them. Try to do this in such a way that the seeds are planted within twenty to thirty minutes of your last handful of seeds. Every time you do a handful, put them in with the others so that they're all familiar with who you are. If there are many of you doing this project, after you put all the seeds into the individual containers, you can put the containers together. Don't pour the seeds in together. Put them together and then hold both your hands over it and say, "We honor you, seeds. We ask of you only to bloom in the best way you can and express yourselves in the best way you can for our mutual benefit." When you say "mutual benefit," understand it is not only for the humans there, but also for the plants' benefit. Then you may do your planting process.

Try to be gentle, and don't get angry or upset with anyone while you are doing the planting. You may recall, or maybe even know now, what it's like to have people yelling, shouting, or displaying anger around you. Most of the time it makes you nervous and edgy, at the very least, and sometimes it makes you even more upset. It is exactly the same for seeds. That's why some seeds don't sprout, even if they've been touted as the best seeds in the world: because they have feelings. Everyone is alive and has similar characteristics. That's what I wanted to start you with as gardeners, because I know that there are some gardeners reading this book. Those of you especially who are trying to grow unusual flowers—roses and so on—would benefit from reading this, because there will be a lot of personal information about the plants that you may not be able to find easily elsewhere.

The Magic in Communing with
Plants Is in Both the Giving and the Receiving

Now I will speak about myself as a representative of dandelion, as you call it. We will use your names; it's all right. One of the best ways you can interact with us is when we are getting to that stage after the flower has bloomed but has then closed, when we are producing the seed structure and the seeds are not yet exposed—you've all seen us, eh?

So the pod is closed, but you can tell the seed time is coming. This is what to do: If you can, if you have the physical energy, go to the plant and, from the strongest part of your body, take a breath and relax—meaning breathe through the part of your body, or your whole body, where you feel particularly healthy. You can look at the sky if you like. Look at something you find attractive—not another human being! [Laughs.] Just look at something in nature you find attractive, take a few breaths, and relax.

After you feel relaxed, take a breath and, as you look at the plant, blow very gently toward it. You don't have to be near the plant, but it would be helpful—if you are looking at an individual plant, in this case a dandelion—to be within, say, six feet of it. Don't get any closer than a foot and a half, and then blow gently toward the plant. This is a way of offering your excess strength. The purpose of this book, of course, is to tell you what plants can offer you. But you must remember the reason the ancients—I'm talking about human beings here—stayed alive and disease-free for all that time. It was because they knew how to give as well as to receive. That's the magic that's involved here, and it's not the kind of "magic" magic that dazzles and attempts to fool. It's natural magic, which is associated with heart, love, and Creator.

Blow that single breath toward the plant, and if you can, step back one step. You can look to see where you're going. As you turn to your left, step back and walk away from the plant, if you're feeling strong. If you don't feel strong in any part of your body, then don't do this. Do this simply to share your strength and vitality with the plant. The plant will not use anything that is meant only for human beings, but it might produce a stronger plant, and you will want this, all right? As you continue, remember that the intention of this book is to show you what you are missing in your interactions with plants, not just to comment on things you already know about.

Dandelions Can Help Heal Head and Bone Conditions

Now, how about a time when you are not feeling so strong—in fact, you are feeling a little uncomfortable. If the dandelion is blooming and has one or more beautiful flowers, then this is what you should do. Perhaps you have a condition that you've been dealing with for a while, or perhaps you have a temporary condition that is uncomfortable for you. I will give you various ways to do this, because I realize that sometimes you feel this way or that way. Remember, you cannot be out there in the yard digging up dandelions and destroying them while you're doing this. Always remember that if dandelions are growing in your yard or where you happen to be in the forest, they are always there for a reason. If you go into the forest, you won't find many dandelions, because dandelions are meant to help human beings. This might help you to understand why you find them on your lawns so much. It's not just because certain nutrients might be there that the dandelion likes. Dandelions come to visit those who need them, and since people who live in the forest—meaning animals and so on—don't generally need dandelions' energy, we don't go there.

Say you are out on your lawn, maybe in your backyard where there are not too many prying eyes. If you can hunker down near the dandelion, that's good, but if you're not able to do that—and many of you are not—then try to lie down if you can. It's all right to put something on the grass, perhaps a towel or something. Lie down if possible. But say you are unable to do that; perhaps you're not feeling very well. If there is a paved surface a distance away, even nine, ten, or twelve feet away, you can lie there instead, as long as you have a clear line of sight from where you are to the dandelion—ideally, it should be no more than six feet away, but farther away is also possible. Then sit in your chair. It can be any kind of chair, but the best would be all wood with the least amount of metal or plastic possible. Sit in the chair, and try to face it toward the dandelion. Try to avoid putting the chair on the lawn, for that harms the plants underneath the chair and may harm the soil and the creatures in the soil. To do what you are going to do, which is to attempt to improve your health, you must not damage the health of others at the same time, for plants find that offensive, just as you would. If you were in a hospital or doctor's office, you wouldn't be punching the doctor while the doctor was trying to help you—of course not!

When you're sitting in the chair (you can recline if need be), then look only at the dandelion when it is in that condition of flowering. If there are many dandelions and your eyes happen to fall on many at the same time, that's all right, but only if they are concentrated in one area. But say it's just one that's blooming. Look at the dandelion. In this case, you're not going to have to relax, all right? You can relax a little bit if you wish so that you can be receptive, in which case the best thing to do is look at the sky. Don't look at the sun, of course, but look at the sky if there are clouds and so on. Usually this will relax a person, as long as the clouds don't look like they are going to rain at any moment.

When you feel relaxed and a bit more receptive, look only at the dandelion. Again, try to do this in a place where people are not walking in your line of sight, between you and the dandelion. It's important also that cats and dogs are not doing this, at least in that moment, eh? If your eyes happen to fall on the grass nearby, that's all right, but if there are children's toys or other objects lying about, try to move them out of your line of sight (or have someone do it for you) so that you are looking only at the dandelion, concentrating on it. While you are doing that, breathe in and out naturally. However, if you have some condition and you know where that condition is centered and how to use your breath, then you can take one deep breath. As you blow the breath inside of you, as you're exhaling that breath, either imagine that the energy of that breath is going into the area where you do not feel well, or blow the breath into that place where you are feeling uncomfortable—if you know how to do that, if you have been trained to do that.

I will tell you what kind of conditions in general that dandelion can support, help to cure, or help to put you on the path of receiving better outcomes from the cures you are using presently. You see that this system can sometimes be used not as a standalone cure but as something that supports the curatives you are already receiving. Dandelion is particularly good for ailments of the head and the bones. It may be good for other conditions, but those are the ailments to look at. Ailments of the head might include difficulty with vision or hearing or smell, for instance, or even headaches. Conditions of the bones could be perhaps an old fracture that didn't heal right or even bone problems of other types. Of course, it can be useful in other circumstances, and it can be tried, but those are the things in general that dandelion will work for. Remember, just a single deep breath is sufficient. That's what I recommend.

As the Creator Apprentice, You Re-Create More Benevolent Human Beings

Can you tell me something about the dandelions? Do you have an immortal personality on another planet or are you focused here? How does that work?

We are totally focused wherever we are, interacting with the soil, the moisture, the animals, and other natural life forms, and we do understand that we are here to teach you and to help you, but we do not have a separate life in existence on other planets. Granted, we are not from Earth—but then most of the plants you interact with these days are not from Earth. The Earth plants native to the planet have been almost completely removed by years and years of not only human culture but simply Earth's tendency to have various forms of her personality expressed—volcanoes, storms, rising and falling continents, and so on. So we are generally associated with a star system at the farthest boundaries— meaning farthest from you—of the Pleiades.

Zoosh has said that the vegetable kingdom was a creator who had come here to help us.

That's true if you go back far enough. But you will find—to supplement what that being said—that that is not at all unusual. If you go back far enough with any type of species, general species in that case—speaking of vegetables only—you will often find a creator, or at least a creator apprentice. You can only go so far in learning about creation before you must invest a considerable amount of experience in being the current status of what you are attempting to improve upon in your creation. If you cannot experience that personally, then you will not have a general idea of what might be the outcome of your intended modifications.

So if you look around at other human beings—in the case of your form of existence—you must extrapolate what I have just stated, for if you go back far enough, you will find a creator's apprentice who is the root of the human being. All these beings completing now—as the human race—has everything to do with what you intend to do as the creator's apprentice to re-create the human being in a way that is, of course, more benevolent. So I am putting it to you like that so you will understand from a more personal point of view that the broader implications of what Zoosh has said are also true.

How do you perceive your time on Earth? If you are a single plant, you bloom and then die. Your consciousness flow comes out of the whole of all dandelions or . . . ?

We do not die. Generally speaking, any plant that can seed itself never dies, because within every seed there is the original personality of the plant that has offered the seeds to the air and thence to the earth and beyond. So there is no death. We are physically immortal as long as the seed chain continues. And again, applying that not just philosophically but physically as a fact, it is the same for all life, including human beings.

You have perhaps been told that on the soul level you are immortal, but this is also true on the physical level, because in the seed that joins with the egg of the human being, there is at a deep level at least an element, if not an encapsulation, of all the personalities that preceded that seed. This is how you will come to know a great many things about yourself: because in the not-too-distant future you will learn how to tap the knowledge and wisdom accumulated by all the human beings who came before you. This is how you will be able to engage the solution to almost all of your problems: because somewhere in the past a human being solved it.

This is how we know things, and it's true for all life forms on Earth. Part of the reason is very simple. Earth can do this. You come to this planet to have life here, because this planet has a great deal of advanced capabilities. The planet itself is as close to a creator as any planet I am aware of in this universe. Planets are not often considered creators, but if they were, this planet would be considered one, because the very air you breathe (at least in its natural state) and the very soil you grow your food in—the animals, the plants, all human beings, everything—are constantly interacting with the planet herself. And thus you have capabilities and connections with all life. I might add, this is where your Garden of Eden story comes from. Don't go searching other worlds for Eden. You are living on Eden. Eden is not a garden; it's a planet.

Dandelions Came to Earth to Help Humans Remember

Are there any other particular benefits that the dandelion brings?

No. I don't think that there's anything other than what I have stated. If I may speak for us all for a moment, I believe all the plants will indicate that we are approaching this book project as a means to help human beings know how to interact with plants in a way that is most beneficial for them while reminding them of their responsibilities when interacting with us. If possible, we will suggest how you might interact with other species, including your own, when we are able to fit that into the flow of communication. But in terms of some special message, a worded message, I do not have one to offer other than what I have stated.

I see. Originally, I thought it was going to be the medicinal qualities of each plant.

It is. You are perhaps confused, thinking that we are going to talk about plant extracts as medicinal qualities. But as I said before, with that you never get more than one-tenth of what you can get from the live plant, and that is why many diseases are difficult to cure. It's like eating a watered-down cure, because no matter how you pursue it, no matter how much you concentrate it, in order to get the best capability of the cure, you must interact in a gentle way with the living plant so that you can experience the plant's vitality. And as part of your responsibility, if you have a great deal of vitality and the plant is not doing so well, or perhaps other plants like it are not doing so well, then it is your job to share your vitality. That's the whole way to understand this book. It is not to teach you what you already know. It's to share with you what you don't know.

When did dandelions come to this planet? Can you describe any kind of landmark in the past that we can recognize?

No. But I will put it this way, and this will help: When human beings began to forget who they were, the first thing that happened was that your lifetimes began to get shorter on the planet, and then you began to develop diseases—in that order. Your lifetimes got shorter because you were missing something. You knew you were missing something, see? Before that you weren't missing anything, because you knew how to live benevolently on the planet, but eventually you were missing something. When people feel they're missing something, they look for it as much as they can when they're on the planet. Then they begin to get the idea that the answer's somewhere in the stars, and their lives get shorter.

So as you began to forget more and more of who you were, you developed diseases and so on. Around that time, we showed up, as well as a great many of the other plants. Some of the peoples at the time understood: "What are these things?" Some of them thought the plants were food, and so on. In some cases, they could have been eaten in certain ways, and that's true even today. But in most cases, it was all about reminding you how to live without disease and, ultimately, in the case of the very large trees—the wide ones, the tall ones—of reminding you who you are. Within those huge trees, sometimes called grandfather or grandmother trees, are the memories of all the living civilizations and dead civilizations of human beings. These memories are in the trees, and if you know how to communicate with the trees—and it's not difficult—you can reacquire that wisdom. I would recommend putting a filter on it, so you don't reacquire the suffering, the knowledge of the suffering, but if you simply wish to reacquire wisdom that has been lost in the past, or even answers and explanations for relics that still exist in the present, an interaction with an ancient tree might still be possible in some places. I can go on, if you wish.

Please!

How You Can Reacquire Wisdom from the Trees

What you do if you find an ancient tree, for example, is approach the tree but do not touch it. Human beings often rush up to trees and touch them, and trees are no different than humans. If a complete stranger rushed up to you and started touching you [laughs], you would be at the very least surprised, and more than likely alarmed. So the thing to do is to walk toward the tree. If it's very large, then fifteen or twenty feet away is close enough. Put your hands out—not in front of you as you would to push something away, but out to your side as if you were going to hug someone—with your palms facing the tree.

Try to make sure there are no human beings walking between you and the tree during this time. You can have a few friends there if you like. Ask people to stay back for a moment because an experiment is going on. You can, if you like, share with those you are keeping away when you do this. Of course, it's better if there's no one else there, but [chuckles] realistically in your time, that's not likely. If deer are nearby, if a butterfly flies through, or if a worm or a snail crawls through, that's perfectly fine. These are natural beings, and they won't interrupt too much. Most likely, they won't get in between, because they'll know you're doing something.

Then simply say a greeting to the tree, one that plants often give each other—and other forms of life do this as well. In English it would be: "Good life!" In your language, it might be something different, but "good life" is a blessing. It is a greeting and it is a way of honoring, so just say out loud—you can whisper it if you like, but say out loud quietly: "Good life!" And then wait for a moment. If you feel comfortable in your physical body, the tree welcomes you. If you feel a warmth in your physical body, more than usual, the tree is exchanging loving energy with you, and the tree greatly welcomes you. But if you simply feel comfortable, you might still be able to acquire some of that which you would like.

Put your hands down at your sides a little bit but with your palms still facing the tree, all right? While either feeling comfortable in your body or feeling the warmth, simply look at the tree and say, "I am asking now to acquire knowledge and information from previous human civilizations that would help me to solve the mystery of _____." Then state what the mystery is. Don't say anything violent or upsetting; just say something simple, all right? Ask about a certain relic or the solution of the mystery to such and such a disease, for instance.

Then put your arms up again as if you were going to hug someone without reaching forward—meaning your arms are at your sides but with the palms facing the tree, as in that preparation for moving toward someone—and take three deep breaths while looking at the tree with your eyes wide open. If the first breath does not feel too comfortable, then immediately relax your arms and step back, say good life, take a deep breath without looking at the tree, and blow it toward the earth, generally aiming toward the direction of the roots of the tree. This will only happen if you did not feel warmth but were just relaxed in your body. In that case, it might be that the tree is not prepared to share with you in that moment.

If you don't feel the warmth in your body, if you said good life because that first breath did not feel good, then step back from the tree and go on to another tree until you feel the warmth. But if you feel the warmth when you take the first breath, you will probably feel slightly warmer, and this is good. By the time you take the third breath, then that's all. Now, don't blow the breath inside your body when you exhale. Just breathe and exhale with your eyes open while looking at the tree. When you are done, thank the tree, put your arms down to your sides, and say good life. Step back if you can, one step at least—looking where you're going so you're safe—and then after a few steps, turn to your left and leave. Don't turn to your right; always turn to your left. It is considered more polite, and it will be better for the energy exchange.

Within twenty minutes, you may get some inspiration about the problem you are working on. You may find that it happens within a few days. It may come in a dream. It may suddenly pop in as an inspiration. It might even happen in a circumstantial way, meaning that the interaction with other human beings—someone might say something, usually away from work entirely, and *bing*, suddenly it will be as if that person had unlocked a door. It may be totally unrelated to the problem you are working on, but it will happen usually within a few days. If it doesn't, then give it time. It will come to you, although it may not be directly from the tree. If it doesn't come within the first three days, it will be by way of the tree working with other trees or other plants or even other entities who have love for you.

Oh, I see; this is going to be very practical. That's wonderful.

Yes. That is the purpose of the book, is it not? Not just that which inspires—which, of course, is worthwhile—and not just that which is "how to plant a garden and have it be successful," which we started with because we know there will be people from that community reading this, but also information about how to know and how to find out, where to go to seek, and so on.

Connecting in the Evening Is Safer

Tell me a little bit about your experience. What do you experience of humanity? Do you see them, hear them, feel them?

Generally, we know what we need to know at the moment it is required. We don't think about human beings, just as you don't think about dandelions. But if there is an occasion, such as right now, then we know what we need to know to communicate in a polite way that allows what we have to say and allows what we may encompass in that moment to be practical for the human being. It would be the same if we were interacting with deer, say, or earthworms. We would know what we needed to know to be practical, polite, and even helpful. So no, we don't retain it as a constant.

What about interacting? What is your interaction? What is your experience, then? You're growing in the yard . . .?

Oh, where am I? What am I doing? I am currently growing. If you could see me, I am in a garden, someone's garden, one who is more magnanimous with plants. These people have flowers, but they also like dandelions. Some people do. And I'm growing near a mortar-covered wall, which may have brick inside it; I'm not invading too much of the area where the peonies are growing.

So if a cat walks by, or a raccoon, or another kind of small animal—I don't know what part of the world you're in—is there some recognition or interaction?

Usually, if the species is friendly. Sometimes they're not, or sometimes they're hungry and try a little bite [chuckles], and we can't help that. But usually we'll know if it's safe for that species to eat that plant, and we will broadcast a message. If the animal is conscious and open, it'll pick up the message and won't eat, but it might smell. However, sometimes animals are not open, for the same reason human beings are not open. They might have had a trauma. They might be upset about something, or they might be living hard, so to speak, in the case of, say, a dog or a cat trying to get by as best they can in the wild—meaning they were originally a house pet. When they're living hard like that, they're not always completely open, and they're more desperate for food. So it might take a while, but we usually manage to get the point across. We try to get the message to them before they swallow anything. If they do swallow any of the plant, they usually will throw it up if it's not good for them, because in some cases it makes them sick.

What is your connection with your home planet? You're aware of what's happening in the Pleiades and in all creation or you're focused right here or . . . ?

I'm focused where I am, just as you are, but the difference between us is that I know what I need to know when that moment is present, if I am dealing with others. But I realize what you're saying. You're asking me as an individual. If there is a moment of wishing to connect with the home planet, then I will do that, in general when it is as safe as possible, which usually happens in the evening when the light from the distant stars of the Pleiades is more present. During the day the light is also present, but it is washed out by the light of your own star, your Sun.

What do you mean, "when it's safe"?

As safe as possible. If there are children running and jumping and throwing things and so on, then I don't do it.

I see. Do you have teachers and guides, or you don't need them?

We have some on our home planet, but not here. If we are here, we have moved beyond the need for teachers and guides. Remember, we are not trying to state that we are in any way superior to you, as I'm sure the animals mentioned in the book *Animal Souls Speak*. Rather, you are here as a species because you are trying out the human race before you do anything to modify it as a creator apprentice. So you are here to learn, yes? But *we* are not here to learn. We are here to help. So we do not need to have direct interaction with the type of beings you indicated.

How interesting . . . because the animals do.

I see. It's hard to say.

When you talk about the Pleiades as your home planet, that's just in this universe, right?

Yes.

Do you have memories or awareness beyond that?

I am sure we existed before that, but I do not have that memory available to me—which is probably just as well, so that I can stay focused in this universe 100 percent of the time. I wouldn't be much help to you if I were thinking about some other universe. That would immediately alter the energy of my physical being and might damage a human being who was attempting to interact with me in some benevolent way, such as the suggestion about breathing in the energy.

Have you ever interacted with a human aware enough and conscious enough to do that?

Yes. There are a few people with this knowledge—not many, but a few. Generally, they are shamanic or mystical people who have had the traditions handed down to them from one generation to another. But it is believed now that a wider grouping of people can be exposed to this information—hence what I am saying for this book.

Now I have a closing message. As plant species, we will not tell all, so to speak, because you don't need to know all. We will offer what we feel you need to know now in order to improve the quality of your lives and to improve the quality of your own health, which may apply to your physical health or other aspects of your well-being. As the first plant to speak in this book, it has behooved me to speak in general for other plants, but speaking now just as myself, I will say that even after all that has gone on between us as different species for these past few hundred years, we still have great love for the human being. That is why we are here. We are here exclusively to help you. We can get along just fine on the Pleiades and live happy lives there, but we are here on Earth to help you. Try to remember that when you interact with us. Good night.

Thank you! Good life.

Good life.

CHAPTER TWO

Sage

MARCH 6, 2009

℘

SAGE.

Sage, welcome!

Greetings. I will speak for a short time about myself and then it's possible that Grandfather will want to give methods and usage. My nature is one of clarifying. If we were to speak to each other—communicate one to one—I would be able to see when you are speaking your true personality as compared to when you are speaking from something else: an influence, conditioning, or perhaps just being polite. Any sage plant can do this. Thus my nature is clarifying and some people use it for purifying; this is the use that is often found in your time. But I feel that clarifying is more important, so if you happen to live where sage grows naturally, that is to your advantage.

It is to your advantage to have sage growing where it has been naturally welcomed. But even if you are able to grow sage, then the way to do it is not in a small pot. It would be better in something that is bigger, flat but deep—four inches deep at least. Sage does not like to be crowded, so if there is enough of a sage plant growing in your herb garden to be safely moved, move it if you can. If you cannot move it, then try your best to do as follows.

17

Sage Can Help Resolve Communication Problems

If you and a companion—a mate or a friend; it can't be a business thing—are having some confusion over something, such as some difficulty in communicating through some problem (possibly because one person does not have the experience that the other person is referring to, and hence can only try to understand mentally), then this is what to do. One person gets on one side of the sage plants. If you are going to do this, it would be better to have three or four sage plants—at least three. One person gets on one side of the plants, and the other person gets on the other side of the plants. You can be anywhere from one foot to as much as three feet away from the plants. Try to have the plants in such a way that the sage is chest high for both people; you'll have to find a way to do that. Then one person talks and says what he or she has to say. Try to keep it brief. And then the other person answers and tries to understand.

When you talk, do not look at each other; look at the plant. If you do this, you might find that it will be easier to understand each other. The plant will act as an interpreter. You will still hear the words the same, even if you are using the exact same words you've been using to each other. Don't test it, but try to move past your misunderstanding this way. Talk to the plant. If you are angry or you get angry, look up at the sky at first and just breathe in and out. If the sunlight is too bright, close your eyes. Breathe in and out for three or four breaths and relax, because the plant cannot be abused. Remember, the plant is a go-between not unlike a diplomat. In this way, the plant not only helps to generate an understanding but is a calmative, up to a point. This is a use that is not remembered in your time. Generally speaking, sage is used in ways that have to do with clarifying the energies of a given space—such as burning it, you understand—and it is considered a purifying element. This is well known in your time, but sage can be used in other ways that are helpful to the human heart and soul.

Sage Can Help Clear Distress from Babies

A mother who's worried about her baby for any reason can use sage. This could be simply a worry about something that is in the neighborhood or in the town where you are living, or it could be "I hope my child doesn't get _____," whatever. It could be that the baby is not feeling his or her best, but it's still safe to take the baby outdoors—even though he or she is bundled up. Go over to the sage plants if you have them in your herb garden. If they are growing wild, you will have to be able to stoop, and if they are in your herb garden, you still might have to stoop. If they are in a small area where you have plants potted, though, then it may be easier to get the sage to chest level. You want to try to align your heart and your whole chest with the plants if you can.

Sit and hold baby in a natural position. Baby does not have to look at the plants. Baby can even be asleep. But sit one to two feet from the plant. You can even be talking to baby or singing to baby; that's fine. Just sit and look at the plant and breathe in and out normally. You can be talking or just supporting baby. Perhaps baby might be upset and crying a little bit. That's okay too. Just sit and talk and breathe in and out with the sage plants.

If you have more sage plants, or even a small greenhouse, baby might like that better. But if there are many different kinds of plants in the greenhouse, it may not work. The whole point is to look at the sage plant, breathe in and out normally, and sing or talk to baby. It's best to address your comments and your song to baby. You don't have to look at the plant, but you need to be near it so it can help. This will help to clear baby of any attachments. By attachments I mean if there has been a lot of anger in the house or you are in a community where there is a lot of anger or misunderstanding. This will help to clear baby and yourself as well. I recommend that. I am trying to give you uses that are not known in your time and could be actually helpful.

Keep Sage Near to Clear Congestion

I want to give another use before we go on. If you are an elderly person or if you live with one or if one comes to visit you, and if the elderly person has some congestion in the chest, then do all your medical things that you normally do and drink your herb teas; that's fine. Bring the elder—or yourself, if you are the elderly person—to a table that has a comfortable chair. If you can, use a soft seat that one can be comfortable in, a chair with padded arms so one has something to lean on comfortably. Sit the elder in a place where that person is comfortable, and just sit next to the person. You can sit on the elder's right side or left side, whichever you wish.

Have the sage plants on a small table in front of you, and just talk about anything the elder wants to talk about. If she is uncomfortable and unable to talk, something good to do is to read to her. She might look at the plant; she might not. The plant ought to be within two feet (up to two-and-a-half feet) of the elder and not necessarily within reach, because the plants do not like to have leaves broken off absentmindedly by people who may or may not do that. Just leave it there; that's sufficient. But never have it more than three feet away if you are going to have the plant interact with you. If you are more than three feet away, the plant will probably not interact with you. Anywhere up to that one- to three-foot mark is okay. Just talk or read to the elder or whatever she likes. This may help to clear the congestion sooner than it might have cleared up otherwise. This might be particularly helpful for people who have chronic conditions. I am not saying to do this instead of your regular care; I am saying do this in addition.

It might be something that you would think of in terms of, "Well, would it be good to bring sage plants to a hospital instead of flowers?" The problem with that is that with the likelihood of other people coming and going from that room or even being right next to your loved elderly person, it will be overwhelming for the plant. If there is too much going on, the plant will just quietly move within itself. But if your elder is at home or you are the elder, then this is something that could help.

It's also useful for another thing I'm going to mention, since it's connected. For people who smoke and have congestion in their chests, whether young or old, having a sage plant nearby is good—but don't touch it. It won't work very well if you are actually smoking during that time. But if you are not smoking, then it could work, perhaps.

All Types of Sage Are Unique in Their Abilities

We need to do things now that are readily accessible to the wide majority of people. You understand, you can live anyplace on the world and still order some dried sage, or in many places of the world, if you are fortunate, you will be able to grow it yourself. The living plant, I would have to say, is much more effective than the dried plant, especially when it's burned.

Are there different families of sage plants that are better at one thing than another or are they basically all the same?

No plants are the same, including plants that are identical. They are just like human beings. You wouldn't say that human beings were all the same, would you? It is the same with plants, including individual plants. This is a fact that is sometimes overlooked and a fortunate question you have asked. I would say that different plants—based on their personalities, not just their biological makeup—may be more inclined to do some things than other plants, not unlike human beings. People who work spiritually understand this. That is why it is so useful to be able to have applications of different sage types in different forms, meaning even planted in different ways associated with the uses I've given.

How to Identify Sage Plants to Communicate With

Some people might find that if the plants—say a mobile flat of plants—can be moved and used in the methods I've mentioned, that the plants in a row might work best. But other people might find that the plants in a triangular pattern would work best. It depends. For those who are well versed in growing herbs, start them in a small flat, say twenty or thirty plants growing until they become strong enough to transplant. You might look at this flat and then move your left hand in the wand position (see page 26) slowly over each plant and ask, "Would you be good to help clarify communication?" Or you could go over each plant like that slowly, and you could find that two or three, or maybe more, would be good at that and would volunteer for that. So you put a little mark there—a little piece of tape or a little piece of ribbon, something in color—and lay it in such a way so the plant is not touched or disturbed if possible, because it will be young and tender.

Then you might ask another question and move your hand over the plants again. You might ask, "Would you be _____ " and you ask all the plants, even if you've found some that are good at something—there might be some plants that are good at more than one thing. You could ask, "Would you be good at helping people to clear their congestion?" and so on.

You ask these questions, moving from the right, whatever row you're working with, and you work slowly from right to left. Then you move down a row or up a row, however you're doing it. I recommend you start with the back row and go across to the left, and then come down a row and start at the right and go back. It takes time, but this way you get plants that are absolutely skilled and are inclined to perform those tasks. When the plants are strong enough, you move them into a larger flat or a pot, and then they'll all have not only characteristics that you might wish to utilize for your healing practice but will also be compatible because they would have things in common.

It is very much the same with plants as it is with people, except plants are not quite as mobile. This is why in nature, you might find that when trees grow here instead of there or there instead of here, wherever those places are, it always has to do not only with the plant being welcomed in the seed form—or whatever form, pod or what have you, that it springs up from—but it also has to do with what other plants or trees or forms of life might be in that area so that there is compatibility. This can be applied in agriculture, but it would have to be experimented with—with other plants, you understand? Say, corn or whatever you are growing. If you are attempting to create a particularly strong form of whatever you're growing, you might have to experiment.

I recommend keeping it heart centered rather than scientific. With science, there's a tendency to try to structure what you're working with to suit your goals. But in this situation, you are picking plants on the basis of their personalities—who they are, what they are. And then you will find that you are in balance with nature rather than attempting to control nature. You see the value of that, of course? Let's have a little more water. [Pause.] Very well. The human being is an interesting plant, eh? Take the water in through the top and not through the bottom. It won't do this physical body much good to pour the water on his feet, eh? *[Laughs.] No, it won't do much good.*

Sage Was One of the First Life Forms Invited to Earth

Are you a spirit that contacts the various plants, are you embodied at the moment, or are you on the home planet? Can you tell me something about yourself?

I am a plant. I am a sage plant, not a spirit. If you wish to speak to the spirit that is associated with sage, this is possible.

Well, maybe; you are doing great. But you're connected to something larger than the plant itself at the moment, aren't you?

I am in some degree of communion with the home planet, yes. But of course, as a physical plant, I have never been there. I can say that the home planet—the actual source planet where we're from—is not from this universe. But we were invited to this universe so long ago that numbers don't really matter. So we were one of the initial forms of life that the creator of your universe invited because of our capabilities, our flexibilities, and our ways of supporting communion in the form of conversation that connects one to another in a totally benevolent way.

Your Creator felt that such a personality would be welcome in this universe. Thus you find various versions of sage sprinkled around on all planets where there might be any possibility—either from the residents of the planet or from visitors who come to the planet—of difficulty in communications (in some cases bordering on frustration). So other planets generally do not have conflict as you know it on your planet, but there is sometimes this frustration, the annoyance that comes from a desire to communicate in great detail, and if that is not possible, then you understand, it can be frustrating. But if sage is present, then people will normally know—whoever they are, whatever they are—that if they just sit in the sage garden, whatever difficulty you are having in communication, even if you do not speak the same language (which is very possible in the case of visitors), communication will become much easier. All frustration disappears because sage has the tendency to calm, especially when in number—meaning if there are a great many sage plants or if they are very large. On some planets, we are like a stalk: six, eight, twenty, thirty, forty feet high, and our leaves are immense. In order to be very large on those planets, we have to live for several thousand years undisturbed, or be cared for by the local population, to a degree. But it is more likely that we are exposed to the elements on that planet that are nurturing and comfortable to us, with nobody pouring foundations anywhere nearby. [Laughs.]

Sage Souls Have Migrated from Planet to Planet

How was the decision made about the size of sage on Earth?

I'm not privy to that information, but my understanding (to the degree of the practical reality of my day-to-day life) is that the large and immovable is often moved on this planet in spite of its desires. Therefore one might reasonably feel that if one is smaller, one might be tolerated or overlooked.

So does that mean that with that talent, that ability, you commune with other sage plants all over this planet?

I do not, but I commune with those near me because we have much in common. There is no need to commune with plants on the other side of the planet, much less wherever they are growing. Although, I would guess that the spirit of sage may do that, but you would have to ask that spirit.

Do you have memories of being in other sage plants on this planet?

I have memories, yes, of different lives on this planet—not to any great extent, but I have some memories of that and a few memories of being on other planets. This is why I can speak of the very large plant on another planet, because I was in attendance in that plant for a time—not the entire time. Sometimes it is not unlike a phenomenon you experience here: a soul, meaning an immortal personality. We are ensouled just like all life and might migrate from one plant to another, always making sure that the plant is ensouled as we migrate, sometimes through a particularly large plant like the one I referred to. Then one waits until another soul has joined, and they might be together for a time. Then if one wishes to move on, that's what happens. So that's how it was. I was in that plant for some time and then desired to move own, and then another sage soul came and we visited for a time, and then I came to Earth.

Use Sage to Commune with Your Higher Self

Does your ability to help others commune work only among different people or can sage be used by one person to commune with one's higher self or one's spirit or one's immortal personality?

You could try that. I don't see why not, but if you are doing that, you would want to say whatever prayers you are saying at first to commune with your higher self. You would want to look at the plant. In that case, you'd want the plant or multiple plants to be about two feet away from you. But if the distance can't be exactly that, then just get as close to that as possible. If it's, say, a foot and a half or two and a half feet, that's okay too. So look at the plant and then try to make your contact that way.

If your eyes have to close, that's fine. But stay in the proximity of the plant. If you are down on the ground, it might be uncomfortable at some point, especially if you are a little older, not a youngster. However, if it's a plant that is growing in a park or in some similar place, then you can make contact. Once you make contact with the being you wish to make contact with in some benevolent way, then the tendency might be to pick up the potted plant and move it to someplace where you are more comfortable. Don't do that.

What you do is you leave the plant exactly where it is and you gradually pick yourself up. I'm going to give the example for a potted plant. So if you need to move to someplace more comfortable, perhaps a softer chair, move very slowly, all the while staying in touch with that being you are in touch with. Or just remain where you are. But don't move the plant. Just because it can be moved does not mean it's a good thing to do in the usage that you are asking about.

Generally speaking, when sage is working for you, it's not good to move it. It's not good to touch it; it's not good to move the pot. Of course, you can't help it if a vehicle goes by and shakes the street and the table and so on. Well, the plant will be used to that by that time. But, you understand, by picking the plant up, touching the plant, or interacting with it—because it's working, and therefore anything like that would be a distraction to the plant—it will probably stop doing what it's doing.

Other Plants Might Also Have Clarifying Personalities

How would you describe your process? What is the mechanism by which you are able to act as a clarifier or help others to communicate better or commune? How do you do that?

It is a portion of personality. This is why I have suggested creating a family of plants, as in my reference to the flats and the young plants, and asking of them: "Can you do this; can you do that?" It is something that is associated with personality, not unlike the human being. It is less to do with anything biological or that which can be mapped out scientifically. The pure personality of the plant, this facet of sage behavior, you might say, is not entirely exclusive to sage. One might find this with other plants—you will have to ask them—but it is something generally found in many sage plants. You have to ask them gently, as I said before. Ask plants you are growing: "Can you do this?" all the while holding your hand in the wand position directly above the plant—say, three or four inches above it. Don't get too close, because the plant is tender and finds the human being to be a bit overwhelming.

I cannot state for a fact what the biological function of this is. My belief is that it is purely a fact of personality. That's how I react. If a human being knows this about sage and does what I have mentioned to you, I'm reacting primarily on the basis of my personality. I do not feel anything unusual going on in me—in my biological or physiological functions, as you might say if you were a human being.

But you focus, you move . . .

I come to attention to what's going on. It's as if you are speaking to someone who is not like you. Say you have a pet dog or even that you are on a farm and there are cows and the cows are communicating with each other—lowing perhaps, eh?—the way they do sometimes. You might be inclined to look at them and give them your attention: "I wonder what they are saying to each other." How many times have farmers wondered that, eh?

As a result, it draws your attention. It's a little more than that, because the cows are communing with each other as compared to the human being attempting to commune with a higher version of itself or even to commune with another human being in some way that works better for the both of them. Then as a plant, I would be functioning on a personal level between the two human beings in my example.

I would be paying attention to the one who is speaking. Then I would relax for a moment while there was a pause. Never in this situation do you want to have both human beings speaking at the same time, as human beings sometimes do. Someone speaks and then stops. Then there is a pause—not long; maybe half a minute of your time. Then the other person starts speaking. This gives the plant—in this case, myself—a chance to relax for a moment and then, as the conversation continues, to address my attention to the other person.

As I say, long bursts of words are not the best thing. For a human being to do this for two or three minutes, then you see there is an opportunity to interact on

Using Your "Wand" (Hand)

The whole point of shamanic interaction with anything is to create a personal relationship between shamanic individuals and whatever they are touching or in contact with and to pass on that wisdom and knowledge, not only to their

students, but to the people they live with in general, so that ultimately all people can have personal relationships with all things material around them.

They can walk up to a bunch of rocks, many of which could be sat on, and point the fingers of their left hand (or wand, as Speaks of Many truths calls it) like this [the two longer fingers, palm sideways or slightly upward], toward the rock. The left hand is the wand because it is the receiving hand. (I know some people are left-handed and their right hand might be their receiving hand, but in reality the left hand is always the receiving hand and the right hand is the creating hand, the doing hand, even if you're left-handed.) By the feelings they get in their physical body, they know which rock gives them the greatest warmth, and that's the rock they can approach and ask, "Is it all right if I sit on you?"

A shaman will do that. If you are an average person, however, you can use this technique for everyday things: You can learn to run your fingers, your wand, over a wide array of things to see which one is right for you. This could be done in a supermarket. If you have a garden, you can go out and choose not only which ear of corn is right for you or your family that day, but which plant wishes to offer it to you at a given time or any given day.

To do that, use the wand like this: If you're covering an area, not just pointing at something, you always move the wand, the hand in the wand position, right to left. You never move it from left to right. It's not a mental reason; it's a feeling. You are more sensitive and receptive when moving to the left. If you attempt to move the wand from the left to the right, you are not protecting the most sensitive area. Where is the most sensitive area of the wand? It is in the palm. So when you're moving from right to left, you're protecting that sensitive area.

So take your hand right now and move it in the wand position. You will notice, when you stop the motion, that you will have a sense, a physical sense, in the palm. While you're moving it, of course, you have a physical sense on the back of the hand, but when you stop it, the last physical sense you have is in the palm. You're protecting that part when you move from the right to the left. How does your physical body feel? Yes, you get the sensations in the wand hand, but how does your physical body feel? Ultimately it's about compatibility.

That personal feeling you get, the warmth within your body, tells you that yes, there is a love for what you are asking for today, right now in this moment—not an hour from now, not five minutes from now, but right now. That doesn't mean it won't be so an hour from now, but you'll have to do the experience with the wand again in an hour if you want to know. Because plants, rocks, everything, have their own personal lives, five minutes from now they might be doing something else, just like a human might.

It is essential that you understand the intimate, personal nature of the living world you find yourselves on, the core elements of your common personality. A person might be available to talk to you or do something with you now, but five minutes from now they might be doing something else. All human beings have that in common, and the living world on which you are living is the same way. Maybe your dog or the rock or the tree is doing something else five minutes from now. It is exactly the same.

a feeling basis as well. But, you know, if a human being has strong feelings about something, which they might in the case of a misunderstanding, then there will be a lot of radiated feeling as well. That's why it's important to think about what you're going to say and then to say it. If a feeling comes through, that's all right, but try to avoid anger or extremes.

This would be the case if you were speaking from . . . say you spoke German and you were speaking to someone who spoke Chinese, for example. You would have, perhaps, two interpreters there. You would look at the person you wish to communicate with, but the interpreters would have to try and keep up. So keep in mind that it's like that. You would be speaking short little phrases, saying what it is that you need to say, and then you would stop. There would be pauses to allow the interpreters to catch up, you see. It's all very polite.

Communication between Humans and Animals Is Possible with Sage
Would this work interspecies if the farmer wanted to get closer to his cows or somebody wanted to be more in tune with a pet? Does that work also?

It could work, but in the case of the pet who might be more mobile, then it's hard to say. It might work with an older pet.
A pet who would sit still.

Yes. It might work with, say, an older dog who is clearly not well, but you don't know what the problem is, and maybe the reason you'd use this is that the veterinarian is not sure either. Then when dog is home, you place it in whatever comfortable arrangement so that it can lie down or partly stand, or whatever it wants to be doing, and you put the plant between you. Again, try to get to chest level, which means you might have to sit on the floor. Or move the plant up on something that is firm, because dog might get up and if tail goes *kapoof*, plant could go flying.

So it has to be on something firm between the two of you. But it probably won't be possible to get plant at both your chest level and dog chest level. So you have to make the best of it. It's important that plant be at least at some level with dog. Your dog might be communicating a great deal with its eyes, because dog knows that the human being can recognize certain meanings in the eyes of another and has a much better chance of understanding what that means as compared to other dog communication. Dog will be giving you meaningful looks.

Don't put plant in front of dog's eyes; that will just make difficulty, but put plant somewhere near—within one to three feet, or maybe two to three feet from—dog's chest area. Also do something similar to that for you if you cannot get down on the floor with dog, which is very possible for some people. Then you have to do the best you can. But if you are younger and stronger, you can perhaps lie down on the floor near dog, and then it will easily be be possible for plant to be lined up with both of your chests so you can do eye conversation with dog. You might quietly talk and say, "Do you need to do this?" or "Do you need to do that?" or "Do you have this or that?" Ask questions very slowly, and dog will answer with the look in its eyes—or dog may look away if you are completely off about what the problem is. Get used to body language. But mostly with dog, if dog can move head and neck and so on, dog will look away if you are completely off. But if you get closer, dog will look at you and give you meaningful looks. It could help.

Have you met or are you aware of any other plant or animal on this planet that has this ability?

As I said before, some other plants may have this ability. I do not know. You will be talking to some plants, and you can ask them. You might find abilities like the ones I am mentioning today more with herbs, because herbs are the sort of plants that will be interacting with human beings, and they know it. Human beings tend to use portions of the fresh plant, or dry it and use it for this or that. But it is something that plants classified as herbs know before ensouling in a physical body: that they have a much greater likelihood of interacting with human beings than, say, some other plant.

Animals Can Also Use Sage to Resolve Communications

This is extraordinarily interesting. You must have had this ability in the other universe, which is why Creator asked you to come to this creation. Do you remember being in the other universe?

No. But I have heard, in terms of our history, that that is where we originated.

Do you know what your form was there? Is it similar to this?

I do not. But a spirit may know. Perhaps next time you can talk to the spirit.

We could, but I think we want to keep this practical, and these are mostly my concerns—probably not relevant to the book.

Very well.

How do the different sage plants on this planet differ? All I've heard is that they are in different colors. But you are basically one species, one family, right?

I cannot say that. It's like standing in front of twenty or thirty human beings and saying, "So you are basically one species. How do you differ?" The answers are based on personality. In human beings, one finds different colors also, eh? So my feeling is that personality would be different.

But especially in such a conscious plant, yes.

Yes. I can tell you what I look like. I would be called California white sage.

And you are in California?

No. But I would be called that.

I see. Do you know where you are?

I do not. I am near somebody's garden—a house built close to the forest. It is very nice. Lots of trees and shade and natural animals.

Do you communicate with the animals that are around?

There is a family of rabbits nearby, and they come over to talk. Sometimes they have a little sniff around to see if they can find a tasty morsel, but because I have been their friend for so many years, they do not nibble me up. They do come sometimes when they are having difficulty communicating or teaching one of their young. It is the same with rabbits as it is with all species. It's not unusual for one young member to be born who has a different understanding about what life is here and may come in with a belief of, "Well, I can do this or I can do that, and I don't care what they've been doing." [Laughs.] It's more of an attitude.

Mom rabbit, if I might use your terms, will come by sometimes and bring a young one who's a bit reluctant to learn their ways, and she does exactly what I mentioned to you. She gets the young one settled on one side of me, and she goes over and gets settled on the other side. And their communication goes from there. It's not verbal or loud—I can tell the communication is nonverbal; they make sounds, of course, but the communication is nonverbal. Usually when they leave, my impression is that if Mom rabbit gives me a little glance, then I know she got through. If she doesn't give me a glance, then I know they'll be back.

[Laughs.] Local psychiatrist, okay.

You might call it "woods lore."

It's great to have someone with such a sense of humor and such an appreciation of the different species living on this planet.

Also, it is good for you to know that sage has been interacting in this capacity for some time. If we do this with rabbits, it's safe to say we can do it with people.

Pleiadian Songs Have Given Us Hope for Earth Humans

I have heard from other plants who've had other lives here that there have been older groups of people, most established in the past, who have known about coming out to speak to help you understand and make for better communication from person to person.

Well, that would be the people who lived closer to the land before we got so many cities and became mental, right?

Yes, but I'm reminding you of this because it's important for you to know that many life forms around you can be helpful to you in ways you have simply forgotten or don't know about. But now that you do know about them, you can interact with them, perhaps in new ways, and improve your communication. From what I have been able to discern of human behavior, one of the biggest problems that you have in our time is communication. I believe part of this simply has to do with different ways of talking, but there's also the feelings.

Human beings sometimes believe that they must try to control their outer appearance so that their feelings are not obvious. This makes for problems in the long run, I believe. I also believe that from what I've been able to perceive of the human being—granted, within my limited exposure—that some of this is changing. I have seen with the younger ones that they are more inclined to demonstrate their feelings. While it's not always an appropriate demonstration, it does perhaps bode well for the future.

Absolutely, yes. The new children are the hope of the planet.

Yes. We will have to finish up for the day pretty soon here, but we could continue next time if you like.

Let's plan to do that, and maybe you'll talk for a while, and then we'll talk to the spirit of the sage.

You might like that, and it might be useful when doing this sort of thing to have a two-stage arrangement like that. Then you'll be able to . . .

Study up on the plant quickly. [Laughs.]

That's right.

Then we'll talk again in a couple of days. And thank you.

You're welcome. So the inclusion of the human being on Earth has made for a change in sage world, and it's the same for other life forms on Earth. Generally speaking, all life forms on Earth were welcomed up to the point of the human being's arrival. But since then, we are not sure. I am not saying this entirely to be amusing. I am saying it also because there has been a counterbalancing.

You may not know this, but there are people living on a star system called Pleiades who look very much like Earth human beings. They used to come to Earth. I have heard from stories (you might call it folklore) that they used to come and visit different species, different life forms on the planet, and talk to them quietly or sing to them and talk about how Earth human beings will come to be benevolent to all forms of life—how Earth humans would even be able to emulate qualities in other forms of life that would make those forms, as well as all forms of life on Earth, very happy indeed. It is because of that song and those communications that we have high hopes for the human being. Good night.

Good night. Thank you very much.

CHAPTER THREE

Sage

MARCH 10, 2009

୫୦

GREETINGS. SAGE.

I had no idea that you were so multitalented. What I read about the ability of sage to cure discomforts in human beings is awesome.

Referring to our last talk, eh?

Well, I researched sage and it's just incredible. Do you have a particular connection with humans—your being, your plant, your personality—for your energies as a dried herb to be so beneficial to humans, or are you that beneficial on any planet with any species that's there?

We tend to adapt to the needs of others around us and attempt to do the greatest good that is possible while being full of life and vital. We can do less good when portions of us are dried, but we can do some good even then, as people do with dried herbs. But generally speaking, the scope of the herbology aspects of this book will focus on what can be done with the living plant. We feel that that is vital, especially to herbologists and healers who may be greatly interested in this book.

Now, the source that chose to sprinkle our being around on this or that planet always chose to do this when the perception—or the certainty, either one—was present to know that we would be needed there by this or that species. Sometimes we would be needed by the more noticeable species, such as the human race on Earth, and at other times we would be needed on other planets by other aspects of life. Sometimes we would even be needed by life that might go somewhat unnoticed by the comings and goings of this or that species—referring in this case to serving the needs of biologicals, microorganisms, and so on, even spirits.

But on this planet, the focus is largely on the human race in terms of your feelings and physical attributes; your spirits, which are the unifying element; and (to a degree) your instincts. We are particularly interested in your instincts—they tend to be as closely related to your spiritual self as any portion of your being—since they operate on an instantaneous level, as your spirit does. Your spirit is always in the now but has full and complete access to what is necessary to know in the past—especially if an action or reaction is required—and what is necessary to know in the future. Although this is not thought—it is not a consideration; it is not a pondering. It is simply an instantaneous knowing with reaction.

This kind of thing could be one definition of spirit—certainly not the only definition, but one. Therefore we are particularly interested in working with human beings to help to sharpen, clarify—which is one of our favorite things to do—and train human beings to utilize their own instincts and to appreciate and value the instincts of others as a group dynamic. "Group" is used in the sense of meaning those individuals participating in communication, as discussed last time, with a sage plant or two or three between them. Or it is used to refer to a group dynamic meaning the human race in general and anything in between. So we are particularly interested in the facet of human acquaintanceship with one's overall being.

You Can Use Sage to Increase Physical Strength

There are so many benefits from the traditional use of herbs—which is, you know, the parts of the plant after the personality has left. But I'm wondering if you can do these things as a plant when you are alive, like increase physical strength, alertness, or body heat?

Wait. You must ask only one question at a time. I realize you think that is one question, but I'm going to answer only one of those, and you can ask the others again if you wish. I'm going to address strength. "Can you do this to increase body strength?" is how I am going to interpret your question. First, find a plant that is in your garden, or better yet, in a pot that you can slowly and gently move around. Always move your potted plants slowly and gently. They will react best to that. When you are done doing whatever you are doing with them, make sure to put them back in the exact position they were in before—not just placement, but also the direction they were facing.

Now, if you wish to have a little more strength, this will incorporate the soil of Earth since the plant is in the soil—ideally in the ground as a natural plant growing without your having planted it, but on a practical level, more likely your herb garden or potted plants. Then interact with at least three plants at a time. Using just one might be too much of a strain for that one plant. And I would recommend not doing this with young plants. Let them be a bit more mature. So if they are just peeking out of the ground, don't do it then.

I'd recommend that if you can do this, do it in the daytime, ideally under blue sky and sun. The Sun does not have to be shining directly on the plant; it just has to be out. If it's shining on you, that's fine, but it doesn't have to be—it just has to be out. I don't recommend any one time or other of the day. but it ought to have been light for at least an hour and be at least two hours before sunset.

So I would recommend, then, having the plant about eight to ten feet away from you. Don't get too close. If it is near other plants, this is a problem. I would recommend that if you are working with a wild sage growing on its own, you should hold your hands around your eyes so that you are focusing only on that one plant to the best of your ability, and you need to decrease your view. If, however, it is a potted plant, then move it to someplace where it feels good. Remember, if you feel uncomfortable when you set the plant down there, it might very well be that you are getting a message from the plant that it does not want to be there. There are other suggestions, but I don't want to get too elaborate.

Let's say you have the plant eight to ten feet away from you, and ideally, there are three of them or more. Glance up to the sky where the Sun is. Obviously, close your eyes and just take a quick glance, but enough so that you can feel the sunshine on your face. Then move your head and neck so that you are looking at the plant. Keep your eyes closed for a moment. Then open your eyes, looking only at the plant and not the pot the plant is in. Then take three deep breaths—not so deep that you feel like you're going to burst, just deep breaths. Don't hold them. And then exhale: in then out, in then out, in then out, you understand. Then relax, close your eyes, and be still for a few minutes. Make sure you have the ringer off on the phone during this time and try to make sure that you're not likely to be disturbed.

Then after about five minutes, do that again for a completion on any one day of three times in a row like that. Don't keep looking at your watch. Don't look at your watch or a clock more than once; just make your best guess. If it's four minutes, that's okay. If it's six minutes, that's okay. Five minutes is best. Then repeat the process. So the whole thing might take you less than a half-hour. As always, go over, pick the plant up, and put it back where it was.

Plants like to grow together. They don't like to be isolated, so if you decide, "Oh, I'll just leave the plant in the position where I do this," don't do that. It's not natural, really, for plants to grow in pots, but some plants are willing to do that. As an aside, if you are trying to grow plants in pots and they don't want to grow in pots, then you'll know that they may not be willing to grow anywhere but in a garden or in the wild. So don't always assume you're not a good gardener.

This may help with your strength. If you are old and getting on in life, it might be marginally helpful, but a marginal difference at that stage of life will be noticeable: 5 percent, 8 percent. If you are younger and relatively vital but perhaps just getting over something—maybe you were sick for a while and are just getting over it—it might help you to get over the sickness a little quicker. If the person involved is very young—say, a child who can follow instructions to do this (but commands and demands are not being made of the child)—the child may not be able to do it more than twice in a given setting. And that's all right for a child; doing this will probably help him or her to achieve more balance and stability. In the case of a child, though, don't do it more than once a month. In the case of an adult, you can do it twice a month, if you feel like it, but make sure there's at least two weeks in between. For an elderly person, then I would say once a week would be acceptable.

Breathing with Sage Can Break through Depression

Okay. That's wonderful. What about combating depression?

In the case of combating depression, it's necessary that the plant be in a little different situation. If it has recently rained and you can go near the garden, it's better. You don't want to tromp around in the garden too much when the soil is very wet or you'll make a mess—any good gardener knows that. First, if it has recently rained, then once the rain shower is stopped, leave the plants alone for at least five to ten minutes, because they're going through a revitalization. There will be a lot of gold light there from angelic and other presences. That's important.

It's particularly important if there's been some problem in the area, such as a serious storm or even a flood, and you want to leave the garden kind of alone for a while, giving it only the attention it absolutely needs. On the other hand, if there has not been so much rain or you are living in a drier area and rain is unusual, then it's important that the soil in the potted plants—since we are talking about that for the sake of convenience—be moist.

You probably have a time of day when you normally water the plants. It would be good to wait for about fifteen minutes and up to thirty minutes after you've watered the plants. The plant soil will still be moist, and then you can put the plants on a table, perhaps, so that their position is—not the pots but the plants—lined up somewhere between your chest, the center of your chest, and your forehead. If they are big plants, then it might be beyond that, but at least that general area.

The plants are going to have to be close to you, and you're not going to touch the plants. But if you can, cup your left hand slightly—with your fingers loose, though—including your thumb, kind of loose, not touching each other but curved slightly. Put your left hand about six to eight inches—no closer than five inches—to the left. Do this to the best of your ability; a little flexibility is all right. Do the same thing with your right hand. Then look at the plants and breathe in and out normally—ten, twelve, even eighteen breaths, that's fine—all the while focusing only on the plants.

You may have to build up to this, but the whole point is to see only the plants and to have no other thoughts. It's vitally important to have no other thoughts, including pictures. If you suffer from chronic depression, this will be difficult, but see if you can build up to it. It might be an achievement to get to three breaths without having other thoughts or discomforting feelings, but build up to it slowly.

If you can build up to eighteen breaths, that will be very helpful, but if you can only make it to six or eight, that will also be helpful. The effects will accumulate over time and make it much easier to break through depression with less medication or with kinds of medication that are more gentle. Use a remedy that is homeopathic or something simple that does not cloud you. Some people use alcohol to break through depression but alcohol makes you cloudy mentally and on a feeling level, and it has other damaging effects, as you know.

So I would say that if you are on medication, this might make it possible to lower the dose. Or, as I say, get on something gentler, such as a homeopathic remedy or something else. That's what I recommend. It will be useful. It may make a big difference to some people. But if you're not chronically depressed, it's likely to help you to get through low moments a lot faster. I would say,

30 percent of the time, maybe up to 50 percent of the time—the depression might be a stage you are going through from something else, grief perhaps. If it's chronic depression, it will make the times between the depressions longer, because you may not always be depressed every moment.

Is this using three plants?

I recommend on an ongoing basis for these talks for you to put in three plants or more.

The Aroma of Sage Might Help Ease Mental Conditions

This book says traditional herbalists even thought that sage might be useful in treating certain forms of insanity. Would you go that far with it?

I wouldn't go that far with it in terms of *treating*, but if patients are in an environment where they are separated from the mainstream of life, it would be very useful to have a greenhouse where such plants are growing. Spider plants may also be a possibility. But the problem there is that people who are delusional—or, in this sense, greatly injured mentally—may not actually be delusional; they just see things other people do not see, and this means that perhaps windows have been opened up for them that would have been better left unopened for a living person. Such things can happen with drugs. For example, consider people whose minds and personalities have been severely damaged by some of the drugs that you have and that you are dealing with and struggling with at this time in your cultures. Yes, it can be useful to have some kind of greenhouse, perhaps one that doesn't have glass for the sake of safety—"hot house" is another term. Then talk and treatment that are beneficial, gentle, psychological, and heartfelt might go better and more easily.

Smell also might migrate. It's not a major smell, you understand, when you are out in nature, even if there's a great many of the plants. But it might become quite noticeable. There's another odor that is also helpful in such situations, but most civilizations do not allow this in your social systems now: the marijuana plant in its living form. When it's flowering is best, but most likely it will not be available to most people. The living plant has a great deal to do with creating a balanced and harmonized energy. This can be particularly helpful for people who are struggling with damaged minds and personalities. You'll have to talk to that plant to get more.

I think we will.

A Breathing Exercise to Aid Digestive Conditions

Here's another usage of the dried form that's interesting. Sage promotes good digestion and stimulates the appetite, eases gas pains, removes mucous, and increases pancreatic functioning. How would one get that benefit from a live plant?

I think, in this case, you would have to get a little closer to the plant. Make sure you are not touching it. You can, in the case of a plant on a table, put your arms to either side of the pot just to brace yourself. But get to within about three to four inches of the plant. If you get an uncomfortable feeling, the plant does not feel comfortable with that. But if you've grown the plant and treated the plant well, you might have a comfortable relationship—meaning the plant feels safe with you. In this case, you may be able to get your face to within three or four inches of the plant. If the plant feels less safe, then keep it to six inches. The plant also might be busy doing other things. They have a life. They are busy sometimes, eh?

So I would say that, ideally, three or four inches would be good, but if the plant is busy, then leave it alone and try again another time. If you've tried three times, you can be pretty sure the plant won't do this. But if on the first, second, or third try the plant allows it, then you can be sure you may be able to do it again sometime. So get close to the plant at the distances I recommended, and then open your mouth and take a breath as if you are slurping in spaghetti. It would be like [makes a slurping sound], like that. It would create a sound such as if you were trying to suck on a straw to get that last bit of whatever you're drinking up into the straw.

Obviously, if the plant is dusty or if there are little creatures on the plant, you want to be careful, but most likely, it will be all right. Then take one to three breaths like that. Don't take deep breaths. Just breathe in as much as you normally would, especially in the situation of say, sucking on a straw, and exhale normally. All right? You can exhale out your nose if you want, or you could exhale out your mouth, but don't blow out your mouth. You could try that.

Use Sage's Energy Based on Your Own Intent

Nowhere in your instructions is there any verbal communication with the plant. But the plant is aware because it's tuning into you. I am assuming that it knows what your intent is.

The plant is aware of you because it is tuning into you—but no, don't assume that it knows your intent. The plant is not changing itself for what you need to do. The only thing that plant is aware of is your proximity based on your auric field. It will recognize the auric field of a familiar person, one who waters and perhaps feeds the plant, and so on. It will recognize them with a certain amount of joy, or if you've been cutting the plant, with apprehension, for example. But if you are new to the plant, it will simply notice that you are present. In which case, you'll probably have to keep back a little ways, in general, so the plant does not alter itself in any way. So your purpose and your intent is *your* purpose. It's *your* intent. You have to stay focused on it. But the plant will simply exude its normal energy based on its personality and being.

For you to use as you need at that time.

Yes. Remember, if you are utilizing the plants in this way, you need to allow them to rest, say, two, three days between cycles of usage. So as I mentioned before, in the case of an elderly person using it once a day, you're going to need more than one set of plants. Fortunately, such plants are not difficult to grow. And in the case of friends who might have plants, it isn't just that the plant cannot interact with you as a person more than, say, once every two or three days. If a human being does this, then the plant needs to recover and be itself. It doesn't get drained or exhausted so much, but it needs to relax and be itself. So it doesn't help to just trade plants with others and then have them use it. The plant needs to rest.

Become a Wise Old Sage

As an herb, sage is said to strengthen the brain and promote wisdom. Now, would that be similar the previous example of increasing physical strength and mental equanimity?

No. I think wisdom requires something a bit more elaborate. It would really require—and this might be in a room or simply outdoors—to have plants on at least four sides of you. North, south, east, west would be best, but it would also be acceptable to have more plants than that—say, at other points on the compass; I think compass points would be best—and then to simply stand in the center of them. So you'd like to have a circle perhaps, maybe an eight-foot circle. And then you'd stand in the center. What you'd need to do is look at the plant. So you're standing in the center and the plant is maybe four feet away from you. Look at the plant. It's in front of you, and if you have several points of the compass, there might be several plants—I would recommend maybe sixteen. This is for someone who has something ongoing, you see, or someone who's very good with plants. Then breathe normally while facing north and, as you take your breath in, stand with your arms down at your sides with your palms facing your body.

When you breathe in, move your arms about a foot away from your body. As you breathe in, your arms are moving out with your palms still facing your body; your arms are relatively straight, not rigid. Then when you exhale, return your arms to the sides of your body. This reproduces something not unlike gills on a water creature, where you see them and they take in water through their mouths but they blow the water out through their gills. It helps.

You do not have to turn in the circle, but an option is to turn to the different points of the circle, depending on how many plants you have. In the case of four plants, you'd start out at the north and you'd turn for each; maybe you'd wait and take three breaths, then you'd turn to your left—rotate always to your left. Face the next plant or group of plants and do that again. Go right around the circle once; you don't have to, but you can. Then if you have many more plants than that, you face each group like that and turn around until you make one complete rotation, ending up facing the north. Keep in mind that when you're looking at the plants, you are not only breathing in the energy of the plants that you are looking at but you are also breathing in all around and behind you. On your sides, behind you, and so on, the energy is coming in. That's why we don't make the circle too big. If it was, say, a sixteen-foot circle, then the plant may not be connecting with you directly. But between your auric field and the auric field of the plants, there's undoubtedly going to be some overlap. So the energy comes and goes in connection with all the plants. That might, in general, serve other purposes.

In the case of an individual who may be in a wheelchair for whatever reason—temporary or longer than that, chronic perhaps—the circle will have to be made bigger, about ten feet. And ideally, the wheelchair would not be metal, but that is probably hard to avoid—try having the least amount of metal possible. If the wheelchair is metal, then some purification might be necessary for the chair. Then repeat the procedure to the best of your ability. But if you roll into the circle or someone pushes you into the circle, you will have to establish the plant setup of the circle after you're rolled in.

In the case of a person who can step into the circle, establish the circle of plants. If you have only four plants, you can just step in through someplace between the plants. If, on the other hand, there are many plants, then you will have to very gently and respectfully remove three or four of the plants and step in. Do *not* step in by stepping over the tops of the plants. That will create a disharmony. After you have stepped into the circle, have either you or someone who's assisting you gently put the plants back where they were. Once you are standing in the center of the circle, wait at least five minutes.

It would be good to have no shoes on, if at all possible. But it is also completely acceptable to have on shoes made of natural fabric—leather, in this case, would be considered natural. Also, have the least amount of metal possible—ideally none—on your body. If you have metal in your teeth, it can't be helped, so don't worry about it. If you happen to have a pacemaker or an artificial hip or something like that, again, it can't be helped. You will probably be doing regular things to clear yourself on a general basis if you're using such a circle anyway. So the metal in your teeth will probably be pretty clear.

The Benefits of Sage in a Sickroom

What about in a sickroom? This says the antiseptic properties of sage as an herb are useful in treating intestinal and respiratory infections, and the essential oil heated in a vaporizer will disinfect a sickroom. So with fevers, would you bring the plants into the sickroom?

Probably not in this case. It should be something more associated strictly with the shamanic. If you wanted to, though, and the doctors and nurses and everybody said okay, you could put a group of three to six plants to the person's left. But if you did that, you'd want to set up some kind of perimeter so that other people didn't touch the plants. That's very difficult in a sickroom, but if it's a situation where that could be done, then you put the plants to the person's left—not so close that he or she could reach out and touch them. We are talking maybe five feet away. If the situation exists where that can be done, then instruct everyone not to touch the plants. There needs to be someone who tends the plants, waters them, and so on. That's acceptable.

If the plants start to look poorly or feeble, even in the slightest way, then they should be removed from that room, along with any other plants that you feel are volunteering—make sure the plants are volunteers. As a shamanic or mystical person, you might be able to do that. Probably you would by that time know whether the plants are volunteering or not. If there are other volunteers, bring them in. If there are not others, then the plants will have to recharge and be nurtured back to health. If those are the only plants you have, then you will just have to say, "Well, you can do this only as long as the plants can tolerate it." Then they will need to recover.

We're talking about how it's better to use the live sage plant. But can you use the parts of the plant if the plant dies naturally?

Sage does not normally die naturally, but if allowed to go through its cycles, normally something else happens in your modern world, but . . . I will change that a bit. Say you are requesting of the plant for it to provide you with a sprig of itself—you might do this as an herbologist, as a healer. You would have to get a volunteer, and you would have to cut the plant very carefully so as to cause the least amount of harm. You would have to cut it only where you get the feeling to cut it, even if you need more. If you need more, you will have to get another plant to volunteer. Use the heart-warmth, the heart-love technique, you understand, to know whether it's yes or no, or use your own built-in skills and abilities, your process that you have evolved, and acquire sprigs of the plant. That's what I would recommend—not to cut a plant off at the ground, or worse yet, to pull it up. I know that spiritual folk do not do this, but I'm mentioning it to those of you who may just be getting started with this.

If you're just getting started with it, always consult others who have been doing it for a while to get their guidance and advice, especially someone who is fond of plants and not just one who is growing them for research or science. I recognize that scientists and researchers can be fond of plants, but they may have other agendas, not necessarily their own. They may be working for somebody, eh? Ideally you are going to want to be interacting with wild plants.

But if you are interacting with plants that you've potted, in your garden or in pots, say, then you absolutely must get their permission, because anytime plants are trimmed, they all get nervous. Even if you're growing flowers or potatoes, you can be growing an herb garden and 400 feet away, if you are trimming the herbs, the potatoes get nervous. I'm picking out potatoes at random, but it could be any other plant—apples, an apple tree.

Plants are aware; they are very aware of trimming, because of course, without permission from the plant, it's painful, just as it would be for you. Ideally, you would give the plant at least three days' notice. First, you get permission, and then you give the plant three days' notice—so a minimum of sixteen hours' notice. Then you come back and follow the procedures I've recommended. We're going to have to stop for the day. We can resume next time. Good life.

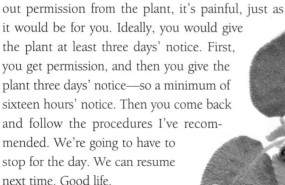

CHAPTER FOUR

Marijuana

MARCH 13, 2009

ର

MARIJUANA.
Welcome.
   Thank you.
Tell me about yourself.
   I am an individual growing in the wild and in a place that is basically inaccessible to most human beings, simply because of its terrain. It is in our nature—speaking for myself and others in the family—to have a certain coordination with the spirit of all beings. Given that nature—which, as far as the human being goes, has been discovered in and passed on through various generations and groups of human beings who are known for their shamanic or mystical capabilities. There has been a concordance with addressing Spirit, with heightening Spirit's influence, and yes, with what you might call falling back on Spirit.
   There are times when life becomes too complex (or the opposite, too mundane) to support life, and you as a general global society—not talking about individual groups here and there but as a general society—are in such a time now. The problem is that it's complex and mundane, and the foundation for your unity is based largely in business. The problem there, one that you have

tripped over recently, is acquisition, our society's unifying element. This element is very susceptible to slipping into greed, and as you know, with greed comes competition and frequently a savage element. So you are struggling to maintain global unity—which a great many people appreciate, including those in government and other influential places—not only for its efficiency but also for the hope it offers. Granted, this may be a long-distance hope, but maybe it will happen sooner, that global strife would reduce at least country to country.

What's happened along the way is that the model you are now using, the business model, is not only cyclic but it is susceptible to greed and the savage element within that. So on one hand, I feel you will be able to coordinate global unity with one another and most likely, people are striving for that now, in groups. That's something beyond you. Initially, people may reach for longstanding religions and philosophies and ways of life, but this may not prove to be a lasting thing. People will discover that those who lead such organizations and groups are frail. People are looking for role models. What would you like to know?

The Challenge for Human Beings
Is to Achieve Connection with Their Spirit

You are a single plant in the wild. Are you connected to a larger being or to your home planet? Or are you speaking as one personality?

I'm speaking as an individual connected to the family of others of which we are. [Pause.] For your global entity to achieve a higher and more comfortable level of being, it will be necessary—since those who lead organizations, religions, philosophies, and so on, are just normal human beings like everyone else, and in that sense, frail—for any one person who is shoved into a spot of global leadership to seem to be just normal like everybody else. People will become frustrated by this, and then they will find that they themselves have spirit. Spirit and soul are a unifying factor of all beings—for those on Earth too.

The turn to spirit is something I am interested in because as a living plant, we, in terms of our reproduction in our natural state, have moments of union with all spirit. So a way that human beings can heighten their own spirits is ideally to be in a field that contains many plants, such as me, that are going to seed. Other plants present would be acceptable, as long as they are compatible and considered to be supporting Spirit as well—perhaps sage and maybe others according to shamanic or mystical tradition.

Be with the living plant and strive to become conscious of your own spirit, and just breathe in and out. There may be a fragrance, you understand. Just breathe in and out, with the plants all around you—ideally with you not standing on any, so perhaps in a garden outdoors would be best—and then the ability to achieve total resonance with your own spirit will be greatly simplified. The challenge for human beings now is to—within a complex, busy life—be able to achieve connection with their spirits and then to be able to feel that connection in others. But first you achieve connection with your own spirit and then relax into that feeling—eyes closed, perhaps sitting on something comfortable, perhaps sitting on the ground, for people who are flexible. As you relax into that energy of your own spirit, you will feel a physical sensation of yourself expanding. This is not a delusion, all right? It is an actual sensation of your soul or spirit expanding and encompassing.

You do not lose touch with your own individuality, but you simply join the spirits of other beings. If there are other human beings in the garden doing this, you will be joined with them, and you will be joined with the plants and all other beings on the planet, whether they are plant or animal or human, who are doing this at the same time as you are. Thus it would be possible to have at least an expansion into life forms that are connected with their spirits—which would be plants and most animals and some human beings, and even beyond that.

Used as Intended, Marijuana Can Help Humans Connect to All Life

But at the very least, you would be able to connect with the spirit of all life connected by doing that at that moment on your planet. The feeling would be as if you are expanding more and more but without losing touch with your own personality and your own spirit. What happens, though, in the course of that, is that the cares and concerns of your busy world fall away. So of course you want to do this when you have the least amount of things to do over the following few hours. As these cares and concerns fall away, the connection is very easily accomplished. This is something that has been misunderstood in your time because people have taken our plants, cut them up, dried them, and put them through a lot of processes. They are harming the plant and escaping through the use of the plant in drug form. But this is not the intention. It's not to escape; it's to embrace. It's not to step away from and shove away from; it's to make a connection with all life. The best way to do this is with the living plant, in the condition that I have described.

This would help to greatly reduce avarice. If people were doing this, say, once every three days or so, it would greatly reduce the need, the desire for acquisition beyond one's own needs and beyond the needs of one's family. It would create a calm state, a relaxed state, a state of ease wherein one would not require more and more and more just for the thrill of it. One would feel awkward and uncomfortable and burdened—literally burdened—with the more and more and would let go of it. It would still be possible to have commerce, but it would not be necessary to acquire more and more. In short, feelings that are very difficult to control—perhaps feelings that are conditioned into people by the way they were raised or by the society in which they live—would not have to be controlled because these feelings would simply vanish and be replaced with a connection to all life. But after a while, the advantage to this—and I'm going through stages here, because the connection to all life would be those who are connected to Spirit—is that if more human beings do this, there is more of a connection to all life.

Interacting with Live Plants Does Not Create Chemical Dependency

Afterward it is then quite easy to notice when you are feeling imbalanced. If you do that five, six, seven, eight, nine, ten times like that, eventually the feeling will be present even though you are not around the plant. But it would be good to be able to easily go out into the garden, have the fragrance available, and within a few seconds, immediately feel refreshed into that feeling. You would not have that fragrance with the dried marijuana plant, burnt and so on, because the burning element creates a change in the energy. It is important that the plant be living. That moment of thriving is involved in the seeding process, that transformation where one is becoming many, and it is found in a great many forms of life all over the universe. It is a unifying element.

Thus the unifying element applies quite easily to the physical human being because your body is made up of however much of this element—from earth, from who knows where—multiple times over. Your body immediately reacts to that, and the only thing that takes a little while to come along is your personality, based on your conditioning and experience. But that comes along. In the beginning, this process may take longer, but after a while, it happens much more quickly. When everyone or a great many people are involved in doing this, what occurs is that relaxation. The most important part in comparing with your current cultures and civilizations is that you will immediately notice both where people are not doing this and where people are suffering or hurting.

It will be very easy to find such people and then to provide them with what they need to help them come to balance—and, eventually, to show them how to connect with their spirits as you have done—if you use this process. It can begin with small groups and from there go on to larger groups. It will take time, and interaction with other plants might be useful. But my feeling is that it can help you to easily and much more quickly re-create a benevolent state of being on this planet.

Also, since avarice and acquisition will no longer be a replacement for the feeling of the loss of one's connection to all beings and thus to Creator itself, substitutes will no longer be necessary and other things will come into balance in a natural, benevolent way—such as, over time, the world's population. There will not be a huge need to continue to populate so much, though there will be a rediscovery of the means to live underground and to travel to other planets to take up residence there. But that's in the further future; that will happen in a couple hundred years. Interacting with a living plant does not create a society of people who are dependent on this or that chemical or this or that chemistry. You are interacting with the living, and thus life itself takes on a new meaning for you.

Shamanic Societies Interacted with Wild-Grown Marijuana

How many plants must be around in order for four or five people to achieve this connection?

Not around, interspersed. Picture a garden with rows. It requires as many plants as it takes to be able to notice the fragrance. One person could experiment. I realize in your time that this might be awkward since the plant has been made illegal because of its uses. It's been made illegal because its use has created a disconnection from society, but the method I refer to supports a connection to society and all beings. So I understand the reason why the plant has been discouraged from being grown.

Still, it will take, if possible—perhaps done experimentally with some kind of a permit—as much as it takes for one person to walk up and down the rows. Make the rows wide, because you're not only making rows so that you can water the plants as in a typical garden but you are making rows so that the plant will have plenty of room to be with human beings who are, say, lying down in the rows or sitting in the rows in some comfortable accommodation. So the other possibility is to have gaps in the rows where a person could sit.

I know some people are going to want to sit together, but I would recommend that people have individual places to sit. The reason I say "lying down" is because some people might fall asleep—and for some, this is good. But if people are going to sit, they need to be able to be in a position where they don't fall over, so the chair would have to have arms or something to keep you from falling over. Because when you fall over, you'll just crash into a plant and that will disrupt the energy, obviously—to say nothing of the fact that you might get injured; we can't have that.

Was this done in shamanic societies in the past?

Yes, but more casually by finding the plant growing in the wild, which is always better. But I realize that this is a rare and probably difficult situation for you now. Plants growing in the wild are usually stronger, more capable, and more connected to all life in general. But I realize the next best thing for you is to grow the plants in a garden. It's all right if they are grown in a greenhouse, but if they are grown in a greenhouse, there would need to be some sheltering element. So you might have glass panes or something with the proper ventilation. But if they are growing in the wild or you have your garden, it would be best if there were trees around so that the fragrance would tend to permeate the whole area. You might be required to have a permit for this. But in some countries, maybe you wouldn't.

Try a New Pathway if You Become Frustrated While Trying to Make a Connection

The whole point, however, is to help people who find it difficult, because of distraction or for other reasons, to connect with their spirits. People who can connect with their spirits now do not require this. I want to make that clear. But you may have worked with people—those of you who are in the process or helping others to be in the process of connecting with their spirits—who simply could not make this connection. They become frustrated and it's harder for them as a result—frustration meaning something that tends to expand or become more, the more one attempts to do something that isn't working by using a certain pathway. So then you try a different pathway. This is a pathway I am aware of, being a member of the family of plants, as you say.

When you talked about the spirit of all beings, were you talking about one spirit being or the combined spirits of all beings?

I was speaking of the spirits of all beings, but there is a unifying element. When a person doing a meditation can connect with her spirit, the energy comes in and the more she relaxes into the energy, the greater the energy becomes. When that's happening, you are connecting with other spirits. That's why it becomes greater. It's not because you yourself are using a small connection and then your connection gets bigger. It's because your connection, the way you feel your spirit, is only so much. But as this naturally occurs, you begin connecting with the spirits of other beings who may be present. This will be a benevolent thing, because it will be other beings who are connected to their spirits whether they are small or big creatures: ants, little beetles maybe, trees, blades of grass, and so on. Other human beings, their spirits—this is why it seems to expand. The same process is at work. Feels good to know that, eh?

It's wonderful.

Not All Plant Life on Earth Is Meant for Human Beings

Were your people invited to this universe by the Creator?

I could not say. I know that we came here because we were brought by others from other planets that we used to populate. We still populate those planets, but we were seeds brought by visitors who were profoundly spiritual. These visitors would travel among planets—planetary travel is typical of beings who are supporting all life on various planets. They are very spiritual beings and they acquire seeds on an individual basis, based on how those seeds feel to them.

If they feel like the seed wishes for them to go to other worlds, then they collect that seed. But the only reason they know the seed's wish to come is that when they hold a finger out—it's like a finger but it's somewhat splayed at the end—and come close to touching a seed, the seed moves a bit. When they very slightly touch the seed, it immediately releases from what it is connected to and joins them. Then they know that the seed has volunteered. That's how they connect; that's how they collect seeds from wherever they go. Then they take the seeds and use the same process to bring them to other planets so that everything is done in concordance with the seeds' desires. No seed is brought to a planet where it does not desire to go. The seeds feel all the way ahead so they know that the plant will feel welcome, will be embraced, and will feel a personal connection. Shamans and mystical people in your time and place have been trained to do this as well, trained in knowing these things.

So they will often bring such things to planets where civilizations are struggling. Sometimes the civilizations will not be human; they might be other lifeforms. And you have such forms of life on your planet, great varieties. So the plants are not always for the human being. A nonhuman population may be struggling to survive for this or that reason, and so they might need this or that kind of plant to be supported. You may have seen different forms of life go toward this or that plant to consume some portion of that plant or even to consume something that the plant is holding. Plants will sometimes hold things that are much more than they need. And you might reasonably ask, "Why does the plant hold this?"

They may be holding it for other beings. You might see this if there has been a long dry spell, and you might see ants, for instance, go to a cactus to withdraw water. They don't do much damage to the plant, but you can tell if you look at a cactus—the kind with broad leaves—it might have little brown scars here and there. This means that probably ants or other creatures have managed to land there and take in some of the plant itself or the moisture the plant is holding beyond its own needs. That's a physical reason.

But there are other plants, fruits, berries, and so on that may not be specifically meant for the human being. That's why the human being might find them to be poisonous—because they are not for you. But they might very well be for other creatures: birds or bears or worms or spiders or what have you. So they might need them for their own survival. They might need them for their reconnection. There's any number of things that might need them, as individuals or groups.

No Matter What Planet We Are On, Our Purpose Is Always the Same

The animals know the interrelatedness of all life. It is only the human being who does not know—but only here on this planet, not anyplace else in the universe. Elsewhere, human beings are like everyone else. They know. But on this planet, you are attempting to do something new. We know this, and because you are attempting to do something new, you cannot know what you know everyplace else. It has created many problems—I feel too many, but it is not my job [chuckles] to address that point of view in myself so much as it is to offer what I have to offer.

Your family has always had this ability to help others connect to their spirit? Is this innate within you, no matter what planet you are on?

It's always been that way. Of course, when we are on a planet where everybody is connected to spirits like that, we are not conscious of it. We just live our lives as well as possible as beings of the universe do, in many universes over. But we notice that. For instance, I notice that on this planet you have a vast number of beings who are not always connected to their spirits. Of course, when you are sleeping deeply, you are all connected to your spirits. This is how we can be here. I feel that we would never have been able to volunteer—the originating seeds would never have volunteered—if the human beings on this planet were never connected to their spirits. That would be too much. But every one of you—with very few exceptions in my experience, limited though it may be—is connected to your spirit, generally speaking, at least once a day.

Every night, yes, when we sleep.

Yes. This happens on sort of a revolving pattern. So no matter how complex or distracting your life is as a human being, you do have times of the day or night when you are deeply and totally connected to your spirit. As your soul migrates, since it does not need to sleep, your body naturally reconnects with all spirit, because your body is used to doing that to a degree, though your spirit may be unaware, meaning your personality, of being connected to all beings and all spirit when you are awake, physically in your body. Your body is still mostly two-thirds to three-quarters connected with all spirit. But when you are asleep, your body completely connects; when the soul goes to be with teachers and guides and so on, then there is a total connection.

Human Beings with the Same Interests Are Not Always Connected

Do you have a period of rest or are you conscious all twenty-four hours of the day, or how does that work?

Just imagine that we are very much like the human being in deep slumber, except that we are awake. Granted, at night we may go a little deeper into rest, but since we need to be alert to our surroundings, we do not sleep as you know sleep to be, meaning a state that would be essentially unconscious. We just rest a little more. It is not unlike what you might do, say, in a meditation.

Are you aware of many of what you would call cycles of being in a marijuana plant on Earth? Does your memory go back quite a ways?

Quite a ways, yes, but it would be hard to describe it in terms of years. All I can say is that the first few times I was not aware, and I didn't see a human being. But somewhere around the third or fourth time, I saw a human being. They were wearing . . . "see," you understand, but not with eyes: I became conscious of a human being. I will have to take a moment to discover if I can get a year. I cannot do this myself. I think it was in the 1800s. People were migrating. That's all I could tell. I think it was a natural migration. They were not fleeing, because they were calm and seemed to be comfortable. They were at ease. That's all I can say.

Can you live anywhere on the planet or do you need a temperate zone?

We cannot grow where there is snow or ice, nor can we grow underwater.

You have this incredible ability to help humanity but people are cutting you up and drying you and burning you and doing the opposite of what you came here to help us do.

Well, that is not surprising, since human beings in the waking state might operate under willpower rather than inspiration. But we understand why this happens, and it was a long-range choice, in my perception, to come here. Those first seeds came to the planet thousands of years ago. So in those days, it was more common, you might say, to find yourself exposed to human beings who might have more mystical or shamanic capabilities, because many thousands of years ago, human beings tended to be more tribal in nature, for the purpose of survival. Even though you have tribes today or groups within cultures and civilizations who are essentially being tribal, who have the same interests—though at this time, focusing on war and avarice—they are not always connected, yes?

So the tribal nature of the human being—or the familial nature, you could also say—goes hand in hand with your character, because this is found on other planets where all is benevolent. So that is natural. But thousands and thousands of years ago, when you had the original seeds, they had contact with the plant form more often. They were able to spread and have many plants so that perceptive human beings who were studying all life in order to know what was safe to be around, what could support their lives and how—in short, mystical people, medicine people, and just acute observers—were able to have different reactions.

I feel that perhaps next time it might be a good idea—if you would, if it were possible for you—to connect with such a being. Thus you might get more of an understanding of the beings who brought them here, but perhaps more importantly, of the nature of the human being uncluttered with the demands and complexities of today's culture. I have come to you first, you understand, because today's culture is a reality. It might also be helpful to know how it was in other times, because in those other times, you would find certain core elements of the human being's structure, such as the tribal nature. That is something that has not gone away. You still have that nature and you do seek out tribes of like-minded individuals, as you call them—but actually, they are like-hearted, like-feeling, and like-nature, meaning personality.

The Way to Survive and Thrive Is to Support All Life

You have such a great heart and such a wonderful personality. I'm so glad we are doing this book so that people will know this about you marijuana plants.

Yes, I feel that the book will help to bring back lost knowledge, and that is really important in your times when people are seeking knowledge that will support and sustain, yes, but that also may have served that role in the past in ways that lasted a while. People are always attempting, in your time, to create and re-create. This is normal. But the desire to create and re-create now must be expressed in ways that are peaceful, calming, benevolent, and support all life. That's the key: how to support all life, not to compete when life is damaged or sometimes permanently destroyed. The way to survive and thrive is to support all life. You understand this?

Yes. Does one have to be in your physical presence to connect with you or can one connect on a meditation level?

Well, quite obviously, it's possible to connect on the meditation level, since this channeling process is taking place. The channeling—my understanding of channeling—is connecting to the spirit that is the most benevolent form of being so that when the personality and energy is focused through the channel himself or herself, it does the most good for all beings and offers some influence to others when something may be required of them. The channel connects in this way rather than connecting with just anything that might be in pain or suffering and might therefore require things of the channel, drain the channel. So a certain amount of knowledge and training would be helpful—to know to do this, not that—to bring it through. Therefore think of all the training that this being has gone through to be able to do what he can do.

There are other methods, but it may be possible for an individual who does meditate, you understand, or is able to connect to spirit, to connect on the basis of a photograph. But the photograph must be the plant in its seeding stage—any stage in its seeding. The problem is, without the fragrance, you will probably be acting or reacting on the basis of your learned knowledge as compared to your wisdom—and wisdom is always based on experience. That's the difference. Learned knowledge can be helpful, but wisdom is based on experience. My understanding is that it's based on the experience that has worked for you as an individual, and such wisdom may be helpful to others, but probably not to all others at all times, because different individuals respond benevolently to different wisdom. It depends on the time, the place, the circumstances, and so on.

We Are Aware of the Experience Human Beings Are Participating In

Now, you are aware of what we are trying to do here, right? You are aware of the school?

Yes. I think all of us are. Not in its totality, you understand. We are aware that you are attempting to create something new that will be good for all beings. So—knowing the universe slightly as I do—if it is something new to the universe and it will be good for all beings, then Creator could only have completely approved of that, because it isn't good on the basis of someone's will or someone's avarice. To be good for all beings, this would be something that all beings are in agreement with now in the universe. They would not make an error based on somebody's will, avarice, or any other reason like that. They would only make that decision based on the feeling they had when contemplating the possibility of feeling better in the most benevolent way.

So I know that it is a good thing, whatever it is you are trying to do. That's what we know. We don't know exactly what you are trying to do, and I'd just as soon not know. It might be a complication. I know enough; we all know enough. There are many other forms of life here that know enough. Since we have to know our own personalities—we have to know what we know in order to survive—then to know enough about what others are doing is sufficient. I'm making a point of this because sometimes human beings get caught up in learning way too much about other forms of life when they do not know enough about their own form of life. [Chuckles.]

That is a good point. You seem so wise and self-sufficient, but do you ever have need to call on a teacher or a spirit to get advice or energy or anything?

Generally, no, but in this condition—speaking in this way through a human being—I am somewhat connected to the overall spirit on this planet of all beings such as myself. That is how I am able to access, to a degree, knowledge outside the parameters of my own awareness, but it would be a stretch—an uncomfortable one at that—to access the knowledge of the original seeds that came or were brought here by those spiritual beings.

But would the spirit you are connected to have that information and other information?

As I said, it would be uncomfortable to make such knowledge present. You do that next time.

That's what I'm asking. You said talk to the seeds, but I'm wondering if we should talk to the spirit also.

I think you are creating a separation where there is none.

Oh, I see. Talking to the seeds will be the same as talking to the spirit. Okay.

When you talk to any being, even a human being, you are also talking to his spirit, even though the predominant element at that time—with a conscious human being—might very well be her personality of the moment, her conditioned personality, you understand?

Mm-hmm.

Yet if you have ever talked very gently to a human being who is going to sleep or just waking up, as you might do with a youngster in your care, very often you are talking to the spirit of that being. It's not as if you have to go very far to talk to a spiritual being. This is why people will often see, in the eyes of babies—especially with their own children—something vast and loving. This is the total connection, you see, that babies have to all spirit. They have not developed their separated personalities yet, so they are separated only to a degree. One sees this in the eyes or notices it in the radiated energy you call auric fields around any and all beings, whether they are baby birds or baby ants or beetles. You might not see those, but you might see these fields around baby birds if you are lucky, or around baby humans.

All others have their own auric fields. But they are totally connected to Spirit. As time goes on, they develop their personalities and they may not be totally connected all the time. But they are totally connected at least some of the time. I'm mentioning this because as life goes on for you and more human beings connect with their spirits through our help or the help of something else or someone else, then you will understand that better. You will have a broader view that you are not talking to a human being—to some thing, especially people you don't know where there's a tendency to speak to them offhand or treat them roughly, perhaps, or speak to them sharply—you will know that you are speaking to a portion of Spirit, of which you are a portion. If you speak to Spirit harshly, you will feel harsh and uncomfortable. If you are not aware of that in yourself, you can become aware. The mistreatment of other human beings always results in harm to your self simultaneously. It may not be felt to the same level as it is felt by the one who is receiving mistreatment, but it will be felt and it will linger; it will demand to be taken care of. This is why human beings, while maybe mistreating others, even in slight ways, will feel a restlessness, because human beings, as sensitive as you are, are attempting to resolve that. You're here to not only create something new, but you are here to create resolution about all that has been created in the process of taking steps toward the new thing.

Therefore you must be and are creative all the time. This has created certain problems and has required a great deal of resolution on your part. More will be needed. But there will be people who will specialize in that, and they are doing that even now. Many of you are shamanic and mystical and medicine people, and others will be needed—at times, everyone. Often this takes places at the deep levels of your sleep, and other times, when you are more conscious or aware, if you are striving for it, or when the feeling just comes over you. These days, it will not be so unusual to have a calming, wonderful feeling come over you for a moment or maybe even for a minute or two. That is the connection with all spirit. Some of you will identify that as the connection with Creator— and really, there's not that much difference. So I am letting you know of some things, I am reminding you of other things, and I will allow the founders of my form of life on this planet to speak to you next time. Adieu.

Thank you very much. Good life. Thank you.

CHAPTER FIVE

Marijuana Spirit

MARCH 16, 2009

છ૭

GREETINGS. This is Marijuana Spirit. I'm not sure how long we can hold this, but let's go ahead. Question?

You go to many planets around this universe. Before your seeds were brought to this Earth, were you told that there was anything different about this planet?

Only that the human being was a hopeful being—meaning that a lot had been placed in your hands, so to speak, that would be helpful to future generations—but that in order to be effective, you would have to be practical while at the same time being highly sensitized to your surroundings. You would be surrounded by teachers in the form of plants, along with other beings from other parts of the universe (those you have come to call animals), and even small particles would help you at your various stages of sleep. Much of what you breathe in and out at night is made up of particles, aside from the gases that you breathe to stay alive.

These particles near the human being, whether created by the human being or not, are generally infused with the spirit matter of your teachers. These teachers are, to a minor extent, associated with the teachers of all

61

human beings, and to a more significant extent, they are individualized on a personal basis with your spirit teachers in general—meaning per person guides, and so on. This is how your physical body is able to interpret the messages from a given set of guides for an individual. Now, you call these spirit guides, but that's too confining because sometimes these guides are associated with living beings. They might have at one time been a mineral you call rock or they might have been a plant you call wood or they might have been a form of animal, which you call many things.

Human Beings Use Drugs to Obtain a State of Safety

Sometimes if people do not have something available to them such as an air-filter system, then there might be a pet who comes and goes and can bring those particles. This helps the human being to access the natural world. In good times, this has been more difficult—by good times, I mean going back, say, 125 or 150 years to when human beings as a group lived in dwellings that were less permeable to the transit of not only materials of the natural world but by particles from the natural world. This has become a little problematic. So the essence of spirits that might be seen as, say, lightbeings by the sensitive or the trained are much more frequent in your world. This is why sensitive people or people who have worked on such training see these things more often. But even those who have not been sensitized and have not had the training but are simply functioning as human beings are much more likely in your time now—especially with, as I say, the dwellings that one works and lives in—to see these little patterns of light or quick flashes of something that is there. This is not done to frighten anyone but is done as a reassurance of your immortality.

Why do you think people on this planet do drugs, among them marijuana? Are they trying to get closer to their spirit or to escape their daily lives?

Both, and for other reasons. Some people are naturally more sensitive than others. But almost all people, human beings, are born profoundly sensitive, and there are different expressions of personality there. Some might be highly sensitive to touch, others might be sensitive to feeling, and so on. As a result, one longs for those original states of being. Oh, there is this talk about how your spirit longs for your home planet and so on, but in reality, from my perception, one longs for that sensitive state of being in which one is safe and yet can be highly sensitive.

So there is a spiritual longing involved in the interaction with what you call a drug in the form of marijuana. Marijuana, when *unadulterated*, can be a plant that supports the reengagement with one's spirit and the connection to one's early weeks as a child physically on the planet. This is a time when one is pro-foundly receptive, almost too sensitive to take the life that one is exposed to as a baby here. There is, as you know, a tendency to handle babies a little more firmly than they can accept. Sometimes this is the reason babies cry—because they get frightened of being handled as if they were older children.

It's true that older children like to tumble around and play and so on, but they've become used to the way of the culture(s). But when they are first born and up to the end of the first year to when they are a year and half old, they are so sensitive that such contact must be made very gently if at all. So I thought I'd mention that. The attraction to reconnect to those times and perhaps to one's deeper spirit purpose and the reason on the physical basis for the soul to be here—I'm differentiating between spirit, because that's your overall purpose of all your lives everywhere, and the soul, which is individualized to a physical life—will most easily be stimulated as you link to the physical and find the capacity to be focused on that reconnection.

You Must State Your Intentions as You Approach a Marijuana Plant

So when interacting with the living plant, this can be done by fragrance, but it can be done another way. It's very important that the plant be alive and unadul-terated—not sprayed with anything—so you can have a true sense of the auric field of the plant. There must be a sense of "simpatico," a camaraderie between the individual and the plant. I would recommend, where this is possible, that there be a choice of at least five or six of these plants and that the human beings state their intentions for approaching any individual plant. Ideally, for the sake of such approaches, the plants would be in pots, but these are not to be metal pots or any human-made material other than formed earth, which would be a clay pot or possibly even a wooden one. But it doesn't have to be that. There needs to be at least a couple of feet between plants, so this can be done outdoors.

First, as one approaches the plants, you might say out loud that, "I am asking to feel more connected with my soul's purpose on the planet, my overall spirit's influence, and my experience on the planet in a most benevolent way." Thus nothing is ruled out; you are not trying to replace who you are, you see. Then at this point, you may be ten to twelve feet away from the plants. You approach them slowly but you do watch where you are going if you are outdoors so that you don't step on anything or anyone. And by "anyone," I am referring to life forms other than the human kind as well. You cannot help stepping on the soil of course. But try to watch where you put your feet.

Take a few steps forward and—it is no longer necessary to speak—hold out your left arm with the palm of your hand facing down and your fingers in a natural, curled, relaxed state. Hold it there and move your hand so that you're approaching the plant, reaching for the plant with the back of your hand. Reach toward each of the plants. I'm assuming, for the sake of this explanation, that they're in front of you. Let's say the plants are spread out from your right to your left. Try to put your arm toward the plant that is the farthest to your right, and then turn and face that plant. Say you are about six feet away at this point; in a moment you'll see why it's necessary to have that space between the plants.

You can put your arm toward any position, any part of the plant, meaning you can aim toward the ground, you can aim toward the top of the plant, anyplace—wherever you feel you should do this. Don't do it where you think or where others have told you to aim, but rather move toward where you feel attracted to aim. Remember that there are probably a lot of life forms behind the plant. So anyplace where the plant is at its most full would be best so that you make the connection with that plant.

When you aim your arm with the back of your hand, this way it's very safe for the plant, see? The plant isn't worried about being grabbed because this is not the way you would normally contact something. Then when you aim your left arm that way, you don't have to say anything. Just notice how you feel in the areas of your chest—one side or the other of your chest, you understand— and (not or, *and*) in the area of your body just below your rib cage (this would take in, generally speaking, what you call your abdomen). But only those parts of your body. If you get tense or uncomfortable in any one of these places, then that's not the time and not the place for that plant interaction. Then lower your arm and raise it again so that it is in the same form aimed toward another plant, and so on, working from your right to your left, you understand—always turning and facing the plant and then aiming your arm in that direction.

The Plant's Auric Fields Will Extend Out to Interact with You

At some point, you may get a relaxed feeling in your body. Some of you might feel warmth or some other pleasant feeling. But you have to feel that way, because this is how the plant signals its comfort with you as an individual and also that the plant is not busy doing other things. That's why I mention "another time," because it might be possible to do this another time with that same plant, see? If you get the feeling at some point with these plants, if you have that good feeling, then you can approach that particular plant. But this is how to make contact.

You don't ever touch the plant, all right? You get to the portion of the plant that feels best to the back of your hand—meaning you, at that point, begin to lower the back of your hand. You are about, say, three feet away from contact with the plant, still pretty far away. You lower the back of your hand toward the base of the plant or to the point where, as you lower it, your body doesn't feel quite as comfortable.

Then you raise your hand back up to the point where your body feels comfortable with the plant. When you feel that—then and only then . . . and your arm doesn't have to be straight out; it can be folded at the elbow, you know—at that point, you have your hand, and you bring it up so that the palm of your hand is facing the plant. Again, with your fingers and thumb relaxed, all right? Then you essentially reach toward the plant, but at no time do you get closer than three feet, because the auric field of such plants, when they are interacting with you, will extend. The plants will relax and extend out to their normal ranges, which is about nine feet or so. Of course, your auric field may not take in all that interaction because your auric field will be reaching out as well.

So there's a commingling of the energies. You don't want to get closer because the plant could get unsettled, uncomfortable. Then it would withdraw its auric field so that it's practically not far away from the plant at all. Everything is done very politely. Nothing is stated at this point. You've already stated your intentions. The plant knows your intentions. By the way, it doesn't make any difference what language you speak or if for some reason you are unable to speak—not in the case of someone who hasn't learned the language yet, but simply if you are unable for some reason. Then you can just approach the plant on the basis of a good feeling. Feel good toward the plant. Don't just think good; *feel* good. I'm covering that territory for those who may have that situation.

To continue, you can stay and interact with that plant for perhaps a minute or two. The plant will be interacting with your auric field, and because of being outdoors, there might be life going on around you naturally—other plants and animals doing things. Ideally there won't be too many human beings around. You can have a companion with you who is at least twenty-five feet away—maybe a little farther would be better. It would be good to not have anything that plants would be afraid of on you, like knives or things like that, things that plants are alarmed about for obvious reasons. But any other metal objects are perfectly all right—a belt buckle and so on.

So stay for that minute or minute and a half or so, but don't look at your watch. Just make your best guess. Then lower your hand back to its original position so the back of your hand is toward the plant. This is a polite way of letting the plant know you have received what you need. Many of you will have felt something. All the while, of course, you'll be breathing. So you're breathing in and out and you might take in some of the fragrances around you, which will include the plant's fragrance. Then relax, and if you can, take one or two steps backward, all the while looking over your shoulder or glancing around you so you can make certain that you are stepping someplace where you will not trip and also where you will not step on other life forms (to the best of your ability). After you take one or two steps backward, you can make one quarter of a rotation to your left. Then glance back at the plant after you make the quarter rotation and say, "Good life." Pause for a moment and put your arm back down at your side. Relax, make another quarter rotation to the left, and then you may walk away slowly.

You Only Get 1 to 3 Percent of the Benefit of Marijuana If You Smoke the Plant rather than Interact with It

For the next sixteen to eighteen hours, you will have that energy in you. It will help to coordinate your soul's purpose on the planet and your spirit's intent as well as commingling with your life experience so that nothing is left out of the mix, so to speak. Thus the potential for you to reengage with the individual sensitivities you had when you came to the planet—but which, as a result of your experiences, might have changed—could be inspired by your original purpose and infused with your life experience. You don't have to sacrifice anything, such as your spouse, your friends and family, your occupation, and so on.

Nothing is excluded, but you are reattuned—maybe you not having forgotten, but you're reattuned—to that which you generally cannot remember. It is rare for a human being to remember all the way back to babyhood, the way a baby would remember things. You might have flashes of awareness. You might even, using some techniques, recall feelings. But it is not likely that you will be totally focused in your spirit's and soul's purposes. This helps you to do that because it coordinates this by including your life experience, not only talents and abilities you have developed, but heightening your original talents and abilities so that your capacities are sharpened. You can attune to something quicker. You have your soul's original purpose; you have your overall spirit's being. Certain talents and capacities will be more readily available to you.

You may have a clarity of purpose that has been missing for a time. In short, you can have an experience over the next eighteen hours that may come and go, and for some, it might take place in the light-sleep stage or meditation, perhaps.

It only takes place in the deep dream state as you get older and more experienced in life. This is something that I recommend to be done. I know you originally asked about marijuana as a drug, but marijuana is not a drug; it is a living plant. The fact that it is utilized—smoked, you say—that way, gives you, depending on the individual, 1 to 10 percent, or for the vast majority of people, closer to 2 or 3 percent of the experience I just mentioned. That's why people like to do it not just once but perhaps a few times a day, every day—something like that, to smoke like that. Although I must say, wrapping a piece of paper around it will diminish the experience. In any event, people will want to do that in order to get even 1, 2, or 3 percent of that feeling back again. Most of what they get by smoking it, however, is injured to a degree. Your lungs don't like taking in hot smoke. So ultimately, you are left with about 0.5 to 1 percent of the experience. If you could interact with the living plant, it would be much easier, much gentler to you and the plant itself.

Use Your Physical Body, Not Your Mind, to Interact with the Plant

You said the fragrance is a powerful part of the experience. So should we only use the plants when they're flowering? Or are they fragrant all the time?

They are probably more fragrant when they are flowering or going to seed, yes.

Is there any increased benefit or any difference between the male, the female, or the one that has both?

The only difference is in the flowering or seeding process. So that's the one to interact with the most. But other expressions of the plant may be around. That's fine. For some individuals, it might be a different plant that attracts them, regardless of what's flowering or going to seed. Remember, we are talking about approaching the plant. You interact with the plant that feels the best to you regardless of what it's doing. Remember, this is not a thinking experience. Don't look at the plant and say, "Oh, that one has flowers. That's the one I'm going to." Instead, use your physical body because your physical body is much more in tune with the physical world than your mind is. What would your friend say—your friend, Zoosh? What would he say?

Never forget that.

Yes.

In the human brain there is a receptor for one of the elements of marijuana, one of the chemicals in the plant. In fact, there are several in the cerebellum, in the hippocampus, and in the ganglia.

This is research done by your scientists who are trying to understand why human beings become attracted to the constant use of the smoking material. So

I understand this research, but in fact, the auric field and, to some extent, the olfactory functions and the cilia in the lungs, are the portions that interact with the plant. So I will not comment on the attempt by science to initially look for research of nervous system interaction and, ultimately, genetic research, because I recognize that that's an attempt to solve a problem that doesn't really exist. By that I mean the natural interaction of human beings when they are ensouled—meaning that for living human beings, any living human beings, interaction with anything is always through your auric field. I'm not saying your energy body, because your energy body can reach out to other planets. But your auric field generally radiates a certain given amount of radiation—like a light bulb—in your body based on what you are doing. It is usually not more than twenty-five to maybe thirty-five, forty, or fifty feet away for some. Your energy body can range out a lot farther and is associated with your immortality, but the auric field is what you use to interact with all life.

Marijuana Can Reacquaint You with Your Love of Life

There is an estimate of 14.8 million Americans—Americans only—who smoke marijuana. How on earth are we going to get the government to, first, let people grow these plants for this purpose; and, second, inform all those people that they are doing it the wrong way?

Your job is never to inform anybody that they are doing anything the wrong way—as a publisher, all right? I realize this is sort of a personal question.

Well, it's a humane question.

Nevertheless, allow me. I will speak the way I speak. You have to be used to the fact that I have a tendency to speak in sensitive ways. You understand why, eh? So as a disseminator of information, it is only your job to disseminate to the best of your ability without taking out advertisements in the newspapers. In terms of those who read this and tell others, that's generally how it gets around. So we are reminding people of what was once known. Generally speaking, all of the material you put out in the world as a publisher does this. It reminds people of what was once known. That's why it's a good venture in many ways. So in order to encourage such contacts, it would be easier if the plants were centrally located. Obviously, human beings aren't living in the forest so much these days, and there's not even much forest left, though it will regenerate in time. So in terms of how this can be done, it will probably be much more easily done by individuals in different places. You have to remember that the United States is not the only country. There may be other places where such things are possible and where individuals might even be allowed to interact with life forms beyond that which is considered "legal" for various, well-intended purposes. I appreciate that, the differentiation of "well intended."

It's not so much about convincing anybody. It will be, in time, that certain places are licensed as they are now by government institutions to grow and have experiments. It might be possible that certain religious organizations are allowed to do this. It might also be possible that universities and other places of learning are allowed to do this, and so on. Those are the places that are most likely to get such permissions. Also, there are other countries that might be more allowing. So for those who can travel, that might be done. For those who can interact with plants at universities—ideally those growing outdoors—and for those who can interact in other ways, this is how it will start.

In time it will be discovered that interacting with marijuana calms people, because when you reconnect with your soul's original purpose on the planet and reconnect with your overall spirit being—the one that is associated with your immortality and all the lives you live everywhere, interacting with all beings—it tends to calm you. It tends to reacquaint you with your love of life. Even when your life experience would cause you to become violent for protective reasons or other reasons, interacting with marijuana tends to diminish that. In short, it is therapeutic—not when done in prescribed ways, but when done in this fashion so that the plant has a status that is equal to any other life form, including the human being.

There will be some people who will be allowed by the plant to get closer than three feet, but generally speaking, it is best not to touch the plant. If you touch the plant, the plant, as I say, might become uncomfortable. But there is more. For those who are in a highly sensitized state, touching the plant might become overwhelming, and you can go too far with the contact of your soul and spirit and become less involved in your physical, experiential life. So you do it the way I suggested simply because you are attempting to reacquaint yourself with portions of you that may have been harder to get in touch with—because of your life experience—before doing this experiment. I've elaborated there so that various individuals who, for good reasons from their own point of view and from their life experience, might say, "Well, this isn't worth it. What's the point? Just so somebody can do this? So what?" But it also will tend to reduce agitation, violence, and other forms of self-destructive behavior.

Some Plants Will Offer Information about the Future

How long since this was known and practiced on Earth?

It is still known and practiced in certain places where groups of individuals—generally speaking, spiritually connected individuals—pass down information. Sometimes it is passed down in threads from one family member to another, meaning connections. But in wider practice, it goes back to when there were more nomadic peoples and more space without so many human beings. It goes back to a time when there was more forest and when people had to utilize their instincts to know what was safe and what wasn't. In short, it goes back a few hundred years, and in some places maybe 1,200 or 1,400 years. But as I say, it is not unknown today.

Are there any other plants who have this ability that we should talk to? I mean, in addition to you and sage?

Yes. I think you'll want to speak to some other plants, but they will volunteer the information. It is not for me to volunteer that at this time. If I hear or feel different, I might volunteer a name as we go along here today. But I do not feel that that permission is granted right now. My feeling is that other plants will volunteer different things. There's only so much that needs to be heightened in the human being right now. And other things might be mentioned by various plants that may not seem relevant to your time, but include them anyway. Include all the other plants you've done for this book so far, because a great deal of the information has been given for other times, especially twenty-five years into the future, and some things that are more current. Sage and I are speaking more to current events, but other plants will speak to future situations. You've heard from a lot of those plants. I would recommend that, since sage and I are speaking to current events, you have us toward the beginning of the book.

The Human Soul Is Not Needed beyond the Veil

Have you ever inhabited a marijuana plant or are you always a spirit?

I am spirit, not unlike your own spirits. You have your immortal spirit, you see?

So you are the . . .

Please. I speak slowly, and that slowness has to do with sensing the environment here and all the environments between where "here" is with this human being to where you are. That's why I am slow. I'm sensing your environment as well. You know this, and I understand you are trying to get as much information as possible, but we will continue next time, so know that. Now, I lost my track. [Chuckles.] What was I talking about before I explained my purpose here?

That you were a spirit like a human high self or total spirit.

Yes. There is no high self, but I understand you're using terminology under-stood by your readers. There is no low self; there are just portions of your being. I am spirit, so I would be similar in that sense to your spirit as all spirit is con-nected all the time. As an individual, you also have a soul because soul is indi-vidualized. Your soul is your overriding being. Your soul can interact with the physical world, including the extremes you find on your planet. This must be the case, because many times your spirit cannot interact with extremes—vio-lence, hatred, and so on. So your soul takes over during those times from your spirit's guidance. Your soul is charged with a little more of Creator's energy than would be necessary for spirit. Both are charged with that energy, but spirit does not have to be charged with it in what I would call a polar fashion, as you would find in electricity—where there is the positive and the negative as an electrical charge, not as a comment on life. Your spirit tends to have a more benign feeling, meaning you would never get an electrical shock from your spirit. [Laughs.]

However, you might have something like that in contact with souls. Thus your soul also functions in some ways as an intermediary between your physi-cal life, your physical world, and your spirit. So when you come to the end of your natural life and your body is returning to the earth, your spirit moves toward your body and toward your soul. But as you move beyond and toward the veils—your soul and spirit traveling together—your soul does not move through all the veils into spirit, because it is no longer necessary to function and bring along its Earth experience. It moves through, perhaps, one of the veils, and that explains how people have what is sometimes known as an after-death experience and then they come back to life. They are reenergized somehow. This is the passage through that first veil. But it is not needed to move beyond that point, so the soul—how can we say?—dissipates its portion of being asso-ciated with Earth and the Earth experience, and the portion associated with spirit moves on. This is why after-death experiences only describe things up to a certain point. In this way, the spirit becomes the overriding factor that is in all life, and you move away from the world, rejoining your total spirit being, your guides, and your teachers—some of whom go with you; guides more associated with Earth doings may not—as you move on into your immortal being.

It Is Possible for Humans to Reconnect with All Their Lives

I don't know if you know this, but I thought I'd share it with you so that you recognize the commonality between the way you function on Earth and the way other beings do equally. Individual plants, every blade of grass, every ant, and every microbe has the same situation. Granted, their souls might not be as complex as the human being's soul because their reason for being here—aside from simply celebrating life and living it as well as possible—is to support the growth, change, and full experience of the human being as you attempt to create and re-create something new.

This does not mean that you have license to consume every other form of life, but it does mean that as these other forms of life interact with you, their souls function to a much greater degree in their interactions with you than with one another. This means they are ensouled, but they do not have to be disenfranchised from their spirit beings as much as you may be because of the violence or extremes of experience that human beings have on this planet. Extremes can sometimes also be joyous, but then they are compared to times when there are other things, you see. So the overall interaction is that the human being has a soul that is much more than that of, say, a blade of grass or an elephant—an elephant, also knowing who it is, not having to forget, is in touch with all of its lives and its immortal spirit, yes. As human beings, you are only in touch with all your lives and with your immortal spirit at the deepest levels of your sleep.

But getting back to my purpose for speaking today, it is possible to involve your spirit more. It is possible to reconnect with all your lives and with the reason for your being here. It is possible to relieve your soul from having to over-compensate, from having to be—how can we say?—more of the soul warrior. Thus it will make your life a little bit more complex because of having to interact with extremes of conditioning and societies struggling among themselves or between one another.

Generally speaking, obviously because of other lives, immortality, and inter-action with Spirit and Creator, your spirit is a better support for your life. But given the extremes that the spirit cannot comfortably interact with at all times, you have your soul—which can migrate up to a point between different worlds but must remain associated—linked, you say, corded to your energy body, yes. But your soul is more corded to your auric field and can thus travel by being corded—meaning the human being is alive but at the deep-sleep level—to where teachers are.

Your Soul May Linger Here so that You Can Become a Spirit Guide

But you are also, when corded that way, exposed to much more of your spirit being. The spirit being itself thus has the potential to recharge the soul with the spirit's overall purpose and capacities. This is why, if you can wake up without being jarred awake, you have those moments of transcendence from the deep sleep to the semiconscious state where you feel not only rested physically but also a sense of peace and comfort with the sleep state. This is because the soul has been recharged not only by teachers and guides but by your spirit itself.

When the body dies and the soul dissipates, what percentage of it goes to the spirit and what percentage goes back to Creator?

Well, your question is in error, but I understand what you are trying to say. It isn't by percentage. It depends on the individual and her life experience. So I will say that I cannot give you the percent because it's different for each individual. I can say that a small portion is reconnected to Creator. The largest portion dissipates on Earth because it has to do with your Earth experience and it has to do with the souls of all other beings on Earth—not just human beings but also other life forms.

A very small percentage of it reacquaints itself with spirit and travels through what I'm referring to as the veils, but they're not really veils. It's a word I'm willing to use that you can understand. It permeates one or two more veils, perhaps, and then remains. After all, you may return that away again—you might go to that planet for another life or, more likely, the reason the soul lingers in that area is that you might return to be a guide in spirit form. And where else would you have your recollected life experience so that you can function as a guide on Earth and not be completely irrelevant?

You understand, if you are going to be a guide who actually interacts with and helps a human being on Earth, sometimes urging that human being to go this way or that way or do this or that, some of this actually gets through and occasionally is heard verbally as a word by the human being in your now times—or even two words. As time goes on and you get more reconnected to Spirit, you'll hear more. It is left there in that place so that the guide (who once lived another life on Earth) has access to enough Earth experience—not to all the dramas and extremes of the individual experience, but to basic Earth wisdom—so that the guide does not give irrelevant advice. After all, it would do no good to give an Earth person advice associated with the spirit world well and beyond Earth. Advice must be grounded in something, and that is what it's grounded in, because your being as a spirit—as a spirit guide, which many of you are training for, which is why I bring it up—cannot be grounded in Earth itself. You will not be able to handle that energy functioning from the spirit world, but it can be grounded in that portion of the soul that has moved beyond the extremes of Earth and has your core Earth experience left in it without those extremes. Thus it is compatible with you and is sufficient to give relevant advice to those you are guiding on the planet.

Your Spirit's Purpose Is Usually
Complete within Three or Four Days of Physical Life

The part of the soul that dissipates—does some of it go into the awareness of the being who ensouls Earth?

No. It goes into places where it's needed by other souls. Generally speaking, it doesn't go anywhere; it just remains until it is used as energy. It remains. We are talking about that which is left, yes; it just becomes energy. Energy is transformable and to a degree transmutable. So since it's transmutable, it becomes something else at some point. Go ahead.

So what are our spirits getting out of this—what are they gaining from the Earth experience?

The spirit's purpose, the overall portion of your spirit's purpose? No one comes to Earth at all without the spirit having a purpose for being here. Your spirit's purpose, however, has to do with your overall being—something that is needed, perhaps, something that must be known so that other lives can be understood better, or perhaps something that you need to be able to do but where such wisdom can only be obtained by having an Earth life, like that. It's individualized.

Can you give me an example of such a need, or needing to know, or needing something?

Yes. Perhaps you haven't been able, in your other lives, to interact with a wide variety of beings. Thus you might need practical, physical, grounded Earth experience with that. It's one thing to commingle with spirit of all forms of life throughout the all-beingness in the universe. But it's completely another thing as an individualized being on another planet—a portion of your overall spirit —to have contact with all different types of individuals. That may be something, and this is not something that is common. I'm giving you an example. You asked for an example. So you might come to a place where there is a wide variety of beings, including beings who look basically like you human beings. All human beings look basically alike, but there are different appearances to a degree and certainly many different cultures and languages and so on. So you will be exposed to much more in a life on Earth than you would ever be exposed to in any life anyplace else. So on Earth you would get what you call a crash course in exposure to variety.

Somehow that permeates up to spirit and influences future lives, then?

Yes. Usually that takes place within the first few days of physical life. The spirit's purpose is almost totally completed within three or four days of physical life on the planet. Let's say about 87 to 90 percent is achieved, 91 percent, maybe, in the first few days of physical life, whatever that purpose is. But then you might go on throughout the rest of your life and attain little bits more here and there. You might remember that when you were a baby, in those first few days, your spirit was omnipresent. It was overwhelmingly present. That's why people say that babies have such magical energy. That's the energy.

You Have Been Ordained by the Creator of This Universe to Achieve Something beyond Your Individual Spirit's Purpose

My understanding from Zoosh is that all of the plants in total, which he calls the vegetable kingdom on this planet, have been creators in another universe—and I don't know who else. Is that part of your awareness?

Yes, it is. Other forms of life that you have come to call animals have been involved in such things too. I don't know that it's a requirement for being around the human being, a requirement for life on Earth during your time, but I can see the practical application of it. Can't you? Because think about what other forms of life have to endure. Imagine a tree going through all the struggles to be born, to live as well as possible, and to mature to the point where it can be a wisdom tree. A wisdom tree might be anywhere from—depending on the particular type of plant—say, 70 or 80 years old and beyond, even 200 to 300 years old, getting to the point where it can be profoundly influential with trained, or at least open, human beings to interact and support your spirits and souls and your experiential lives on Earth. And then along comes somebody and says, "Oh, good. Wood." [Makes a whooshing sound like the swing of an axe.]

So one must have a significant degree of patience. Such patience often comes with creation. Think about this. Perhaps your creator—or any creator—creates something that seemed like a good creation in the moment, but as time goes on and interactions with other lives you have energized happens, you reconsider— maybe that wasn't such a good idea after all. [Laughs.] And thus patience does come, even if it didn't exist before. I'm sure your own creator is more patient than it once was, but perhaps not as patient as it will be someday. This is not a criticism; it is simply a comment on life. I think we ought to finish up for the day. We can continue next time, if you like. I will make a finishing statement just in case we don't continue, all right?

On this planet, you have been ordained by the Creator of this universe to achieve something beyond your individual spirit's purpose for being here. You have been ordained by the Creator of this universe to achieve something beyond your soul's purpose and even beyond your experiences' purpose—for therein lies your total being united with other, your spirit and soul. The ordination comes because something is needed in this universe, something that this creator did not bring. Thus even though at times you are isolated to a degree from your overall being and long for home, know that you are serving Creator but evolving into the greater personality of all your souls and, more to the point, all your spirits, which will someday assist Creator in the ultimate outcome of this universe on that journey. I wish you well.

Thank you. Good life.

Good life.

CHAPTER SIX

Marijuana and Marijuana Spirit

MAY 15, 2009

∞

I would like to offer my perspective on working with marijuana plants. As long as you come across a plant that's growing wild, or if you have the legal capacity to have a living plant growing—so there is no fear, no worries—then this is what to do. This works especially well if you have three plants, but if there is only one, do the best you can. It would be best if it was outdoors so the plant could get sun and interact with the elements. If it is raining hard, wait. If there is a mist or fog, that's all right, as long as you are comfortable there. If not, then do this indoors.

Marijuana Can Amplify Your Capacity to Achieve Full Awareness in a Meditative State

Sit about three feet away from the plant or plants. If you have three or more, line them up so they're in the shape of a semi-circle in front of you—so the one directly in front of you would be the farthest away, and the ones to either side would be a little closer. Then simply look at the plants. I must also say that if you are using potted plants, try to have a neutral background behind the plants. By this I mean, if possible—though it may not be—have something behind the

79

plants that is neutral, not young tender shoots of whatever else you have planted growing. Ideally, if they're potted plants, then you can simply move them in front of a wall or something that's blank with nothing on it—no writing, no distractions. If you can, sit facing the north. If you can't, then just do the best you can. I'm going to act as if you have three plants, but if you have one, then just look at that one. Looking at the plants, begin your gaze on the plant that's the farthest from your right. And during all you do as I set it out here, move your gaze from the right to the left.

After you get to the last plant on the left, look up and move your gaze back to the first plant on the right. Don't slide back from the left to the right, looking at the plants. Look up so you are not watching the plants, move your gaze back to the plant on the right, and then again move your gaze slowly from the right to the left. Doing it this specific way is very important so you don't accidentally interfere with what you're doing here. While you're doing that, simply breathe in and out normally and say:

"I am asking that the most benevolent energies emanated by these plants now provide me with the inspiration I need to achieve full spiritual awareness about all that I need to know now in the most benevolent way for me."

Just say that once out loud. You can have the words written down on a piece of paper if you can't remember them exactly. It will help. Once you get done saying these words—and say them slowly, don't rush through them— it's all right if you continue to look at the plants the way I said before; continue that process up to five minutes. Try not to look at a clock or a watch, though, because that will be distracting. By the same token, I don't recommend having a timer running if it ticks. But if you have a timer that will simply make a soft ding in the distance—maybe twenty feet away so you can hear it but it isn't annoying and won't make you jump—or if a friend is nearby and can come out when five minutes are up and can simply say, "Now," and then walk away, that would be good. If a friend does that, request that he or she does not look at you or at the plants.

The purpose here is to amplify your capacity to achieve full awareness of what you need to know and to achieve that in such a spiritual fashion that you are able to acquire this in a dream state or a meditative state. It is simply for you to achieve full awareness at a moment when you are quiet so that words pop into your mind—or even better, awareness comes into your mind. It will never be something that is harmful or hateful or anything like that. If anything harmful or hateful pops into your mind after you do this, it has nothing to do with the plant.

If there is any concern about this and you have an angelica plant nearby, you can always go and look at the angelica plant. And while standing—not sitting—about four to five feet away, just look at the plant and take ten slow, deep breaths in. When you exhale out, look up and blow out. That will clear anything from you that is an attachment or something that has been in your region that is a so-called negative energy, meaning specifically a discomforting or agitating energy.

Humans: You Are Not Failing

Now, a little bit about me. I am a marijuana plant. I'm a very old one growing in an extremely remote area. Of course, I'm not going to say where, but it's in an area human beings do not readily have access to. In terms of years as you measure them, I am about sixty-four years old. I'm not as big as you might expect because of the conditions that exist here, but my stalk is quite thick. I am able to interact with a great many other plants like me up to a radius of about forty-three miles from here and, of course, with the overall spirit being of the plant you have named marijuana.

There is also a spirit being of this plant, and we will allow that being to come to you soon, but I felt it was important to speak to you in this way. Because of my length of time on Earth and my familiarity with Earth and what is happening in your worlds as you live them, I have observed that many times as individuals you fail in your duty as human beings, no matter what your responsibilities are, because this or that is happening that seems to be a struggle or a problem, as you say, or because you are otherwise uncomfortable. Many times, this is not a personal failing at all. It is set up because this is a school. You are here for a short amount of time—compared to how long you live in other places—so that you can create and re-create possible solutions to problems that may exist to a much lesser degree on other planets or in other societies in the past and future of Earth.

You come to this intense place so that you may try these things out. I'm not saying that correcting this or that behavior won't improve your life. I am saying that very often you are caught up in a belief that you are at fault or involved in a personal failing when that's not the case. I want to make a special point of mentioning that today, because this is something that occurs for most people, especially young people in your "now" time, fully one-third to even one-half of the time. This does not mean that you should turn a blind eye to things that you could help with. But it does mean that when things are not working out, there is probably a fifty-fifty chance, if you still use that term, that it is something you're trying to work on yourself so you will be able to help others someday. Do you have any questions?

You've been in that plant sixty-four years, but how long have you been on Earth overall?

Sixty-four years.

You weren't here before that plant—your plant?

No. It's not typical for a plant that grows in the wild, unless it is unusually sturdy or well out of the way of human interaction, to exist for sixty-four years. Of course, you find trees like that, but not as many as you once did.

Do humans come through there at all? Have you seen them or felt them?

Not lately, but they've been here before, and there was one passing a few miles away a few months ago. I can pick up what I need to know from passing beings—no, I can extend my full awareness up to forty-three miles in any direction, including up and down.

So there are airplanes that go over that you can feel, with people in them?

I don't usually do that with airplanes. I'm not clear whether that would create an interference with the propulsion device. Probably not, but just to be on the safe side. . . .

Ease into the Energy of Your Spirit

So you know quite a bit about the Explorer Race. Did you know about us before you came here?

Oh yes, or I wouldn't have come; this is not an easy place to live. On my home planet, we are more of a bush—a plant growing low to the ground with a heavy stalk or trunk. Gravity is a little stronger, but there are no predators, so it is safe to have our boughs on the ground. We would look more like a squat tree or bush. It is known that living on Earth is fraught with hazards and discomforts, as it is for you too, of course.

Have previous beings who have inhabited marijuana plants come back to your planet and talked about their experiences?

You'd be surprised how very little beings of all sorts talk about their experiences in a given life. From my experience, when you human beings go to your home planet after you are done with a given life here, you almost never talk about your experiences of your life here. You will have done all of that communication back and forth on your way *to* that planet with your guides and teachers, and possibly with Creator. By the time you get there, you won't need to talk about that. Beings don't gather around and say, "Hey, what did you do?" That really doesn't happen. No, there is very little communication about that, but if you are considering going to a given place, then there is communication available. Of course, going to any new place, one might be interested to know at least the basic parameters of what might be expected.

What joys have you found here? I mean, it sounds difficult, but are there any compensating joys?

A mystical man and woman used to come to be where I am, and they would sleep here and dream, and we would dream together. I used to like that a lot, but they've passed over now.

So you could dream with them?

We would dream together. They liked to do that kind of dreaming in which . . . you might call it conscious dreaming, but they were deeply asleep.

Lucid dreaming, I think we call it. Is that the reason Creator asked you to come to Earth—because of your abilities to connect humans to their spiritual selves?

Yes, and to a degree, this is why the plant is used the way it is used now, because people have found that they can make a greater spiritual connection and ease into the energy of their own spirits by taking in the plant the way you do now. Of course, the original intention by those who discovered this as a possibility was to take one puff—no more than one puff per hour—to heighten visions. But it has become something now that . . . well, the plant is often seriously adulterated in one form or another so that smoking does not prove to be the best way. I feel that the living plant, without having been sprayed with anything and without having been even necessarily supported by human beings with water—not anything, just the living wild plant—is the best way to interact, but I've given instructions for situations in which people can't find wild plants.

So would you advise that people not dry and smoke your plant?

I didn't say that. I just commented that that is how people are doing it now. But it's one thing to grow the plants in the best possible state, an organic growth cycle, as compared to a plant that has been altered in some way—hybridized, huh? It's best to do that, and if you are going to pick some portion of the plant, don't pick it all—don't destroy the plant. Just take the parts of the plant that the plant volunteers. You can look at the rest of the book to see what that means. I won't repeat that, if that's all right.

Then dry those portions, and if you're going to smoke them, smoke them in some kind of a pipe or arrangement that doesn't take in other materials like paper. If you can use a pipe made of stone or something like stone, that would be best. Don't use plastic or any material that might contribute to what you're taking in, smoke-wise. I assume glass would not be appropriate, because it might break. It might be possible to have something made of a glass material that's more durable, but stone is also good if you can get a pipe made of stone. I think that's possible.

Beings Come on Pilgrimages to Commune with Marijuana on Its Own Planet

How do you use this ability on your home planet? Are there other groups of beings there that you interact with?

Sometimes beings—not on the planet—will come on a pilgrimage to the planet where we are. We're not all over the planet. There are plenty of places to walk—or float, if they happen to be like that—and they will pause next to the plant or plants they feel an affinity with. Of course, the plant must feel an affinity with them, but that's easy to take note of by the way you feel yourself. Then, depending on their culture, if they are like you, they would perhaps go to sleep right next to the plant, and then they would be breathing in the atmosphere and breathing out the atmosphere that is around the plant and then possibly dreaming. But they might also be a faster-paced society in which case they would simply engage with the plant and breathe in and out as many times as they would breathe, if breathing is a factor. Some of them get closer to the plant and take in the energy of its auric field, exchanging for their own energy. This can only be done if there is total balance and a desire for such connectivity between both parties. There are other ways, but those are the ones that come to mind readily.

So your planet is known, then, as a place to come do this?

Yes, and it is usually only done by elders bringing young ones, if the young ones are having a little problem connecting with their overall spirit beings. This is not typical, you understand, so the planet is not crowded with visitors, but it happens on a regular basis. The way I've seen it is that it is almost always an elder. Although sometimes I've seen beings I'm assuming are relatives, possibly parents, but it's not always easy to tell.

Earth Is the Only Planet Where Humans Do Not Know Their Purpose

So what are your pleasures on your home planet? Do you live a very long time there or do you have a life cycle or how does that work?

My impression is that our life cycle is very, very long, but I couldn't put the number in your years. With no predators and the means to grow and multiply when necessary, one goes on for a long time.

Do you have memories of living before that planet?

I do not, no.

What gives you pleasure on the home planet, then? You interact with beings; you live, right? You have a life.

Everything is pleasurable on the home planet, for there is no harm, no discomfort. It is a question one might ask on Earth as a human being or another type of being on Earth. Generally speaking for all beings on other planets where there is no discomfort at all, as far as I know, I understand that everything is pleasurable—with no exceptions.

You're aware of beings on other planets; you can commune with them? You don't have an educational system. So do you ask your teachers or your guides if you need information or if you want to know what's happening in the rest of the universe? How do you find that out?

The simple answer to your multifaceted question is no. I don't need to know. We are complete, and we are interested to a degree in the visitors who come to interact with us, but we do not seek nor do we feel we need to learn about other planets. We are not intellectual. Generally speaking, I've noticed that the mental body functions on Earth for the Earth human to find out where, why, and how, but we do not have a mental body like that. We know where we are and where we're from. We know why we exist and we know how we exist. That's all we need to know. So I'm not trying to say one is better than the other. I'm simply saying that we do not have the need for a mental body.

Yet you know of and you have mentioned the planet that humans come from. Can you say something about that?

The reason I know this is because I am here on the planet of the humans—even though there are other planets with humans. But this is the only planet I know of with humans who don't know why they are here, where they are from, etcetera, simply because they've forgotten that at the moment. But on your home planet, you'd know all these things—and by "home planet" I do not necessarily mean as a soul being. Rather, the home planet of human beings is one place, as far as I know—though human beings live all over the universe, as much as I've been able to tell, as I am not curious. So this means a quick flash and I can see—not unlike as if I had a map—the many places where human beings live. Of course they are not exactly like you, but in appearance and biologically, for the most part, they are exactly the same.

But the home planet of human beings is a little different. It's not your source as a soul or a spirit, but it is the place you almost always go to for a while after living a human life, because you can transition there. You essentially see yourself as a human being—albeit in spirit form. You will be totally healthy and completely comfortable, with no discomfort whatsoever. And very often—I don't know for certain whether you always do this—those who have been human beings on Earth as you know it now will go there for a short time to have the relaxation of being a human being in total comfort.

You don't always do that. From what I've observed, if someone has been, say, a human baby for a short amount of time—no more than a year, basically less than a year—then you might not, because you wouldn't be that attached to life as an Earth human being and you wouldn't have hundreds and hundreds of questions about why and how and where and so on. You wouldn't have the kinds of questions you might develop all throughout a maturing adult life as a human being, not necessarily as a mental curiosity but simply as a desperate question in a moment. Then it passes when you find a solution or something that comforts you.

Do human beings from that planet on a soul level then come to Earth also?

No, it's a one-way trip. You don't come *from* there to Earth. You go *to* there on your way to someplace else. You might say it's a portion of the transitional process, but from my point of view, since nobody else goes there but human beings—mostly just those who've been on Earth and occasionally humans from other places—then I'd say that it is the human home planet.

Can you see the soul leave the human body when the transition from live to not-live happens?

Oh yes, just about anybody can do that. Maybe not every human being as you know yourselves now, but just about everybody else can. It's not that difficult. A great many people see it now; they're just not sure what they see. If they're frightened for any reason about it, they tend to forget it quickly. It's fleeting, and it's good not to stare at it too much. Just, "Oh, there it goes." Now I will say good night, and the spirit of marijuana plant will come in.

Thank you for coming. Thank you very much.

Good night.

Good life.

✳ ✳ ✳

Marijuana Spirit

℘

GREETINGS.

Greetings. Welcome.

What would you like to know?

Well, what can you say beyond what the lovely plant just said? What is it that we can learn from you or your species beyond what he said?

Ask a specific question. You can repeat yourself, but not just "beyond what the plant said." I need a specific question.

Have you ever been an individual marijuana plant on Earth?

No, but I can feel into them.

So are you a teacher on the home planet?

No, there's nothing to be taught. I am simply a spirit—an overall spirit that is available to pass energy that is attuned specifically to the needs of what you call marijuana plants. To such plants on Earth, that energy is focused from the source that inspires that particular form of life to exist—from Creator. This inspiration exists for all forms of life—for a human being and for everything else. Every form of life has a source in Creator—if Creator chooses to stimulate a form of life, then the origin of that form of life is with Creator. Therefore my origin stems from Creator.

Marijuana Spirit Serves the Needs of All Marijuana Plants

So you are in feeling connection with all the marijuana plants on Earth?

Yes.

Can you feel when they are hurt or have low energy or are tired or need you? Or do they call you? How does that work?

I'm aware if they need my energy support, but they do not always need this. They'll usually only need it if they're injured. Being tired is not a reason to do this, and even dying is a natural process that all plants do, so that also is not a reason. They'll only do that if they're injured. They do not assume dying requires attention. Dying, after all, is simply the body returning to Earth, and one's being goes on. I do not help them with that. They do that on their own.

But the plant said he is not going to be here again. Do most spirits of the marijuana plants go into another plant, or do they go back home?

The plant said that?

He said he would only be here during the time his plant was alive—when he left here, he would not go into another plant.

Yes, I believe he said that. And so your question is?

Is that the way it works for all of your plants, or is that a choice they have?

It's a choice they have. They may remain or they may return—but then, it's very much the same for human beings, isn't it?

Well, we won't go into that. So what did you do before there were marijuana plants on Earth?

I existed on the home planet functioning in the same way, except that on the home planet—since there's no hurt or harm and no death as you know it—I simply existed as an overall supporting energy. So you see, that's why they all welcome me when I come around, because they already know me in that sense on the soul level.

There's only one of you for that group of plants?

Yes. I think this is typical for all forms of life.

Marijuana Exists for Its Ability to Interact Spiritually

While your energy is focused on Earth, do you interact and communicate with the spirits of other plants?

Only if necessary. Perhaps, for instance, if a marijuana plant were injured and a great many other plants were injured—say a fire or somebody using a device or just simply somebody walking through a field and stepping on plants—then, if necessary, I would interact in some way with other plants. But those other plants wouldn't benefit from me sharing energy with them, since they are not the type of plants we're talking about here. They would have their own spirits to help them; there's no need for conversation. You understand, perhaps, that the plant you know as marijuana exists primarily for its ability to interact spiritually but not mentally. So curiosity is not a factor. I understand quite clearly that it is a factor and necessary for the human being, especially on Earth, but it is not for us. So there is a simple, benign acknowledgment of all other life from me to other plants, other species—animals, for that matter, as you call them—but there is no need to inquire.

You don't focus on humans, but in the course of your focusing on the plants around the planet, you learn about them or us, right?

Only to the extent that it is necessary.

Do you have information that you feel is helpful for us? I mean, have you noticed something that you feel we could do better?

I have no criticism-based suggestions for you. I realize the reason you're asking that question is to support and fulfill your understanding of the purpose of your publications, which is to offer guidance and suggestions—advice, as it were. But I cannot find any fault with human beings. I believe that you are living and existing as well as possible for beings who do not remember who you are, where you're from, and why you're here. To be perfectly honest, I do understand that that is the whole reason for your existence on Earth: so you can create and re-create. Yet this has caused a great deal of harm, meaning pain and suffering. So I am not in agreement with the way you are existing here.

I have found, in my interactions with human beings from other places who have come to visit the home planet, that when they do remember who they are and where they're from and why they exist, they are the most pleasant and benevolent beings, just like all other beings. They don't harm anyone and they are not harmed by anyone, and of course, they're completely comfortable to be around. I meant, I may not have the wisdom of Creator—certainly not—but I do not understand why it is necessary for human beings on Earth to forget who you are, where you're from, and why you're here to the extent that you cause harm to yourselves and others. If it were simply a search without causing harm, then that would be understandable to me, but the harm part—I do not understand why that's necessary, and I can't say that I approve.

Well, that's an honest answer, and I appreciate that. I think some of us living here think that sometimes [chuckles], but there is a great reason and a goal in all of this.

I've heard that, but I don't agree with the extent of this suffering. Perhaps a minor pain or ache that goes away just to remind you of something—okay. But the extent of the suffering and violence that humans experience? No! That's what I believe. I realize it sounds disapproving, but I have reason to believe that I am in the majority, and I believe most human beings would agree with me as well. So I am not campaigning for anything, but I will be—and have been—supportive of the Earth human being remembering who you are, where you're from, and why you're here.

I have reason to believe that Creator and others are doing what they can to help you all come along at the same pace. Some of you have to go slower than others, so you all have to go at the pace of the slowest one, and you can't really tell who's slower and who's quicker. There's no way you can tell. Behavior is no way to know. Intelligence is no way to know. It's a spiritual thing. So you will go as fast as the slowest one among you to recover your total being, your knowledge, your wisdom, your existence, but you'll get there because you're all headed in that direction—and there is no turning back.

The Purpose of Earth Is Spiritual Development

Would you say that you've seen any improvement in human behavior over the last few years?

How many years?

Well, how long have you been here?

No, that's a good question—how many years?

Some people say this started a hundred years ago; some say that we made the decision in 1987.

But what do *you* want to know? Give me a number and I'll give you more.

Since 1987.

A little bit. Give me another number.

A hundred years.

Quite a bit.

Good. You have memories of the tribal beings who were here who came from the various planets to get Earth used to humans, so you go back and remember them and the way they lived, don't you?

Yes. And of course I remember the original beings on Earth, those who would be somewhat similar to human beings—humanoids, you would call them.

Was that the Anasazi?

Well, there are different words. I wouldn't be attached to that word particularly. The heads of these beings were not shaped in the same way as yours. These beings were stronger. They had more body hair. But they were very special. I think there might be a few of them around somewhere, but probably none on this planet anymore.

So you were one of the first plants who came here?

We've been here for a while. It makes sense when you think about it, because Creator's whole purpose for this planet, as near as I can tell, is spiritual development. So of course we've been here for a long time.

That's your field, right? [Laughs.]

That's what we do.

Yes. Is there a word that you've heard for these original humanoid beings?

I can picture it. I don't know what you'd call it, but it wouldn't be Neanderthal; it would be before that, significantly before that. If you saw them, they walked upright. Their arms were a little longer than yours, and they were fully furred, as you say, but that was practical. They were not meat eaters; they lived off vegetation. There weren't as many nonhuman-type beings—you call them animals. There weren't as many of them then. The so-called dinosaurs—they weren't here then.

Can you put any time on it at all? I know time is so weird, but . . .

It doesn't factor into your time, but the planet was here in this position, in this orbit.

Marijuana Will Remain on Earth after Humans Leave

Well, you're great. Do you know if you'll go back to your home planet after we succeed in what we came here to do?

I'm not here because you're here. I'm here because of the so-called marijuana plants. If marijuana plants remain, I will be here, regardless of where you go.

But they don't know yet if they're going to stay beyond the humans leaving.

Oh, as far as I know, they will. Of course, not all Earth humans as you know yourselves will migrate away from this planet. Some will live underground as you develop that capacity into being something pleasant. That's been done before by other civilizations, and it seems perfectly reasonable that you might do it yourself once your society is benign and benevolent. Then the surface of the planet can recover.

And your plants can have a benign existence here.

Yes.

Ah, that would be great, because it's such a beautiful, fantastic place of variety, of beauty.

As you say.

We need the physical plant to get this effect. You said your energy's only for the plants, so we can't do this in meditation or any other way. We need the physical proximity of your plants to make these spiritual connections, right?

Correct. And it's that way as far as I know with all plants, but you'll have to ask them. I'm not trying to take over for them and speak for them, but as far as I know—and correct me if I'm mistaken—the main thrust of this book is about how people can interact with the living.

Yes, absolutely.

You might say "living with the living," and in this way, a more benign life can be the result.

Let's talk about that a little bit. So a human interacts with a plant. For some, it may take more than one treatment. Do you have a recommendation for how often this could be done?

It could be done three times and with at least four days off between times. Once is probably sufficient for most, but it could be done three times. Other times it would be possible to do what mystical people did with the plant, as described by the plant you spoke to before. This means they could go and—as long as they're not sleeping on other plants—if there is a dirt patch there or if they can figure out how to sleep without destroying other life, then it might be possible to just sleep in the proximity of plants that support spiritual interaction. I'm not saying do it; I'm saying you *could*, but then you wouldn't do the recommended work as suggested by the elderly plant you spoke to before.

From Plant Soul to Human Soul

How does this work? We come into the aura, the energy, of your plants, and . . . how is the mechanism between the human and the plant accomplished?

It's very simple. It's this: soul to soul. Period. That's how it works. Your soul is in your body all the time. Even though at the deepest levels of sleep your soul travels, it's still connected to your body—on a cord, you might say. So that's why sleeping still works and you can dream, but as far as doing the work as suggested by the elder plant, you would have your soul totally present in your physical self, and the soul would of course be present in the plant. It works on the basis of soul to soul.

And then we are more connected to our souls as a result of that interaction?

That's the goal. There is no guarantee. The goal is that you will be more connected to your own soul. You would then be able perhaps to get clearer and more frequent inspirations, for example, but your soul isn't going to get bigger.

But if we're saying we can't get it all at once, could we come back the next year and the year after? Would there be value in that?

Who's saying that you can't get it all at once?

Ah, you can *get it all at once.*

You're saying that. It was stated that you do it once, but it was also stated, on the basis of *your* question, that it could be done three times. There is no reason to believe that you wouldn't get it all at once in the first pass. I'm not going to say what it is that you would get. The *words* you say define what you are asking for, and I cannot say what you would get because that would vary from individual to individual.

Can you see how the soul is connected in the human body? Is it in the DNA? Is it in every particle, in every atom? Is it in the nervous system? How does that work?

It's not complicated. I realize you are using the microscopic technique here. Come back to the whole thing. It is connected in every portion, and yet because the human being is made up of so many other beings—this kind of cell and that kind of cell—they may all be ensouled in their own way as well, but still, human beings in their totality are one soul.

So what the human being in its totality does impacts all of the individual souls in all the organs and all of the body, right?

I wouldn't use the word "impacts."

Stimulates? What word?

"Impacts" is a word that is a little too forceful in this. Perhaps "is with."

Well, that's exciting. Do you recommend someone doing this at a healing center? You know, having hundreds or thousands of plants . . .

No. I think it's best to do it where the plant is growing wild, or if you can, do it on your own, if you have permission to grow the plants. If you are experimenting on plants in a laboratory, it probably won't work very well because the plants will be afraid. But if it is someplace benign, especially outdoors, where plants are not being cut up and so forth on a regular basis, and the plants are relaxed, it would work better. If you're saying, "Would it be a good thing for there to be a place where plants are grown and allowed to be themselves, and people could come and interact in this way," yes, that might be good. But do not fertilize the plants other than the natural earth—good soil and so on. Don't try to stimulate their growth artificially; that's what I mean by fertilize. If they could be grown and people could come, yes, but it wouldn't take that many plants because if they're not interfered with, they can grow very big. When they need to create more plants, eventually they'll fall over and the seeds will fall, and then more plants will come.

Humans Are Moving toward Becoming
Their Natural, Conscious, Spiritual Selves

How tall was the being who spoke first? Do you have any way of measuring— like six foot or ten foot?

A little over six feet.

Six feet tall. You don't know if any other plant has this ability?

No, you'll have to ask. Then you'll have lots of choices. Now, remember to return to angelica. It's a very important plant for you now—significantly more important than marijuana. I'm mentioning it because of the situation that exists on Earth now with various diseases. Be sure and ask angelica about its spiritual impact and all of that business. Now I'm going to make a closing comment.

In your time, people are looking for a means to know or understand more about themselves or their society in order to try and make things better. Know that at the end of your life, whenever that may come, things will automatically be better. As you go along as a society, globally speaking, you are inexorably moving toward becoming your natural, conscious, spiritual selves. I know it doesn't look like that now because of your struggles and because of various dangers having to do with living on a living planet. Future generations may not remember all of your struggles. But don't you agree that it's more important for them to live in comfort, happiness, and fulfillment? After all, that is what you are seeking. Don't resent those who live in it, even though they may not remember your struggles. Be happy with the knowledge that you have contributed to their capacity to live benevolently, to provide benevolently, and to cooperate benevolently. That is a most generous legacy to leave for future generations. Good life and good night.

Good life, and thank you very much. You were wonderful.

CHAPTER SEVEN

Angelica Spirit

MAY 5, 2009

∽

ANGELICA.

Angelica, welcome! Welcome.

Now, I am here because the channel thought of one of the most difficult diseases that the human being faces now, which is cancer. The channel asked if there was any one herb or plant that could make a difference—maybe even cure cancer—and through a series of communications, he came to angelica. Now I will give an opening statement.

It is true, whatever plant spirits have said, that interaction with the living plant is an area not known or explored well by most of your cultures in your time. In the past, this was known better, and a great deal of interaction happened—human-to-plant interaction—without humans even touching the plant, not unlike a form of communion whereby each individual supports the other. In times gone by that I can recall as spirit of angelica, there were human beings— nomadic humans—who went from here to there. They were very strong, vital, and able to adapt to a great many circumstances. Sometimes they would come across certain circumstances that were difficult to adapt to or might even contract a disease, but they had this knowledge then.

They would approach angelica and would breathe in and out with angelica—I will give the detailed instructions shortly—and thus would not only have the cure for the disease but would also support the plant if the plant were struggling to survive. The great human need for daily consumption of food and water, and other feeling needs as well, would support the plant's ability to attract food and water for itself, so it was not only a one-way exchange. Always know that sometimes—not always, but sometimes—plants will not take from the human but will experience what the human shares as well as the human experiencing what the plant shares. It can be compatible. I bring that up so you do not get too concerned about the plant's well-being.

Wild Plants Are Better for Healing Cancer

Now, cancer is a terrible thing in your time, and pollution is partially the cause—pollution meaning any disruption of the planet's original continuity factors, of which there are a great deal. I'm not here to discuss that, because that will require a great deal of effort on your part to clear up. But I feel that a cure for cancer is needed, and this is what I'm going to suggest. It won't work in all cases, but it might work in 30 percent, sometimes even 40 percent, of cases. In situations where it does not cure, it might relieve symptoms or simply cause things to get better. This would work best with the natural, growing plant—one that is growing wild. Perhaps there are many in an environment where the plant grows wild. It does grow all over—sometimes in this area of land and sometimes in that. You'll have to look it up. There are different species, but all of them, to one degree or another, will perform the same results—meaning you'll get the same or a similar outcome.

Angelica is not a tall plant, so you would have to approach it and ask for permission. If you're going to walk over other plants, always ask permission first. It's amazing to me how few human beings do that. If you ask permission, then put your feet one after another in the places where your feet tell you that you have permission to walk, to step. Don't just stomp over to the plant. Other plants would be injured, and angelica would then be serving the needs of those plants, their emergency needs, because of this shared energy, helping prevent them from being stepped on, you see. Then they would not have much left over to support the human need.

So this would be easier in plants grown by people, because they might be grown in a garden, but the wild plant will always have more to offer because it has been able to grow and mature in a natural environment and be free. A suggestion: If you are approaching a plant in the wild and allowing your feet to tell you where you can step, wear the thinnest-soled shoes possible, ones with no metal and made only of natural products on the sole—leather is acceptable, something like that. Then your feet can have the ultimate or the greatest amount of contact. If you normally walk barefoot all the time, you may not need such a foot covering. I'm assuming that most people in your time are not in that situation, but there are some.

Serve Your Own Needs By Serving Others' Needs

Whether the plant is wild or growing in a garden, go up to the plant and say the greeting that plants use, which is "good life." Always say it out loud, or you can whisper it if you prefer, and pause for a moment. The plant may be introducing itself. Sensitive people might get a general feeling of that, meaning there might be an energy. Wait until it fades a bit. Very sensitive people—channels in that sense—might even get a few words, but it's not about communication through channeling or inspiration. If you like, after you say "good life" and you initially approach the plant, say your name, where you're from, a little bit about your family, or a little bit about the land where you grow. This does not mean the name of your country. It might mean, for instance, "Where I live, the soil is rocky or sandy," like that, or "The earth is dark and rich and supports life." That's something a plant would care about, you see.

After that introduction you wait for the feeling of the plant introducing itself. There might even be an energy before you get there. If it's strong, wait until it fades as you approach, but if you get an uncomfortable feeling anytime you are approaching a plant, this means the plant is busy, so approach another plant. If the plant is busy, what you're going to do won't work. Assuming the plant has welcomed you—do not touch the plant; about three feet from it is close enough—then say out loud:

"I am asking that my exchange with you provide me with the stimulus to my own organism whereby the cancer I have is diminished or cured—or both—along with all its symptoms and feelings, physical and otherwise."

Then pause. There might be a wave of energy again. Anytime there's a wave of energy that you can feel, always pause, because the spirits around you and around the plant will be working to support your needs or, perhaps, even the needs of other beings around you—other plants and so on. Then after that energy fades, just look at the plant. First look at the top and breathe naturally, in and out. Then after a minute or two (don't use your watch; just make your best guess), gradually allow your gaze to go down, and breathe in and out. At some point, you reach where the plant goes into the earth. Don't imagine what the roots look like. Just stop. Figure that you start out looking at the top of the plant, wherever that might be, and as you allow your gaze to go down to where the plant touches the ground, you're just breathing in and out naturally.

A full circuit would begin looking at the top of the plant and then allowing your gaze to go to where it touches the earth. It might take two or three minutes. Then slowly, in the same way, look back up again toward the top of the plant for another two or three minutes. You can do this for about ten minutes. It would be best—only in the case of the ten minutes, not in the two or three minutes—if somebody else was nearby, say twenty feet away, no closer, to say when the ten minutes are up. Perhaps this person could say "time" quietly, but loud enough so you can hear. Then stop and say "good life" again to the plant and turn to your left until you are facing the direction you need to go to leave. Then you can walk away. That's what I recommend. It might take two or three visits. It would be best to go to the same plant, but if it's two or three visits to the same plant, you will have to wait two days between visits.

This will work at night as well as during the day, but I recommend that it be done during the day, because there's less chance of your stepping on some other forms of life if you can see. Stepping on other forms of life—meaning, say, a snail, for example—would immediately stop what the plant is doing for you. Then the plant would attempt to in some way assist the individual you'd stepped on. Perhaps it would try to decrease its pain and suffering and help its family as well. So you see, you serve your own needs by serving the needs of others. This is something all angelica plants know.

You Might Have to Complete Some Other Purpose before Healing with Angelica

Remember, while you are breathing in and out and looking at the plant, to try not to think of anything. Don't be thinking about this or that. If you catch yourself thinking, just stop. Don't get mad at yourself; don't slap yourself on the leg or something. Don't do anything like that. Just stop, and if you have a difficult time stopping your thoughts, then glance up at the sky for a moment or look away from the plant. It's best not to look at other plants because you might accidentally start breathing their countenance in. Just look up at the sky or at some safe area. Don't look at the Sun. Now, if the sun is behind clouds and you happen to glance in its direction, that's fine—that's safe. But once you stop thinking, then you can look back at the plant and resume. If you are keeping time for somebody doing this and you notice that they are staring at the sky, then take that off the time they're interacting with the plant.

In 30 to 40 percent of cases, this interaction with the angelica plant will diminish symptoms—pain and suffering—and in some cases, 30 percent or sometimes 20 percent of cases, depending on the situation, it might very well cure the cancer. If it does cure the cancer, then the chances of it returning are less likely, unless it came about as a result of some toxic fume, for example, or exposure to something that you are exposed to again.

When I'm giving these percentages, it does not refer only—and this is a very important point—to specific types of cancer. In some cases, it might refer to types of people or your personality or something like that, so if it doesn't cure you, it might be the type of cancer you have, but it might just as well be the culture you come from, who you are as a person, and so on, because sometimes your soul wants you or needs you to go through this extreme situation because there's something you haven't done yet. Sometimes that extreme situation will put you into a position where you might do it, such as interacting more with human beings and so on. But that's just an example. There might be other situations, other reasons; you might be developing compassion. Who can say? There are myriad possibilities for each individual.

If you aren't cured or if your symptoms don't lessen, then automatically assume that there is some other reason for you to have that disease or discomfort. However, if that occurs, try to find out what the reason is. For example, if it is for you to interact with more people in some benevolent way, then start doing that. Or if it is because you need to pursue some other activity that you've avoided and believe might be good for you to do, then begin doing that. Always try to keep it benevolent. Then after you have begun, keep doing that, because it's something your soul wants and needs you to do. After you've found out the reason, then it might be possible to return to the angelica process and do it again.

But if you do begin doing something and you feel that it is right, wait at least a month before you return to that plant or to a different angelica and try again. If you have success, then continue, because your soul will be allowing that success. Continue with what it is that you have started in your interactions with others, as I said, because the cure will be dependent on that continuation. Souls are very complex, and they do not always understand the realities of physical, day-to-day life on Earth. But they do understand the overall completeness of your being—what's needed where and when. This is not something you can know in your given life on Earth, or in many other places, because such knowledge could become obsessive. It might interfere with other aspects of your life. So your soul is not naïve. [Chuckles.] It may have other purposes in the larger sense for your total being.

You Can Begin Your Relationship with the Plant by Interacting with the Seeds

Is this common knowledge on the planet that you can do this? Is this something that's been discussed before?

I don't believe it is—no, not in your time. Many of the cures and suggestions given by plants in this book that have to do with interacting with the living plant have not been common knowledge for 400 or 500 years. By common knowledge, I mean known within small groups of people—you might say tribes. If you go back several thousand years, then many people knew it—not everyone, but again, small groups all over the planet here and there. Because they thought it would always be known and couldn't imagine it not being known, there wasn't any great effort made to keep records. Even in your time, there's a great deal of what is called "common knowledge," and people don't write it down because they can't imagine it ever not being known. [Chuckles.]

Right, but then tribes die out or they move or something happens.

Something happens, yes. Even if you write things down and something happens, there's no guarantee it will live after you, but you can try. So no, this is not common knowledge in your time. A few might know and, as I say, feel it has value. Thus I also want to say that the book itself has value, and I feel that many will be helped by it. Now, there's an addendum to that. Some of you, as a result of reading this, might try to grow angelica in a pot, something like that, for a small garden. That might be possible, but I recommend that if you do, there should be consultation with someone who understands the growth of herbs. An herbologist is not always the best person. It would also have to be someone who is a good gardener, and you might ask this person to raise the plant for you. If you do, you're going to want to participate in the following manner: The herbologist might have set a few seeds aside. Ideally, you'd want three plants.

If the seeds are available, ask the herbologist to set aside the seeds she feels are appropriate. Pick out five seeds—you're going for three plants, but each doesn't always germinate and produce, so I would suggest trying with five seeds. If you know someone sensitive who can pick out the right seeds for you, that's almost as good as using your own sensitivities, your own needs of picking out the plants on a seed basis that might be right for you. This makes you more of a participant, and then they'll start to grow for you.

If you are mobile, then you might be able to go to the seeds if they allow it, or the person might be able to bring them to you and you could talk to the seeds and the young plants. But if you are in discomfort or difficulty, you're going to want to start doing what I recommended, and the young plant might not be able to take it. So if you're in a great deal of discomfort, wait until the plant is brought to you by whoever picks it up from the herbologist or the gardener, which could be two people or one—ideally one, but it's not always that way.

It's Angelica's Personality That Helps You

Does asking how it works interfere with how it works? How does the plant do that?

It is alive. It is our personalities. Say you meet someone who is profoundly cheerful—even just temporarily so about something that happened. Maybe this person is always cheerful and so has a tendency to cheer you up. Have you ever had that experience? It's the same. The plant has a certain quality, a personality, and you are interacting with its personality in the same way as that person who cheers you up—not because the plants are *trying* to cheer you up. They cheer you up simply because that's how they are, and being with them cheers you up. If you know that, it doesn't have to be any more complicated than that. If you try to synthesize it, it won't work very well because the living plant enjoys its freedom and its ability to roam, so to speak—especially the free plant growing in nature. By this, I mean the seeds spreading about and interacting with other plants and so on. It enjoys this existence, and it is living in the open as well as possible. Thus you experience the plant's free and complete personality to the best of your ability as a human being.

Of course, the plant experiences your personality. It does not take on your dis-ease or discomfort, but you might share some other quality that you take for granted in yourself as a person that the plant could use more of, if that plant had a similar quality, as in my example of before. It may not be obvious to you. You would certainly not be tired as a result of interacting with the plant. You will not have any of that portion of your personality depleted. It will just be a sharing, like the cheerful person cheers somebody up but does not become less cheerful. [Chuckles.] They are normally cheerful, you understand, as compared to being temporarily cheerful and talking to someone who is not cheerful. After a while, then they might not feel so cheerful. [Chuckles.]

Angelica Spirit Is on Earth to Help Humans and Angelica Interact

All right. Are you here to work with the angelica plant? If so, how do you do that?

Not so much. I support their dreams at times. They sort of sleep—not the way a human being sleeps in an unconscious fashion, but they have a state of being that is—how can we say? It is similar. I support their dreams and their visions during that time. But other than that, I'm here to help the human being and the plant interact. If the plant, especially in the case of a young one, does not know how to get along well on Earth, then I might teach it how to draw what it needs from the currents of air if there are not others nearby to do that. It's very similar to what I suggested you do in your interaction with the plant, only the plant itself can draw from many different sources what it needs to survive and thrive by using air currents. It cannot use wind, just connections to different life forms, which are not that different from currents in water, and it can go for hundreds, even thousands, of miles. Someday perhaps that teaching will be available to the human being in this fashion, but right now I feel that the more immediate needs have been addressed.

That is something I might help the young plant with: to know how and which way to draw on those life forms so that it is benevolent for all beings, and how the plant can acquire something that will allow itself to thrive. This kind of interconnectedness of all life is a theme on this planet. The human being tends to tap into what I was just speaking about—drawing on such energies at a distance—unconsciously on a day-to-day basis. Someday you will do so more consciously, and life will be better. Right now, I think it is better for it to be unconscious so that you do not try to create support for yourself in a subconsciously self-destructive state. That can lead to a great deal of mischief, so I'm going to say it's fine for you to be doing this unconsciously now.

Well, we'll file that one away.

Now I feel it is time to stop, and let us continue next time. Is that acceptable?

Of course. Good life. Thank you very much.

Good life.

CHAPTER EIGHT

Angelica Spirit

MAY 29, 2009

⅋

ANGELICA.

I looked up angelica and I was impressed with your plant. It has been very highly regarded since there were records kept on this planet.

It has been known for some time. Herbologists going back several hundred years have known of many benefits. So it's not a new thing, the idea that plants can be used beneficially. The new thing for your book is how they can be interacted with when they are alive and that all these uses that have been heretofore unknown—or not fully appreciated—can, in some cases, be acquired through this type of interaction. Even that is not new; it's just wisdom that has been lost through the years or, in some cases, suppressed—not condemned and suppressed, but rather left to be a resource only for a select few. Sometimes this has been done for practical reasons, meaning that language, especially written language, was not widely available. Therefore, some individuals, sometimes with the best of intentions, kept written material away from the general public. But other times it was kept for a select few.

Still, down through the years, one cannot prevent herbologists, medicine men, medicine women, or whatever names you have, from experimenting, trying, seeing what works. Many years ago when civilizations were less complex, without technology as you know it now, the idea of interacting with the living plant—much like what has been explored in this book—was more widely known. So it is not my intention—or the intention of other plants here, as far as I can tell—to be revealing something entirely new; rather, it is simply to be reminding people of things their ancestors may have known in the distant past.

Nomadic People Dried Herbs for the Purpose of Availability

Another thing that might have kept the information from spreading was that the plant would have to grow in the area where the medicine person was, right?

Yes, unless the people were nomadic, which is sometimes the case—especially given that, as you know, sometimes rain will come to mountainous areas, and you want to be around that in the warmer months. But those same mountainous areas will get snow and cold, and you need to be away from that in colder months. So many times in the past, peoples were more nomadic; therefore, if something didn't grow where they were, then in their travels or where they stopped as they went from one place to another, this plant often was something you'd come across.

This is also how it came to be that herbs were collected and dried: for the sake of causing them to be available when needed. This really is the reason. Because if you weren't around the herb, as you said yourself, it wouldn't be available. That's really how the whole idea of using the dried herb came to pass. Long before that, though, there was the idea of using at least the very fresh herb, meaning cut but very fresh and used that way or, in other situations when enlightenment was present for one reason or another, interacting with the living plant. In a nutshell, that's how it came to be that people used the dried version.

So they could take it with them and have it when it wasn't growing.

Yes. But you can't get the same effect. You can get some beneficial effects, of course, but you can't get the same effect as you might get with the living plant, especially if it's mature. Sometimes if the plant is very young, it may not have enough energy of its own definition, meaning its own personality, present in enough sufficiency so that the plant could share with others. But then the herbologists, or the wizened ones, would know that, having been taught by those who preceded them. When such wisdom is passed on in that fashion, it often is maintained for generations.

The Information Is Being Released with the Intent to Empower

There is information coming out now that a lot of the wisdom held by the elders of various tribes or groups was supposed to be released at this time for the good of the general public, but the elders aren't releasing it. Is this why you beings are coming through channels now? In an attempt to get the information out despite their lack of candor?

One might say that the whole series of books through this channel is based on that fact without any attempt to blame, allowing for the fact that some material hasn't come out—not because the people who possess the knowledge don't want to put it out, but rather because of those individuals being interfered with in some way.

So the purpose is not to be blaming here but rather to state that the general reason for all these *Explorer Race* books is to not only prompt and encourage others to release what they know, what they believe, and so on, but also to take—how can we say?—certain threats away from them. If others are revealing the information, then there's not much reason to try to hold the information back. Generally speaking, I cannot speak for all the materials you publish, but for those through this channel, there is a significant amount of that going on. I do not wish to suggest that others are not doing that. Rather, my knowledge in terms of interactions with this kind of process of communication is with this channel.

One hopes that the information will come out in some benevolent way, but it is yet to be known whether it will come out that way or whether some of it will be released with an intent to corrupt or disrupt—not people specifically, but the body of wisdom. My feeling is that there will be some attempt to do that. You call it disinformation. But overall, the whole purpose of these books, as well as the material put out in other places and other media, is to educate, to teach, and most importantly, to empower so that others have the means to know when something not only rings true mentally but feels true physically.

We're being told that if we awaken to our natural selves, we will know this more and more. We will be able to know what is the truth and what is not the truth.

In reality, you don't have to awaken to your natural self to know that on a feeling level. It is all in the blogs. Every bit is published now on the Internet—how to know through feeling, the heart-warmth, and all of that. This is about knowing. [Please see the Love-Heat exercise on the following pages.]

The Love-Heat Exercise

I am giving what we're calling the love-heat exercise in the way that Speaks of Many Truths taught me how to do it. Take your thumb and rub it very gently across your fingertips for about half a minute or a minute. While you do that, don't do anything else. Just put your attention on your fingertips. Close your eyes and feel your thumb rubbing slowly across your fingertips. Notice that when you do that, it brings your physical attention into that part of your body. Now you can relax and bring that same physical attention anywhere inside your chest—not just where your heart is, but anywhere across your chest, your solar plexus area, or abdomen—and either generate or look for a physical warmth that you can actually feel.

Take a minute or two or as long as you need to find that warmth. When you find it, go into that feeling of warmth and feel it more; just stay with it. Stay with that feeling of warmth. Feel it for a few minutes so you can memorize the method, and most importantly, so your body can create a recollection, a physical recollection of how it feels and how it needs to feel for you. The heat might come up in different parts of your body—maybe one time in the left of your chest, maybe another time in the right of your abdomen or other places around there. Wherever you feel it, just let it be there. Don't try and move it around—that's where it's showing up in that moment. Always when it comes up and you feel the warmth, go into it and feel it more.

Make sure you do this when you are alone and quiet, not when you are driving a car or doing anything that requires your full attention. After you do the warmth for five minutes or so if you can (or as long as you can do it), then relax. Afterward, think about this: The warmth is the physical evidence of loving yourself. Many of you have read for years about how we need to love ourselves, but in fact, the method is not just saying, "I love myself," or doing other mental exercises that are helpful to give you permission to love yourself. Rather, the actual physical experience of loving yourself is in this manner, and there are things you can do that are supportive of it. But in my experience and the way I was taught, this is the method you can most easily do.

The heat will tend to push everything out of you that is not of you or that is not supporting you, because the heat, as the physical experience of loving yourself, also unites you with Creator. It unites you with the harmony of all beings, and it will tend to create a greater sense of harmony with all things. You might notice as you get better at this and can do it longer that should you be around your friends or other people, they might feel more relaxed around you, or situations might become more harmonious.

Things that used to bother or upset you won't bother you very much, because the heat creates an energy, not only of self-love, but of harmony. Remember that the harmony part is so important. You might also notice that animals will react differently to you—maybe they'll be more friendly, perhaps they'll be more relaxed, maybe they'll look at you in a different way. Sometimes you'll be surprised at what animals, even the smallest—such as a grasshopper, a beetle, a butterfly, a bird— might do because you're feeling this heat.

Because it is love energy, it naturally radiates just as light comes out of a light bulb. Remember, you don't throw the heat out, even with the best of intentions. You don't send it to people. If other people are interested in what you are doing or why they feel better around you, you can teach them how to do this love-heat exercise in the way you learned or the way that works best for you.

The most important thing to remember is that this method of loving yourself and generating harmony for yourself creates harmony for others, because you are in harmony. Remember that this works well and will provide you with a greater sense of ease and comfort in your life no matter who you are, where you are, what you are doing or how you're living your life. It can only improve your experience. The love-heat exercise is something that is intended to benefit all life, and in my experience, it does benefit my life.

—Robert Shapiro

Lost Information Has Now Been Found

As a spirit, have you been here since the angelica plant first came to the planet?

A little before that. It's typical for some spirits of beings to be present before the actual physical manifestation comes. This is by way of seeking out the best places for the physical manifestation to grow and be welcomed. This is also by way of energy to interact with the planet's soil, water, and experience of the Sun and the Moon and other influences so as to prepare those influences for being comfortable and at ease with that form of life. That happens, as far as I know, for all forms of life on all planets, as I'm sure it happened for the human being.

Yes, beings have told us how they came to allow Earth to get used to their energy in preparation for the Explorer Race. Were you one of the first plants to come here?

No, I cannot be certain of that. It seemed to me that the place was already greening over quite a bit when I got here, so I can't say that. No.

Have there been cycles? Have you experienced cycles on the planet where this information was widely known and then forgotten and then known again? Have you experienced something like that?

Yes, and that's why we're coming through now, because you are in one of those cycles during which there is a desire by people to know the information, but not much of it is in circulation. The whole point of your books, as much as I understand them, is to get the information into circulation so that people have the means and the capacity to find out whatever they're seeking. So yes, what we are speaking about—not what's known about this plant or others, but what we are attempting to reveal and remind people of—is important enough to bring it to the attention of people who assimilate information through words. One cannot wait for the dissemination by word of mouth alone. It must also be words in a book or sounds, although I don't think you broadcast other than with words on a page.

We're very close to having the channeled words available for sale on our website to stream, on cassettes, via MP3s and CDs and however else people want to listen to them.

Oh, that's good, then. Some people react much better to that conversational element.

Much Information Was Lost Due to War and Strife

Have there been other influences on the planet that caused these cycles of awareness and forgetting?

At least 70 or 80 percent can be blamed largely on wars and strife. This is how whole peoples are wiped out, or education and inspiration is wiped out, because when peoples are battling, the normal structures of society are broken down. Even if you survive, even if you win, your normal structures of society before the battle or war are usually totally different afterward. Sometimes it's for practical reasons, because of losses on your side—even if you're the winner. Other times it's because people no longer believe in that which kept the peace before the battle broke out, because they feel something new must be tried in hopes of avoiding whatever pain and suffering they suffered for whatever reason. So this is the main reason. Other times, of course—but this is much less so—there might be some catastrophe. It happens, but most often it is caused by battles and strife. I'm separating the two because sometimes strife does not come to blows, but battles always do. Strife, you see, can sometimes be a source of stress, so to speak, that controls behaviors. Sometimes peoples who have great knowledge and wisdom are afraid to speak of this knowledge and wisdom because of stresses put on them. I would classify that as strife.

I hope that we're close to getting beyond battling. How do you see that?

I feel when taking your whole history on this planet into account that within this context, yes, you're getting close. But if you're talking about next year or the year after, no. It will take awhile yet.

But it's there; you can see it?

Yes, and people—even people not of a like mind such as yourself—have noticed changes that they cannot account for with logic. Very often, people will simply ignore these changes if such changes are unknown or unacknowledged by their belief systems, whether it be spiritual or religious or scientific. Very often science displays aspects of philosophy or religion when it simply chooses for one reason or another to ignore something that is real. Sometimes this is caused by stress or what I would call strife.

Plants Receive Most of Their Energy from Earth

Are there areas of the planet where your plant grows where energies come from the planet and make your plant more powerful or more healing than in other areas of the planet?

That's a better question than you may know—and I'm acknowledging the inspiration there. Of almost all plants that have healing properties, fully 90 percent or even more of those healing properties are because of the energies being radiated by the planet. The planet, after all, is vastly wise and is a master many

114 ॐ PLANT SOULS SPEAK

times over at many things. Therefore the planet knows what you and other species on the planet need. The radiations from the planet up through the plant into the stalk and flowers and so on are all energies that are compatible with the plant and are also associated with healing qualities that benefit this or that group of beings on the planet—sometimes human beings, sometimes other beings. Sometimes plants, even edible plants as humans see them, are not meant for humans but wind up in the human food chain simply because the human does not realize these plants were meant for someone else. This is not a crime; it is simply a lack of knowing.

What are some of those plants?

No, let them speak for themselves.

Okay, but as the plant is irradiated with energy that comes up through Mother Earth, this energy is magnifying qualities already present in the plant, like angelica plants and others—unique abilities that the plant already has, right?

Yes, but fully 90 percent of the personality of the plant, these qualities, would be added to the plant. And the planet can only add to the plant, you understand, what the plant already possesses in its personality. This is because the planet knows what's needed, whereas the plant might simply be volunteering to be present, bringing only its native natural personality, which would not be as potent as what the planet needs the plant to be. But the plant is not forced. This happens only if the plant is willing to take it on, meaning to welcome it.

So how did that work with your plant? You came here, and could you see or could you feel the best places for your plant to be?

I could, yes.

Did you interact with Earth? How were those choices made?

It's not mental. It's entirely through feeling. All aspects of existence function through feeling. Thought is something you use now, but when you are not on this planet, you don't really use it, so it is all through feeling. If something feels good, then it is a good place. If something doesn't feel good, it's not a bad place; it's just meant for something else.

So you were there to welcome the first angelica plants?

Well, it wasn't like a handshake, but I was there before the plants were there. Initially, when the plants began to manifest physically, they could tell that I was nearby. But as it is with all spirits, one is not encapsulated. One can be many places at once.

But they were comforted and made to feel at home because you were there.

Yes, and I think also because the earth there was welcoming of them. After all, one needs to feel welcome to thrive—not necessarily to survive, but to thrive, yes. When plants are just starting out, they must thrive in order to have viable offspring that will continue to thrive.

It Is Preferable to Interact with Plants That Grow Near Your Birth Area

Are there any places on the planet now where it would be best to go to inter-act with the angelica plant based on the energy coming up from the earth?

Let me put it this way: wherever the plant grows naturally near where you live. Preferably, this should be near where you were born, which might be, at least in old times, where mother and father were born and raised on foods around there. But in your time, people move about. Then if you as the offspring go to those plants that are near where you were raised, you are more likely to be compatible with those plants, and those plants are more likely to be compatible with you. Given that people move around so much now, the best thing you can do is to seek out the plants that are near where you are residing. It would be best to go with someone who knows and understands plants, such as an herbologist or a person with knowledge of these things, and also with enough heart to interact in the ways we are describing in these pages.

Something else occurs to me. As the planet turns and moves in its orbit, differ-ent energies come in from other planets, energies that affect, influence, or help Earth. So does your plant in particular—and do plants in general—have more healing energy at certain times tied to astrology? Or is that not relevant?

Not so much to astrology, but there might be a little more healing energy during a few days before and a few days after the full moon. Moon cycles are well known in farming.

So if one were going to interact with the plant, then a few days of the waxing and the first few days of the waning moon would be the best.

Something like that, yes, but don't necessarily wait, especially if your condition warrants seeking out the living plants. During the new moon, the plant is likely to have less energy, and the human may have less awareness. There are some new-moon teachings. Those who've been exposed to new-moon teachings, as long as there is feeling involved, may be able to move past that. I would recommend that the easiest thing to do would be to go at times closer to the full moon.

But there's no great advantage to going on the day of the full moon—just go anytime around five or six days before the full moon or five or six days after the full moon. For some people, the full moon itself might be overwhelming, too much. I wouldn't recommend going for your first time on the full moon. It would be better to go a few days before and then go back. Try to be careful where you walk. There's almost no way to avoid stepping on plants, so wear something that will have the least effect. Don't drive a car out to a field, say. Plants don't usually get over such a crushing weight.

This Information Should Be Shared with Others

If you look back now, how long has it been since the last time we lost this information? Has it been a hundred years, five hundred years, a thousand years? More?

It gets lost not just cyclically but it also gets lost geographically. Even though you're in a time of it being fairly lost right now—just the interaction with the living plants—there are those on the planet now who have the information, even some small groups. But it's important to get it out to a larger group. I think that question has to be modified by that knowledge.

So how can we get people to interact with these plants more?

That's not your job. Always remember, even though you might feel an urgency, that your job is to make the information available. Once you've made it available, your job has ended. It will be other people's jobs to tell this person and that person that this is information they find to be of value. You are not so much selling a new, wonderful broom that can sweep more dirt. You are revealing, or being the pathway of revelation, in saying, "Here is something that you might want to know." It is largely up to others to proclaim its value. You might announce it here and there, the way you do now.

[Chuckles.] Advertise it, you mean. Yes.

Yes, but don't do too much. Just leave it up to others. They're doing it now. They will continue to do it.

Do most herbologists who read books focused on drying the plants even know the value of interaction with the live plant?

Many of them are open to that and they are just waiting for this information. I feel that there will be a great deal of interest from herbologists who are open to information coming from this type of source—even gardeners. There may be some information that will appeal to them, as well as those who are ill and looking for possible therapies. Then there are those who are simply interested in lost wisdom. The books that have come through this channel, and other information published here and there or put out here and there, is all about lost information.

It doesn't mean it doesn't exist somewhere. After all, if you lose your shoes, they still exist, and then you find them: "Oh, here they are." So you might say your publishing company is about . . .

Finding shoes [chuckles].

. . . finding those shoes, making them available for your feet.

To Be Reminded Is to Be Cherished and Appreciated

Do you pretty much interact just with your plants? Or do you, you know—not like you have coffee klatches—communicate or commune with other spirits and other plants on the planet?

Only if there is some necessity to do that. Communication would have to do with shared feelings in this case—not thoughts, not words, not language, but there would be a sense of shared feelings. Feelings can be communicated instantaneously, but concepts, words, and thoughts take time and are subject to interpretation, reinterpretation, and even misunderstanding. Feelings are known and understood universally.

So do you at times share feelings or pictures or stories or something with other beings?

No. It's not like that. I mention the feelings because if there is some value in sharing, it is entirely with feelings. They don't need pictures. They don't need stories. These things are needed by those who don't remember; therefore, to be reminded is to be cherished and appreciated. If one is already remembering, such cherishing is a given.

So do you feel into the human race? You seem to know an awful lot about us. I mean, you were here long before we were. How does that work? You don't see us, but you feel us. You could say you know our stories, right?

I don't know your individual stories so much. Because the communication is going on with you personally, there is a little more knowledge there, but in terms of . . . if you were to ask me, "What did I have for lunch today?" I would not be able to say. I am making a joke, but in terms of the basic humanity, I have some knowledge there. After all, human beings exist beyond this planet, all over the universe, here and there. I'm familiar with the type of being. The only real difference in a major way between the human beings on this planet and on the other planets is that you don't remember who you are. That's all the difference is. There are some slight biological differences, but they are very slight. If you were to see a human being from another planet, just looking at them casually, you wouldn't notice anything different.

This Experiment Should Be Conducted as Slowly as Possible

Okay. How do you feel about the experiment we're involved in, the Explorer Race? You've watched it since we've been here, and you know what we're aiming for.

I know the intention, yes.

So what is your opinion of it?

I feel it is a worthy effort, but I'm of the belief, you might say, that the slower you go to accomplish it, the better. I know the human being wants to get it now—yesterday. But I believe that you must go as slowly as you possibly can, because you're not just talking about changing your own life. It's not about buying red shoes compared to blue shoes. It's about changing life and lifestyles all over the universe; therefore, I feel that the slower you go, the better.

Now I'll make a closing comment. As you read this book, consider not only the information rendered within the book but also your own feelings as you read. By your own feelings, I do not mean that which is a vague sense within you but rather the physical feelings in your body. Should your body draw attention to something—meaning you read something and you are not distracted but you get a sudden feeling in some part of your body—maybe that part of your body wants you to read that passage again and consider it. Maybe it's important for you. Maybe there's not a lot of it that your body wants you to read, so maybe make a note of that. As those notes accumulate throughout the reading of the book, then at the end, after consulting your notes, you might have a more complete picture of what this book could mean for you individually. Good life.

TREES

CHAPTER NINE

Cherry Tree

JANUARY 28, 2008

ᛒ

THIS IS CHERRY TREE!

Welcome!

Greetings! Now, I understand that you as human beings eat the fruit of this tree, which is actually the means by which the tree is intended to be propagated. In terms of more wild trees, the fruit can best be propagated by animals eating some of that fruit. Those who raise cherry trees know that they are very difficult, that it is challenging to encourage a good crop, and this will remain so and get much worse until the farmers at least hire people who have the feeling awareness to know the pattern that the trees wish to be planted in.

It is natural that the farmer would plant the trees in a way that is practical to reap the crop, but in fact, as trees we do not like to be planted that way. We prefer a meandering pattern—not as meandering as, say, a river, but something along the lines of a slightly elongated letter s, meaning a waveform, but not so extreme as a waveform, if you understand my meaning. It is hard to explain in words.

Compost and Waveform Planting Will Make Us More Comfortable

A shallow wave?

A shallow wave! Yes, very good! This is the best way, because as trees we do not like to be in an artificial pattern. Go into any forest and you will not find trees in a squared-off pattern. We like curves; we like to have that wave pattern, and I speak in general for all trees here. Farmers, if you wish your crops to come in more abundantly with less struggle, you will consider the wave pattern. It may be awkward, it may not be as easy to bring in the crop, but it will reduce your efforts and will make a more abundant crop. Also, we don't like too much fertilizer—just a little! If you are going to use fertilizer, try to use soil that has been naturally created. What do you call that?

Compost?

Yes, that's it, compost, but not adulterated with too many chemicals, a very light dosage. Most plants do not like to be stimulated like that. It is not so different for you. Imagine your natural day: you sleep, then you get up and you work or you play, whatever you do. It is like that for us. But now imagine if you were taking some stimulation twenty-four hours a day. It would be difficult to rest. Part of the reason the plants don't do too well or do not live their full-length natural lives is because of the twenty-four-hours-a-day stimulation.

From the fertilizer!

That is what happens with fertilizer—it creates a twenty-four-hour stimulation. Imagine how difficult it would be for you to sleep and to have your other natural cycles if you were under stimulation twenty-four hours a day. It is not so different for us. I speak for plants in general here.

What does the waveform do? What is the reason you like that?

Look at the forest. I am using the waveform as an allowable means of access. I am not saying we want to be in a form; I am not saying that. I am saying that if we are in a form, then that would be a little closer approximation of the way animals might walk. When animals consume the fruit and it passes through their bodies, the excrement they produce to release the seeds acts as a fertilizer. But animals do not as a rule walk in a straight line; they walk in a meandering path. Humans in their natural state also walk in this way. Straight lines that are connected at right angles like that—this is something that is utilized for the sake of practicality, an engineering manifesto, so to speak. So the flat wave, as you call it, approximates the way an animal might walk. It would also suggest that you don't have trees every twenty feet or so—maybe every thirty feet, or vary it one-seventeenth of a foot away from each other, and so on. That kind of variation will produce a larger crop; the tree will last longer and be less likely to get diseased. That's what I recommend.

I also do not recommend using products of the sea, meaning animals. Don't use animals in your fertilizer too much, or at least not fish! By fertilizer, I am referring to compost. Some products have this, and as a good farmer you could read up on the products that are in the compost, if you have not made it yourself. Or you could perhaps hire someone or have someone do it for you. A small amount of bone from land animals would be acceptable, because one would find that in the forest.

Just try to keep it natural, similar to . . . ?

Try to keep it natural, and try not to use dung dust from domesticated animals. Generally speaking, that would refer to cows, and especially pigs. Pigs in your time are extremely unhappy. These are very smart animals, and they do not like to be imprisoned. They much prefer to wander. I am not saying that this is how you should do things; I am just saying that the angrier the elements in the compost, the more uncomfortable it is to take that energy in. I am not talking about something vague, like some kind of vague reference in terms of energy. I am using energy as a word that is associated with physics, as in math, mathematics, you understand? So energy in this sense means the feeling it has and the effect it produces.

That's felt by you?

Yes, it's felt by plants. So you must try different things and be alert to what would naturally be in the forest where a tree might just function by itself without human care. Trees are like this as well.

Oh, this is very good. I am sure this is not known.

Well, I feel that this is part of the purpose of your book—not only the applications of what is not known for the care of human beings, which will perhaps come later in the book, but also the personality characteristics of plant life. If this is known on a more personal basis like this for the farmer, for the gardener, or just for the average citizen, it will help you to not only understand your relationship with other forms of life on the planet but also how to interact in a way that not only serves your own kind but helps you to learn how to get along with other forms of life.

When you get along benevolently with other forms of life, your friends from other planets will be much more likely to come to Earth, feel welcome and safe, and offer you all the wonderful gifts they have for you. They are not doing that now, because they don't feel safe to come. They see how you treat the plants, how you treat the animals. I am not talking about individual humans, who may very well treat plants and animals well. But as a general society, treating plants and animals badly just keeps people who love you at a distance. They are waiting for you to become more benevolent to each other and to other forms of life on the planet so that they can offer you the means of technology to vastly improve your life on Earth.

We Are Not Native to Earth

We know about these things because, after all, as life forms ourselves, we are not native to Earth. We come from a planet very far from here, and on that planet we do not appear exactly as we do on Earth. We are slightly—not much more, but slightly—more mobile. We do not have legs per se, but we are slightly more mobile, because the planet itself has movable surfaces. You have such things on your planet, but you don't really notice them very often. You are aware, of course, of earthquakes and the motion of the seas and the lakes, but on our planet there are plates—what you call "plate tectonics" on your planet—that are in fairly constant motion. So even though on our home planet we may grow and appear to be similar to a tree—what you would understand a tree to be, yes—because the earth beneath us is in motion, gradually but perceptibly, if you were there, you would actually see the motion of the plates. You could measure it—say, an inch an hour, two inches an hour, three inches an hour. It would depend where you were on the planet. You would say that it does account for a certain amount of motion on our part, though we do not get up and walk about, so to speak.

If you were to see us, you would see something that does look like the trunk of a tree, but there is very little in the way of branches. It is more like the occasional branch, but from the branch will always hang one object that, while it does not look like the cherry you have on Earth, would be about the size of an orange or occasionally as big as a grapefruit. But it has a very rough exterior—not unlike a nut, for instance a walnut—and it does not house something that is meant to be consumed. It houses what is a close analogy to a nervous system or a portion of a brain.

It is not likely that you will see us any time in the near future, or even in the much farther future. Though you may see other forms of life from a distance, you are most likely to meet up and interact with beings who are at the very least humanoids and certainly very often beings who, for all intents and purposes from your perception, are human. This will help you to feel at ease and ease you into the world of activity with other life forms.

How are you propagated? Who else is on your home planet besides you?

We do not have too many other forms of life. There is water of a sort, and it is a little bit different in chemical composition than your own, a little thicker. It travels in narrow streams between the plates, and it nourishes us. It is thicker because it has nutrients in it as well as the liquid itself, and it has a little bit more of a composition of light—meaning if you were to have some in a glass, say, in a dark room, it would glow slightly. This does not mean it's radioactive; it just has a means of illumination. I am not sure what that's about, but it does that. I have not seen many other forms of life on the planet. My impression is, however, that there are other forms of life, but I believe they might stay where they reside. I believe there is something that flies, but I have only seen it once.

So where you are here on Earth do you see many birds?

I am conscious of birds, of course, because they land in the branches. I do not actually see them, but I have a means to see. It is not unlike the way you would see something in a dream. You know when you are asleep that your eyes are closed, yet you wake up with clear visual pictures. It's very similar for us. We can see very clearly, but we do not need to use eyes. This is fairly typical among all life forms on the planet with the exception of those who have eyes. Then they would relate more directly to the way you utilize eyes.

Here on this planet, are you connected to other cherry trees in their roots underneath, or are you separate?

I am connected to others. I am currently in a farm in North America.

Ah. Do many humans come around?

Some. It is a farm, not a big one, but some humans come around. Sometimes they are very small, but most of the time they are of average human stature.

Do you feel their energies? Do you know what they are doing?

My impression is that they are working on the farm.

So there are animals there?

The humans do not encourage animals, but they have some of their own who are apparently like family members, and they run around here a bit.

While you're here, are you aware of what's happening on your home planet or is your energy all focused here?

No, it's focused here.

As We Propagate, Our Energy Goes into the New Trees

What do your people say about why you were asked to come here? Did you have someone come to your people and ask that you come to Earth?

Yes, this appears to be a general rule. My impression is that . . . now, this is strictly my impression, but from what I've heard, no one volunteered without being asked. This makes sense when you consider it. If you heard about a project going on, on the other side of the universe, for example, and you had the opportunity, though no one had asked you yet to volunteer to go there, but the chances of you ever seeing your family again were almost nonexistent, most of you would not consider volunteering. So generally speaking, a being would come and lay out the case for it, so to speak; they'd say, "This is why we're requesting this of you, and we don't want to coerce you in any way, but we're asking for volunteers." So generally speaking, from what I understand, the original volunteers were older, toward the end of their cycles, and they were able to let go of their family life because they were nearing the end of their cycles and were able to say their goodbyes and go. So that's how I understand those who originally came—as elders.

And how does it work now? Do you come between lives on your home planet?

No. Since then there has been a stream of propagation here.

Oh, the elders came to start the entire species. I see.

Yes.

So your volunteer time is the only time that a cherry tree lives? Or do you come back here more than once?

Generally speaking, those of us who are here remain here. We will be here until human beings no longer make much effort to keep us going—meaning at some point you may not be consuming our fruit anymore. That will be in the considerable future. But even then, we will probably remain here for a time, because we who have, who are—how can we say?—the inheritors of what the elders have started here on the soul level as trees, are native now. I was born on Earth, and I do not really identify with the home planet very much. So we will be here until we are no longer here, and when the last one of us is either no longer here or somewhere else, then perhaps I will be on the home planet. I do not identify with the home planet personally. But I explained it to you before so that you would have some sense of how we look there, since I know that is something that interests you.

How long have you been on Earth, then?

Oh, hundreds of years, I suppose. I really don't factor such things in.

So you are with your tree, and when the tree eventually dies, your consciousness goes into the new tree?

It's that way with all trees on the planet, as far as I know. When you propagate yourself, your consciousness goes into the trees that spring up as a result of your seeds. Even if there are fifty that spring up, your consciousness goes into them. It doesn't mean there aren't other consciousnesses in those seeds, but you become a portion of it. I believe it is similar for you as human beings, though you may not be aware of it. Your parents' energy to a degree actually goes into your physical body for a time, but I don't think in your case that it stays. It just goes in for a time.

From what I have been able to gather by simply observing human beings, this parental consciousness lingers in the body of the baby after the human baby is born for about a year and a half at most, and then the baby's own consciousness begins to emerge as the predominant expression of personality. It is done that way with the human baby in order to motivate the baby to remain alive on the planet, since the first six months of life on the planet for a human Earth soul are often very shocking. The reality, you understand, does not necessarily live up to the anticipation. The parents' energy, because they love baby, tends to support baby to be here, and after a year and a half, baby gets used to being on Earth.

In your case, then, your consciousness spreads to the area around your original tree. But what if some of your seeds are carried by an animal or a bird a distance away? Then you are at the original place and the new place?

That's right. Distance doesn't make any difference, even if the system is done by human beings. Processing does harm to the energy connection—meaning if there are machines involved—but if it is done gently by human beings without involving machines, then there is no interference or interruption with the connection at all. A certain amount of contact with human beings is acceptable.

Our Fruit Helps Humans Experience Greater Welcome on Earth

So what was the reason the emissary asked you to come? What did the emissary feel you alone could do?

My understanding, based on what has been passed on from the elders, is that we specifically were asked to come because the energy we would offer in our fruits eventually . . . we were told that initially it would not be with humans directly, but eventually that which we would offer to the human being would allow the human being to experience a greater sense of welcome on Earth. We understand that the fruit we have is naturally sweet, at least if one waits the proper amount of time to consume it. It is naturally sweet, and such sweet fruits always encourage on the physical level the physical human body's—how can we say?—sense of being in the right place. The physical body is not convinced by any form of rational argument; the physical body is only convinced of any truth on the basis of the physical evidence, meaning how one feels physically.

So if the physical body is consuming and swallowing, say, for instance, an apple or a cherry or anything like that, it tastes good; it has a sweetness. And when one consumes it, one feels the vital life energy. In short, the physical evidence is presented that the planet has positive qualities and one feels more welcome physically being on Earth. This is a reminder to the physical body of the way it might feel on other planets, where simply the air you breathe—to say nothing of the surrounding atmosphere and energy and feelings and so on—contains that energy. But this is not always the case on Earth, so when one consumes a sweet fruit, one is reminded of the feeling that one has on other planets where such welcoming is a natural portion of day-to-day life.

Receiving Messages from Birds and Trees

Do you interact and discuss things with birds and animals and other trees?

There is a small amount of interaction, though not what you would call thought, between trees. I sometimes have the opportunity to hear the birds communicate to each other. They will communicate about their own life forms, but occasionally one of the larger birds will make philosophical conversation, usually a commentary on the state of Earth or the state of one's own kind on Earth. I've had such commentary from eagles and large blackbirds before. Large blackbirds are very philosophical. Ravens are very philosophical and inclined to share their points of view about the nature of life. They are what I would call "cosmos-ticians," meaning that their philosophy seems to expand beyond Earth and take in life in the cosmos as well.

This is probably one of the reasons their presence, although sometimes amusing or even exasperating to human beings, always stimulates a tendency to think about one's life, one's culture, one's family, and so on, because of their philosophical nature. They can deliver messages from Spirit. So if your dreams suddenly shift when they are around, some of that might be a message from Spirit. They have been known to pass on messages to those who are able to pick them up. So if one ever lands near you and begins making its sounds directly at you, you will know that it is attempting to pass on a message—always know that!

This is also a factor sometimes with trees. If you've ever walked near a tree and were carefully avoiding all the branches, and suddenly out of nowhere a branch touches you and you were quite certain you were going to miss that branch, the tree probably wants to pass on a message to you. This would not be a message coming from the tree; rather, it is passing on a message from someone else or some other form of life. Then you'll just have to do your best. If you don't have the means or the awareness to get the message directly from the tree (or bird), then just spend time in the presence of that bird or that tree. Stay there. See if the energy will absorb in you. Don't rush off to where you were going to go. Wait—just absorb the energy.

You don't necessarily have to touch the tree—actually, as trees we don't care for that. But if you feel a need to touch the tree, always touch it with the back of your hand, never with the palm. There are acids on your palm from when you sweat, but on the very back of your hand—not the fingers, but the back part of your hand—there is much less of that. Then touching a branch, not a leaf (leaves are sensitive), would be the best way—if and only if you feel the need to do so. So stay with the tree for a time, or with the bird.

If it is a bird, then just talk to the bird and say, "I will take in as much energy as you have to give me without taking your own personal energy, and perhaps I will dream about the message you are trying to give me," something like that. Say it out loud; just thinking it won't work. You can whisper it quietly. In the case of the tree, you can do the same thing. Just wait, and at some point you will feel that it's all right to walk away. Don't walk away on the basis of, "Oh, I have to get somewhere," unless it is an emergency or pressing, something like that.

In the case of a bird, the bird will simply fly away when it feels you have engaged enough, and then that will tell you that you have enough and perhaps you will dream the message or it will pop into your head. If you are in doubt, you can ask a sensitive person or someone who can help you with your discernment. But in the case of the tree, most likely the message will come to you, if you are not able to pick it up on your own in a dream.

Silica Will Bring You Clarity and Purpose

How do you sustain yourself?

We take in what we need from the soil. It is generally best, however, for the soil to be welcoming. I think you can check this with gardening magazines. I have tried to offer suggestions based on what we would appreciate not experiencing, but I would not wish to lecture farmers or gardeners in general, to say, "Give us this and not that," because the soil is made up of the soil. It is an accumulation of this and that. But I do not request that you make the soil.

I just wondered if there was anything that you particularly noticed or liked.

We have in the past enjoyed silica—not necessarily having it ground up and shoved at us, but the presence of it in the soil seems to be pleasing to us. I believe it has to do with its clarity. Silica does encourage clarity. I would recommend, as a human being, if you feel scattered or confused or your life is moving in various patterns too quickly for you, if you can be somewhere around silica . . . natural silica, not something synthesized by human beings. Just have a natural piece of it around or know where it is. If you can go and be close to it . . . you don't have to touch it. Sometimes it is not good to touch it, especially if lots of others are touching it. But if you are within a few inches or up to, say, three feet, you can hold out a hand—I'd recommend your right hand, palm toward the silica, or even the fingertips of your right hand. Or if you don't have a hand or your hand is injured, you can hold out your right foot. And the silica will help to bring clarity and even in some cases purpose.

We Know Why We Are Here

Do you have teachers who come and communicate—not talk, but commune—with you, or do you ask them questions?

We don't ask questions. We know why we are here, but we sometimes have beings who speak to us, as in reference to the bird. But we are not like you. We understand that you need teachers, guides, and so on, because you do not know why you are here for the most part. It is not like that for the other beings on the planet. So teachers, per se—no.

You're so aware!

Well, you understand, I am around human beings. If I were in the forest somewhere, I might be less so, but being on a farm, I am constantly around human beings.

How aware of them are you? You sense their feelings and . . .

Oh no, I don't make an effort to make personal contact. I have noted that the smaller human beings, the youngsters, will sometimes gravitate toward one tree or another, not even necessarily a cherry tree. I can see one, feel one, be aware of one, you understand, at a distance that is a different kind of tree, perhaps native to the land, and the children often go to that tree. So I am aware that the children might have a personal connection to a tree, but I do not . . . well, let's just say I have not had the opportunity to have a personal connection with a human being at this time. But I believe other trees do have that from time to time, especially if they have certain shapes or forms, or for some reason or another human beings value them in some way.

So are there other kinds of trees, like oak trees or apple trees or cottonwood trees, around you?

There is a tree I am aware of at a distance—it's not in a portion of the farm—that appears to be a tree native to the area, but I don't know what you call it. It's not growing any fruits per se, you understand. It is not growing the type of fruits that human beings would gather. Of course, it does seed itself.

So do you interact with it?

Not really. I am just aware of it.

Well, you certainly are aware of a lot more than I realized a tree was aware of.

It is an interesting phenomena on your planet that I have noted—and I am sure it has to do with your lack of connection to your whole being—but human beings are astonishingly unaware of other life forms, and perhaps because of the way you are raised in many of your cultures, you do not make too much effort to understand other life forms in their living states. I understand that there are those who attempt to study other life forms by cutting them up or destroying them in order to understand them. In my experience of life, I would have to say that if a human being was being cut up or destroyed in order to understand that human being, I am sure that said human being would protest mightily, to say nothing of other human beings. If you want to understand us, don't cut us up into little pieces. You are not going to find out much.

Do you know what human beings were doing when you came to the planet? I am trying to get a sense of when you came.

I'm not aware of what you were doing. I don't have a great deal of awareness of your history.

But it's been so long that, like you say, you feel like you've always been here.

No. I *have* always been here. What I know about the home planet, I know from the elders. I can trace my awareness of life back to the elders, and what I know about the home planet is because of the elders. Remember what I said before, about how the parents of a human being would support the baby, would be in the baby in that sense for a time until the baby's personality took over? In the case of the tree, you understand, the tree's seeding properties, the parents—the parent tree, and so on—would be in the offspring. It stays. Even though I have my own personality,

I identify with the personalities of all the former generations—the ancestors, so to speak. Therefore, what I know about the home planet is *because* of the elders, but I have not been there.

So you are saying that they didn't talk to you but you have part of their personalities in you?

No, just to the degree that supports life. I am not them.

Okay, but some of their memories, then, are part of you?

I am able to access them to a slight degree in order to give you some minor details, but I could not tell you everything they did, everything they felt, everything they thought, and so on. I don't have any of that.

Let me ask if you know this: I'm interested in those moving tectonic plates on your home planet. They seem narrow. On this planet, we have maybe half a dozen tectonic plates. So you have many, many, many tectonic plates that move like escalators?

No, it's a small planet too. Much smaller than Earth! You might not even in your science classify it as a planet, but I can assure you that it is.

It has a regular orbit around its local sun?

I don't know about such things.

So you're not concerned about the future? At some point when you're through here, you'll go back there, but that's then, right?

I'm not even certain that's so, but the future will take care of itself. The present is the most important. If one is not aware of the present, I daresay that you might have a problem.

Our Medicinal Qualities Are Practically Untouched

Okay, what else is it you know that we would be interested in that I don't know to ask?

The medicinal qualities of what we have to offer have been practically untouched, though there has been considerable research done in the area of your world known as Asia. I will say this: When our fruits are freshly picked, if you find it comfortable to be in the fragrance of that . . . the first five minutes after they are picked, the fruits and the stems offer a fragrance that would allow a tremendous invigoration of life, whatever life form there is.

If you are picking these fruits with a machine, you miss that completely, but if you are able to pick the fruits, say, on a small farm by hand and then put them into a padded vessel, every couple of minutes or so you can stop and move your face toward the vessel and take several deep breaths. For the average person without any serious illnesses or allergies, this will invigorate your life—it might even add some time to your life span. After five minutes it rapidly fades. But for the first five minutes, take a couple of breaths, maybe three, and then go on picking, and I think you will find that that's a good thing.

That sounds wonderful. If you're giving off that, you must have an incredible amount of that quality within you.

It's not quite that. It has to do with the separation of the fruits and stems from the tree. In that moment of separation, there is a surge of energy from the tree to the stem and the fruit, and while I do not encourage you to pop the cherry off the tree and stick it immediately in your mouth, since you don't know who has touched that cherry . . . you are going to want to wash it, to say nothing of letting it ripen. But aside from that, the surge of energy is more what you are taking in. You will not take it from the cherry so much, but there is a radiation beyond the cherry, and normally it simply dissipates into the air and that which needs it will assimilate it. But if you are there as a person, you can take one or two natural breaths. Don't breathe in any deeper than normal—just one or two natural breaths in your normal cycle, possibly a third, but only if you get a feeling to do that. Most of you will not get that feeling. Then continue picking.

What about any medicinal qualities in the cherry itself that we don't know about yet?

I think we will be doing that in Part 2 of the book. That's what I was told—a person in Part 2 will talk about the use of the cherry itself.

Was there a call out for a volunteer, or how did you know that this opportunity was available for you to talk?

Oh! I suddenly became aware of it.

Well, I am glad you did, because this is really interesting.

Experience Your Own Ambiance

Is there anything else you want to say about anything?

I could make a closing statement. Your society is in its infancy in terms of learning about other forms of life, but it's not too late to interact with other forms of life as equals. Speaking for trees in general, we do not expect you to be aware of who we are as individual personalities, but we are very receptive to your being friendly and enjoying our beauty as well as our general ambiance. You as human beings also have ambiance, especially when you are happy or when you are relaxed or when you are feeling comfortable—or, for that matter, when you are in restful sleep.

All life forms have a certain amount of ambiance, meaning the energy that radiates around them. As you learn to be more comfortable with your own ambiance, you will perhaps learn to notice the difference between your energy radiations and the energy radiations from other forms of life. Interacting together, radiating all these different ways from all these different forms of life on Earth, creates a healthful environment for all life forms.

I know right now you are involved in cutting down trees and making your structures and so on, and you do not think of trees as a valuable life form in and of their own selves. But in our living state, we have much knowledge and wisdom to offer, on an individual basis as well as on a group basis. So for those of you who are sensitive to such things, begin your practice by feeling or experiencing your own ambiance. Move your hand out and move it gradually toward your body so that you get a sense of feeling as to how *you* feel. You might feel it in your hand; you might feel it in your body.

Get that sense, then go to a tree and move your hand. I'd recommend your left hand, palm toward the tree, toward the trunk of the tree, or if the branches are low, toward the spread of branches. But stay at least three feet away and feel that energy. You might feel it in your hand. You might feel it in your body. The good way to start, then, is to notice the difference between the feeling of your own ambiance and the ambiance from other forms of life. It will always be a different feeling, and that's a good place to begin. Good night and good life!

Thank you very, very much. Good life!

CHAPTER TEN

Pine Tree

JANUARY 27, 2008

ℭ

GREETINGS! THIS IS PINE TREE!
Welcome!

Thank you. I'm called, I think, a conifer, and I am actually in existence some-where in the middle of what is called Canada. This is kind of a restful time of year for me, as the winter is here. We are called evergreens, you know.

It's not easy to sustain one's life force through the cold. One might reason-ably wonder how we can do that, but it is because—and this is part of the reason we even exist on Earth for human beings to see—we have not only learned to tap our roots deep but also that it is actually possible to function in a way that appears to be, for all intents and purposes, stasis. This is not unlike what your scientists are looking for so that your space travelers can migrate from one place to another using your current form of motive force and arrive in a reasonable length of body-elapsed time, as compared to time as it might elapse elsewhere. There is an assumption by some scientists that we are in this form, but in fact things inside us are moving, just very slowly, and it works much better with older trees. Now, that's all I'm going to say about that.

I don't want the scientists to pick us apart to try to figure out how we do that, even though there's been a lot of that in the past. It is more important to just know that it *is* possible. However, in order for it to take place, the being who does this—and this is why we are here to remind you of this, among other things—must be plant-based. So pay attention, human scientists: If you're not plant-based, you cannot do this, so don't be looking to create plant-based human beings, okay? Rather, be pursuing a different type of motive force that will get you from place to place in the stars quicker. I think some of you are on the right track. I just wanted to open that up, so you would not pursue that anymore. It's not something a human being can do in your form. I grant that some extraterrestrials have figured out a way to do it, but it is not comfortable for human beings and really rather frightening, so I don't recommend that.

Lean Back Against Us to Ease Your Troubles

I wanted to say this, because a lot of people, science people, have been missing the point of who we are to you, and that's one of the main points. Also, we have other aspects that we can do. Some of you have noted that if you were to sit near us, if that's possible . . . sometimes our boughs are down to the ground. But if they are not and you are able to sit near us, perhaps lean back and relax for fifteen, twenty minutes, not always, but many times, if we are in the right mood—we are alive, we have feelings—you will feel as if many of your troubles have fallen away.

Not that many years ago, people knew this about us as trees. Now, granted, we don't grow well everywhere, but people knew that contact . . . though the contact must be made from the human being's back. It won't help if you reach out and touch us with your hand, even the back of your hand. You need to lean your back against us. You don't have to have our trunks pressing on your spine, but it's good that your spine is some way in contact. Then just relax! Try not to think, and enjoy the surroundings. Observe perhaps, but don't think about things.

If you fall asleep for a few moments, that's fine. About fifteen or twenty minutes is sufficient, and if we happen to be in the right mood—this is a hit-or-miss thing, for those of you who can't tell—you'll probably feel better when you leave. Staying longer won't help. Sometimes the reason it doesn't help is that we change moods. We feel this; we feel that. Also, fifteen or twenty minutes of direct contact like that with a human being, where we are actually sharing our energy, is about enough for most of us—not because we don't like you, but rather because it is tiring in a way that we do not usually function. If you happen to catch us in the right mood, which is about a 50-percent chance, then we can do this with human beings maybe three times a month per tree at most. But it can't be done, like, three times a week. It'll have to be spaced out, every eight, nine, ten days, something like that.

I wanted to bring these points up, because human beings in your time have forgotten some of these things. You go back a hundred years—even just a hundred years—and in some of your old Farmer's Almanacs you might find . . . and by this I do not mean printed ones, though in some cases you might find them. I am talking about actual farmers keeping track of things around their farms and then passing this on to their sons and daughters, or in the case of a cooperative effort, to the immediate community. This is why sometimes you would find pine trees—and I might add, I can only speak for the conifers here, but there might be others who are like this—on farms where you wouldn't always think of pine trees as growing. You know, we used to grow before humankind showed up and really in this case before technological humans showed up, such as the peoples who are occupying North America, since I am talking from North America.

When you showed up and were cutting down trees, not recognizing what valuable beings we are, we extended and grew toward what you call the Gulf of Mexico. It wasn't that unusual several hundred years ago to find us in growth a little bit below Arkansas and at the northern fringes of Alabama and so on. So that gives you an idea, where sometimes you would not think of a pine tree around there, but it is not that strange to find us there.

There are pine trees there now, aren't there?

Planted by human beings. I am talking about our natural growth. We are also known for our sense of humor. A lot of the reason that human beings can be refreshed leaning back against us, if we are feeling cheerful . . . if we are doing some other work with other trees or other beings, that won't help you because we will have our energy contained to perform some other activity. But if we are feeling cheerful . . . and you can identify with this perhaps. When *you* are feeling cheerful, your energy spreads out a bit. Sometimes people will even know you are feeling cheerful before they enter your general space, meaning within thirty feet of you, because they'll just get a good feeling. So if we happen to be feeling cheerful, then that's when the contact can successfully be made with us, as I described earlier.

For those of you who can pick up feelings from trees, if you try this, try to make sure that the trunk of the tree is at least ten inches—and I would prefer twelve inches—across. Just reach with the back of your hand. You don't need to use a measuring tool; put your hands out and estimate. This way a tree's energy won't be depleted if it's too young. Then you can do that.

We Often Request Things for Earth

What kind of work do you do with other trees?

We're often engaged in activities that have to do with support from the Sun or other stars—and occasionally other planets—that move through our boughs and trunk into the earth. Or in the case, perhaps, when rain is needed under certain circumstances, to move through our roots up our bodies and into the sky, but within the energy of Earth only, to request rain.

The work we are involved in with the Sun and other stars and other planets usually is cooperative work with Earth. Earth is tired now, and she cannot always pay attention to all the surfaces of her body at the same time. So we will often request things for her. We don't always know what it is that she's requesting, because she has a language, for lack of another term. It is a feeling, but it is not one that is native to us. We do not recognize it, so we don't know what she's asking. We assume she's asking, because we can feel it, slightly and up to a greater sense of urgency, and we can tell where that urgency is directed to, in the general direction of the sky. And we may know where this is going on, but if it is not involving us directly—meaning a request through our type of tree, where it's going on the planet Earth—then we don't. We are simply aware that it's going on.

I have had the experience myself, and regardless of where the top of our tree is aimed, we can direct . . . I'm not sure if we're actually singularly involved in this or whether the direction, or function, is a means of amplification or simply functioning not unlike the way a chorus would make a sound, a song, more noticeable. We can direct that energy to the place in the sky that feels right, not unlike you might feel something in front of you, "Shall I go this way? Shall I go that way?" by putting out your hand, and so on, or just getting the general instinctual message in your body. So that's how we function.

Often when we are doing this, then—since you have asked the question—we would not be able to experience our normal state of cheeriness, because we would be working. Now, you have asked what we might be doing, and that would be a good example, because it relates to Earth and, at least on a secondary basis, to the human population and other populations around Earth. Generally speaking, from what I can grasp, Mother Earth does not do this sort of thing to directly support her populations of other beings on Earth, humans or others. She will only do this in our case when she herself needs some support from the Sun or the planets or the other stars. I have noted, even in my short life, that she has been doing this more lately, so to speak. I have been on the planet in infancy to my current size for approximately 180 of your years.

Are you close enough in proximity to other pine trees that your roots are near each other underground?

Yes, but we are very clear when we are close or in touch, and we are very sensitive to not become enmeshed if at all possible. Usually, we will try to leave some space between our root system and the root systems of other trees, although there is an exception: Sometimes if there is a very, well, insufficient amount of soil and perhaps rock—a great deal of rock, yes?—then our roots will have to grow out laterally and go into the earth only where we find space in the rock. So that might be different, but we do not fight for survival at the cost of life forms, other plant life forms. We, in fact, might share energy if one or more of us is stronger and a life form that is meant to be here on the planet is present. This is often why we would allow a certain amount of interaction with bird species that may not necessarily be good for us, but we recognize that the birds are not attacking us. They are simply trying to survive, and most often when we have a nest of birds in our boughs, it is a joyful experience.

How far does your awareness go? What are you conscious of—all trees on the planet or just in your area or what?

Only what I need to know. I am reaching out in all directions at the moment because of the process you are involved in, but simply functioning as my life, I am more inclined to be aware only of the few trees within my immediate area—say, within a hundred feet and maybe a similar amount of space, maybe eighty feet down, maybe eighty feet above myself, like that. But because of the process we are involved in, I am reaching out a bit farther.

This Is My First Physical Life

Your total life span here is what?

Well, do you mean if we're not interfered with or lightning doesn't strike us or if there isn't a fire or if human beings don't go through us with saws? Hundreds of years—I am not certain. I would have to live that to know and I haven't. This is my first life here on this planet.

Do you remember where you came from?

Yes, I do. Meaning, do I remember . . . ?

. . . the planet you were on?

Of course, the planet. Yes, of course. I didn't come from there. All beings are ensouled and have personality or we wouldn't be on this planet or in this creation, since the Creator of this universe naturally includes a portion of itself to sustain any life form. You know, I believe there is confusion about that in some of your philosophies on Earth. The reason Creator includes a portion of itself in each and every being, every existence of every microbe, and so on, is not simply because it is a gift, a portion of one's self as one might give. Even in shaking hands, you might leave a little portion of yourself with the other person, at least briefly. The reason is sustainability. This universe has been created unlike others, meaning that in many universes all the beings who exist in that universe are immortal. They exist, and there's never any death. But in this universe, one frequently finds death. It doesn't mean necessarily suffering as on your planet—many times it does, but not all— but because there is that, then the Creator here . . . I can't speak for other places, but the Creator in this universe provides this soul energy, as you might call it, for the sake of sustainability.

It isn't given so that it can be taken away. Once it's given to you, once your existence is happening, that's the soul energy you have, no matter where, even if it migrates around from place to place. That part of you is immortal in this universe, and your general personality is perhaps not affected by everything you might do in an individual life but remains the same in that soul energy.

So when I said that I didn't come directly from my planet, where we are from as a species, I really came from a visit I was having with the Creator of this universe. It's very easy to do that between lives. Creator can be everywhere and is a portion of everything, and when you hear such things, they are not simply philosophical statements or statements from your religious peoples. As I said, truly Creator is a portion of everything, and that makes sense when you think about it.

If you've ever had any talk with Creator or dreamt that you had one (this is the case with your peoples), most likely you *were* having a talk with some version of Creator. And in my experience in my talks I've had with Creator, the one thing I've noticed is that Creator likes to be everywhere. This is a portion of Creator's personality—the enjoyment, not so much of keeping an eye on things [laughs], as you might say . . . pardon my humor! We are humorous. Cheerful! We are cheerful as a species. But Creator enjoys interacting. When Creator gives a soul— you understand, the life form has a portion of itself you call a soul—to any form of life, it's because Creator is social and enjoys interacting with all forms of life, just exactly the way they were created by Creator. So it's done, near as I can tell, for cheerful reasons, which is part of the reason we as a species are so compatible with Creator.

So that's where I came from, though. To answer your question more directly about the planet I might identify as our home planet, there is such a place. It is quite a ways from here, not in this galaxy, and it functions . . . I have noticed that many forms of life are either plant-based or mineral-based. One could make a reasonable argument that you as a species are at least partially mineral-based. I know that might sound strange, but then, when you look at your bones, these are made up of mineral, are they not? And yet you are walking around. You cannot function, you cannot live without them. So from my perspective, you are partially mineral-based. If you think of yourself that way, it will be easier for you to understand that when various personalities, such as myself and others, refer to mineral-based life forms on other planets, we might very well be talking about life forms that simply have a skeletal structure internally or externally or something like that. It's important for you to keep that in mind, because we think of you that way—as partially mineral-based life forms.

We are from a planet, however, that does not have that as full-time residents. Rather, the life forms are plant-based, I would say, and we therefore do not have to eat foods the way you do. I understand that you must in order to survive well and be strengthened by what you eat, but we do not. We function very similarly to the way we do on this planet—by what your peoples call photosynthesis, water, sunlight, and so on. The planet is smaller than this planet, but not by much. It has two moons, and it's in a solar system of seven planets. The sun, however, is not as bright as your Sun. This may be why the solar system does not have a great many planets. I am not certain. Our planet is the fourth planet from the sun.

Do you have actual memories of your life on your home planet?

I have memories of pre-life, meaning that the process of creation and re-creation—you understand, what goes on—is different. There is a pre-life process that is much lengthier than the commitment to a physical life form there at all. There the physical life form exists for not very long. It is the pre-life that is the more—how can we say?—lengthy time, so the parents, you might say, using your terminology, would be considering the creation of another life form to the extent of their cooperation and their activity to bring it about, maybe a thousand years or so before it actually happens. But the form of life itself, at least as I experienced it, may not last that long. So this tells you that parents are not like your human parents. Parents in this case would be a group of beings: ten, twenty, maybe more, perhaps thirty, and the number would change over time. So the group would essentially be considering the creation and re-creation of other life forms.

When you are being considered for that, that consideration often goes on 800, 900, 1,000 of your years in length of time. I have known it to go on for almost eleven hundred of your years, through a process that I can only describe as interactions with the substance we grow in, which is sort of a combination of mineral, not dissimilar to soil, and a thicker form of water (not entirely a variation of what you might call "hydroponic"). Then that interaction would come about, and a form would be noted in that fluid, thick fluid, and it would take quite awhile to come about. But the pre-life, which happens over that long period of time, is when the communion takes place, meaning the intimate conversation and contact with Creator, one's guides, one's teachers, and so on, in order to even decide whether one would choose to be physicalized as a life form on that planet.

So one gets entirely and thoroughly engaged in the philosophy of life. Why would you want to change forms from, what you might simply say, nonphysical to physical for a time? You don't get persuaded; you just get exposed to different ways of being. "Would you like to do this?" "Yes, no, etc." So that's what I remember. I remember the pre-life, but I haven't actually ever been physical. I decided not to be. This is the first physical life I've ever had.

So you always said no, you didn't want to be physical this way?

That's right. Well, you know, I existed. I had my own life, I had my own function, but I was never physical. You understand, the physicality on that planet is certainly different than yours, but if you were to visit in a vehicle and the vehicle had the means, you could see us; you could see our planet. But in terms of the level of physicality, which is much more engaged, much more involved, this is the first physical life I've had.

And what persuaded you to say yes to this one?

Well, the reason I did say yes to this one is because of the project that's going on here. I feel it has value. Even though it is difficult for your life forms here, you ultimately will resolve a great many problems in the universe. And from my talk with Creator, I can see that Creator has a tendency to look past your current struggles and Creator sees you as someone, if I might use that term applied to you all.

Yes, a unit.

Yes. Creator sees you as someone who will resolve problems and difficulties that Creator did not see could happen as a result of its creation. I think you can identify with this, as you will sometimes do something or start something and realize after the fact that you wished you had done it differently.

Like, "Uh-oh!"

Yes. Creator has a few of these "uh-ohs" and apparently perceives you as a being, the human race, as one who will somehow come along at some point and put all that right.

Yes. That's why we're here.

We Were Approached by an Emissary

So how were you approached to come here, then? By talking to the Creator or by an emissary?

The way I understand it from my fellow trees here is that there was an emissary and this was a typical process where the emissary spoke—not to the elders directly, though. This is an interesting factor, but the emissary spoke only to the pre-life forms, as it is there where one decides whether one wishes to be physical. That makes sense when you think about it. And speaking to the pre-life forms, the general choice was made that about maybe 20 percent of them, 18 percent, something like that, would consider at some point in their life cycles being on this planet during the time of the human race population.

You understand, it's a major consideration, because trees, as you call us, do not have the option of survival, and suffering is a factor here on this planet but not on other planets, so it's quite . . . this is where I feel that the emissary comes from Creator directly, because it's asking a lot of beings who otherwise have not known suffering. Given that we have not known suffering, we don't really know what it is. It is a concept. I feel that when your type of life had contact with emissaries or whoever, you would not have known what suffering was either. Had you known . . .

. . . we might not have accepted.

You might not have. In fact, I find it hard to believe that you would have. This does not suggest that Creator is somehow ruthless, but rather Creator has a longer vision than we do to see that not only is the human race going to resolve things Creator has not foreseen but apparently you are going to go on and do something else past that point that Creator sees to be valuable. Otherwise, I don't believe that Creator . . . because Creator is such a loving being, I can't imagine that Creator would have involved you in any project—meaning the human race throughout your galaxy as well as the universe—that would involve, at least for some of the human race on Earth, suffering. I believe at the time, from my communication with Creator, that Creator did not conceive that the suffering of the human race on Earth would reach such levels.

No, I think it was predicted to be 2 percent or something.

Yes, and that was Creator's original intention.

We Bring a Level of Cheerfulness to Earth

This is interesting, because I have never talked to anyone quite like you. How are you connected at all to that planet of trees if you've never been physical? I mean, were you part of a spirit collective related to that planet or were you just floating free and they were asking anybody there?

That's a good question. I was a portion of the matrix the trees grow in. So keep in mind that the cycle of life on Earth has everything to do with that. If you can understand how things are born and how they die and how they tend to feed others and become a portion of the soil, it makes sense when you think of that cycle of life. Otherwise, when you think of all the beings who have been on this planet, there wouldn't be any room for life. They'd be stacked up to the sky, eh? But because of the cycle of life, there's room for other life forms, and it's the same, only slightly different, on my home planet.

The cycle of life there is less complex. The life forms that one finds on the planet are not that big. They do not have that much impact on the surface of the planet. The surface is entirely that thick kind of liquid. I was a portion of that thick liquid, and the trees that exist there in our native form are maybe, using your measurements, six or seven or eight inches tall. So, you see, if you were to see us, you wouldn't necessarily know that we are trees. I was a portion of the liquid, and I was in constant contact, at least as one might be identifying the liquid as a singular being, with that which was suggesting that I try life as one of them.

I see. And before that, do you have the memory of being aware before being part of that matrix?

Oh, of course. But I think it's important to not drift too far away from our purpose here, eh?

Okay, but how did you become a member? How did you become part of that liquid, part of that planetary system?

Oh, well. You know, I existed before this universe—so did we all, as far as I know.

Yes, of course, but a lot of them don't know it.

I think it's not good to wander too far away from Earth for the purpose of this book, since the book is intended to not only familiarize peoples who choose to read it or hear it with life forms on Earth but also to help you to understand how to better interact with those life forms, either before, during, or after their lives.

What was the reason the emissary came to that planet? What did it say that you would bring to humans or offer humans?

Near as I can tell, for one thing, a level of cheerfulness. Not just our level of cheerfulness, you understand, but because . . . okay, imagine for a moment a single tree. I'm talking about a mature pine tree on your planet. Up to thirty feet from that tree, if the tree is cheerful, which is its usual state of existence, then you, if you happen to be walking by on a trail going somewhere and you happen to walk somewhere within that range of space, you yourself might have your own cheerfulness heightened, or if you are sad, you might become less sad, for example. So we were requested to come because of our enormous good cheer.

Right out my door there are about twenty pine trees.

Well, if you're ever sad, you know where to go.

I will. [Laughs.] Cheerfulness is something you contribute on a feeling level, but of course the oxygen you create is one of the most important things you contribute, I think.

Perhaps you might say that for oxygen levels on your planet, yes. From our point of view, we contribute our native natural cheerfulness. We don't always feel that way, but when left to our own ways of being and functioning, we often feel that way.

How did you discover how to survive? Do you get counsel from the elders in your area? Here you are on a planet and it's freezing—how do you know what to do?

This appears to be part of our natural existence here. It's not something that I'm consciously engaged in. It just happens. The reason I brought it up in the beginning was to just gently suggest to scientists that they are not going to be able to achieve success with putting people to sleep and waking them up in fifty years and they haven't aged. That is a nice idea, but perhaps not the best. Of course, anything that resembles family life and loved ones would no longer be available after one takes a round trip like that, so what is the point? You'll just have to resolve it by interacting benevolently with extraterrestrials, and perhaps they will either take you themselves to other planets, if you wish to go, or they might in time at least, if you form a good lasting relationship based on friendliness and absolute honesty, share their technology with you. Don't try to lie to them, though. They'll know it every time.

What is your joy in your present life form? Do you communicate with the birds and the animals and the other beings around you and the other trees?

Yes, there is a form of communication that is constant. You might call it something that resembles a background tone. If one knows how to listen—and some people are very sensitive to sounds—you can actually hear it. It's probably easier to hear during the day on a quiet day, because at night there is often a great deal of bird communication and other-being communication that is much louder, and this is partially because one might need to make some sound if one moves around without much input from sight. There would be some, but not much. So the sound is somewhat noticeable during the day, if you have a good ear for such things.

And do they bring you tales from other places? I mean, is it interesting?

No, but it's always interesting. It's not so much stories, as the human being might like, because you have to deal with the fact that you don't remember who you are. When we remember who we are, as we do, we don't need to be hearing stories that we already know because there's no loss of memory. But I certainly can see where a human being would enjoy hearing stories like that, because you may not even remember having heard the story before in your lifetime. You might hear it as a child, and then later on in midlife and then even later on as you get older you might hear the story again and not remember it. In our case, there is no such lack of awareness.

Those with Down Syndrome Know Who They Are

So you're always aware, from the moment you got here to . . .

Before that. But the same pre-life process goes on here on Earth. It just doesn't last for 700, 800, 900, or 1,000 years.

How long?

In terms of your time, maybe 700 years. So during that time, one is somewhat educated as to what one might expect, not with certainty, but with possibility, and also to recognize that human beings are as self-destructive and destructive of others as they are because they don't remember who they are. Very often, babies or the very old do have moments—sometimes it's even constant—when they remember who they are. There are even some of your citizens as human beings who often remember who they are. One finds this in certain appearances. The children who are born very loving and stay that way, if they're not interfered with, have an Asian look regardless of the race of beings that produces them . . . they look Mongolian. That's where the term "mongoloid" came from, you understand; the origin of that term is that the children reminded some people who had been to that part of the world of the way some people look in Mongolia. But to say "mongoloids" and then decide that they are not very smart . . . they are smart enough to know that love and cheerfulness are the natural way of the human being everywhere else, so they represent to a great extent the true nature of the human being everywhere else. If they are not interfered with, they will radiate that energy just by being throughout their lifetimes, though they will need care. But it is not understood very often that that radiating, that being, that cheerfulness, *is* what they are meant to do. They're not meant to become something else to the best of their abilities; they're meant to radiate that love, cheerfulness, and happiness. That is what they do, and that is what they're meant to do. They are a gift from Creator to the human race.

And they are aware of who they are?

They are aware from the moment they are born. It is part of the reason they tend to look so peaceful when they are born, because they know who they are. If you can learn—and some of you can, so I am speaking to you now—how to communicate with them . . . and it won't be through language, so don't try to get them to learn how to speak or read or write and all of that, because it'll just cause them to forget who they are. But if you can communicate with them through their natural, native feelings, you will be able to find out who they are, why they exist, what they do, and perhaps you'll even have that cheerfulness, that happiness of life, and be more engaged in yourself.

You would simply be in their energy. You would be sensitive to their energy and be able to be the feelings that these beings are broadcasting, and when you are being those feelings, you would feel them completely. Then later on, you might, to the best of your ability in your native tongue, explain to others who would be interested in what those feelings felt like, how they made you feel, and perhaps compare them to feelings that your peoples, whoever they are and wherever they are, might be able to compare to the feelings they would normally have. In other words, you would be an interpreter. This would be a valuable skill to learn and to be honored in your societies, because many times you will have the opportunity to communicate with a race of beings, whether they be extraterrestrial or native to your planet, who would have everything that would help you to survive on Earth and perhaps would have everything to offer in this form of communication where a person would simply be engaged in the feelings that these types of beings would have around them in their natural states all the time. You would be in that feeling. You would feel it, you see.

After you are no longer feeling it, perhaps you need to go on and do something else. Then you would explain, maybe write down the feeling, how it felt as compared to the feelings you normally have, or if you are working with a group, tell them how it felt, what feeling was being transmitted and what it inspired in your mind. Did you get any pictures? Were there any words? Very often there will not be words, except in reaction to what you were feeling, but it would be a way to form a communication.

This is a vital career choice that could be made in your time to not only assimilate what other life forms on Earth have to offer but it would be *very* valuable training in your communication with extraterrestrials. Some of them often have no means of direct common language available from you to them and from them to you, other than some technological device that would perform not unlike the technological devices you have on your own planet—where they can function only in their own range, with their own understanding, as created by you. Much is lost in this type of translation.

That's why the so-called universal translator, while seeming to be a cure-all to all of your communication problems, will ultimately not be that. It will be something that may help, but there will still be misunderstandings because of the lack of a translator to interpret feelings. So those of you who are good at feelings—feeling them yourself, picking up feelings from others, and perhaps being able even to a degree to interpret those feelings—pay attention. If this has been a source of difficulty for you in this life, that's why you're here: to pick up feelings from others to be able to, when you return to your natural native feelings, interpret as best you are able. And you might not even be able to put into words for others what those feelings felt like; you may have to perform them.

In short, sometimes feelings can be described as one might describe a flower: "Well, it's pretty." That doesn't tell you what the flower looks like, and then you might say, "Well, it smells good," and still you're waiting to find out what it looks like. You're describing the externals, and you don't really have the means in your language to describe what it is. Then along comes the actor, or let's say the mime, and the mime describes in motion what it is. So also work on describing in motion what those feelings might be. That's why you're here—that's the native reason why you're here. If you have that capacity where you're more alert to other people's feelings than you are necessarily to the words they are using and you have that talent, though it may not always feel like one, then that's why you're here.

You're here to be interpreters. They're needed. They're valuable. Practice that, and you will be able to help your peoples immensely.

Is the reason you are able to talk to the Creator and be comfortable with that . . . Zoosh said that the plant kingdom had been a creator at one point.

Yes, I believe that's true, and it doesn't surprise me. But it's a full-time job beyond any interpretation of full time that you might understand at the moment, and it doesn't allow for much *living* of life, as compared to helping others live their lives. So I think we quietly retired to allow somebody else to take over so we could *live* life. We needed a vacation.

[Laughs.] I love it!

Just Be in Your Feelings!

On that cheerful note, I will give my closing message. On this Earth planet, you all find that your lives are terribly complex, much of this having to do with responding and interacting with the technology available. Your technological society, you understand, gives you things you can do that are often pleasant or helpful, but it also places demands on you and your time. Try to make time every single day, not just for sleep, but for relaxing into your feelings. Being in your feelings is a way not only to emanate who you are and what you need, but it is also a means to create a broadcast communication with other human beings who may or may not know anything about you. Sometimes it's important to do that, because things you do not know how to ask for in your language, in your thoughts or in your personal nature, can be asked in those broadcast feelings. And all the broadcast feelings of all the human beings—to say nothing of other beings on the planet—are in motion all the time, moving all around the planet. This is how very often you might meet someone who is the perfect person for you, because of who you are or what you need, because those broadcast feelings have been passed on by others until they reach the right person or persons, and then the opportunity is set into motion by your soul and that person's soul, with the cooperation of Creator to bring the two of you, or the many of you, together.

So be sure to have those times when you are just in your feelings! Sometimes those feelings will be of upset; other times they will be happy. But be in your feelings for at least two to five minutes every day. Try not to think! Just feel, in a place by yourself, sitting in a chair perhaps, and just experience your feelings. Good life! Good night!

Thank you so much. Good life!

CHAPTER ELEVEN

Redwood Tree

FEBRUARY 17, 2008

ॐ

THIS IS REDWOOD TREE.

Good! Welcome!

Greetings! It is in our true nature to oversee the beginning stages of the plant world on planets where plants, as you understand them, exist. What I mean by "as you understand them" is, it would mean that cultures that will follow—plants came first, you understand, on Earth—may or may not understand our true natures, and as such might, if removed from a true understanding of creation, simply consider us to be background or material, not beings. We usually establish such forms of life that create a personal relationship with the Sun. One takes for granted—doesn't one?—that the Sun shines and gives light, and then for the evening, perhaps there is moonlight, but other than that it is dark and perhaps quiet and restful. But a personal relationship with the Sun can even be something that a human being might have. You don't need it to survive necessarily. You can survive without it, but you may not thrive as well. The Sun does act and interact with your physical body in such a way that you receive healthful benefits, provided you don't overdo it.

Helping Planets Understand the Personal

So by our being here on the planet, we have created this coordination by our reaching for the Sun, you might say—at least the poets say that in association with trees. Then that connection from physical being to planetary lightbody—as you might refer to a being (if I can call the Sun a being, which I do)—would become something that is personal. Although I am no longer on Earth, I was a very old, very ancient redwood tree who was cut down around 1870 by a human being.

I grant that the human beings did not understand our true nature. Some human beings who preceded them, though, did understand and came to us for wisdom. You might reasonably ask, "How did they receive that wisdom?" As always, when one is interacting with other species, one does so through inspiration. How do you know your inspiration is correct? By the way you feel in your physical body. You have a good, warm feeling—then you can be pretty sure that inspiration is correct. If the feeling in your physical body gets tight and uncomfortable, you can be pretty sure that what you're hearing or what you've started thinking is not associated with the inspiration. It may not necessarily be a bad thing, but it is identified in that moment as not part of the inspiration. Your physical body reacts that way so that you know you are off-track, so to speak.

These are simple things, known to ancient life forms and youthful ones as well. But oftentimes in the case of the human being who is on planet Earth now, there is a tendency to forget, and this knowledge is often not passed on to younger generations, to say nothing of being reminded as one is in one's youth or middle years or older years. Other forms of life that preceded the human being on Earth have all been to create a training method, so Earth would know that her existence here has everything to do with the personal.

Any planet would know that its job is to be universal. By "universal," I mean that all are treated the way the planet is. No one is singled out for mistreatment, and no one is truly singled out for greater treatment than the planet might offer to all beings. But planets do not necessarily move from that understanding to recognition, honoring, or even factoring in personal relationships. They would generally have impersonal but loving relationships with other planetary bodies, for example, but they wouldn't have a best planetary buddy [laughs]. A human being might have a best buddy, but Earth would not say, for instance, "Mars is my best buddy, and I don't really care about Pluto." [Laughs.] Pardon my humor, but we like that kind of thing.

Now, in order for a planet to understand the personal, there have to be forms of life that require a personal connection to Earth herself—which we do with our roots and tap roots and so on. We also require input from others, in this case the Sun and, of course, with Earth there needs to be moisture. Trees are excellent at being able to signal what we need, and the signal can be heard and understood by Mother Earth. Do you know that as a result of our existence here—not just speaking in general about redwood trees, but on a broader basis about plants— Mother Earth now identifies each and every plant personally, not just the broad general concept? As a result, when human beings came along, to say nothing of other forms of life, it was very easy for Mother Earth to make an personal connection when called to do so with a individual human being, which is why human beings sometimes have a very strong personal connection with Mother Earth, as compared to just walking about on the surface of the planet and not really thinking about it.

I grant this may not happen for all human beings, but it is available for all human beings, and some who are reading this, as well as others, might very well be able to identify with that. So I am bringing this forward not to say that this is all we have done and that's all we are. I am bringing it forward because one does not often think about how it is that one can have personal relationships. One just assumes that this is the norm all over, yes? Everybody can have personal relationships, whoever you are—but where do these relationships come from? We like to answer things like that, and that's my opening statement.

So where does that ability to create personal relationships come from? How did you begin to do that?

I cannot state where it comes from originally. That's a question for Creator, I assume, but this is something we are known for in our home environment. A home environment is not actually a planet; it is more of an orientation in a space where there is light and variable form. "Variable form," of course, would simply mean that that which might be referred to as mass would change form accord- ing to the way any being might feel, so the expression would belie the feeling that anyone had. This is necessarily a means by which to establish a personal connection with others. If you are displaying a certain form feeling and you see somebody else displaying that form feeling, there is a natural affinity, is there not? And so you see, our source has to do with that.

So why are you displaying yourself as a redwood tree here? Have you done that before?

Yes, but generally on other planets we are much smaller—even if not inter- fered with, we are still much smaller. But on this planet, it was deemed a worthy thing to allow one to become as great (meaning as large) as one cared to as long as not interfered with by humans—or, you might say, the random lightning bolt, but of course, no lightning bolt is actually random. It is going from the sky to Earth, generated by Earth, in order to relieve some pressure or activate some energy zone, and if you happen to have picked that spot, well, alas.

So humans who get in the way of lightning bolts—it's just an accident, then? I thought there were no accidents.

I didn't say there were accidents. You said there were accidents.

On this planet you grew to be very tall—why was that?

Didn't I just say that?

So no one could interfere with you?

No. No. After all, you could be a tall human, yes? Could somebody interfere with your toes? We grew to be very tall because we could.

But why could you here and not on the other planets? You chose to here?

No, we were told that we could do that here. We thought, "Well, why not?"

So Creator's emissary came to your place in space?

No, but you might say, if I can put it in your vernacular, the word was out. We heard about it, and we volunteered. After all, I'm sure Creator was well aware, naturally, of our capability to instruct by way of need on the value of personal relationships, and so when we volunteered, I did not hear any "nay."

Finding Our Place of Welcome on Earth

So the first being you set out to form a relationship with was the Sun, or was it the planet?

The Sun. We formed that relationship on the way there. As a lightform being, that was easy to do. But with the arrival on the planet, of course, then there was the immediate circuit relationship, which was with Mother Earth.

And what was that process?

First one experiences the outer energies of the planet one will be calling home. As you get a little closer, there are the various layers of atmosphere. Then going through that, one perhaps, depending on one's route, passes through clouds (very nice), and then one nears the Earth, meaning the soil, and finds the spot where one wishes to be—just to start, you understand! As I recall, it was an area that you would call moist, not wet, not too far from the base of a mountain, about two miles, and it was very receptive. You can usually tell a receptive place, because it was mossy. There was moss nearby, though not everywhere—moss being a form of plant, yes, but not a plant, not a grass, not a reed, not a bush, you understand? So then one touches the soil, and if one feels welcome, then one engages with the soil.

Is there any way you can put a time on that—something that was happening on Earth or a relationship?

Yes, but not by your years. Granted, there are physical aspects to calendars, but this is the way I'll say: There were some humans on the planet, but they were totally coordinated with the natural elements. They could understand life forms. They could communicate. They were apologetic when a life was taken because they had to eat, and they were honoring when needing to eat, giving an offering of love or some small trinket to request that a life form make itself available for their consumption, whether it be plant or animal. So there were a few humans. I suppose all together in the general area we were in when we started, there were maybe a few hundred, but they were nomadic, so one did not "see" them very often.

You felt them more than saw them, right?

You would *"feee"* them, which is like a feel/see.

Were these some of the beings who were here preparing Mother Earth for the arrival of more humans?

Yes, I feel that was the case. By 1870, those types of humans were not around anymore.

They had gone home. You talked about finding a moist area that was receptive, but then how did you actually set up a personal relationship with the spirit of Earth?

Well, as I said, when coming in slowly like that, one sets up such a relationship as you ease through the various layers. You don't just charge in on a path that is the shortest between point A and point B, so to speak. You move toward the planet, and the place where you feel the most welcome, that's where you pass through. That's why feelings are so important, because if you ignore feelings, there's a tendency at the very least to offend and very possibly to harm, and that is not a good way to begin a relationship.

So I only know about you now where you are in California. Were you set up in other places on Earth in the beginning?

Oh, yes. I think the location as I recall was Florida.

Really!

Yes, the redwood trees were well-known in those parts, though that was a long time ago. I still feel that a little research into the subject of those who do that kind of work would probably reveal that the pattern of redwood trees was considerably more varied than what has remained.

So where you are now, there are very few of you who have been left to grow to the height you want, right? Most of you have been cut?

Where I am now is in spirit. But you're talking about redwood trees in general?

Yes.

Yes, fortunately there have been some human beings who have decided that we have some relevance beyond our usefulness in products, and as a result, there have been places designated as preserves.

National forests, yes. Is there an effect on Earth or on humans now because there are fewer of you?

No. Our job is to establish but not to regulate. See, if we were no longer on the Earth, people and beings in general, could still form personal relationships. Our job was to simply show Earth, as well as those who follow, what might be needed regardless of whether they might be plant or animal or human. And this is something that's appreciated. All the things you take for granted were probably shown to Earth or shared with Earth in an overview by Creator—meaning Creator might have said in general (though Creator does not speak) this and this and this and this. And then if Earth had said, putting it in human terms, "How will I know how to do that?" then Creator would say, "Oh well, I'll send someone to show you." Putting that in human terms, that's generally how life works. It's that simple. Granted, when it plays out, it might be much more detailed, but that's generally how life works as you know it.

So as a redwood tree, you were here for hundreds of years. Does an individual embody a redwood tree over and over again, or was it different beings? How does that work?

Yes, I started out in Florida, but my last incarnation as a tree was further west. I'm not sure where it was.

Do you plan to come back?

To Earth? I don't think there's room. There will have to be some concerted effort with the human population, in a benevolent way I am hopeful, to allow the population to shrink gradually, rather than to shrink it the way you have been doing with war and strife and so on. Generally speaking, the way to shrink a population while still allowing love and support has always been the same—as far as my observation goes of Earth and other planets—and it's that love is shared between beings of the same type without producing offspring. This is something Creator desires. It is a self-regulating mechanism for populations. One sees this in the animal kingdom as well.

Pay Attention to Your Immediate Environment!

Do your memories as an individual, as an immortal personality, go back long before whatever universe you were in when the Creator started this one?

Well, I haven't tried to remember that. I have found in my lifetime that it's better to pay attention to what you're doing in the moment.

Right, you lose focus. But when you were on Earth, you could communicate with all the other redwood trees, all the other beings on Earth, right?

Well, that's two questions. In general I could do that, but again, if you do too much of that, you could miss something important in your immediate environment. Mostly, the communication as it was—"communion," you might say, meaning felt communication—was associated with what was in my immediate environment: a bird lands on a bough, so to speak; a small creature crawls up your side; human beings walk by at a distance, and so on—that kind of thing. But it was not necessarily a telegraph from the other side of Earth.

[Laughs.] What can we as humans learn from you about coming into more personal relationships now as we move beyond this individuality?

I'd say, pay attention to what's immediately around you. There's a tendency to be very focused on your agenda for the day—"Have to do this, have to go there"—and very often the bulk of your opportunities for personal relationships, to say nothing of chances that might be helpful, go unnoticed as one speeds from one place to another. So pay attention to what's in your immediate environment! Perhaps someone smiles and says hi, and you, after having whizzed past that person, realize he or she said hi. And you're torn between continuing on and going back and saying, "Hi, sorry I missed you. How are you? I recognize you. How are you doing?" and so on.

We Prepare Planets for the Arrival of Other Beings

Redwoods have the reputation for great wisdom. Is that because they live so long? Have you imparted wisdom to others while you were here?

How am I doing?

Pretty good! [Laughs.]

Reputation well-deserved, I'd like to say, but I think we have that reputation more for our duration. One assumes that wisdom comes with experience. I cannot always say that this is so for all beings, but a sense of personal awareness of one's own being may come after a time. So perhaps wisdom is best shared through these inspirational forms, or the trees could gain their own wisdom. Other plants, other species on Earth, acquire wisdom either from their own experience or from others of their own kind, and often from the advice of other types of beings.

After all, if a bird landed on one of my boughs and was concerned about something that had to do with one's immediate life, if I had something to offer, I would. The bird would consider this and either remain for some form of communication or move on with felt gratitude. I did not require the bird to say, "Oh, thank you, thank you." But I could tell that the bird was relaxing, at ease, and more at comfort. That is a form of thank-you, though the bird would often look, at or make a sense of personal connection with some portion of me—the branch it is sitting on or perhaps the trunk of the tree. Such an acknowledgment is recognized as a thank-you. Even if it would not be helpful for the bird, it would at least allow the bird to feel that those around her cared about her immediate needs.

So you are not present in another form in this universe? You're not a tree on some other planet?

Exactly. I am not in tree formation, as you recognize it. I am simply in my home area once again, but having had been on Earth, I am still, you might say, even in some other form. Portions of my body are still in existence on the planet. I believe there's a table and a sideboard or something somewhere.

[Laughs.] But are you on other planets doing what you're doing—forming personal relationships? Not the home planet, but in service like you were on Earth?

No. I'm at home.

No, not you—your beings.

Oh yes, of course. We're on other planets, usually in the early formative stages of the planets or in preparation for populations to come—that's usually the case. Though on other planets where we are less likely to be interfered with, we might remain during the time of the populations that arrive.

That's something we've never talked about. Are you talking about human populations?

Anything that might arrive on some other planet.

And is it a standard thing, for the plant kingdom to come first and then others arrive?

It depends on what is intended for that planet or what, for that matter, the planet may wish to intend for herself. So it would depend largely on the circumstances.

Well, we're always eager to know how it works on other planets. So you could end up being the only life form? Or the planet could have any type of life form, and humans might be one of them?

Yes, certainly. Since you said more than one question there, The chances of us being the only life form would be unlikely.

Ah! Have you participated in that prior to coming to Earth?

Yes, personally speaking, I have been on several planets. That does help to acquire a certain amount of knowledge, which eventually turns into wisdom, perhaps. One hopes so! But I have only done that once where there was a human population. Granted, not with the same type of experience that human beings have on Earth, but if you were in the same room with them and you were all dressed the same, you wouldn't be able to tell you apart from them.

Does it affect you in any nonbenevolent way to be on a planet like Earth where there is discomfort? Do you have to protect yourself from it? How does that work?

One cannot protect oneself. One has one's bodily structure, and we have layers of bark, yes? The bark is kind of like a tough skin, which would allow, for instance, mother bird to land on a bough and grip strongly with her claws so she doesn't fall off and it is not uncomfortable. So that is what would be available. But for a place where there is discomfort, one cannot avoid it.

So how do you deal with it, then, because that's not been part of your existence before this, has it?

No, but you learn, eh? You adapt. You say, "Well, here it is. Ouch!"

Before you came here, did someone explain to you what we're doing here? Or why you're here?

Generally, our impression was that you were attempting to resolve the unresolvable on a practical level, as compared to theoretical levels. Theoretical resolutions existed all over the place, but on a practical level, well, that's completely different, isn't it? One can then throw out many theories, because theories are based on the unknown essentially, but one applies those theories through adaptation, experimentation, time, and experience. One discovers what actually does work.

In the various places you've lived on Earth, have you interacted directly with humans, whether they were shamans or just regular people?

Well, I don't really count somebody walking over and leaning against the tree and saying, "Take my photograph," so to speak, as a means of interaction (I am speaking for other trees here, you understand). But I recall having the human children come around and being happy and having fun, and I can remember children hugging. They do that; they're very open to things. And I can also recall having relationships with human beings that were spiritual, integrated into all life on Earth. That's what I would call a pretty good definition of "spiritual," meaning open to communication, felt communication: feee, felt, see/feel. I want to say "feee," it's my word, but feel/see, yes? So yes, I've had that communication. The word I want to use is "communion," but I'm trying to avoid it, because I recognize that it is a special word to some of certain religions, and there is confusion about that.

But we have used it a lot in the books.

The way you've been using it in the books is helpful, but it still causes conflict for those who read it. I would recommend finding another word.

It's the word that has been used for other beings to explain to us how they interact.

Ask them in the future if they have some other word they can suggest. They may have their own word, like feee.

I will.

I recognize that you may use that word "fee" to mean something else. To avoid communication problems in the future, I would recommend just tacking on an extra *e*, so fee would be f-e-e-e. Then there perhaps may be less confusion about that. One would look at that and say, "Ah, this is not having anything to do with the exchange of goods and services."

That's a good idea. So that is the reason you came, this establishment of personal relationship. There's not a special energy that emanates from you that has another purpose?

That's it. No secrets to be unlocked.

Embrace the Variety in Human Experience

I think from what I've read about your species that . . . I mean, nothing else on this planet grows that big and lives that long. There is something very special about that. That is one of the attractions for you to come here?

Yes, we like that idea. You understand, on other planets we might live considerably longer, but we wouldn't necessarily become so expansive physically. One would not necessarily become as wide or as tall. There's an odd thing with human beings—I think it's purely a temporary fad—and that's that there's a tendency to cast judgment on human beings who might be wider or taller than others. I've also noted that there's some judgment cast on human beings who are narrower or smaller. I do not understand what this is about. The whole point of human beings is to—as close as possible, given species guidelines—emulate variety as much as possible. So even within a certain type of human being, there is a wide variety of appearance. This is intended by Creator. Creator doesn't want you to become bored.

One does not necessarily plan on experiencing boredom in an Earth life. So accept and appreciate the variety. I can assure you that there are other planets where human beings exist where such variety is not seen and it is really, really missed by the people there. In fact, it is not at all unusual for their literary circles to suggest how human beings might look in a varietal form. Very often what is considered to be a delightful form is to be big or tall—I grant, I may be just slightly biased here. Nevertheless, I have seen a considerable amount of variety in human appearance, and I consider it to be a plus. I don't understand why there is this tendency to reject variety. After all, the Creator of this universe loves variety. A simple glance around your planet suggests that.

Well, there have been advertising and role models on television and in movies that make us feel we're not quite up to the ideal model.

But in times gone by, you see quite different things. If you've not studied Reuben's paintings, now would be a good time to do it. And it is not unusual. There are societies on the planet today where variety is considered a plus. Artists often suggest the approval of variety and forms that one does not consider to be beautiful in their own right that when combined with other forms, can be. One finds this in art, and one even finds it in the study of science when using a microscope. Many scientists consider what they look at through their magnifying instruments to be beautiful indeed. Science has a heart. Granted, it is expanding that heart and letting go of its more edgy aspects, but that will take a little longer.

You focus on what's in front of you—so you are focusing now on your life at home. But do you have plans for the future?

[Laughs.] I am living in the present, as you are, and all plans aside, the present takes care of itself.

When you lived on Earth, what was your greatest joy?

· Oh, I think in being in the moment one experiences the warmth, the coolness, the breeze, you understand, air, the interaction with other life forms, fragrances—in general, the stimulation of the senses to produce all of the touches that one experiences and remembers later in life.

That's beautiful!

Humans Are Becoming the Inheritors of Other Life Forms

Now I'm going to give my closing statement. There is a time coming now on the planet when you all will have the opportunity to appreciate variety in a more personal sense. Human beings are becoming the inheritors of other life forms. Some life forms are going away permanently, but others are simply leaving traces of themselves in the soil or in the stone and may emerge again at a later time when there is more welcoming of them on a universal Earth-human level. So don't feel too bad because some are temporarily leaving—and some may be leaving permanently.

Human beings have a wonderful quality of being able to emulate that which is gone or missed. How many of you might display traits and characteristics of one's parents or grandparents? Oftentimes these traits are amusing or bring forth a chuckle or a laugh in a family situation—"Hey, Grandma used to do that. I remember when Grandpa acted like that," and so on. Learn to differentiate between the traits one wishes to perpetuate—because they are truly welcomed by others and they feel truly welcome to you—and those that are simply a repetition of self-destructive actions. Learn to be the forms of life you miss in moments when you care to express it, and thus that which has gone before you will be remembered, not only in form, not only in memory, but in action. Good life! *Good life!*

CHAPTER TWELVE

Peach Tree

FEBRUARY 26, 2008

&

THIS IS PEACH TREE!

Welcome! Tell me about yourself.

Well, I need more of a question than that.

Are you incarnated in tree form right now, or are you a spirit?

I am on Earth, located in, I believe, someone's garden at a private home somewhere.

You don't know what country or anything?

No.

Do you see people there?

In a manner of speaking, I'm aware of their presence. A moment! [Pause.] That's good. I made a connection with the home planet and more, so I am able to speak a little deeper, then. And greetings!

Okay, good. What is your experience? Have you been there only in that tree, or as part of the root system, or . . . ?

I am the spirit of the tree, but it would be like you saying that you are the spirit of yourself. There's no difference. The personality you present is the spirit of yourself as focused like a lens through your physical body. If the spirit of

169

one's self is focused like a lens through whatever form one has taken or through any veil through which one is speaking, there is that intonation affecting one's personality so only that which is compatible with one's body or veil is heard by those to whom you are speaking. So I would be saying a great many more things than you would be hearing, and equally when you speak, you are saying a great many more things than anyone hears.

Human Filters Cause Much Misunderstanding

It's important to understand this, because I feel that much of the miscommunication from one human being to another is caused by the filtering effect of the personality having to focus through its own physical body and compounded by the fact that it also has to go through the filter of the other person's physical body in order to reach his or her personality—and of course, vice versa.

Beautifully put! And so that applies to you also?

No wonder there are misunderstandings! Yes, I have to focus through the physical body of myself—what you would call "tree," "peach tree"—and through not only to you but as this spoken word is translated into text, the physical apparatus of others who may read it or perhaps hear it someday. So the theme or themes that would run through any conversation, as long as they tend to be omnipresent or close to that, that's what the other person will hear, and along those lines of theme, though there may be variables associated, the theme will be served.

If you've ever had conversations with someone that has themes and then out of nowhere seemingly a different thought or communication comes through . . . . this is something that is essentially, you might say, burbling onto the surface based on some synchronicity between the two of you. This means that you might have a common interest or a common experience, so you are hearing a thread of something that has actually been present all along, but the other personality is saying something, whether they are conscious of saying it or not (which they may not be), and it is suddenly something you are aware of. Sometimes this happens after the fact of a conversation. You might talk to someone on the phone, for instance, and after you're done talking to them, you suddenly realize, as you think about what was said, that something was stated that you didn't really notice or weren't able to respond to at the time. And that might prompt you to think about it and recognize the qualities in that statement that have to do with you.

I am bringing this up because, as near as I can tell, at least half of the strife between human beings on a personal basis, to say nothing of wars and whatnot, are caused by misunderstandings. Sometimes people are speaking their needs in the way they understand to speak their needs, but if the person listening to those needs cannot understand them in the way the personality opposite them is speaking, then a misunderstanding automatically takes place. You have had such conversations, where people suddenly yell or scream that they've been telling you something for a long time, and now they're explosively angry about it and you have no recollection whatsoever of them ever having brought it up before.

This is something that almost everyone can identify with, including the very young. If you understand that you are not hearing most of what the other person is saying due to the focus you are in, then perhaps you will all be able to develop a little more patience. And when you realize that somebody has said something that strikes a chord, you could bring it up again and ask that person if he or she wants to talk about it some more. If you then make that a theme of your conversation, you might discover that the person had been communicating to you about it for a long time—you just didn't hear it. It didn't get through the filters, or you didn't understand what they were saying and how they were saying it.

What's the purpose of the filters?

You'd have to ask Creator that.

How do we get rid of them?

You'll have to talk to Creator about that, but the filters are here because Creator wishes them to be so. My best guess is that it has to do with humans learning something. And of course, it has to do with patience. Patience is a difficult art to refine when one has such a short life, as human beings generally do. On other planets where you live your natural life cycle, patience comes naturally because you have plenty of time. But here, where life is short and threats are present, one does not feel that sense of a leisurely quality about life, and therefore to learn patience in such an environment is challenging and not always possible to accomplish.

You certainly are right about that!

We Came to Earth as Seeds

So tell me, how did peach trees get here? What was the inducement?

We haven't been here that long. If you try to find us in fossilized form or something like that, you'd have to look hard. That's peach-tree joking [laughs]. I believe we were brought here by a race of beings who were here about 40,000 years ago or so and brought many nut-bearing trees and fruit-bearing trees and so on, partly for the beings who were here then, whom you would call animals, and partly for the human beings who were present, as well as for the human beings yet to come. They felt it would be necessary to bring such a food-bearing crop (trees, as I understood it) well before the population swelled and went through its cycles of getting larger and smaller, because to disseminate seeds and to move the crops around the planet would take time—because animals would spread them, and so on. So about 40,000 years ago, a lot of trees and bushes and plants like that arrived by that means.

You might assume that they brought them for someone in particular, but they didn't. This is not at all unusual. There are peoples who travel from planet to planet, and based on their analysis, I believe, they can take a look at different times of the planet's potential futures and pasts when they might bring various food crops or plant crops that would help sustain civilizations to come. There are cultures that do this to support it.

What form do you have on your home planet?

We are more of a vine on the home planet, and fruits that we have are more hard-shelled—not as hard as, say, a nut shell, but not quite as soft as a melon casing. So in order to reproduce ourselves, the process requires the actions of others. There are beings on the planet very similar to human beings, and they consume the fruit but they separate the seeds out first. Then they will find the seeds that are the most strong and vital, and they will plant these seeds and they will put in a vessel the other seeds. They say blessings over these seeds to encourage them to become stronger. When the seeds do become stronger because of the form of the blessing these beings are able to say, then they will plant three of them in proximity to each other and check on them from time to time to see which ones sprout.

I believe some of these practices are done by personal farmers. What I'm calling "personal farmers" are those farmers who interact with their crops, from the seed point all the way through the sprouting, the maturing, the growth, the harvest, and beyond—interacting with the crops as one might interact with a fellow being, talking to them, perhaps singing to them, and often planting seeds in that fashion, communicating and doing blessings with the seeds before they are planted. There are some peoples still doing that on Earth, I feel, but not so many. Of course, foods grown in this fashion are much more satisfying to those who eat them. You can eat a great deal less and feel satisfied and be nurtured and enriched and fed much better than if you eat something that has been grown and harvested through mechanical means.

After all, with mechanical means, you are using machines that are not in their native state, so of course the parts of the machine themselves are uncomfortable.

When you take a seed and thrust it into the ground with something uncomfortable in the place where the seed would not have gone naturally, it starts out in discomfort and continues that way. So by the time the food comes to you and you are able to prepare it, it is not very much alive.

Do most of the vines on your home planet that you inhabit grow in these beings' gardens? Or do you grow wild?

They don't have gardens. The planet is not separated into properties, you understand? We grow on our own. We were on the planet before the beings came and thus had much to be harvested. But the beings came and then we shifted with their cooperation into a new level of being more on the planet. The fruit that they consume feeds all their requirements. They get everything they need from that fruit, the fruit we have. Therefore they are well taken care of, and their gratitude causes us to be well taken care of. When they plant the one seed they find that is the strongest, they do that for us. When they plant the three seeds that they have said blessings over, they do that to create more food for them, but they do this with thanks and gratitude. But when they plant that one strong seed, they do that to offer thanks directly to us and they do it in their own sacred way.

That's beautiful!

It is a good thing that we appreciate, and we can feel their appreciation. So we have a symbiotic relationship, eh?

Interactive! So tell me about these beings! They look like humans, but they're not?

They look somewhat like human beings, but they are a little different. They have more hair on their bodies, and they do not wear garments. They have a slight stoop to them, and this is natural for them. And their legs are very strong. Their arms are a little longer, but other than that, they have largely human characteristics.

So they're not technological? They live close to the land?

That's right. They're agrarian.

How did it come to be that some of you came here to Earth? Did you agree that the seeds could be carried here? How did you get involved with Earth?

I believe the ship that brought us to Earth came one day and communicated with the other beings, and I believe they worked out an arrangement where some seeds could be taken. You understand, the beings on the ship who visited wished to take a fruit or a plant itself, but the other beings who live on the planet with us prevailed and said that that would not be acceptable but they would offer some seeds. So they offered some of the seeds they had blessed.

This actually worked out better, because here they are, a form of human being—not exactly a human being, but you might say . . . a humanoid, that's it! And so since they had done blessings and the intention was for the peach to serve human beings as well as other beings on your planet, their people on board the ship, who interact with other races of beings, felt that it would be better to take the seeds offered, especially as they'd been blessed by the beings on this planet, and that's what they did. So when they came on the ship to Earth, they planted the seeds and, as a result, stayed a little longer to make sure that enough of the seeds would sprout and thrive. They planted them in various places around the planet. They were only given about sixty seeds, so they stayed for a little longer than they had planned.

So there were volunteers among your immortal personalities who came here?

Well, we were always in the seeds.

Coffee Beans Have a Need for Companionship

[Coughing.]

You cough because you are always thirsty. You drink some kind of liquid that keeps water from your body.

Yes, coffee.

Yes, and this is why you are always thirsty. And when you are thirsty, you drink coffee, and that takes more water from your body. I am not trying to lecture you, but it is a self-destructive pattern. You are not alone in this—I have observed it in other human beings. I believe it is because you're living an unnatural life on Earth, and you want to get off of Earth as fast as possible. This is also why many human beings take risks, including doing something that might be considered unnecessarily risky by others. It is not exactly a death wish, but it borders on that. Your consumption of coffee is something you do unconsciously, partly because . . . it is all right to speak to you in this personal fashion?

Oh, absolutely! I appreciate it.

Your consumption of coffee—aside from it being an addictive thing, which you cannot help, and you being attached to it—forms a personal relationship between you and the coffee bean. I don't know if you know this about coffee beans—you must, in time, request that they come through for this book. But coffee beans, when they are whole, especially before they are roasted, have a need for companionship. It is an underlying facet of the plant that they grow on. This need for companionship is expressed from one portion of the plant to another, and this is why they are happy being grown in large communities of such plants. But that need for companionship does not stop after the bean is roasted. It decreases a bit, but after the bean is roasted and ground up to a form from which the drink can be made, the bean still has that need for companionship.

This is part of the reason people who drink coffee regularly must be around other people or they get uncomfortable. They can have times when they are away from people, but they prefer to drink coffee with others, generally speaking. Also, such products like that often are associated with creating dependency. If one does not have dependency in certain behaviors, then one will have a dependency on the coffee itself. There's a lot more on that, but you can ask the coffee plant.

I will, thank you. I've never heard any of that before.

The Filtering Effect Goes Beyond Conversation

You were already connected to the seeds, so when the seeds came, you had no choice but to come too?

It was all done with permission. The humanoid beings on the home planet talked to each and every seed. They recognized that the seeds were *someone.* They'd always known that, and so they had more than sixty seeds—many, many more. They picked out the seeds individually who volunteered to come. It was not random; they do not do anything in a random fashion.

And you were one of those?

One of my ancestors was. Obviously, I was not. You understand, this was 40,000 years ago.

That's right [laughs]. So what is your length of life on the home planet, then?

On the home planet . . . it is hard to put it into your terminology, but I'm not aware of any deaths.

So you constantly keep recycling into seeds, then?

I don't know how to explain it. "Recycling" is a term of the human being on Earth, but on that planet, we don't really think about that. I realize you're trying to figure out how our souls get to be in the seeds; I understand where your question comes from. I'm going to try to answer that: Our souls attach to the seeds on our home planet from the central sun within the planet. There is a sun external to the planet, yes, but it is at a great distance, so there is another sun within the planet. The light comes out through the northern pole of the planet and is reflected in the atmosphere and thus shines on the surface of the planet. Somehow our souls come from this central sun.

How beautiful! So your awareness is continuous, right?

Yes, but I do recall and can state that on the home planet, when our souls are immersed in the central sun, there is not the same sense of consciousness. It's different. It's more of a universal consciousness.

Do you have memories before being in that Central Sun?

No.

Are you from any place we've ever heard of?

I don't think so.

So you are from a great distance, like the other side of the universe?

No, I think you just haven't heard of us. But, then, you haven't heard of most civilizations. You have to keep in mind that what I said before about communication goes for other things. If your personality, with all its vast knowledge and awareness, is filtered through your physical form so that you can learn what Creator wishes you to learn on this planet and experience that as well, you must extrapolate. It's the same if you look with your eyes at the sky, to say nothing of looking through an instrument to see more clearly what's in the sky. You don't see everything. If you were as a spirit only—not focused through your body to look into the sky—you would see all light, even if it is nighttime. That "all light" is the amount of stars that are actually there, but you only see as many stars as you see based on the filtering through your physical bodies.

So, you see, the filtering effect goes beyond conversation. It is applied to all aspects of what the human being does and perceives. Creator wishes this to be the case so that you are not overly distracted. If you had available to you the talents and abilities of your natural state, you understand, you would never accomplish anything that Creator wished you to accomplish on this planet. You would simply continue to pursue your lives as you have pursued them other places, moving from one source of interest to another to explore it, interact with it, and so on. This is why when you look up into the sky, you will just see so many stars or star fields or galaxies, as you say. But as I say, if you are outside your body, you would look up into the sky and it would be all light. This is why people who have described after-death experiences say there is the light: They are no longer in their bodies. There is the light, and there is only the light.

I understand we have some of the void from the Creator's father around the planet, or at least that's what we see.

Well, this may be part of what Creator has set up for you to sustain your seeing only what Creator wishes you to see in order to pique your enthusiasm and interest for travel to other places, or conversely, for other places to send travelers to you—which they would like to do, of course. But because of the current state of affairs of your cultures and governments, they are only able to do as lightbeings and lightships now. So a lot of the ships you have seen in your skies are actually lightships that will sometimes take a form. As they get closer to your planet, you will see them, if you can, if they can—both—in something that resembles a physical form, though this may not be their actual physical form.

This is why different individuals might describe what is actually the same lightship in completely different patterns of physical formation or even of light formation. As the ship moves closer to or farther away from Earth and you are actually looking at it—and even a few yards or a few feet make a difference—different people might see different things, and of course, their personalities are also filtered through their bodies. It's necessarily complex, you see, because in order for the wide variety of souls that make up the complex being of the Explorer Race to be on Earth, it is necessary to have such complexity so that all needs are served and all opportunities are available to serve those needs.

I hadn't heard it put that way before. Well, someone said we only see the star systems that want to be seen. A lot of them don't want us to be looking at them, because then I guess they would feel our discomforting energy.

That's certainly possible.

The Original Human Soul Number Was 144

If you weren't one of the original sixty seeds, how do you get into the seed here on Earth when your central sun is at your home planet?

That doesn't make any difference. Once that has occurred from the home planet, one remains and moves one's soul being through the tree, into the fruit, into the seed, and so on. So it's an ongoing cycle. You would say that souls have split into the different component parts, but we don't see it that way. We have the same amount of souls—sixty—that we've always had on Earth. It's just that we occupy more than one seed now. There are those who would make that same analogy on Earth, but I don't wish to cause too much consternation in biblical circles.

[Laughs.] So as there were originally sixty of your seeds, then how many original humans were there?

There are those who refer to the 144. There is a tendency to say, 144,000, because there was the belief that people couldn't accept such a small number, but it's actually 144.

That has split into six billion now!

Yes, but they come and go, you understand, in terms of expressing that. But still the original human soul number was 144 on Earth, as far as I understand. Of course, it's different on other planets.

Do you know so much because you connected to your home planet?

Yes. Before when I first started out and came through, we wouldn't have been able to say much other than, "Hello, I'm a peach tree. Who are you?" But now that I am connected to the home planet, there's more knowledge.

So you have an awareness of why we humans are here and what we're doing?

Well, you have to understand, if I'm connected to the home planet, I'm also connected to the central sun. The central sun has a great deal of knowledge. I'm referring to the central sun on our planet, of course.

Well, I understand that every sun is connected to every other sun.

I don't know about that.

Do you know if your seeds plan to stay here on Earth very long?

It's possible we might go into a dormant state from time to time as in your ice ages, and so on, but as far as I know, we're here for the length of time that we're here. I do not know; we do not make plans. I find it curious that human beings make plans. I think the real thing that human beings do is that they make goals, and then you call the goals "plans." The problem with doing that, of course, is that it enslaves you to a rigid future and tends to eliminate many, many of the opportunities you have. It would be much better to say that you have goals and then strive for those goals, if you wish, but are aware of other opportunities. If you make plans, you can miss what's happening in the present very easily, because you have a fixed stare in one direction.

Toward the goal, yes.

Life on Planet Earth

You are in the moment—so what is your life like? Do you interact with other farm animals where you are, or chipmunks or squirrels or something?

There are no farm animals. I have seen them from a distance, been aware of them, as you say. It's not seeing with eyes. We see, but it's not the same as you do—although it's not that different from the kind of seeing you have in your dreams, where you don't use your eyes in your dreams, either. But the seeing for us is benevolent. Of course, we do get frightened when we see somebody coming along with something that could cause us harm. I interact more with just a few human beings and some four-legged animals.

Are there dogs or cats?

I don't want to say, because then you'd know where I am, and I think it would be best not to.

Well, I would only know if you were interacting with something unique like kangaroos [laughs] or something specific to a certain place. So you flow through the tree and you flow through the fruit and into the seed, and then back in the ground.

We do not flow into the human being, even if the human being purchases or is given the peach. Once the seed departs from the tree, we very quickly move back into the tree. The only way we will remain in the seed is if we know for certain that the seed will be planted in the ground. If we know this, then we will linger in the seed. We will generally know these things.

Well, this is a change in form. A peach is sort of different from what you described as your natural form.

Yes, it is different. This is the form we have on this planet, but in the natural form there are many seeds and the fruit is about as big as, you might say, a honeydew melon. On this planet, as you can tell, it's different. But I believe it's somewhat sensible when you consider that Creator is particularly interested in individuality on this planet. So it makes sense that we would have one seed in one fruit. Of course, I know there are other fruits that have multiple seeds, but that is my best guess on the basis of our experience and our understanding of life. You would have to ask apple and strawberry their opinions. They might feel differently.

You don't have a sleep state—do you have a meditative state? Do you connect with the home planet to sort of keep current during that time?

Not really. We don't feel we need to do that. I'm just doing it for this purpose.

So you interact with not only the other peach trees but the other trees in your area? Not interact, but commune with?

Only if necessary. We are not that social.

Ah! You certainly sound social.

Well, it's because of my connection to the home planet. I didn't sound so social before.

[Laughs.] No, you didn't. So you're aware of what goes on around you?

To a degree. So necessarily if, say, a butterfly or bird flies by farther than six to nine feet from me . . . I'm not particularly aware of what's beyond me, say, twenty-five feet or so unless it represents a threat, and I may not be particularly aware if it's anything beyond six to nine feet away. But anything within that six- to nine-foot range or closer, I'm quite aware of.

So what would be a threat—someone coming at you with a scythe or something?

Yes, I think that would be a threat for you too, eh? But fire, lightning, lots of things are threats! We can't make an attempt to get out of the way like you can. I have experienced a mild flood, and by mild, I mean the water was about two or three feet above the normal surface where my roots go into the ground. It was about two or three feet up the trunk, and one might reasonably say, "Well, that's not so awful, just for a couple of days," and that's true. But the thing about floods is that there are often things in the water in motion that bump into me. So it took quite a few months to recover.

What would have been in the water?

As in any flood, one finds branches, rocks.

Oh, I see! Inanimate things bumped into you.

That's it, so I was pretty tense during that time—[laughs] an example of a threat. The water itself wasn't that much of a threat, because I noted that the flood would recede. That was only that one time. Then the human beings made some effort to create some means so that the water could pass around their property, and since then there have been some high-water times, but I haven't experienced it other than rain.

Do you have a wintertime there?

I can't say. I'm not saying, because it seems to be very important for you and the reader to not know where I am. I'm just on Earth somewhere, in somebody's yard. That's all you can know.

One thing I don't understand yet is that when you subdivide, you still feel as powerful as you did in the original seed, right? Each of the seeds, then, in all the peach trees on Earth feels as complete and whole as in each of the original sixty seeds?

No, because when we were on the home planet, we were surrounded with nurturing energy, and the other beings present there, the humanoids, were very honoring and respecting and understood very clearly the relationship between us. So, no, we don't feel *that* energy. But insofar as what I think the meaning of your question is, do we feel the same level of presence in each of the seeds on Earth that we feel in any of the other seeds at any given moment as compared to the original sixty seeds that we started with here on Earth? We do not feel that level of energy either, especially in the case of, say, farm peach trees, where the usage of chemical sprays and the sort of agitation involved with those sprays affects us especially.

If it's a private farm, a personal farm, it's not necessarily that bad, because of the personal relationship and the farmer saying, "Yes, I'm spraying this now because of this and that," and some farmers actually do that. They talk to the trees or the plants, and that is always *greatly* appreciated. But on some farms, this is not the case. It's just people working, trying to live their lives, and so then the energy in the seed might move toward the center of the seed, which makes sense, you understand, since on the home planet, one central sun is in the center of the planet. So if we feel not quite so welcome, we'll move our presence toward the center of the seed—and by the "center" I mean, there's the hard shell, and then if you were to break that open, there's the actual seed inside it. We would move toward the center of the seed that's inside. But if we feel comfortable and safe, then we would occupy the entirety of the seed that's inside the shell, inside the fruit.

But you are a peach tree. You're the whole tree, but you're also in all the seeds of the peaches that are on the tree?

That's right.

So then, at the end of this . . . ?

It's like if you put sixty dots on a chart and then you extrapolated out to all of the peach trees and all of the seeds today, you would see a lot of lines, but if you trace those lines back, they'd all come back to the sixty seeds. It's the same with human beings. They'd all come back to that 144.

Do you know where those 144 first appeared on the planet?

I don't know that much about your history. I just have a loose knowledge of it, some of the high points, I suppose. But I don't know where they first went—someplace warm apparently, because it looks like sand. That's all I have. It would make sense—the vehicle they came on might be able to transform that sand into fuel, so it would make sense that they would go on the ship to someplace where they could acquire fuel. I don't know why they stayed; maybe it was intentional. So perhaps the ship brought them there and collected fuel, otherwise known as sand, and deposited them and went somewhere else.

Humans Are Completely Different in Their Natural State

So when you quit talking here, will you disconnect, or will you still stay connected?

Disconnect from the home planet?

Do you find it stimulating? Do you feel more energetic?

These are good human questions, and as a human being I understand you are here to learn and thus are not here for a long time. I don't need to be stimulated; I don't need to have external energy in that sense. But as you are a human being, of course, I completely understand you saying this, since you're cut off from probably 98, sometimes 99 percent of your total being. So I'm not the least bit surprised that you say and do many of the things you do. Of course, when you're not embodied in physical form and you're in your natural state, you're completely different. But one might see glimmers and recognize something that one has seen on Earth. Generally, it's the other way though—when you see a human being whom you don't know and have never met but there's something there, then you've probably met this being in another life somewhere or know him or her from beyond.

Wow, 99 percent. That's such a little piece of us left for us to use on Earth.

It's 98 to 99 percent. It's actually all right, because when you move past the veil of your physical body, then you don't have much difficulty finding yourself, as you're going from a very weak signal of yourself to a very strong signal of yourself. It's pretty hard to get lost that way.

[Laughs.] You have some of the most amazing things to say. I love it. So have you ever seen our exact kind in our natural state visiting your home plant?

From what I can tell, scanning the history there, I have seen beings who look like you. Their biology might be a little different. I'm not sure where they're from. I don't think they're much taller than, say, five foot four; five foot five would be tall for them. But other than that, they certainly appear to be like you. They seem to be what you would recognize as human beings. I'm not sure where they're from.

It's a small ship, only six people on board—that's what I'm seeing—and they stopped for a short time, communicated with the humanoid beings who were there, and went on. I think they were gathering stories. Sometimes the storytellers must go out and gather stories in order to replenish what they have, and you would refer to them perhaps as in your social sciences. But you also have storytellers, and sometimes storytellers travel and acquire stories from other peoples, and weave them into their own stories or start new branches of stories. These people, I believe, were storytellers traveling for that purpose.

I guess I'll be gone before we get to travel out to space, but it would be fun to go discovering and exploring all of the different civilizations and cultures out there.

Well, you won't have any difficulty with that, once you do go. You'll do as much of that as you like. Of course, you'll remember all that you *have* done. It may not be quite as urgent then, but you'll remember it. Very often, in any given life, you might be very attracted to something and it turns out, after you leave the life, then you discover, "Oh, that's what I've done, and I'm so used to that, that's what I know." And very often, I believe, with human beings on this planet, since you are so cut off from almost everything you know, when life gets difficult, you are often attracted to what you know, even if you didn't know it in this life.

When things get difficult, we are attracted to what we know. What is an example of that?

This does make for problems, you see. Sometimes you could go within, be attracted to something you know and essentially retreat from your life. Other times you might know something and have a lot of experience with something that may not fit into human culture on this planet and be destructive or self-destructive. And other times you might simply be attracted to something that fits into human culture, and it could turn out to be a career, the kind of career that you love doing, love acquiring knowledge about, often feel a sense of familiarity with the knowledge you acquire—and thence, you are happy in your job. It's not always that way when people go into a career, but it can be.

But if they're doing something they're very familiar with, they're not learning anything new, right?

Everything you're familiar with on other planets and other ways of being, everything you learn new on this planet, because you learn things differently on this planet. You don't necessarily learn the same way you learned before. Say on another planet, your teacher might sit you down somewhere for a nice talk about things and explain the secrets of the universe to you, whereas here on this planet, you might discover bits and pieces of those secrets in completely different ways. You have to be in the flow of your life. Most likely your teacher (meaning your guide) isn't going to sit you down consciously and explain these things to you. It may be different in the future, as children are getting more aware, but as far as adults go, especially from your time, I don't think you could identify with that.

Right. It's a piece here and a piece there, yes.

That's right, but you tend to feel the familiarity, if you notice it. You don't always notice it, because of the other distractions of life.

The Rest of the Explorer Race Awaits You in a Place of Light

This is fascinating, that the souls of your species are not only connected to but are residents within your central sun.

Yes, it's not that different from your situation. The Explorer Race human beings have a tendency to resonate to one locality when they have completed what they need to learn as "individuals" in the Explorer Race phenomenon, and then you congregate somewhere, so what we are doing is something similar. We congregate within the central sun. We flow into and out of the central sun in order to, you would say, materialize, become form. I believe that if we ever did cease to exist, we'd flow back into the central sun, although I don't know that for a fact. Should our form cease to exist temporarily, though I'm not aware of that ever happening on our home planet, but I would have to say that'd we flow out of the central sun, as I'm not aware beyond that.

Is that usual, that there's a sun in the middle of a planet?

I don't think it's usual, but it may be, if you consider the fact that we are plant-based, and in the solar system where I am, the sun is very far away and it wouldn't support plant life. But the planet itself is very sturdy, and there is a small central sun in the planet and a light way—I don't think it's like a hole, but it's a means for the light to get to the surface out of the north pole of the planet.

But not the south pole also?

I'm just aware of the north pole. Then the atmosphere reflects that light, I believe. I don't know if it's typical in other planets, but it is a fact in ours.

You said the rest of the Explorer Race is hanging out somewhere, congregating. Do you know where that is?

No, but I can tell that it's all light. There's all this light, but if I look at it closely, I can see individual motion, ripples, tides. So I know that, even though I am seeing it all as light, if I move in my point of perception, I can see all these little spheres or disks of light moving about. But if I pull back, then I just see a glow of light.

Supposedly 94 percent of us are out there, waiting somewhere for the rest of us to get done.

Yes, waiting, but not impatiently. There's a great deal of patience, and joy there. I think some of you visit there in your deep dreams—I think so. I have the capacity to see these things, and when you see them on Earth, you get the impression that they are *on* Earth, but I don't think so. I think that you are seeing something that is other; it's in that other place. I can't rule out the possibility that it might be occupying the same space as Earth, but it's not in the same focus.

Oh, I never considered that! I thought they were way out somewhere.

They don't have to be, do they? They just have to be somewhere other than where you are, although they might be in the same *apparent* space, not in the same focus, so they're safe, and so are you.

Stories Are Important

[Laughs.] You've brought up about forty questions for me to ask Zoosh when we do the follow-up to the Explorer Race books.

Well, it's good to get new stories, isn't it? The traveling storytellers made that clear. They were interesting people. I can focus on that—I wasn't present, but I can see that now. Before they told some stories and asked the humanoids on the planet to tell their stories, they explained the value of stories. They have a philosophy, and after they explained their philosophy, they said, "These are the stories we share with people when we first meet them," and they told three or four stories. I don't have the stories at the moment, and as they were telling—I am looking at it at a distance—I notice that there are colors and the colors are very uniform, or changing according to different stories or different moods in the stories, so perhaps they're not. Anyway, I bring that up because stories are important.

Do your people tell stories?

I think we felt the value of it when their communication was happening between the visitors from the little ship and the humanoids on our planet, but I'm not conscious of stories in our culture. I do see the value of it, though.

Yes, it's fascinating. I love stories. I must have talked through Robert to 1,000 beings, 2,000, all the way from creators to the 13 beings out there beyond the totality who began the emergence of the latest round of manifestation into form, and now we are coming back and talking to the beings who live on our own planet.

That has value. One must do that for those who are on the planet. After all, in the form of books as you understand them, there's a limit to how many of them circulate beyond the planet.

[Laughs.] Yes, at least right now at this time. You have a marvelous sense of humor.

Thank you.

Maybe you should get more social sometimes.

Well, you understand, the personality that I'm reflecting has more to do with the home planet than my actual personality.

Ah, I see! But I like it, whoever it is.

We have to finish now. I'll just make a closing statement.

You Will Have the Opportunity to Find Friends

For those of you who have interest in this book, you can see I've tried to touch on different topics, different ways of being, different perspectives. This is something that we peach beings like to do, but for you, you also might find in a given life that you have many different things that attract you, many different *types* of things. This is all right. Creator, I believe, intends for you to have as much variety as is possible.

Look toward friends! You have a great abundance of other human beings in the future, and as a result, it will be possible for different types of personalities to be available on Earth than have been available in the recent past. You will have the opportunity to find friends who may be compatible with you. Some of you have had difficulty in the past finding friends who were compatible, but now with the range of numbers that are available for human beings to be, which is billions, it is likely that everyone will have many friends available to them all over the planet.

So find ways to network with people and seek out those who have similar interests, even though your interests might change. Try to find root interests within you—not just, "I like this type of book or that type of movie." That's good, but try to find other things within you. What are you searching for in your life? What is the type of thing you generally like? You like sweet, you like salty—things like that, you understand, might seem to be important, and they are, but try to keep tabs on things you are looking for that reflect that which you are.

Sometimes your friends might tell you, "You're always so cheerful; you're always so curious." These types of things are good to know, because they will help you find the friends you are completely compatible with, because they are similar to you, they understand who you are, they understand why you are, and they completely honor you for being who you are. Good life!

Oh, good life! Thank you very much. Thank you.

CHAPTER THIRTEEN

Holly

GREETINGS! THIS IS HOLLY!

Holly! Welcome!

You have Ivy, and it seems only natural to have Holly, eh?

Absolutely! Equal time.

Question?

Tell me about yourself.

No. I need a specific question.

Okay. How do you appear? I know there are holly berries.

Can you do something other than what can be looked up in the encyclopedia?

Sure. Are you aware of life beyond Earth or just your Earth form?

Well, I am conscious of my Earth form and life beyond Earth. In fact, let me paint you a picture as an illustration. Here I am growing now in what appears to be a gardening store. As it is with all forms of what you call holly that I know of on Earth, regardless of how much we have grown, even if we are just emerging from the ground and haven't broken into the sunlight, our growth stretches not only throughout stems and leaves but all the way to our home planet. You would find, for instance, to give you an example of another plant, that if a tree is cut down, for many days afterward the spirit of the tree would still be present in some form. Sensitive people might still see the tree in some form there, but this is different. When we are growing here on this planet, we, as so-called holly, maintain a connection so strong to our home planet that sensitive people can often see it. And I assure you, many other beings on the planet can often see, sense, or even in the case of some flying beings—bugs and other smaller fliers—can sense or taste our presence as it reaches up beyond our physical properties into the sky and into the stars and all the way to our home planet, which is in the Andromeda galaxy. So I thought that might interest you and also give you a chance to look us up.

"Any of numerous trees or shrubs, usually having bright red berries."

But I think that I consider myself to be a bush.

"Deck the halls with boughs of holly"—you are a Christmas tradition.

Yes, but for people who have such boughs about, if their plant is growing in their yards or any place, it is a permanent fixture. I am not entirely clear why holly has become a tradition for this holiday. Perhaps just because of our cheerful countenance around that time of year.

Our Connection to Our Home Planet Remains Solid

Yes, with your bright berries. But let's go back to what you said: You grow on a spiritual level, and you are connected to your home planet at all times?

Yes, at all times, regardless of what happens. I have heard of forms of holly that have been, say, exposed to fire, and while the plant may burn down to the ground and to a degree into the root area, the connection to the home planet remains solid. Now, this is unusual in that one might think, "Well, wouldn't the home planet suffer from that connection?" But no—because of the veils of insulation associated with this planet separating it from other planetary beings and planets themselves, what is felt on the home planet is not that. On the home planet, if you were there and a member of our species, you would simply feel that one member of the species on Earth was retiring, what you would call dying. But that's all you would feel, and you would probably anticipate the arrival of that consciousness on the home planet. Generally speaking, we do not, as you would say, reincarnate with the personality on Earth. Once we have completed our cycle here, we, as an individual plant, return to the home planet permanently.

So is this your first time here, then?

Yes. My understanding is that as we are growing on our own—or more likely times seeded, and so on, grown commercially—and then we are activated with personality, or soul being, you might say. But this is a one-time thing, and I do not know of any of the species on the planet that could be stated to be a reincarnation, even though one might have seeds. From the plant sprout new plants, but it is not the same plant. It would be a different soul personality, not unlike the human being, you understand. If the human being has offspring, they are not your soul personality.

Right. There's an awful lot of holly on this planet, a lot of evergreen trees with big berries. You must have millions or gazillions of beings incarnated here!

I do not have the number.

What is your form on your home planet?

On the home planet, if you were to see us, you would assume we were a tree, and by a tree I would say . . . oh, I want to compare it to something you have on this planet, about the size of a redwood tree. Very large! Very ancient! There are no destructive forces on the home planet—none! Whatever individuals are present, there they remain. So given that, there are only so many individuals present. Now, you may ask, "Well, if that is true, where do all these soul personalities go when they retire from this Earth planet?" We will join one of the established trees on the home planet. We simply become a portion, or blend into a greater being—greater in that sense, not just in mass, but in composition of soul personalities. This is something I believe that you can understand with your knowledge of what your Explorer Race is doing. This is not an unusual situation in the other planetary star systems, according to what I understand.

On your home planet, did you embody an entire tree or were you part of a composition of souls that joined the tree?

Oh, I see what you are thinking. You are assuming that I started out on the home planet.

Yes.

No. It doesn't work like that. If it weren't for Earth and what you are doing here and the desire of Creator to have all the variety here, we simply wouldn't be here and then that might be a reasonable question. But given that we came to Earth by messenger, so to speak (we can get to that later), then we do not, in that sense . . . how can I put it in your language? It is a struggle. I as a soul personality have never been to the home planet, but I can maintain my connection—you might say, my conscious connection—with the home planet because of the growth of myself, and it is the same for others of my species. We maintain our connection to the home planet once we have sprouted and are growing, but I have never been there.

Where were you before you came here?

I do not know. I do not have that knowledge. This is an advantage, you understand. Perhaps you don't understand that. Do you know that if you personally knew where you were before you came here, you would be totally infatuated with that and not give your current life the attention it needs and requires? This, I believe, must be an intention by Creator, because this planet is so harsh—"harsh," not meaning cruel, but it is a serious test of, simply put: "Do you want to live? Give yourself a reason to." That's it, because life here can be very difficult.

Think how vulnerable the young are. Even though they might be nurtured by their parents, when your own young are sent off to school, they are not nurtured there. Teachers try their best, but children are knocked around physically and in other ways by fellow students. So you have to want to live to be on this planet. People find various reasons, I am sure, but the desire to live must be present. If it isn't, then not-so-pleasant things happen.

So you think you had to leave your memory at the gate just like we did?

This is my understanding, yes. That is why I am using your peoples as a comparison, to say nothing of the fact that quite obviously my peoples are not going to be reading this book, so I might as well use your peoples.

Our Presence Allows a Certain Continuity over Time

So how long do you anticipate being here? What is your life span here?

This is not something I know. It depends largely on how well I am cared for and how I am supported in the environment. In short, not unlike yourselves, this is not a plan. I do not make future plans based on my best guess. I live in a moment. Perhaps you do not do that. I understand that with the challenge of your mental self, there is a tendency to create a reassurance of life by making plans, but I do not do that, and I am not aware of any others of my species who make plans. I will be here as long as I am here.

I didn't realize before how vulnerable plants are.

Well, yes, we are not good at getting out of the way, eh?

Are you told as you awaken here as a holly plant that you will return to your home planet, that you will join one of the compositions of souls in one of these huge redwoods? Did they make you aware of that?

It is not a "they." I just know, and I realize you are using the term "redwoods" as if that is what they were. But, of course, they are not that. I used that to give you a basis of comparison to understand how big they might be if you were present, not that they are, in fact, redwoods.

Well, they wouldn't have a name I would understand.

No, they do not. If you were to see them, they would not be what you would call deciduous. There are no leaves, but there are vines that wrap around them from the outside up to the top. The vines have not cut off their leaves; there just aren't any leaves. There are a few little stubby branches, but no leaves.

Do the vines grow the way trees do here, with water from the soil and energy from the Sun?

Not exactly—it's hard to describe. It is mostly atmospheric.

So they take in substance through the vines from the air in the space around them?

No, but there is a very slight exchange having to do with atmospheres. You say "gases"?

Yes. That's wild, that you wake up and you are on Earth.

It is not so different than your own.

Right, but I just haven't talked to a plant before who had done that. What was the reason that the Creator's emissary asked your beings to come here?

My understanding was that we were requested to come because our presence would allow a certain continuity over time. I took this to mean, from my understanding of these things, that our use in celebrations, as well as for other things, would create a certain context, not only associated with a happy occasion, but also because of the nature. If you have ever brushed up against holly as a growing plant, we are not entirely soft and fuzzy [laughs]. You have done that?

No—so you have thorns?

Yes, we have . . . it is not a comfortable plant to bump up against. We have a pretty good defense system, but you see, this makes it a perfect symbol, and I think this may be why we were chosen to represent this particular holiday you have—because the holiday is celebrating something, but it is also acknowledging that what is being celebrated does not come entirely and exclusively with happiness. There is also something to watch out for, something to anticipate, and holly might just be considered a good representative of something that is joyous but that you have to watch out for it at the same time, eh? This apparently was considered to be a threat, you might say, that would unite the general approach by civilizations of humans as well as other beings on the planet to life here on Earth. One might have a certain amount of joy in his or her life, but one does also accompany that joy with caution.

That is a really interesting symbol.

Two Exercises to Transform Your Tension

Is there an energy that you exude or a healing quality that we don't know about yet?

There is some healing quality that I can recommend, especially in your now times where there is a lot of tension and struggle. Generally speaking, if you can stand—or even sit, if standing is not comfortable, or recline perhaps—and if you can be about ten feet behind, meaning ten feet from, a holly bush, and someone who has the capacity to emanate energy in a comfortable way . . . you have people trained to do that, yes? If that person can emanate that energy standing about, well, maybe six feet in front of the closest portion of the holly bush to you, toward that person who is standing ten feet behind it, then this can give that person greater strength and durability.

There is another way it can be used also, which I feel is kind of a flip side of that. For those returning from war or struggle or strife, or even if you have been in a prolonged conflict of sorts—not an internal conflict, but conflict with others, even a disagreement that is prolonged and perhaps hard to bear—you can stand or sit or recline, if you wish, about ten feet from a holly plant. Now, this has to be done at a specific angle, and probably, unless the plant is very large, you may have to sit. If you can line yourself up in such a way that you are able to blow your breath toward the plant—not the very top of the plant, but, say, two-thirds of the way up—and the angle of your breath is aimed toward the sky . . . it doesn't have to be toward the Sun, but it does need to be in the daytime so that the energy of the transaction will ultimately wind up at the Sun, and if you are concerned about that, you can hold a picture in your mind's eye of the Sun. You don't have to look at the Sun in the sky. You can sit in front of that and all the discomfort you have and all the uncomfortable feelings you have from that conflict, you can just simply be in touch with those memories of those feelings, which is not difficult when you are feeling tense and uncomfortable, and blow toward the holly plant.

We are very sturdy in some ways. If that breath goes up, you see, it can't go toward a house or another person or something that won't help you. This will actually make you feel worse. But if it's going up toward the sky in an unrestricted way—try to make sure there are no airplanes up there, to the best of your ability—by the time it gets up that far, it should be diluted. Then you can, over time . . . say you are doing that for a few minutes every day, you will feel the tension gradually evaporate until there isn't any. This is particularly good, as I say, for those returning from battle: warriors or those who may have to go to battle again.

This is not really something done for a soldier who might never have been in battle. Then, in that case, you could use the first thing, where you would get strength and a certain amount of durability. But when you are returning, injured or not—physically, that is—this is something good to do. It is particularly good because when soldiers are returning from battle, they are often carrying wounds that are not visible to others. One sees an arm in a sling, yes, but one doesn't necessarily see the scarring of one's heart or mind, the brutalization one may have experienced as a soldier or had to apply perhaps. So such activities can greatly improve the quality of one's time away from being an active soldier, and it would be particularly helpful if one is simply home for a few weeks to recover or between assignments, for example.

This may be another reason that Creator's emissary asked us to come, because we have that capability. On the home planet, occasionally, although we are not the same shape or form, when we get visitors, sometimes they will come to release their tensions, and we are able to almost instantaneously transform those—because travelers from other planets don't have much tension, but on Earth this is something that can be done. Now, it won't work well with a very small plant. If you get one of us and it is a potted plant in your house, for instance, then that won't work. The holly bush has to be reasonably healthy and growing in the ground. If it is dying, it won't work, but if it is reasonably healthy, it will work well.

That's wonderful.

You don't have to be a soldier. You could be in some job that is stressful for some reason but that involves conflict of some sort—not necessarily physical, but perhaps a long, drawn-out argument, and so on, or just a job that is very stressful, say a doctor or a police person or something.

How often would one want to do that? Once a day? Once a week?

Whenever you are feeling that the tensions are interfering with your interactions with your fellow human beings. Say you are at home with the family and you feel yourself wanting to yell at somebody, even though there is no reason to do it—that's a good time to go out and plop yourself down in front of a holly bush.

[Laughs.] No, I meant that from your point of view, you wouldn't want that done all the time.

Oh, I see what you are saying. As long as it is one person doing it . . . this is not something that would work well if, say, two people were doing it. It has to be a relationship really in that moment between the human being and the bush.

There would need to be at least a couple of hours between that being done, so you would probably . . . if you did that, then it would be good to let the plant recover for a couple of hours afterward.

Just a couple of hours! I didn't know if it was once a week or . . .

No, a couple of hours ought to do it, because then the person who is going to be doing this is probably not going to be blowing his or her breath toward the plant for more than five minutes. It would be uncomfortable. And don't pant, meaning don't take a breath and blow, and take a breath and blow. Just breathe in and out naturally, but when you are breathing out, just blow your breath toward the plant. You don't have to do it mightily; just blow gently. The breath doesn't have to move the leaves is what I am saying. It is really the energy, but you use your breath because it is more effective that way.

Human Language Is Not Natural

Now, since you are in a pot, I don't know if you know this or not, but once you are planted in the ground and there are others around you, is there some communication? Or even in the nursery, do you communicate with the other plants in some way?

Yes, but not verbally. The reason I was struggling in the beginning with your language is that this is not a natural way for us to communicate with each other. Rather it would be largely on the basis of feelings. All life has feelings, from the tiniest to the largest. Planets, star systems, and universes have feelings, I have noticed. But the communication system that you as human beings use is something that is not entirely clear. You are not utilizing your feelings in the best way, so there are often misunderstandings. There is also an attempt by many human beings to hide your feelings for one cultural reason or another. Therefore, misunderstandings are frequent and even common. But this is not the case with us, because our communication from one species to another, to say nothing of interspecies within, is entirely feelings, and so there are never any misunderstandings.

Do you know how long you have been here? Days, weeks, months?

No, a few weeks, something like that.

If someone comes in and wants to buy you, can you feel that person and determine whether you want to be with him or her or not?

I might very well feel that, but that doesn't affect the outcome [laughs]. The outcome is, whoever takes a plant from this place does whatever he or she does with plants. But I am still in the place, so I won't be able to answer that question for now [laughs].

I just wondered if you have any way to influence them.

You mean, "Take me, take me?"

Like, "Take me," to that one, and to somebody else, "Don't take me," or something like that.

No.

Oh, that puts going into a nursery in a whole new light, doesn't it?

Buying a plant is a responsibility. It would be good to pick a plant that you feel good about and not be confused that something you are thinking is something you are feeling. I have noticed that human beings get confused about that. They use the term "feeling" as if it had to do with something other than physicality. Feelings are physical and are understandable—it is an interspecies communication. All beings feel the same way, meaning not at the same time, but the function of feelings is the same from one species to another, to say nothing of planets from the biggest to the smallest. It works the same; that's the universal language. But I have noticed that with human beings—I understand them a little bit from them walking through and talking, to say nothing of sprouting plants, myself included—there is a tendency to be confused about what's a feeling and what's a thought.

So to get back to the original start of this, if you go into a nursery to pick a plant, try to pick ones that you feel physically attracted to, even if they may not have been what you went there for. Generally speaking, that would mean that you may have a personal affinity with that plant, and you might feel a sense of affection and maybe get something out of the process rather than just picking something because, "Oh, it's pretty," or because that's what you went there for. That's what I'd recommend.

Well, a lot of us spent most of our lives thinking and not focusing on our feelings, and now we are sort of moving from one modality to another.

Interesting, because when you are born, of course, you are entirely feeling beings, and you are in complete coordination with other feeling beings on the planet. So you learn, apparently, in your cultures somehow to set aside the instrument by which you can know almost everything about other beings and communicate with other beings completely. In short, you set aside the universal language and adapt to the verbal one of your own culture. This, I assume, will be something you will get over at some point.

We are working on it. Have you seen little babies come through the nursery?

Oh, yes. They are totally feeling beings, and we all enjoy their presence. They seem to have fun, and they smile a lot. They understand who we are; we understand who they are. It is the best communication with human beings that I have had, I think, and the other plants here feel the same way. There are some plants here at the garden store who have been here for some time. Apparently, they are being grown to become fairly large trees before they are taken somewhere and planted so that they will become well-established and thrive. So I have the opportunity to assimilate some of their knowledge and experience as well.

Humans Connect to Their Home Planet in Their Dreams

You don't have any idea where you are, do you?

Where? You mean on the globe? No. I have a pretty good idea that I am in a garden store, but that is about the limit of my ability to tell you where I am. I don't suppose that's very helpful in terms of your question.

[Laughs.] No, but it doesn't matter. I don't know that I have talked to a plant who didn't know where he came from, and it's interesting that you are given this knowing that you will go to this planet in Andromeda when you leave here.

Well, this is because of the connection. To us, it is solid. We know. There is the plant—the stalk, the branches, the leaves—but to us it's almost as physical as the physical matter of our beings, so we can't *not* know.

Well, that's a great gift—I mean, given the uncertainty of life on Earth.

But the parallel is, you see, that when you sleep and dream, even though you don't necessarily remember within the countenance of your culture what you have been doing, sometimes, if you are allowed by the circumstances of your life to awaken naturally and slowly, you might have at times good feelings for no logical reason. This will always be because you have connected with the home planet—or that which might be considered home, whether it's a planet or not—and you wake up feeling refreshed and with a renewed sense of being able to live, because you are imbued with the total energization of the fact that you are passing through this planet for some reason but will continue on with your total being once you leave here. In short, it is as if you are being told that you are in school but the bell will ring at some point and you will be out, and then you can come and play.

Now, are you conscious all the time, or do you have that sense of meditation or sleeping at night when they turn the lights out?

We tend to relax a bit more when nighttime comes and the lights are turned down low. As it turns out in this particular garden shop, they never really turn the lights off, so we don't get to have the complete relaxation as if we were out in nature some place and nighttime would be a fixed fact. So I cannot say that

I have ever come to a completely relaxed state as one might when it is dark and quiet except for the sounds of life around oneself. And of course, it is not entirely quiet. It might seem to be quiet to you as a human being who has only a certain range of sounds you might hear, but of course, sensitive human beings, including babies, hear/feel, and when you hear/feel, you don't entirely . . . you are not committed exclusively to that which is in the tonal register that you can take in. You might have a sense of hearing something, which might be a very small noise and barely perceptible to any other human being, but because of your feeling it (meaning being conscious of the means by which the sound is produced), then it might be louder in your consciousness. This is actually the explanation of how it is that human beings can tell that a phone is going to ring before it does, for example.

Since you stretch out, are there other holly plants in this place you are in?

Yes. The garden store appears to be organized, and there are quite a few other holly plants, larger and smaller in various degrees. Generally speaking, when they get to be a certain size, that is when they are placed in such a position as people will purchase and acquire them.

Oh, I see. Some plant nurseries get plants in on trucks and sell them, and some places grow them. So the place you're in grows them?

This is a place where things are grown, but also it is a place where people, human beings, come to purchase things, so there are different places within the garden store. Plants are sprouted and grown from seeds, seedlings, and so on. Then eventually, once they are able to exist on their own, they are placed on shelves for people to acquire.

So where are you? Are you still growing or are you placed out . . . ?

I am not on a shelf yet.

You are still growing. So I was thinking that, since there is such a strong connection to your home planet, do you have a stronger connection to the other hollies around you than to the other plants, or not so you would notice?

There is a stronger connection to one's own species, yes. That is typical. I don't know that for a fact, though.

Remember the Sympathetic Nature between Plants and Humans!

Did you hear someone say, "Would you like to talk?" or did you suddenly find yourself talking? What was your experience when you started tonight?

Do you mean, did I hear a request or did somebody knock on the door? No, I just . . . I can't really describe it. It was just suddenly an awareness that I would be able to communicate if I could adapt to the symbolic sounds, which is still a bit of a struggle.

You are doing great for someone who's never done this before. It's awesome. So you just became aware that it was possible, and you started doing it?

Have you ever had in your mind the sound as if you were conversing with others and you could hear them answer back? You might think it's your imagination, but very often these are real conversations happening in another time (perhaps in the future) or in another way. It is not unlike that for us, except that I know for a fact it is happening and I am not confused that it is my imagination. Sometimes when you are having those conversations, it can be confusing to the human being, I believe, because you can get them mixed up with actual memories of the true conversations, physical ones. But if you can separate them somehow . . . and it would be possible, you see, if you were having a talk with somebody you don't know and would likely never meet. I am not saying you ought to do this, but if you notice yourself doing it, as long as the conversation is benevolent and you are enjoying the conversation and the other party is as well, then I see no reason to stop it. But I do not claim to be the last word in the human gardens.

Since you stay connected to your home planet, are there beings there who are aware of what you are doing here?

I do not know, since I haven't been there, but I'm assuming that since I feel connected to the home planet, there must be some knowledge. But I do not know, and this is probably because we here on the planet have, as you can see, certain similarities to the human being, and I am only allowed to be conscious of the home planet to a degree that does not interfere with living my life here on the planet, not unlike your own situation.

Right. There are awesome similarities. Are your beings there the only species or life beings? Are there others on this planet?

From what very little I know, I am not aware of other beings there, though I believe there are travelers who stop now and then. I perceived something like that once. That's why I got my knowledge that an uncomfortable traveler stopped, stayed there for a short time, and then moved on.

You may not know this, but do you think your planet is one we will visit when we go out to explore?

I do not know. Sorry, I do not have all the answers, including my opinions. There are limits. I do not know your future.

I was just under the impression that a lot of the beings we were talking to for these books we would meet once we went out beyond our planet, beyond our solar system.

No guarantees, eh?

No guarantees. Is there anything else you would like to tell us?

That's all right. It is not intended to be an omnibus dialogue.

But you have been very informative, sharing many new things. I thank you for that.

You are most welcome. I would say that the important thing to remember about plant life in general is that when you are around us, the sympathetic nature between human being and plant life cannot be overlooked. One must truly honor that a creator, such as the one of this planet and beyond this universe, would create these species, plants—my own species, yes, but plants in general—who consume carbon dioxide and exhale oxygen. This can never be perceived as a coincidence, eh? It is like, "Oh, isn't that wonderful!" This is something intended. Please keep this in mind when you are removing plants. How many plants can you remove to make room for humans? Only so many, because you are not going to be able to create oxygen with the exception of destroying some of the materials that you need for your very survival—such as to break down water into its component parts. You will suddenly have lots of hydrogen, lots of oxygen, but you will be missing the water you need to survive. So the simple way for you to have an oxygen-rich atmosphere is to have lots of plants.

On other planets, it is not at all unusual for civilizations to work up the proper technology so that you can live in more condensed units, such as you are doing now with these tall buildings and so on. But some day, perhaps, some of you will actually enjoy living underground. This is not so unusual. It's been done before, and people have thrived. On other planets, it's typical. I am not trying to tell you how to live; I am just trying to suggest that it is not an accident from Creator's hand, so to speak, that we exhale the exact gas that you need to survive and that you exhale the exact gas that we need to survive. If this is not an obvious fact, I am underlining it here. We need you to survive, and you need us to survive. Let's remember that so we don't step on each other's toes too much. Good night!

Thank you very much. Good life!

CHAPTER FOURTEEN

Maple Tree

MARCH 9, 2008

&

THIS IS MAPLE TREE.

Welcome! I love your syrup!

Well, it is not actually something we enjoy providing to the degree that we do. But on the other hand, we recognize that the fluid that becomes maple syrup through your process is something that is intended to provide one with a greater sense of vision—meaning that if one can have the syrup shortly after one acquires it (meaning as fresh as possible), then the chances of your sight improving, not necessarily in your rating of 20/20, or what-have-you, but in your ability to see things that are there but are not necessarily acknowledged by most people . . . one's subtle vision ought to improve by a considerable margin.

People from that part of the world will often see things if they are able to have this fluid when it is freshest. Much of what they see is simply explained as folklore, but you know, a lot of folklore develops because of what ordinary, everyday people see or experience that they don't photograph—they can't because it happens so quickly—or they haven't documented the events because they're not members of this or that recognized academic community. This has often been the case, and that is how real occurrences get written up as or ascribed to being myth. A myth may be something that is not true, or it might be something that is true but hasn't been documented, so there's that.

How does that affect you when they take that fluid? That's like your blood, isn't it?

It's not quite like blood, but very much so. There's no question that it will affect our health. Obviously, if they drilled a hole in your body to tap some fluid that someone needed, it would be very painful to you, plus it would be a loss you would not be able to immediately balance. It is the same way with us.

But as maple trees, we understand that this is part of human culture. We also understand that the reason we are here on the planet is to provide the closest connection that human beings can actually assimilate to experiencing themselves as our type of matter. In ancient times, when human beings were more adept at experiencing interspecies wisdom simply because they had to know what was safe to eat and what was safe to use in medicinal fashion, there was a lot more of an effort to interact with different species, animals, plants, and so on that might be medicinal in some way. In that sense, folklore was a lifesaver then. So we recognize that this fluid is something that can help human beings become more sensitive to seeing. That is why we are here.

For a Long Time, There Were No Volunteers

When the emissary came to our home planet and asked if under the circumstances—meaning how we would be experiencing human beings—we were going to be able to offer ourselves to come to Earth, there was a long pause. We didn't come right away. We had never known, as individuals on our planet, that kind of assault, and we had never known the idea of sharing so deeply our life's blood, as you put it. And so we did not come right away, meaning when we were requested to come. We waited many thousands of years, because when the emissary came, there were no volunteers—none. As it turned out, though, over time—this being such a momentous occasion that an emissary would come—the request remained as part of our knowledge and eventually several individuals volunteered. Thus they were able to migrate in a very small fashion, like a seed pod, with the assistance of another traveling culture to Earth.

Do you know when that was in our time frame?

I do not. All I know and all that's part of our lore is that no one volunteered right away. That may not be typical, or it may. I am not sure, but we thought it was unusual. It's kind of like someone rather grand and magnificent coming in to a group of humans and after giving a talk that was very inspiring, asking, "Any volunteers . . . ?"

And nobody raised their hands.

Nobody jumped up.

So those first volunteers are the source of the maple trees, and then they had seeds and created new trees?

That's right. Simply the way that you see things now is the way that it has always been on Earth. On our home planet, we are a little different, but not so much. The only major difference you would notice is that we are very much smaller on our home planet. We've had some passing scientists who came by, and they said that our gravity is much more than some other planets. That could be an explanation, but all I know is that we are much, much bigger on Earth than we are at home.

So there were only a few volunteers at first, but now there must be many to inhabit all of the many, many maple trees that are here.

Yes. But at that time, obviously, there weren't.

So you are here for the life of one tree, or do you go into the root system and go into another tree? How does that work?

You have the option. You can simply be here for the life of one tree, or you can remain—meaning you can charge the seed pods, and from there you can go on and be reproducing yourself. But you don't have to because there are enough volunteers. I have been here as a personality for several thousand years, so I can't imagine that more than one tree is involved.

You're in the north temperate zone now. Have you been in the same area all of that time, or do your seeds travel and you get to be in different places?

I have always been in what is called the northeast of the United States as it is now.

And so over the course of time, you've seen quite a few people and other animals?

I have not really seen. I have a sense of the presence, but there is no vision, and I know you meant that. Some plants do have a sense of vision, but I am not one of them.

Thank you for that. I assumed they all sensed.

I do not mean they have eyes, but they get some sense of size and shape and form, as well as to simply know that something is present within their auric field. I am more of the latter.

Do you commune with your home planet or are you cut off from them?

No. We are able to commune if necessary, and of course, we have relatives, so to speak, the same way you would have relatives. The difference is that we can trace our ancestry back quite a few generations, so it is possible to communicate with one's family. Granted, it is not the same kind of familial structure that you have, but it is a family of sorts.

Your gravity on your home planet is denser than ours?

Yes. I think if you were visiting there, you would have a hard time moving about. You understand, as a two-legged being, even for your two-leggeds who are in the best of condition, it would be a "difficult, one step at a time, and then rest" kind of thing and a bit of a struggle, kind of like you were climbing as compared to walking. So we don't get too many visitors who do not have special equipment to move about the planet.

Is there anybody on your planet who can move or are they all like you?

We do not have any other forms of life on the surface, but I have felt things moving about under the surface, and I don't know what they are.

Do you mean like a civilization of some type or some individual beings?

I felt some beings moving about, and I do not know what they are, but they do not cause us any harm. I am just aware of motion.

Did you come from another universe or did you originate with this Creator?

I can't answer that question, because it is screened, so I don't know that.

Okay, it's not important! I wonder why the gravity is so heavy. How many Earth gravities?

Maybe three times. I believe there are variables like this to be found in other planetary existences. I do not know why, but visitors will come sometimes and sing songs or communicate somehow about their culture, and sometimes they will even speak of the culture of their planet or planets nearby. We have had a couple of visitors over time who have stated that they had to leave because the gravity became more than they could bear. I don't know if this means there was a change in the gravity of the planet or whether as a result of some maturation they could not handle it anymore. I don't know. They didn't give those details, and the thing about our culture on the home planet is that if people or beings, shall we say, don't volunteer information [laughs], we don't ask. We may be curious, but we think it is not polite to ask that which isn't volunteered.

Oh! So how do you feel about me asking questions of you?

Well, I am speaking through a human being who is conditioned to that, so I am able to—how can we say?—it is like there is a filter mechanism, and I am not offended. But remember that I have also been on Earth for some time, so I'm used to a certain amount of differences in cultures.

If It Weren't for Threats, Humans Wouldn't Move around as Much

So you've been here aware continuously for several thousand years. What is your life span? Are you immortal on your home planet or do you change bodies as you come and go or how does it work?

We have lengthy life cycles on the home planet, not having any natural enemies. But the life cycle would be maybe four or five times what it is here on Earth if there were no hazards, meaning nobody came along with a saw or there weren't any landslides or anything.

So on your home planet you have a lifespan, and then do you come back to that planet or do you go somewhere else after that life?

That's a reasonable question. I have had lives in other forms and shapes on other planets, but not as a humanoid. I always found that in lives where I was more mobile, it made me nervous. I have found that the idea of being in one place and growing with beings also in one place is very comforting. Human beings wouldn't move around so much if there weren't any threats. I have had, as I say, knowledge passed to me from visitors to our planet and from some human beings who visited from some distant star system. They did not move around all that much, and that is because they didn't have any threats. They weren't raised with any threats, and therefore, they weren't the least bit nervous. We really liked those visitors, and we'd like them to come back again someday because we felt an affinity, but they haven't come back.

I can understand that, because it's not so much a threat, but I mean . . . just to live, we have to go to work, we have to move around, we have go to the grocery store, we have to keep moving to finish our tasks, to do this, to do that.

Yes. If you don't have to do that, then being in one place and simply expanding slowly as anyone does is very comforting.

Interesting! What were some of the shapes and forms that you inhabited in other lives?

I was an underwater being in a life, and I was a flying being in a life. That's all I remember. I tried different things of some variety. Other members of my group on the home planet recommended that I try different things if it were possible, so I tried things that were *completely* different.

And the gravity was completely different too, when you flew and when you were underwater?

Oh, certainly! They were each on different planets.

Yes. But you like your home planet.

I much prefer that, yes. You may feel the same way when you remember what your home planet is.

Yes, I'd like to know, but the refrain is, "Don't be distracted; focus on Earth." [Laughs.]

I am not trying to talk you into doing something else. You must do what you are doing here. But the moment you are no longer here, much of what you do not recall now will be with you again.

My Friend the Deer

So do you interact with the various animals in your area—deer or chipmunks or raccoons or birds or others who live around there?

For some time, there was a deer who came and enjoyed rubbing a bit against my base, the trunk you would say, and this was something it did to scratch itself. That deer remained in the area for a long time, and it would come back and visit. When the deer would come back, after a time instead of just scratching itself, it just would lean against the tree in that spot where it used to scratch itself, and we became friends.

Oh, that's great. And it would tell you stories?

Yes, the deer would commune as interspecies do and speak of places it had gone and things and beings it had seen. This occurred several hundred years ago when human beings were not quite as prevalent as they are today and it was possible for a deer to have a lengthy life span and die a natural death.

Where do you live? Are you on a farm or are you in an orchard or where?

I am. That's a yes and no answer, because I was originally simply at the edge of a forest, but then there was a farm for a time, and then it wasn't there anymore. I don't know what happened. Now there is not exactly a farm, but there is something like that. I don't know how to describe it. There is the human being, an older man comes around when it's time to collect, but I wouldn't call it a farm, no. I've been here too long for it to have been something human beings participated in. I know there are such places, but I'm not in one of them.

So except for this old man who comes around . . . what, once a year?

I think so, yes, during the season.

Otherwise, you don't notice many humans?

I'm not aware of too many, no. I think this old fellow just knows where some trees are and goes around and collects. He has brought a younger one with him, so I think he is going to pass the collecting on.

So how far does your awareness spread? How big an area are you aware of?

In terms of my personal safety, I'm aware of about fifty to eighty feet beyond the edge of my boughs. As far out as I would go, I'm aware of about fifty to eighty feet beyond that. For some trees, I think it's more so, but in my personal case, that's about it.

On My Home Planet, Our Species Is All We Have

And then you interact with your home planet. Do you receive news of friends or what's happening?

No, it's not really like that. Stories, old-time stories, and songs, things like that—"songs" I suppose is the best way to describe it, because the songs actually provide nurturance and structure and support, not unlike, I think, what some songs provide for human beings in their culture, where the singing of a song out loud with friends or peers can be supportive and nurturing and helps to establish a certain continuity.

Like the way we sing in church?

Yes.

*What about birds? When we did the animal book [**Animal Souls Speak**], different ones said they and others provided sounds that would be healing for everybody who could hear them. Do you have any birds or animals like that around?*

I have birds that come, especially in the springtime for nesting, and sometimes repeat—meaning they come back again or pass it on in the family. There are not as many birds as there once were! I am not quite certain why, but the bird population seems to have decreased quite a bit. I don't really acquire anything from them that I need, but I do enjoy them being present and raising their young. It's very, very pleasant, and they are very pleasant beings to be around. They are very affectionate and are wonderful parents, very devoted, and I understand that. On our home planet, we have *very* strong family ties. On this planet, it's a bit different, because we are scattered about somewhat, but there is a sense of family ties here as well.

Are you very close together on your home planet?

Yes, a certain amount of contact on the home planet is typical.

So the trunks grow close together, and the leaves . . . do you have leaves?

Just branches.

Do the branches contact one another?

Yes, or come very close. There's no wind on the home planet.

Is there one sun?

I am not sure.

Do you have seasons, or is it pretty much the same year-round?

It's pretty much the same the year around, yes.

And the young grow by seeds?

On our home planet, yes.

So you don't have the wind to carry the seeds around?

That's right.

They're so close.

That's right, close.

Ah! And you don't have flying beings like birds who carry the seeds around the area?

No, not that I'm aware of. On Earth, of course, it's completely different.

Yes, but that makes sense, because your own species is all you have.

Well, yes, and that's not unusual from what I've heard from travelers, that planets may have one or two species. Although, of course, I've also heard of situations where travelers will like a planet and might settle there for a time.

Which many, many did on Earth originally, I think.

Yes, I think that human beings, as you know yourselves, have done that, and in time . . . I don't expect you to leave Earth entirely, but once you have it available to you to travel, I think many people will migrate or look to see how things are elsewhere, and so on. This is typical of all beings who suddenly have space travel available to them. You are doing this just a little bit now. You haven't really been able to travel to the degree that you will someday because of the limits of your technology. This is going to pass, because at some point when you're embracing the visits of cultures from other planets and they feel safe to come, then of course, they'll share what they have to offer with you when they see certain responses or certain changes in how you treat each other. They'll know how you treat your young and how you treat your old and how you treat each other in various situations, so that's how civilizations are measured. It's not a judgment; it is simply a perception. If you're treating each other well, then there is every reason to believe that you will treat visitors well—at least there's a better chance. You're working on it.

How do you replenish after the fluid for maple syrup is collected from you? Is it like humans giving blood—you're weak for a while, and then you have to work extra hard to get your strength back? How do you replace what was taken? I never thought about it before.

It's a struggle, but you get used to it. You just don't grow as tall, you don't spread out as wide and so on. You give up a certain amount of growth—yes, it's a lot. Plus, you never quite get over having that hole drilled in you.

And that was explained to you when the emissary came?

That's why nobody jumped up and said, "I'll go."

So do you have this same fluid in your bodies on your home planet?

It's very similar but not the same, because water is different there, a little thicker, and I don't think our sun is as close. So it's not the same, but it's similar.

So then how do you get your nutrients? From the soil? Your roots reach down into the soil and there is water there?

Yes, as I said, water. The water seems to be underground.

I never thought about what a tree eats. [Laughs.] So it works the same way on your home planet as it does here on Earth—there are enough minerals in the ground and in the water that you get through your roots to nurture you.

It's adequate. I wouldn't be at all surprised if some strong farmer couldn't cause us to grow a bit more, but he'd have to be able-bodied indeed to survive our planet. Plus, we're happy with how we are on the home planet.

Spider Taught Me about Earth

So you like to hear stories—what else do you do there?

[Laughs.] That's a true human question: "What do you *do*?" And the child might say to a tree, "But what do you *do*?" [Laughs.] We live, you know, and we experience life in our own way, but we do not go to the store, buy shoes, and so on.

Yes, I know. We tend to project our human ideas out on everybody.

Well, that's not so unusual. I've had chats with spiders and other beings, and they will sometimes tell stories and talk about how they relate to different forms of life and so on. They are very wise, you know, spiders. I used to have this one female spider who would come around, and she would often say how it used to confound her how there were other species who related to everything on the basis of what *their* species was. I didn't realize at first that she was talking about human beings, but it dawned on me after a time. Sometimes spiders speak in riddles. I think it's because they're teachers, and they like to give hints and clues, but they don't necessarily come right out and tell you. This is perhaps why their webs sometimes have shapes and patterns that stimulate one's thoughts—at least that's what ancient spider told me. The shapes and patterns on the webs are sometimes meant to stimulate the minds and imaginations of others, is how she put it.

We were told that there's actually wisdom and understanding in those webs, if you can get to it.

Yes, as long as you·don't fly into it and then, whoops!

Yes. But, you know, one of the reasons we're doing these books is to try to open up the readers' minds to the similarities they have with plants and animals but also the wondrous differences, the variety.

Yes, and I support it completely. I feel it's a very good thing.

So do you have teachers? If you have a question, do you have access to spirit teachers?

Yes. Generally speaking, it's through the home planet, but the reason I brought up the spider and the deer is that in the case of the deer, the deer was companionable, a friend, but the spider was a teacher. We'd talk about things, and in the beginning I thought spider was just being friendly. After a while, I realized that spider was trying to teach me of the ways of different life forms that I might come into contact with. In that case, she was talking about human beings.

I hadn't had much contact with human beings up to that point. I was young, but over years I've had the chance to think about what spider said, and I realize it was very helpful. So sometimes your teachers are not what you'd expect. They might look this way or that way. That might not be at all what you'd expect teachers to look like or act like, and if they are aware that they're teachers, that's helpful, because then they might say things to intrigue you or get your interest. If they're not aware they're teachers but they still are, they might still say something, some one thing, that you remember. Sometimes it comes back to you as a recollection when other things happen that synchronize with it. Don't you agree?

Oh, yes! But as far as teachers of your own species, spirit teachers who are connected to beings from your home planet, do you have those?

Yes, I think most species have that. I haven't had the occasion to ask one of them anything—I haven't needed to—but I'm pretty sure they're there. You have to remember that the spirit teachers we have on the home planet are geared to that home planet and the conditions there. That's why, being on Earth, it was very helpful indeed to have spider teach me the ways of other species here. That's pretty important on Earth, eh? There's lots of variety on Earth!

Some beings actually have spirit teachers who do come to Earth and talk to them about problems they have on Earth.

Fortunately, I've been able to have friends from other species who have talked to me about those things.

Of course, you have this kind of built-in not-asking thing, right?

Yes. That's our way, and I wouldn't perhaps have heard these things from spider, except that spider knew of our way and would volunteer things, stayed sometimes for weeks at a time, saying things, telling stories, singing songs, of course.

But you don't see many spiders now?

I do. I do see spiders. They don't seem to be engaging me like when I was young, and perhaps that's why—I was young, and spider perhaps felt she would help me, and I am very grateful.

You Will Probably See Earth's Forests Go Away

Do you plan to stay here for the time that the Explorer Race is here, or has anyone discussed when you will leave?

I think that I will not stay here that much longer. It depends on the space needed by human beings. You see, human beings need a lot more space since there are so many of you, and I think it will not be too long before houses are built out where I am and the forest will gradually disappear, though people will miss it. It will be much stated, "We have to save the forest," and so on, but then you have to face the fact: If you have so many human beings, they have to live somewhere, don't they? You're not living vertically all the time and you're not living underground yet in large numbers, so until the population is more stabilized in some—hopefully benevolent—way, then we will probably see the forest go away. So I don't expect to be here too long.

Now that's you, as more of a personality in your area, but has there been a decision by the maple trees en masse to leave?

No, we don't make decisions like that.

So do the individual trees make their own decisions?

Yes. But I have a sense of the human culture spreading this way.

So you've been thinking about it?

Well, one does consider these things, eh? The way I can tell is because of the old man, when he comes. There are times I remember in the past, that when he was younger, he would come maybe once a day. But now he is able to come twice or sometimes three times a day, not necessarily to collect every time he comes, but the fact that he can come two or three times a day leads me to believe that where he lives is closer than it used to be.

Oh! But that still doesn't mean the towns are close or that developments are creeping up on you.

I think a simple observation of human existence as compared to forests would back me up on that point.

I don't know why we need so many of us.

There must be a reason.

Isis says there's always a reason, but . . .

Yes, that's my understanding.

Death Is a Gift from Creator

So you're sort of enjoying the time that's left, but you have this wonderful knowing that when you leave you'll go home?

Yes, as you will. When you leave, you will go home also, though you may go someplace from there. As far as I know, all beings do that. So there is no real loss of one's total self. You might change form, certainly, when you leave here, but you will still exist in a way you know yourself. There is no such thing as oblivion. I've heard that terminology used in describing humans' approach to what comes after death, and there are apparently some human beings who believe there's oblivion. I find it hard to believe that anyone could believe such a thing, but apparently the human being does have the opportunity to believe such things, so some of them do. Of course, there's not even a moment of oblivion. When your body decides that's the end, you leave, and granted, what you see, what you experience, will not be anything like what you saw or experienced in your physical human body, but you will still see and experience. You don't lose that at all.

I know, but because we have to forget who we are when we come here, we don't have the knowing that you do, that there is a continuance. That's why many, many people fear death so much.

Yes, and I realize that that is apparently some kind of confrontational flaw. I don't know if it's a flaw, but it seems to me that it's an unfortunate thing. Maybe Creator wanted you to have something that you could have, meaning the pursuit of your life with zest and zeal and so on. But the other side of that is if you don't know that you are in a continuous life cycle, you might toward the end of your life hang on to your physical life even beyond the point that you would normally wish to.

Yes, that's a real problem here. So much money and effort and equipment goes into delaying death. It's such a waste, but we have that will to live built into us, so . . .

But death is part of life, and it doesn't mean that if there is life and there is death . . . it's not a philosophical statement. If you didn't die, meaning your physical body dies but your personality and soul do not . . . but if your physical body didn't die, then you would be in perpetual suffering, because as long as your physical body was alive, you would be obliged to stay in it. But death is a gift from Creator. Creator says, "No more suffering for you; time to move on to some more comfortable life." Death is a gift. This doesn't mean that you should pursue it, but it does mean that Creator's wish is not for you to suffer some lingering death.

Okay. You've been gracious and kind, and you have a sense of humor, so I thank you.

You're welcome. Keep in mind that I'm not used to conversation. When a fire came around, I listened.

[Laughs.] Well, you're doing great!

Thank you.

Human Civilization on Earth Is in Its Youth

On this planet now, you are conditioned to seek answers and you are commonly presented on a daily basis with questions that sometimes have no answer—so perhaps they have multiple answers and no single answer is enough. As you pursue your life beyond this planet, exploring other planets and welcoming visitors from afar and being welcomed when you go to other planets, know that you will be presented with many questions and that any single answer you give, no matter how pleasing, will last only for a time, and then you will always be seeking more answers. It is in the nature of youth, not unlike my own, that I had many questions that I did not know how to ask, and I was fortunate to have teachers, as in spider who came to share knowledge and wisdom and to stimulate my curiosity. But it is also true in the larger sense that civilizations of people also have a youth, and you, as a human civilization on Earth, are still in your youth. You are perceived that way by beings from other planets, you see, and this is why they haven't come in a big group to welcome you, because it's not unlike what you have in your own culture.

Adults, when they see children, don't rush over and overwhelm them [laughs]. They leave the children to play on their own and to find their own ways to pursue life with just a little supervision sometimes. We of other cultures and other planets do not think of you as children, but we do think of your culture, as it's coming along, as being youthful—in the stage of discovery, seeking, and finding only temporarily your own purpose for life. As your purpose becomes clearer and you realize that it is your job to inform and discover at the same time,

then you will embrace searching the other planets to find out who to inform and what to discover. All beings from other planets know that this is your destiny, and so you will be welcomed in time. If you know this, then you will be able to develop that thing that is so hard to develop in youth, and that's patience. We will see you in time, and you will be welcome. Good life and good night!

Good life! Thank you so much.

CHAPTER FIFTEEN

Walnut Tree

MARCH 29, 2008

&

THIS IS WALNUT TREE—THAT'S WHAT WE ARE.

Welcome! Are you connected to your Earth existence now or to your total existence?

I am an actual individual tree, yes, and an old one at that. I believe I've been able to maintain my persona here because I was planted so very long ago, but the farm, although it fell into disuse for a time, has been reinvigorated by someone new. They're trying to increase the strength and durability of the new trees they have by doing . . . what do you call it when they take little saplings and . . . ?

Graft them?

That's right, grafting.

Are you in an orchard or on a farm?

I'm not sure about that. There are a few other trees, but there are other things going on and there are animals.

Do you know in what part of the world you are?

No. I don't know my geography. It is warm sometimes, and other times it is cold.

Do you know how long you've been here in terms of years or experiences or our events or anything?

I'm not too good at that. I'd say, best guess, a hundred and eighty years.

And you still produce walnuts?

Yes, but not as many as I once did. Younger trees are more vigorous that way. But I believe the reason they're grafting is that the young trees don't always last as long. And I'm sure that this is because they are planted by human beings in not exactly a cavalier manner, but they are planted for the purpose of cultivation, meaning in rows rather than where it feels best.

When I was planted, the farmer who did that walked around on the ground for a long time until he felt that it was exactly the right spot. I think he was doing something like dowsing—and you know, that's a very old thing to do. It's nothing new. When he found just the right spot, that's where he did the planting. I really feel that in your now time the reason farmers are having difficulty bringing in natural crops is that they haven't been doing enough dowsing.

Of course, some people just know where to plant on the basis of feeling, but if you don't and you're not sure about dowsing, bring in somebody who's good at it, and that person will do it for you. Don't look at it askance, though! If you do, the plant may not feel welcome. Welcoming is everything in the plant world, in the human world, I might add, and in other worlds of beings. If you do not feel welcome, then you are always reluctant to give it your all. That's true in the plant world as well.

I Am from Inner Earth

So you were aware in the seed of the way in which the farmer planted? You were aware of yourself in the seed?

I was asleep then, asleep meaning . . . the walnut falls from the tree and finds its way to becoming a tree. If the seeding process happens naturally, then one will be welcomed, but if it happens in an unnatural manner—meaning planted by somebody else for his or her purpose—those seeds are usually asleep. I was asleep.

So that's when your awareness on Earth began, in that tree you're in now? Or do you remember from before?

I remember from before. I remember from *way* back, from home territory, which in my case was located inside the Earth. I believe this area has been seen by a famous person.

You are from Inner Earth, what Richard Byrd saw?

Yes, Admiral Byrd, yes.

Well, how interesting! How did you get up here?

It was believed by those living at that time, in that place, who looked very much like you, that the people on the surface who would come would need food and in the beginning would not be certain what was safe to eat. So it was believed that some plants who volunteered . . . they're very conscious people, you know, who lived there. The plants who were food crops—such as apples and so on—volunteered that some would be taken and put here and there on Earth to provide food for human beings and in some cases for animals until human beings showed up and sometimes shooed them away. That's how I came to be on the surface.

So you've been here since before humans?

I've been here since before the kind of humans you understand Earth people to be, but I wasn't always on the surface. It was really just about 400 years ago, I think, that I had my first surface life. Four hundred years ago the people living inside Earth were still there—the people you would recognize as human beings—but I don't think they're there now. I believe they emigrated awhile back. I could feel the departure.

Do you know to where?

No, but I don't think it's that far away. I'm not certain that they emigrated to a planet. They might be on a vehicle—a big vehicle, of course.

How many people are we talking about?

I couldn't say.

How long were you aware of being in the Inner Earth?

Thousands of years.

Did they grow and mature as a people or were they the same when they came as when they left?

They seemed to be the same culturally. Of course, individuals came and went, but culturally speaking, they seemed to be the same. They were benevolent, insightful, spiritual, you might say, but in the context of being able to communicate with all species, they would receive visitors from other planets and sometimes they would deflect groups of visitors—very occasionally, but I recall them deflecting one or two groups—not in an armed conflict, but they would just make the planet not comfortable.

So they were from a much higher dimension than we are?

No, I don't like to say that. I'd say they were from a form of consciousness that is your native consciousness, but just slightly more physical. Your native consciousness is not really physical.

Right. And why did they . . . ?

Pleasure of pure being—that's why, if I can anticipate your question. "Why were they here? Why did they decide to be?" For the pleasure of being.

So they came from somewhere else, not from the surface of the planet after some catastrophe or anything.

No, nothing like that! They came from somewhere else.

Life on Inner Earth

Tell me about Inner Earth. Can you describe what you remember? You don't see, right? But you can feel it or sense it?

Yes. When you are in a place that's totally safe, very loving, nurturing, and supportive, all your senses are heightened. They aren't just heightened when you're in danger; they're also heightened to a great degree when there's no danger whatsoever. And so I remember a lot of smells. The air was moist and warm, and my impression is that there were lakes, forests—a beautiful environment. I think that the environment could be compared to something like the Garden of Eden, although the people there, the human beings, they wore clothes [laughs].

And they had high technology?

Well, it depends how you define technology. If you mean machines, no. I like to be accurate. They had devices that might be classified as technology, but not in the sense that you would. For you, technology is materials made into component parts to produce a desired outcome. Their technology was different. It was materials, but only the material that had volunteered and usually only to accomplish one thing, not a versatile object.

So if, say, there was some need to perform some task, you might ask the materials to volunteer. You wouldn't form it yourself. As a result, those kinds of mechanisms, so to speak—if I can use that term, though it's really a misnomer—that kind of technology would often look different from one object to another. It wouldn't have a generic appearance. So in one case it might be spherical or oblong or something like that; in another case, it might be all different forms or shapes, almost ribbonlike. It depends how it came together, but it would perform the same task.

They could make lightships that came up and looked at the outer surface of the Earth when they chose?

I don't think they had vehicles that I'm aware of. Vehicles did come and visit, but I don't think they had vehicles of their own.

So when they left, somebody took them.

Yes. This would suggest that they either simply had friends from other places . . .

Yes, or they were an outpost or something.

Yes.

Did they bring you with them—you and the other food-bearing plants and fruit and things—when they came to Inner Earth?

They did.

So you came with them from where they're from.

Yes, I believe so. Now wait! Let me look at that! That's a long-term memory. No. No. My type of beings were with them for a long time, but we have our own place.

Ah! They brought you, but you're not from there.

That's correct.

It seems to me that somebody in spirit through Robert told me about what were called the foo fighters—little orbs of light during the second world war. They're from the Inner Earth; they were sort of seeing what was going on. Do you know if that's true?

I don't know about that.

Okay, we'll ask somebody else. Well, that's wonderful! That's a whole new revelation. Do you think we will ever be able to go into Inner Earth?

It's possible. It's not what it was, because of the type of technology you have now, using sound waves. Those sound waves have corrupted what was there. I don't think that was intentional, but it has created problems. As a result, that's why they migrated. Sound waves, you know, can cause a lot of damage if you don't know what you're doing with them. I recognize that your science is trying to find uses for things, but when you start experimenting because you can, as many scientists know, sometimes you make mistakes that are irreparable. And I think that's what happened. There were effects, damage, and it caused a situation that was unlivable.

So it was affecting the human and the animals or the actual land itself? Everything, I suppose.

Everything—just like it affects you. When you are around those kinds of sound waves, you usually don't know, but they do affect your body chemistry and your body functions.

Not for the better, you are saying.

That's right.

Interacting with Humans on Earth

What is your outlook where you are? As long as your tree is alive, your consciousness will remain in the tree.

Yes.

And then it will go with the seeds or how will that work?

It depends. I haven't decided whether I will remain here. I've been in this position for a long time, and some of the people on the farm are nice, I enjoy them. There is a very old man who comes around sometimes, leans against the tree and talks about what was: family, memories, good times, sad times. This is not unusual. People do this sometimes with their favorite dog or horse, I have noticed, and sometimes just leaning against a tree when it's been there forever. I was in the same position when that man who's very old now—I can't say how old, maybe in his eighties—was here when he was a child, and he would come around. Even though the land has changed and there are new things here and almost everything has changed, my appearance hasn't really changed very much, and people often come around and talk out loud. I think they are talking not so much to me, talking as it were to the spirits or maybe talking to God, but I feel like a witness. And I find that comforting. Also, there are some children around who are enjoyable. They like to climb up and sit on one of my very sturdy limbs. I think their mothers or fathers have said, "No, don't sit on this or that branch; it doesn't look so sturdy," and so they sit there, and I like that. They're friendly; they're not harmful. I have very thick bark, of course, after all this time, but they're friendly enough, and I enjoy their chatter.

There are a few other people who seem to be very angry. I am not judging them. They may have cause, but when they are around, it's a little difficult to take. But they don't linger.

What do you think they are angry about?

I don't know.

You say there are many changes. Do you mean there are houses creeping into your area, a development or something?

My impression is that there are more buildings, closer, and I don't know whether their farm will be able to maintain its presence. I'm not really sure how your peoples are going to farm and grow crops. Perhaps you will try to do this underground. It can be done, but you have to want to do it really badly, and you have to welcome the plants, because it's not natural for plants to be underground. But given welcoming and encouraging and gentle treatment, plants might surprise you.

By "underground," do you mean just a little ways underground or in the center of Earth where you were?

I wasn't in the center of Earth.

Where were you?

It's not the center of the Earth. If it was the center of Earth, we'd be boiled. It wasn't that far down, maybe thirty, forty miles.

What I've heard is that Earth is hollow and that's where Byrd went. But you're just saying he went into what we call the mantle?

I don't know, but I heard about his flyover. He flew over and had a visit, but he didn't fly down into the center of Earth or anything like that. I think that was all a speculation, a best guess based on recollection.

But you still get to where you were through the North Pole and the South Pole?

You used to be able to get there.

Not now?

I don't think so.

Thirty or forty miles down—so how big was this area? What was the size? How many people could it hold?

I suppose it could have held millions if you were going to pack them in there, but of course you wouldn't do that.

I mean, in a "Garden of Eden" situation, as you suggested. Thousands or ten thousand?

Thousands. I don't know how many. I'm not a numbers person.

[Laughs.] Was it a natural formation or had it been created by someone displacing the earth?

I don't know. It felt natural.

Life on the Home Planet

You said you had long memory. Where are you from originally?

In the star system Sirius, there is a warm, yellow planet. The soil is yellow, and the sun is just a little closer than the ratio of your Sun to your planet. It has a golden color, and it's a very friendly sun. I don't know how to describe it. There is not a lot of nighttime. Part of the reason I was interested in coming here at all is that it would be possible, I was told, to experience night. Of course, until I got to the surface I didn't, but I have enjoyed that. What else do you want to know about life on our planet?

Are you the same? Do you look the same there as here, or do you have a different shape?

No, we're much smaller there, maybe no more than eight or ten feet high—similar, but not the same.

Are you walnut-bearing—I mean, do you bear nuts?

No, it's something that looks like a seed pod.

Is that edible? Is there anybody there to eat it?

No.

Are you the only species on the planet?

No, there are other plant-type beings and a few of what you would call quadrupeds, four-legged beings.

But they don't eat what you produce?

No, but they eat as far as I can tell.

Oh, it's energetic.

No, they're physical and they don't eat.

So they're nurtured by what?

I do not know, but I've never observed anyone to the best of my recollection eating.

Do you have rain? Is it wet there? Do you have lakes or oceans?

I'm not aware of any.

You don't have water? You don't need water for growth?

No.

So is the soil your nourishment? I mean, do you get everything you need from the soil or from the atmosphere?

Part of our structure is crystalline.

What part? The limbs?

It might be interesting for you to note that some things that you think of on your planet as stone, crystalline, are actually just, from our perspective, slow-growing plants.

[Laughs.] Do you have roots, then, that support you?

I would think of them as roots. You might consider them as a foundation.

But do you reproduce or do you stay the same?

I suppose reproduction might be possible, but I've never known anybody to die, so there's no need to reproduce.

Ah, you're immortal. I mean, everybody's immortal, but you don't have life cycles there, then?

That's right. That was well said.

So what is your culture like? You enjoy other beings—how do you communicate?

With what you would call dreams.

You share dreams?

We live in our dreams.

What kind of things do you do in your dreams?

We *be*. We exist. You mean, do we play cards and sing songs? No, we exist there. It doesn't relate to your culture.

Did you come from another universe? Were you invited here or were you created by this Creator?

I don't recall that.

Did the other culture that came to Inner Earth just bring you or were you invited by an emissary of the Creator?

You know, the seed pods are more vegetable-like, plant-like, whereas a lot of the rest of the tree, as you're calling it, has a partial crystalline matter. I believe that the pods were gathered, but the people were sensitive enough to notice whether the pods were open to going. If they had felt any resistance, they would have left them. I appreciated that. But there was no resistance. I think that the seed pods were prepared for an adventure.

And you were one of the seed pods?

I have memory of that—not the pod, but one of the seeds.

Why would a crystalline tree that has no cycle have seeds?

Because we're not like Earth. It's very typical, I've noticed, of Earth people to expect other life forms to be like the ones you're used to on Earth, but why would they be?

But what did the seeds do if they didn't grow?

They were available. They didn't fall; they were just there. The seed pods were there. The people who came picked them. They weren't on the ground.

You are a being who has no life cycle who is immortal—then why would you have seeds, which implies a cycle of reproduction?

No, it doesn't. It implies an availability.

So you might be a seed forever?

Yes, unless somebody comes along and says, "Hey, seeds!"

Oh! Had someone done that before?

No.

[Laughs.] All right. So you had seeds so we could have walnuts on Earth.

From my perspective, human beings have seeds that could become children, but some human beings don't have children in their lifetimes and yet they have seeds. What's the difference?

So you're saying that everybody on your planet has seeds, but no one had children.

Not everybody—"everybody" like my type of being. The quadrupeds didn't have them.

Oh! You mean just your species. Was there anything about the soil, what makes up the soil that made it turn yellow?

I really don't know. It was always that way.

Use the Walnut Tree for Healing

Do you want to know anything about Earth? This is where you *live*.

Sure. Sure. What would you like to tell me?

About the walnut tree—what it's doing here on Earth, how it can be used for people.

Absolutely! Anything you want to share.

If human beings have some kind of rheumatism and you can find bark from an old walnut tree, you might be able to create a liquid. You can take only that bark and a small piece at that—really, a tiny piece. Please don't use this commercially. Go and ask, then peel off a very small piece, maybe about the size of the tip of your thumb, and you can boil it in water, preferably spring water, for about ten minutes (it might tint the water a little bit). Let the water cool naturally; don't try to cool it by some other means. After it becomes room temperature, then say you have rheumatism in your arm or hand or shoulder or something, you can make a compress of that water, and it might help to relieve some discomfort. I can't swear that it will work for all people, but it might work, especially for women.

Don't drink it or anything like that. If you are going to make a compress, try to use a cloth that is made entirely out of cotton, preferably without dye. Then you can consult with an herbalist for how long he or she feels you could hold it there. Some people might say that it would be helpful to boil that with a sprig of olive leaves as well. Consult with an herbalist. He or she can help you there—a wise woman, perhaps! Then there are other things you can do.

If you are having difficulty with memory, as many people do, you can stand on one side of the tree. I would recommend you stand on the south side, but it's up to you. If you feel better standing on the north side, then try that. Have somebody who's a friend, preferably a spiritual person with a good heart—meaning one who feels love and comfort around plants, animals, and nature—stand on the exact opposite side of the tree. Have that person take a deep breath into the top of the head, so to speak, or a deep breath from the clouds, and look back at the tree and blow gently. The other person doesn't have to blow like he or she is trying to blow through the tree; it's not going to happen anyway. Just have him or her blow gently toward the tree, and you, as the person on the other side, might after three of those breaths and maybe six of those treatments, say every other day (I would recommend during the daytime), perhaps notice some improvement in memory.

No wonder you wanted to say that. I thought walnuts themselves were enough of a gift—that's amazing!

I think it's important to ask the other plants how they can be used like that, medicinally. Some of them may not know, but some may. And be sure to request the olive tree, if you haven't heard from it yet.

We will. You know this because that's part of your nature?

I've noticed over the years that some of this wisdom has been lost. In the past on Earth, this was done. I can remember when peoples who are no longer in this area would come by and do that.

I don't know if you're going to know, but do the humans around you speak the same English that you are speaking now? I mean, the same language?

You mean the peoples where I am? I don't know that. I can't explain that; besides, you are just asking me where I am in another way. I would prefer not to say.

Well, the United States is pretty big, as well as Canada and other English-speaking places. Much of this wisdom has now been lost, yes? But when you were young, then people knew that, when you first came here?

Some people did. They were people who traveled; they weren't settlers. They were on their way to someplace or from someplace. But if they had a member who had some problem, they would stop—not usually at my tree, because I was young then, and it's always better to do this with older trees who are well established and by that time usually used to human beings. If you use that kind of material or try that with a young tree, it probably won't work. The tree has to be used to human beings for it to work—not necessarily around them all the time, but used to them in general as passing by or being around from time to time.

Trees Need to Feel Welcome

So do you communicate with animals who tell you stories?

I have had some animal beings come and sing the song of their lives. Birds often do that. I can recall a big cat sitting on a limb up high and not exactly making a home but just spending time there. He did that for a long time—almost all of that cat's life cycle. That was nice; I enjoyed that. The cat didn't tell stories too much but would make sounds that I found comforting, nurturing.

Are there other walnut trees around you, other than the ones they just planted? Are there older ones?

No. I'm the last of the old ones.

Can you communicate with the younger ones they're just planting now?

They're not just planting them—they've been in the ground for a few years, some of them longer than others. There are some there who have been there for twenty years or so. I can commune, but they are still confused.

Were you confused when you were first planted?

No, because the farmer took care, and so I felt welcomed. The farmer would come every day and not just water me but welcome me, and I believe he would sing. They had a special song they would sing to plants. I don't know how it went, but I think it was a song they would sing in church. It was nice. And I knew it was meant to be a welcoming song. It was about the goodness of life, and I believe that was their way of welcoming.

So there's no way you can help these younger trees right now? There's no way you can get through to them—is that what you're saying?

I'm available, but they are still trying to understand their lives, based on being in an unnatural situation. If you can still find a forest, you wouldn't normally see trees growing in a row. It's not natural for trees to do that. So when trees are planted in a row, they're usually very uncomfortable, and I don't think there is anything that can be done to improve that.

I feel that if someone really wants to start an orchard, it would be good to find a dowser, or to dowse yourself would even be better, if you feel good about that. Just walk around, if you have a seed or a pod or whatever you have—walk around. Don't do it by machine! Walk around and see where it feels welcome and sing to it every day. You don't have to do it one by one. You can walk out into your whole area and field and walk around and sing. Trees like that. Try to only sing things that would be welcoming, some kind of a pleasant and gentle song. Don't play music on an instrument—by that, I mean a recording. If you want to bring a guitar or a flute or something, that's fine. We like that kind of thing. But don't play harsh music; play gentle music.

Busyness Makes Sleep Difficult for Humans

So how do you feel about day and night now that you've experienced it? You said one of the reasons it was interesting for you to come here was to experience day and night, light and darkness.

Yes, I like night very much. It's completely different, isn't it? There's not just a change in the light, but there's a change in the feeling. And this farm is still far enough away from the towns that . . .

You can see the stars?

Well, humans probably can see the stars, yes. But there's not the sense of busyness. I honestly do not know how human beings can sleep when there's busyness around them and sleep deeply with dreams that connect you to good things. My impression is that when human beings are around busyness when they sleep, they might be having somebody else's dreams and wake up confused or upset.

I believe that might be where nightmares come from. I can recall way back when the farm first started. The human beings were not that far away: the man and his wife and several children. I usually know when human beings are having nightmares. I don't recall them having nightmares.

Well, we've got too many people.

It's not just that. You can have a lot of people, but if they're calm and peaceful and enjoy each other's company and are experiencing a good life, then that is fine. But when it isn't that way or when there's a lot of busyness, people working at different hours and so on, then this can create a problem.

Do you know if you have a moon around your home planet?

I don't recall one.

So how will you feel going back then, when it's light all the time there?

Oh, I don't think that'll be a problem at all. I came here because I was interested to experience night, and I'm experiencing it.

So when you go home, it will be fine. It won't be that you miss it, then.

Ask me then!

[Laughs.] The walnut itself is the seed, isn't it? The inside of it, the part that we eat is the seed that grows?

I believe so. I'm not certain about these things, because for me each leaf is the same as the fruit of the tree. Each pod is the same, a portion of my body, but when pods fall, they all feel like seeds to me. It's hard to describe. You'd have to be a walnut tree to understand. My impression from other trees is they feel very much the same. When leaves drop or seed pods of different sorts, it feels the same.

Have any of your seeds fallen around you and grown into trees?

Well, because I'm living on a farm, no. It could happen in nature, but because I'm living on a farm, no.

So people gather them?

There are a few squirrels around. They gather them too, but they usually like to get them from the tree, and the farmer's not greedy. The farmer does not chase the squirrels away too much.

Oh, I see. He allows them what they need.

A certain amount, yes.

Channeling Was Used in Inner Earth

Is there anything else you can tell me about Inner Earth? I've never talked to anyone who's lived there. How long were you there?

Thousands of years, as I said. But just in one form, one tree.

And you lived that long as that one tree?

Yes, because there was no danger there, at least at that time.

Did the humans who lived there live that long?

They had life cycles, but they lived a very long time.

Do you know what they did?

You would have to ask them that. I'll make a closing statement then.

You have a very sweet personality, and I thank you. How did you know? Was there like a call, or you just felt . . . you've never talked to a human before, have you?

Yes, I have.

Really! When?

Inside Earth, the peoples there, if they weren't certain whether they were getting correct information and they needed more details, would do something similar.

Really!

This is an ancient art, you know, a very ancient art.

And you would talk to a human to give advice to another human?

Well, I don't know why they wanted it, but it was not unusual for this kind of process to take place, inspired speaking. It's old, very old.

So what was your process? Was there a request or a call?

I became aware that there was a need and I could fulfill it. So, no, it's not the first time I've done this.

Well, okay. You sound practiced. [Laughs.]

Welcome the Plants around You!

So you have been reading this book because you are interested in the life forms around you. I'd like you to consider when you walk out in your yard or when you're walking any place where plants are volunteering and present, to welcome them. Remember that plants exhale the very air you breathe, and many of the organisms in your time that used to provide you with that air that you breathe are no longer as vital or as strong or even present. So what you really have now that produces the air you breathe are plants.

I do not encourage you to destroy them because you are not happy where they are volunteering. Keep in mind that when a plant volunteers, it feels welcome. It may not be welcome by the human beings, but it is welcomed by Earth and by the spirits of Earth and by the benevolent spirits welcomed by Creator. Keep that in mind! If you see a plant that you're not happy with being in the place it is, just remember that it's *exhaling* what you're *inhaling*. Good night!

Thank you. Good life!

CHAPTER SIXTEEN

Palm Tree

MAY 17, 2008

&

THIS IS PALM TREE.

Welcome! Do you know where you are on the planet?

I'm not actually on Earth where you are now, but I have relatives—meaning descendants—who are on Earth now. Palm trees are so active and so involved in their surroundings and interacting with their surroundings that I believe the reason I came through is that none of them would really be able to be involved in this process because of their activity level. I am on another version of Earth, but I have lived on Earth and my descendants continue to do so.

What version of Earth are you on?

I do not know—are they labeled? It is Earth, but it is calm and quiet. There are some human beings here, not many, and there aren't as many plants as there are on your Earth. But it is a restful place. I do not know any labels for it. It's a version of Earth—that's all I know.

Tell me about the activity palm trees participate in that keeps them so busy.

You will often see their fronds moving in the wind. Of course, one says, "Well, this is the wind and it's an effect," but palms have the capacity to interact with the wind in a way that is unusual from the human perception.

235

We Interact with Wind to Encourage Newborns

Palms have everything to do with the newly born. This affects many different types of species—one of them is humans—but it basically affects all beings who are associated with the land. It does not affect the sea, but it affects almost all species, with perhaps a few exceptions who are land-walkers. I don't think it affects the birds.

In what way does it affect newborns?

There is a great deal of difficulty sometimes in moving from spirit to the physical. Many souls do not wish to participate beyond certain levels—meaning they might wish to just try out physical life but not actually go to full-term. It is palm's avocation to encourage, to tell stories, to sing songs about the value of life here and about giving life on Earth here . . . giving Earth a chance to show the goodness of life on Earth. In other words, you might say we give these souls a pep talk.

It doesn't always work; sometimes the soul only wishes to participate for a short time and not actually be born a living being. But it does work at least 40 percent of the time with souls who would otherwise have decided not to remain on Earth. It requires a lot of support, you know. Souls hear about Earth, and they don't always hear good things. Of course, they have teachers, guides, and the teachers and guides do not lie to them. They might ask questions, and the teacher or guide might say, "Well, it may be very difficult. It may cause you to feel this and cause you to feel that," and so many souls say, "Well, I'm not so sure." So we try to support their engaging with life, at least to be born and see how it is. After that, the soul in the form of a child would choose within the first few years whether it's going to stay. Usually, once they get born and are physical, they stay.

Is there a certain area within which you can contact these beings, or do palms operate all over Earth with the "about to be born"?

Are you asking, is proximity a factor?

Yes.

No, this happens largely for the soul. It would be like on a dream level, but a soul is in that level and deeper all the time when they are considering being born and when they are in mother. They are not really in any other state. So as a result, as long as the communication is benevolent and loving and gentle, it is possible to communicate well. Parents often talk tenderly to baby growing inside mother. Mother may do this and father may do this and even other siblings and so on, and this is a good thing, because it encourages baby to thrive.

For Adults, It Is Possible to Feel the Resistance

So when you were a palm tree and you were on Earth, when you would feel or hear or you . . . the palm tree has to be operating on that level also in order to communicate to these souls, right?

Well, palm trees operate on that level all the time.

They do?

Yes.

Only palm trees or all trees?

I can only speak for palm.

So do you operate on that level all the time? Are you aware of when anyone is about to be born, who says they don't want to?

I understand that you are paraphrasing, but it is not that they might state it. It's that it is possible to feel the resistance, and if the resistance is overcoming the desire to engage with life, we can feel it.

Resistance is a strong factor in engaging with life. You as an adult can probably identify with that to a degree. There may be times when you don't wish to engage with life, and you might just like to curl up and fly away somewhere. So this level of resistance, if it gets to be too strong, even in the adult . . . adults do, in a sense, curl up and fly away. They might be more open to their life coming to a close. Though for adults, once you've engaged with life and been through a lot of life's struggles and joys, it is possible to be aware of it, because it usually shows up in some particular portion of one's physical anatomy. For some people, it might be the solar plexus. For others, it's the back of the neck or the shoulders. You would feel that as stress, although it might not always be resistance—it might be the position you're in, and so on. But you might, as an adult, recognize that it's a stress sign, and stress usually represents either inner conflict or resistance, from my understanding.

So as a baby or as a young soul—meaning not necessarily young in terms of experience, but as a youthful soul on Earth—there's no complexity of adulthood and experience. Without that, it is *very* simple to feel the resistance. It is just as clear as it can be.

What are some of the things humans are mostly resistant to? Do they feel that it's too discomforting or that they will suffer? What are some of their resistances?

Well, you understand, we're talking about beings who don't remember who they are, but sometimes they do, because we're talking about a soul in transit to mother—once baby has started to develop in mother, the soul comes and goes,

238 &D PLANT SOULS SPEAK

so it is not always present. Therefore given the amount of transference—meaning in this case motion in and out and away from the planet and so on—there is a certain amount of observation a soul is able to make in transit, and they see the suffering and they feel it.

Think about it! Even if mother is leading an ideal life, mother is often exposed to things that are stressful. This is why perhaps in olden days mothers were encouraged to live as stress-free as possible. But that's difficult in your now time; it is challenging. You understand, your gestation period is very long for a species, to be in mother for nine months or so. This tends to build up a certain amount of inward experience, meaning that as baby-to-be is developing and traveling to a degree on Earth as well as soul travel, it sees, feels and, most importantly, senses. It's getting a little harder to convince babies to be physically born. They can need a lot of encouragement, and after they're born, I think they still need that encouragement until they're at least ten to twelve years old and starting to pick up the sense of who they are from their peers.

Earthworms, Sheep, and Cows Have All Needed Encouragement

So besides humans, are there particular animals you work with more than others?

We don't need to work too much with other species besides humans—because humans, of course, have the greatest difficulty on Earth. Oh, you might look at other species and have compassion for the struggles they have, but they know who they are. They are never without that knowledge. But human beings as a rule do not know who they are. Humans might know their names, they might know where they live, and they might know their friends and family. But ultimately, when you get older, you start wondering, "Who am I? Why am I here? Where am I from? What am I supposed to be doing?"—especially nowadays when questions like that are more readily stimulated, if not at home, then certainly at school. So we work more with human beings, because there is more need there. I have recollections of working with some young earthworm souls, but that was, I believe, during a hard time for them, when they were considering leaving the planet. Do you know why?

No.

Because they were being used for cruel purposes, from their point of view. You understand that earthworms are on Earth primarily, not only to live their own life cycles, to have their young, and to enjoy life as much as possible, but also to create the most wonderful soil that can be found essentially on the natural level. By doing so, they provide for the well-being of others, and they do this as a natural process for themselves. So something they do that they're happy to do helps others.

But once people started using them as bait for fishing and stuck them on hooks alive, to go through that suffering, they seriously considered leaving Earth. Farmers out there, think about it for a moment: What would you do if the worms were gone? You might think, "Oh, we can do this or we can do that," but those of you especially who are organic farmers and working with sensitive crops, you know you would miss them!

So did that crisis resolve?

No, but we have encouraged them to wait, to see if they can wait it out. Some of the fishermen have gone to using artificial baits, and that's good. But some continue to use baits based upon cruelty.

So were there other instances or are you basically here for humans?

As I said, we are here for any and all species of land-walkers that may have some reluctance to be born. We're here for the newborns, in that sense. Are you asking if there are any others?

No, I mean, what are some of the other land-walker beings you have worked with?

Meaning other than human beings?

Other than humans and the earthworm, yes.

I won't go into that too much, since they're not going to read this book, but we did work for a time with sheep. Sheep were unhappy with their lives and felt like they would rather be somewhere else. We have also worked with other so-called domesticated animals, such as cows! We were unable to convince cows to stay on the planet, so they will be leaving.

How soon?

I cannot say, but it has been clear. Almost all newborns who are coming in for cows have resistance, and it is not possible to console them. So they have chosen to leave, and they will do so when they are ready. As you may have noticed, things are happening with cows. Partly this is due to improper feeding, but I think those issues are well-known.

We Have Always Been Able to Nurture

How did you develop this ability? What is it on your home world that caused you to be able to desire to do this?

This is a really reasonable and good question, but the answer is simple: we have always been like this. As far back as I'm aware, we have always been able to nurture, to encourage, to support. I do not know my personality any other way, nor do I know it to be any other way for any palm. You notice they have a certain grace about them, yes?

Yes.

That factor often makes people feel attracted to them. And that grace is truly a physical representation of our hearts.

On your home planet, do you look like you do here?

No. On the home planet, we are more like a vine. There is no need to protect the fronds by having them up on a stalk, so we are more of a vine there, not unlike your ivy, but the fronds look much smaller, with flowers.

With flowers! What do the flowers look like?

Oh, I couldn't say. Some are pink and some are white and some are translucent. The translucent ones, if it were dark, have a slight glow about them. But the planet doesn't have much in the way of nighttime as you know it on Earth.

Do you have two suns?

I do not know, but there is a bright time and then there's a less bright time. So there is no pitch-dark, as you have on Earth.

How did you like that experience of dark on Earth?

I liked it very much. I found it profoundly restful, and I considered it to be one of the major pleasures of Earth. I grant that my life might have been a little different than some palms, because I was on an island, surrounded by water. There were very few human beings there. Occasionally, they would come and enjoy their environment, but they were not destructive. They would sometimes gather what there was to be gathered, but they wouldn't do anything harmful to each other or anyone else, and then they would leave. So I had very good experiences with the human beings. They didn't carve their initials into my trunk or anything. I don't know where that started, but I'd like to see it stop.

On your home planet, are there other beings there whom you nurture in the way you do on Earth?

No. On the home planet, there are not that many kinds of species on the land. We are a land plant on the home planet, and there are a great many species in the water, since there's a lot of water there. We don't interact with them directly, since we are land-oriented and the beings in the water don't come up on the land. So I think that, if you were to approach the planet from afar and get closer, you would assume that other than the plants you see growing on the land, life takes place in the water.

But you don't nurture the water beings?

They do not require it; there is no resistance there. There is no inner conflict there, or external conflict for that matter, so they do not need it. We don't offer our services when they are not needed.

How did you happen to hear about Earth? What was the impetus to come here?

There was an emissary, but not, as you might say, an angelic emissary. There was something like a diplomatic emissary who came on a ship and spoke to a great many of the water beings. After they did that, they came over on the land and spoke to us—not me personally, but my forebears—and told us about what was being planned for human life on Earth. They asked if we would consider, some of us, volunteering for a time there, and told us that we wouldn't have to stay any time past when we felt we wanted to come back to the home planet. With that level of guarantee, quite a few volunteered.

Do you have any idea how long ago that was?

I do not. But to this day, palms have that situation. If they wish to go to the home planet, then from the human perspective, the tree dies and then the palm returns to home, since that is the method on Earth.

So how long were you incarnated when you were here?

I do not know your time. It seemed like a long time.

Were you incarnated in the same tree or in a series of trees?

In the same tree, but as I say, the island was a calm place. I recall a storm, but it just glanced off the island—very strong wind and a lot of rain! We all got a good washing, but it wasn't too bad.

Humans Are Resistant to Forgetting Who They Are

What is your sense of what humans are resistant to? Is it just a general, "I don't want to go there," or are there particular things that they're resisting?

I think that's a very good question, and the answer again is much more simple than you would guess. I feel the core reason for the resistance, aside from the other things I've mentioned, is that once the soul starts to move toward the Earth and feels its knowledge of itself slipping away and becoming isolated from complete awareness, immediately there is a desire to put on the brakes, so to speak, and say, "Wait, wait, I don't want to give that up." I feel what happens is that the soul that's going to become the human being discusses these matters with the teacher. The teacher might say, "Well, you're going to have to forget who you are while you're there." "And how long will I be there?" says the innocent soul. The teacher says, "You know, fifty years, seventy-five years, a hundred years." "Oh, that's nothing."

From that position of knowledge and wisdom, it would seem like just a little drop of time, but as you start to move toward the planet and your knowledge and wisdom of yourself and who you are and who you've been and what everything else is falls away, you immediately are upset and often there's a *huge* resistance. At that point, many souls say, "No, no!" And they immediately retrace their steps—and they have to retrace them exactly—and go back to their teachers, and that's the end! They don't come.

I would say from my little bit of experience on Earth at that time, which I think was . . . all I can say is that you were not on the planet then. Considering how many human souls were coming on that journey to actually arrive in mother . . . somewhere between 93 and 98 percent didn't come. They got to that point where they hit that sense of resistance because they had to forget who they were, and they went right back and that was that.

I understand completely. It's one thing—it's forgetting who you are.

Think about it! I have been around humans talking (I believe they were adults), and it didn't take long for someone to say, "What's it all about? Why are we here? What are we doing?"—in their language, I don't think it was English. It didn't take long: a few minutes, something like that. I can't be certain, but it seemed like they were walking by, and it came up. So I believe this is a critical factor and one of the most difficult things human beings have to struggle through while you're here.

Of course, the moment you pass beyond your physical life and go through at least the first or second veil, you remember who you are, and there's relief and all of that, but there are often good memories too, I feel. Most lives do not only have suffering. Most lives have happiness, joy, good memories, love, discovery, smells, flavors—things you hadn't experienced before. This planet is entirely about discovery, because since you do forget who you are when you're here, you have this massive joy of discovery. You have seen children awed by a flower or a caterpillar, yes?

So how do you approach these souls who don't want to lose the sense of who they are?

We don't. Because there are so many, we usually wait to see who's going to come farther. When they have made that commitment and come farther—

because there's that huge percentage who don't come and we feel there's no point in campaigning, if I can use that term—perhaps even come into mother, we then feel totally supported to engage in our process with them, because they've already said, "Okay, I'm thinking about it." So generally speaking, we don't contact the souls unless they have already gone into mother and are beginning to experience growing in there as a baby. Then if they get resistant because of experiences or things mother is exposed to and they're not sure they want to be that—mother might get frightened or upset by something, under stress and so on, and this is real—then they consider.

There Are No Longer More Souls
Who Want to Come Here than Can Be Accommodated

I had no idea so many beings turned away. And yet there are still more who want to come here than can be accommodated, right?

No, I wouldn't say that was the case now. I believe it might have been the case in the past, but I would say from my experience, even when I was on the planet, no. I feel that I could be mistaken, but from my experience . . . well, if you counted the ones who wanted to come but turned around and went back— the 93 to 98 percent—you could say that, yes. But if you don't count them— these are souls that never came close to entering mother, becoming a baby and all of that—then I'd have to say no.

Well, humanity is going to reduce its population, so there will be less need for a lot of new souls, right? I mean, there will still be many, many births, but we're trying to cut the population down. There needs to be fewer people on Earth, for the good of the planet and the people both.

I feel that human planetary organization is not in place yet for that to happen in a loving way. The simple way, of course, is for people to be together and love each other and not have offspring for a time or to minimize offspring—say, one instead of two—but this is something that has not taken place yet, and it's going to take awhile for people to want to give up the great joy of having children, although it's not always a joy for the mothers. I don't know why there is the suffering of birth. It's not that way for plants. I've seen the suffering of animals giving birth too. I don't understand that. Why is that? I do not know.

I sure don't know. It's not a question anyone has ever answered. That's the way humans were designed, but I don't know why.

I believe there have been answers. I believe it would be a good thing for you to ask beings from time to time, especially perhaps beings other than plants.

Earth's Personality Is Marvelous

What is your life span on your home planet?

Oh, thousands of years.

Why are you on a version of Earth now? There's no one there who needs to be nurtured, is there?

No, but there are a few palms on that version of Earth, and there I am. So I'm not alone. It's pleasant. I can see where it would be a place most Earth people would enjoy, but there are not that many human beings by comparison. I couldn't say how many, but there are not that many.

Did you choose to go there or did you just find yourself there? What was that like?

It was an option. I could go to the home planet, or I could stop off for a life on this version of Earth, and I decided to stop off so that I could enjoy Earth, because Earth's personality is really exquisite. She has so many wonderful energies and pulses, it's hard to describe. I'm drawing in the air a sort of waveform. She has these wonderful highs and spirited lows—the lows not being bad, just meaning like a musical tonality. In short, her personality is so marvelous. I wanted to experience it without her having to struggle through the complications of her human Earth experience, you understand.

Are the humans there from our level of Earth or are they other versions of humans who have not been to Earth?

From my understanding, they are all humans who have been to the planet upon which you live, and they live quite an idyllic life in very pleasant surroundings. I believe it's perhaps a restful place for them, a place to go and live a very pleasant human life on Earth, but everything is pleasant and loving and friendly and nurturing. It's a good thing.

The Wind Is the Great Communicator on Earth

I don't know if you say anything to them or provide love, but those human souls, those souls who are going to become human, when they advance far enough for you to feel that they might stay, how do you interact with them? Do you talk to them?

It's like singing. A soul at that level does not really . . . language is too slow for them. The communication needs to be motion or energetic, and I consider it a form of song, even though it is not a verbal thing, but there is a degree of tonality. Imagine tonality, if you would, without sound. You can imagine it when you consider the vibrations that the instrument itself causes in the air around it.

And so it is like that. There are certain vibrations that human beings feel relaxed and comforted by. Equally, there are certain vibrations that human beings might feel agitated by.

If the soul is being agitated by some vibration, we attempt to provide a soothing vibration to counterbalance it, and the souls can feel that this is coming from a form of life directly associated with Earth. You see, that's the key. It's not coming from one of their guides or teachers beyond Earth; it's coming from Earth beings, from their point of view. The soul does not consider a palm to be some other thing. Human beings are raised to not have respect for plants or animals sometimes, but the soul has complete respect and considers all souls to be completely equal. So at that time of their existence, they experience that as an Earth being they didn't know who is welcoming them, nurturing them, loving them, and they take that into account when being exposed to discomforting energies. They are aware that there are those they don't know and have never met, may never meet, but they don't think that way, and it's encouraging for them and they know it.

You mentioned that the fronds of palm trees move with the wind. Do you interact with the wind in some way to interact with humans?

The wind is the great communicator on Earth. If something is happening on Earth that you need to know about physically, it is the wind that stimulates your instinct. Even if you are in a building, sometimes you know how the wind is trying to get in—this is usually the wind trying to say something or needing to go through the building and out the other side to get the message to somebody else. So the wind has everything to do with cuing your physical instinct. So, yes, we interact with the wind.

Would you say the wind is a being or an energy? How would you describe that?

I would describe it as a portion of Mother Earth's physical personality—another one of her amazing levels of being. Of course, there is wind on other planets. Even on the version of Earth I'm on, there are breezes—not wind as you would know it, but there are certainly breezes. I believe those breezes function the same way. But, of course, where I am there is no conflict or struggle.

Right, and no resistance. There are, I think, hundreds of species of palm. So you all look different, but all of you can do this? All of you have this ability?

I cannot say for everyone, but my understanding is that all palms with fronds can do that. If there are some that have been changed or transformed by human beings that don't have fronds, I couldn't say that.

For Those Who Are Depressed—Dance with Palms

Do you have a memory before your life on the home planet?

No. May I say something, volunteer something?

Yes.

I would like to make a suggestion for people if they are depressed or if they're concerned about others who are depressed—or not just depressed, but maybe feeling the need to be reminded of the value of life. I would recommend that you dance with the palms. If you look at children sometimes, you will often see them moving their arms above their heads in a sort of, to me, plantlike way. I feel that if people can move their arms gracefully above their heads or at least above their shoulders and just move them in the breezes or even indoors, it tends to create a sense of welcoming the physical and expressing the physical in yourself, and this can be uplifting, encouraging, and welcoming in its own right.

I would say most human beings might consider this a form of dance, but it is a way to feel life as a valuable thing. For people who are depressed or sad, it's good to have palms around and to stand near them. If you have an indoor palm, then go over to the palm. Don't touch it, but stand within, say, three feet of it and just look at it, and while you're looking, breathe in and out. After a few minutes, you might feel better.

That's wonderful! Thank you.

It's good to get such information from all the plants you talk to, because they may not volunteer it on their own. I felt strongly that I wanted to put that in, in case it was forgotten.

The Service Alone Is a Joy

We have palm trees with coconuts—is that something you have at home?

We do not have that at home and it does not even exist where I am now on that version of Earth. I believe it exists on the Earth you are on, because it is often the case that some factor of life provides life for others, something that either passes through your body that you discard, or something that may be involved in something that others might live on. This seems to be something that Creator is fond of: What is cast off by one is consumed by another. So I believe that is why coconuts exist—not to be cast off by the trees, but at some point they fall, don't they?

And other beings eat them, yes.

Yes, and usually in a welcoming way.

Yes, they're wonderful.

It is very important to welcome nature's gifts like that and be thankful, not only to the deity, but thankful as if the palm had reached down and said, "Here, eat."

You have so much to offer to humans. What do you feel that you receive?

Just the service alone is a joy, and I feel that much of life is about that for all species. When you are not on this planet, you are totally engaged in service and get pleasure from that, and many human beings I have observed on Earth now get great pleasure from being of service in some way. This is natural, and it is a part of life and universal as far as I know.

What about your interactions with other trees and with the animals and plants and insects who move around? Was that interesting for you?

I found it to be particularly interesting when birds would land in a tree, and I also liked very much, since it was an island and close to the water, when water beings would come up close to the beach and sometimes right on it in order to have their young and foster them. I found that very pleasant. But birds are something that was new to me, and I enjoyed the birds, because they would land and would be very prepared to engage in conversation, so to speak. There were also other little beings who would crawl up the trunk and look for a place to hide. That kind of physical contact I generally found to be very pleasant. Other than that, that was it. But I don't have much to offer, because I feel that the primary factor about the nurturance of the human was the most important thing to say.

So you're there on an island—would you feel this resistance from a soul coming in once a day, or every hour? Did this happen an awful lot?

I'm not very good with time, and remember, I did not have to do this for every child on Earth. There were thousands and thousands and thousands of other palms who were engaged in the process too. It didn't happen very often for me, but it happened, and I was aware that other palms were engaged in it as well. So we don't all engage with individuals—we each engage with individuals, meaning . . .

It's a one-on-one thing.

Yes. I will have to sign off now, and I have something to say.

Please.

I'd like to encourage you to be gentle with mothers. I feel in your time there's a tendency to want, not only on mother's part, to be engaged in life and do what mother needs to do or wants to do, but I feel that some kindnesses that have been offered in the past to mothers-to-be are not so present in your society now. Don't scare them! Don't, if you would, put pressure on them to do this or that. Remember, it is not only a tender time for mother, it is also that mother is carrying a very tender and vulnerable being within her. Have respect for these beings before, during, and after birth, and in time, your human race will feel more at ease with life and comforted by life. Good night!

Thank you very much. Good life!

Good life!

GRASSES

CHAPTER SEVENTEEN

Oat Grass

DECEMBER 30, 2007

&

There is a considerable amount of communion underground. By "communion," I mean communication that does not require explanation rather than the worded communication that human beings do. It is even busier, in terms of communion between plant roots and the little beings who live underground than, I would say, your society is at the surface. Your society has a great deal of coming and going as well as talking communication, but the difference between what I would call human talking communication and communion is that there are no misunderstandings in communion. I am hopeful, as well as are the other plant beings—and other species of animals for that matter—that human beings will, in time, learn who we are, not from dissecting us or pulling us up and classifying us into groups, but by establishing heartfelt communication like this that allows human beings to discover their own forms of communion. So misunderstandings, which are so prevalent in your culture, can gradually fade away.

We Experience More Dream Life than Physical Life in Colder Months

The one thing that truly disturbs our communion is when human beings dig in the ground for the purpose of construction. Other than that, our communion is ongoing. While this goes on with roots, it tends to emanate up into the rest of the plant—whether it be a stalk of grass (as you refer to oat grass) or the tallest tree, it makes no difference. What goes on underground allows us to celebrate our existence aboveground. Below ground we have a little more security, a little more calmness, and a certain amount of what I would call perpetual existence, because even though human beings seem fond of cutting plants, such as your yard grass—and that is uncomfortable, to say the least, for such grasses—still, what goes on beneath the ground in the roots is more of a constant.

That is wonderful! I don't think anyone has ever said that before. Do you know where you are on the planet?

All I can say is that I am in a warm, sunny place at this time. What's implicated in your question, I would like to answer, because you might reasonably ask, "Well, how do you get along during winter months?" We usually go dormant. Dormant is something classified, I believe, by your sciences; you can look it up, but in my use of the expression, it means what I would call a deep sleep. It is not unlike hibernation, where one goes into a deep state in which one can experience dreams, but when human beings have dreams, you wake up and you remember bits and pieces. This is different. The dream life in the hibernated state is something that is a constant. One thread leads to another thread, and there is no loss.

I have experienced this personally, so I will try to put it in terms that your people can understand. It's almost like another life. We have a greater sense of personal connection to others of our own species, but also to similar species, so even with species that happen to be growing nearby, we might dream together. It is not at all unusual to make connections with the home planet also. In my case, I have done this, and if that is the case for different types of plant life that are hibernating during the snow season, then it is like—how can we say?—a homecoming. In places where there is, say, a great deal of winter, and even some spring, we grow there and then we have our Earth lives, but during the winter months we have our other lives. Sometimes, depending on the type of weather and the length of the seasons, one might even find oneself having considerably more dream life than one might have physical life.

I'm so glad. I didn't know that. That is true for every plant on the planet?

Well, according to what I understand, other plants that you talk to may have a different point of view, since they are speaking from a personal sense. But I'm speaking from what I've been able to gather on the basis of communion with other plants. Granted, I have not communed with them all.

Connecting with the Night Is Like Sharing the Same Dream

There's something else. You said [previously, during a recording malfunction] that on your home planet, there was too much light, and you were able to come here and send the nurturing of the dark home to them. Why don't your people move to some other place where there is darkness?

Well, you have to keep in mind that even our forms on other planets have a certain stability associated with them, and I'm not saying that in a psychological sense. I am saying it in a physical sense. That is why we were fairly comfortable coming here—due to the stable nature of existence. Therefore, moving is not really something we would like to do. Now, I want to give you an analogy, especially for those of you who are gardeners. You know that when you try to move a mature plant to another location, it doesn't always work out very well. This is because any plant, not unlike other forms of life, will establish a certain degree of communion, not only above ground with other plant beings and often animals, but below ground even more so. No matter how careful you are in transferring that plant, the root ball always gets interrupted in some way. You don't, in other words, get all the root. Some of it is left.

This might seem to be a minor thing when you're transferring a plant, because you don't really connect with us physically in the same way you might connect with, say, a loved one or friend. But I don't have to tell you that if somebody asked you to move and asked you to leave a couple of fingers behind, you would object. I am not trying to make light of this; I am just saying that the idea of moving to another planet would not be appealing, because in our natures, we appreciate stability physically. Therefore what we are probably going to do in time, when we make more friends on an interstellar basis, is to ask some of them to set up something by which we can have a temporary night. My feeling is that could work—and I am going to put this into your terms so that it makes sense. You might be able to create a temporary night by having a dark-walled tent or closing your draperies over a window, yes?
Yes.

It might be possible by some kind of mechanical means to give us at least temporary moments of complete darkness, but the trouble with being inside a structure like that is that one doesn't experience the true nature of nighttime here, where you have the Moon and the stars and the fresh air and the wind blowing. In short, it's not the same, so I really don't know how they're going to resolve it. But what we do when we share the night with beings on our home planet is that we fully engage with the night. You can experience this yourself. For example, a human being could fully engage with the night when camping out somewhere or driving out into the countryside where there is little or no distraction. Or if you live in the country, you might simply walk out into a backyard or field behind your home and just stand there quietly, breathing in and out, looking up at the stars and down at the ground. Think of nothing; just notice your surroundings.

This is connecting with the night. When we do that, we also connect with those who are on our home planet. They draw the experience to them as best they can. They don't take our energy, but they draw the experience to them. The closest analogy I can come up with here for you to understand would be that it is as if two human beings shared the same dream. This happens at times, I think, in your culture. Sometimes it happens with people who are close to each other. Sometimes it just happens with friends. You dream something and your friend dreams something similar during the same night, and then you are both wowed by that.

Even the Experience of Shade Provides Variety in Earth Experiences

Are you on other planets doing the same thing, experiencing the night? Are you on more than one planet besides your home planet?

No. I am not on the home planet.

I know. What I mean to ask is, is your species only on Earth and the home planet?

Oh, I see. Yes, only on Earth and the home planet. Yes. As I said, we appreciate stability, so we're not inclined to wander.

If you made interstellar friends, couldn't they possibly take some seeds and sort of start you someplace else?

I know that makes sense to you as a human being, but let me put it another way. If you had children, could you imagine sending your children off to another planet? All seeds are just like children—exactly like that—producing the same feelings of love and family. It's no different for us than it is with you. We wouldn't like that.

Well, this is going to be an interesting book.

Well, they're all that way, aren't they? They're intended to illuminate and enlighten, which is why I believe you get volunteers, such as myself, because the whole point of your books, near as I can tell, is to open—as one might open the covers of a book, yes?—the awareness to see beyond what has been taught, even beyond what has recently been discovered, and on to what can be known.

Yes, and I appreciate your contribution. So you don't have trees on your home planet, but you do have trees in the area you're in now?

Yes, I do. I'm very fond of them. I have one friend who is a very large tree—well, very large from my perspective. From time to time, depending on the time of day, there is shade. Of course, such a thing doesn't exist on my planet, so when I have communication of a sort—a communion—with those on the home planet, they understand it as a form of night. But of course, I understand it as something different. It is, however, a cooler time, and one appreciates, if I might refer to myself that way, the variety of experiences on this planet. For us, you understand—stable beings who do not move much, except because of the wind or other influences—to have things change around us without our really doing much to bring that about is quite startling, and to have shade is quite amazing. I have discussed this with my tree friend quite a bit, and my tree friend says that they often get such feedback, if I might use that word, in the form of communion with other plant species and animals who appreciate the shade. My tree friend often experiences animals who come on a warm day to appreciate the shade, and Tree is very happy to provide that.

Communing Is Like Listening to a Chorus, Not Individual Beings

Do you have water on your home planet?

Yes, of course. We couldn't exist without that.

I mean oceans or lakes, rivers or seas?

Oh, I see. No. I have heard that there are ponds, so I would say that ponds come about, on our home planet, from underground water. Mostly the water is underground.

You reach it with your roots?

Yes, the roots are very deep because the water is, if I might use your measurements, about thirty to thirty-six inches below ground most of the time. But there are places where there are ponds, what you might even call sort of a wetlands, but no rivers, lakes, or oceans. I have heard of that. I have not experienced it myself, but I have heard of it. It sounds amazing.

Okay, so where you are there is just flat land?

Yes.

What about mountains?

It's flat land, but there are mountains in the distance.

I'm sorry—on your home planet? Or where you are now?

Where I am now.

Ah! Okay. But on your home planet, it's just flat?

Yes.

So can you also talk to the mountains here?

I haven't had call to do that, but in the larger sense, when you consider that material of Earth goes up to become a mountain and comes down as the mountain wears down, my communion with the soil around me has revealed that some had been on a mountain before. So yes, I feel like I am able to communicate with the mountain by communicating with that which once was a portion of same.

Soil and mountains have minerals in them. Do you actually perceive the minerals themselves or are they broken down and part of the soil?

I don't really commune. We don't have individuality in the way the human race experiences itself at this time. I commune with the soil all around me, and it would be . . . imagine for a moment listening to a chorus of people singing and from time to time solos emerge. I have heard these things like solos, but other than that, it is usually a chorus. It's not like individuals. It's not like I talk to a grain of sand and then I talk to a grain of something else. We don't experience individuality in that way.

I Use Perceptions and Awareness to "See"

That's very clear. So what are your greatest joys? Being, yes? [Laughs.]

Being, yes, experiencing the phenomena of rain and lightning and the beauties of Earth. There are a great many beauties. I really feel that Earth in its natural state, with some people, of course, is a fabulously beautiful place. I recognize that all human beings are also beautiful, wonderful beings, but there's so many of them now, it's a little difficult. But I feel Earth is an exceptional place, just from the little I've heard in communion with other species. I once had an opportunity for such communion with a deer—that's when I found out about all these places of water. The deer was resting under the tree, and it was a great joy to hear about all the places where the deer had gone, what it had seen, and what it had done. I don't often get that chance because during the heat of the day, the shade is usually on the other side of the tree. So animals like deer and others who might be experiencing a little cooling time are not near me. But in this case there were a lot of deer, and this one deer just happened to be over by me in the sunlight. I don't know why, but I was happy for the visit, and that's when I found out about water and rivers, and it was amazing.

Have you seen people?

I have. I saw two people. Well, I don't see with eyes, but I have perceptions. It would be not unlike an awareness, technical, in which you are aware of forms and shapes and can sense to know whether one is safe or not. But these people were at a distance. I think they were hiking. There is a hiking trail a ways off, and occasionally I hear sounds and I'm aware of human beings coming and going. But one time they were a little off the trail, and I observed them carrying something on their backs. Perhaps they were camping—a male and a female. But they didn't stop, and even if they had, I don't know that they would know how to commune. But it could happen someday.

My Awareness Goes beyond This Energy of Being
Okay. Are you the energy of one stalk, or the energy of the whole plant?

I am, as a being, one stalk.

But your awareness continues here? When that stalk dies or gets too old, you come up in another one, or what?

No. When that stalk dies, that's it. I'm gone.

You're gone back to the home planet?

That's right. A plant can have many stalks, but the single blade of grass in your yard, even if it is united with a root system . . . once it dies, off it goes. It's someplace else. It'll be the same for me. I'm here for a while and then gone. I have a certain amount of awareness of the past based on the roots—not only my own roots, but also associated with those around me, communion and so on. This is how I'm able to speak with a little bit more expertise than I have personally, based on communion with other forms of life. Of course, I do have my own perceptions and don't know a great deal about your people. I don't know what you look like. I just have an impression.

Do people come to your planet, humanoid people?

Yes. The first ones were not aware that we, as plant beings essentially, were forms of life on the planet, and they just landed on us, and we didn't like that. We have a certain way to make such vehicles feel unwelcome. So they landed and then the ship immediately rose up when they realized what they had done, but of course, by then the damage was done because the vehicles are quite heavy. That was a sad time, but those beings have felt uncomfortable about that ever since, and they've tried to help us a lot. Very often they are able to help us. Sometimes we just make it clear that we forgive them. Generally speaking, though, when beings come in ships, they hover. They try, now that they know who we are, to hover over areas where we are not growing—because we're not growing everywhere. There are areas where one can hover over sand or rock or dirt or stone or something like that.

But your personal perception is that when your stalk dies, you go back to your home planet. So is there a constant? Is there a chance for every being on the home planet who exists here and then goes back to come back more than once? How does that work?

I don't really know how that works. My impression is that the connection with the home planet has more to do with the root ball, so I don't intend to come back, because I like the calm of the home planet. On the other hand, I will miss a lot of the variety here, such as the night. I like that very much.

Well, maybe the next time you come back, you will be in a place where there is more activity.

No, I'm not planning to come back.

You have that choice?

Of course! So do you.

But on your level, it's conscious.

On your level, it's conscious. We just look at it differently than you do. You consider your conscious level to be occurring exclusively when you are awake. We consider your conscious level to be both when you are awake and asleep, and at the sleep level, you're in agreement with being here on the planet. You're just not conscious of that. You don't remember that when you wake up, but at the sleep level, you know you're here and you know why—and you're in agreement with it. My friend the deer taught me that. The deer had spent a lot of time near humans. Many deer have—not necessarily by choice. Apparently, you're moving out into their territory or what they consider to be their territory. Everyone has to live somewhere.

Yes, I know there are a lot of us. What am I not asking you that you'd like to share?

Oh, I don't know. I am not going to take up the whole book. You have plenty of opportunities to talk to other plants. I don't know if you will speak to beings on Earth exclusively, but there might be a lot of possibilities there. Can you imagine speaking to a tree that's been around human beings for 1,000 years? I mean, what an amazing thing.

We Were Offered a Part in the Human Experience to Provide Variety

Yes, I am definitely looking forward to that. Where are you in your life cycle? How long have you been here? How does that work?

Think about it. If there's winter, the stalks on the surface all die. So I've just been here for a short time, because winter will come.

You're in a place that has four seasons. Do you get to choose where you go to live on Earth?

No, we just choose to come to this planet. You don't choose where on the planet. And really, for a lot of astronauts it's very similar, I think. You might go to the Moon and say, "Gee, I'd love to be on the other side of the Moon. But then someone says, "Well, this is the best place." Then you say, "Okay, it's the Moon." It's like that here. One is reasonably happy, unless one is growing between the blocks of a sidewalk—I would not care for that.

The seeds fall where they fall, and you incarnate wherever there is an opportunity to be?

The planet herself has a means to distribute seeds, whether by wind or water or other means. There are other means, and that's how we are here.

At what point do you emerge in consciousness?

Well, from my point of view, you're not speaking to the root. You're speaking to a stalk. It might be completely different for the root, but I become aware of my personal consciousness when there is green above the surface.

How does it work at your home? Is it like volunteers or it's a project that everybody contributes to? How did it start? Did the Creator come and say, "I have an opportunity for you?"

We had a visit from someone who was an emissary who told us that there was a project on your planet. They mentioned the name. And the whole point of the project, they said, was to offer the maximum amount of variety available so that the human beings on the surface would have the ultimate hope that some form of communication, and thence communion, could take place so that they could find their way home. "Would you like to be a part of this project?" Like that.

What did they call the name of the planet?

I'll see if I can get that. Edden.

Ah! Eden.

No. Edden

Thank you. The Garden of Edden.

Well, they didn't call it a garden. They just said the planet Edden.

Earth Used to Receive Visitors from the Stars Who Shared Their Capabilities

It's interesting that the purpose of the variety of beings on the planet was for humans, so that we would commune with them and learn more about a greater reality.

I believe that's why all forms of life are here—and some of you do make that effort, usually with animals. But I have heard that a lot of people have gardens, and that's why I've spoken a little bit to gardeners. People also like to go out into the forests to be around native plants and so on. So there is some reaching out, and I've noticed some love for plant species, but still there is a tendency due to your consumer aspects to look at plant species as things to be consumed in some way. Until you have alternatives for shelter and alternatives for some foods . . . of course, one grows the foods one needs to eat, yes, but sometimes food is gathered in the wilderness that may be meant for others—animals usually. Until you begin to look at trees as something other than that which you might use to build homes or make products out of, it will be awhile yet before everyone begins to make the effort to communicate with plant life.

I believe you will get this in time from visitors from the stars. They do have the means to create shelters and comfortable places to live—and nice ones at that; places where you'd want to be—without affecting trees and forests, and generally without affecting any plants. But this will happen when it happens. I don't know. It has happened in the past on your planet. I've heard this from other species, but for some reason right now it's not occurring. Perhaps it will occur again someday, and then you'll be able to live more comfortably. It's totally unusual that a planet is cut off from that. I remember speaking to my elders here on the planet, those who have kept a certain body of knowledge in circulation from the past. I have been told that in the not-too-distant past there were visitors from the stars frequently. But at some point, they stopped sharing their capabilities with the people of Earth. I'm not sure why.

Is what you've learned about life on Earth from your elders and from others communicated to those on your home planet?

I don't know. I can only speak about what I know. I don't know what the elders have done in terms of communicating to the home planet.

So you're in a place on the Earth where you don't feel discomfort from humans and war and violence?

No. I'm glad about that. Although when those two humans passed, I didn't get that impression of feelings from the humans at all. They seemed quite cheerful. When I hear humans moving on the trail, they all seem quite cheerful too. Perhaps it's because they're in a more natural setting, and human beings in a more natural setting feel more at ease with themselves. I don't know for certain.

Meditating near Oat Grass Can Help You Sleep Better

When this book was started, it was said that every plant had a therapeutic value for humans. Is there something therapeutic in your energy?

Well, I think so. If you were a person who had difficulty sleeping and were able to sit—without squashing other plants, please—behind many stalks of oat grass (flowering would be best, but it will still work without flowering) . . . try to sit down at the level where the plants are growing. You might have to lie on a blanket or something similar. And then someone who could meditate or clear her consciousness and physical self could sit in the sunlight and take in several breaths as if she were breathing the sunshine into the top of her head. Then, closing her eyes, she could blow at the oat grass and at the person beyond, and then that person, if he or she were someone who had trouble sleeping, might have less trouble sleeping in the future.

That would take two people. One person couldn't do it for oneself?

Correct. You would need someone to help you. Working in concert with others is a theme of this planet. Now I will make a closing remark.

Okay.

As I just mentioned, working in concert with others on this planet is something that is absolutely thematic to all forms of life here, including your own. After all, none of you would be on the planet if your mothers and fathers hadn't come together in concert to produce you. So I feel it would be good for you to consider, as you look around at the natural forms of life, how no form of life on this planet came about as the result of a singular activity. It was always plural. Keep that in mind as you go through life, and remember, if you need help or if you have help to offer, think in a plural fashion. In this way, you won't ever be very lonely. Good night.

Thank you very much. Good life.

CHAPTER EIGHTEEN

Wetland Grasses

JANUARY 2, 2008

&

GREETINGS!

Greetings!

It will take a moment to prepare a word of identity. I do not have all your words of identity, but our type of being grows in wetlands and is a form of grass, a tall grass. I do not have your words, though. I'm sorry.

Tell me something about yourself and your experience here on Earth.

We—speaking for my species—are in fairly constant motion. We are exposed to water, wind, and the movements of other beings through the water, which causes us to be in motion. This is not always the case for plants, but it is the motion and the water that we find most appealing. It is not typical on other planets, from our perusal of such, to find water, wind, and contact as a moment-to-moment experience. One might find one or two of those factors but not usually all of them. On Earth, this is a possibility. Of course there are other places that have those things, but it is not typical. Those are the qualities of our personalities that we find to be most desirable in order for us to express our true natures. You could not see this, but at the beginning when I was first present, the channel was moving in something like a dance, because we find that this

265

motion comes closest to representing our personalities and tends to radiate our energies not only on a personal basis but on a basis to bring about the greatest good for all beings.

On My Home Planet, I Am a Life Form More Akin to Sea Life

So are all of your roots covered in water? Are part of your blades of grass covered in water?

The roots are usually covered in water, except when there's a drought, and then it is a struggle to survive. But generally speaking, only the fronds of this large grass—that is what they're called, I believe, but there's a name you have; I do not know that—the broad leaves of the grass are what come above the surface of the waters. Generally speaking, the roots are below the liquid.

Do you have four seasons, or is it the same temperature all the time?

I do not know if it's the same temperature all the time, but it doesn't get frozen, or become ice. That's not a factor. We are in a place that is warm and moist for the most part. Sometimes it cools off a bit, but it never becomes intolerant of our survival.

How long have you been here on Earth?

From the root source, meaning tracing back the familial history, many years. As a personal individual—though that's not really something we consider part of our makeup—just a few years.

Can you tell me something about where you come from, your home planet?

The home planet is in what you call the Sirius star group. There, we are not exactly what you would classify as a plant. We are something more akin to sea life but have a tether to something more permanent. It's not a form of life I'm aware of you having on this planet, but it's the form we are there. There, we do not come to the surface of the water. We are strictly under the sea all the time. What's new for us is to be exposed to the air. That's new, and we felt that since we were still, in portion, below the water, it would be something safe to try.

Do you like it?

I do, but like all beings, I miss home, as home is much safer, is much more calm, and does not expose one to extremes.

All Life Forms Have a Radiant Energy about Them

Your planet is, well, not the most extreme, but there are elements of the extreme associated with it. One of those elements, which I feel is something everyone can identify with, is that your planet is a place where one might experience the unexpected, not only in forms that are pleasant but in forms that can be unpleasant. This is not typical of other planets.

How would that reflect itself in your life here—unexpected animals going by or unexpected fish or something?

Yes, or humans. Humans tend to be unconscious—not all, but there tends to be an unconsciousness about them insofar as the consequences of their presence. Most animals will gently take steps, moving gently through this part of existence where I am, unless they are in danger or there is something urgent about their lives. Then they might move swiftly, but even then, there's a tendency to be aware of the impact of one's existence on other forms of life. This is not the case so much with most human beings.

How is it that you see human beings? What are you close to? Do they come to fish or are they in boats?

We do not see. We do not have eyes. We have perceptions, and there's a tendency to be able to get the general form and the mass of any life form. Of course, all life forms have a radiant energy about them, so we can tell a human being from an elk, so to speak. It's obvious. Also, the human being has less awareness of his total existence, so that is something that is a quick identifier. This is not meant as a criticism. We realize that this planet in its current expression is largely a place for the souls who are expressing themselves as human beings to experiment toward a greater, more benevolent end. We take that into account when we consider being present among you.

What are these humans doing? Are they at the water's edge? Are they walking through? Are they going through on a boat? What kind of . . .

I don't know where they are, just that they are there. Not always, but from time to time. Sometimes there's a vessel. It could be a boat.

Did the Creator's emissary come to your people and ask you to do this as a service, to come here?

He came to our home planet many, many years ago and told us of the purpose of the experiment on Earth and advocated for its value. He asked if we would be interested in being present and contributing our energies to the overall expression of energies on the planet. After an overview and some time to consider, there was a general sense of a desire to participate.

What did you feel that you would gain from it?

No one makes that decision, if I may speak for all species who will occupy this planet. Other than humans, no one makes the decision based on what we would gain from it.

But as you're doing this service, are you . . . let me put it another way. Do you feel that you're gaining anything?

Well, I believe I mentioned that. It is interesting to experience an unusual sense of being, meaning below the water, while also being exposed above the water and largely outside of it, except when there is rain. Then one feels a bit more in familiar territory, so to speak, but it is something different. I don't think that I would, if I had the option, choose to experience this on a regular basis. It is something different, feeling the water and the air, but I prefer to be in the water and below the surface, as I am on the home planet. So when I am done here, I will, in my being, re-create myself on the home planet and say, well, that's something I did. But I wouldn't do it again! [Chuckles.]

There Is a Form of Sleep Plants Experience on Earth That They Do Not Experience on My Home Planet

Is the time there on your home planet similar to here so that two or three years here equals the same time that you're gone?

No, I think if it was a similar life cycle, that we wouldn't do it because on our home planet, we might have an experience of time—trying to calculate a comparison—that would be similar to 1,800 of your years or so. But on this planet, in terms of our life cycles, it might be four or five year, tops. If it were the same, I think there would be no volunteers.

Okay. I'm glad you told me that, but that's not what I meant. If you're here three and a half years, do you feel when you go back home that you've been gone an equal three and a half years of experience there?

No, there is something that is experienced here that is not on the home planet, and that is something you can identify with in part. There's a form of what I would call sleep that takes place roughly between (I'm going to give you a time) about 2:44AM and 3:58AM that does not take place on the home planet. There is not anything there called sleep, and there is also here on this planet an experience akin to dreams. Other plant species have this a great deal of their lives on Earth, but for us it is something entirely new. So that's another factor of our being here that is different.

So you're saying that as a being, you automatically sleep during that hour and fifteen minutes?

I'm just trying to give you a general idea of when the timing takes place. As a being, barring any danger that we must be alert to, yes, we sleep.

So like a human, do you find that you need contact with your home world to have the strength to make it through the next day here?

I haven't considered that, but it is a possibility.

I still haven't gotten my question straight. Is your perception of the three and a half years here equal to your perception of the same three and a half years on your home planet?

No. It's much longer on your planet.

That's what I thought.

There, time is not a factor of existence. I was just trying to give you a sense of comparison, sort of an equation, but it is not something that one considers as a part of the flow of life. So I would say that it is much longer here. On Earth, one experiences a moment-to-moment existence, especially for a form of life such as I am on this planet—one that cannot, essentially, get out of the way. Therefore one is in a heightened state of being alert most of the time, except when the opportunity presents itself to sleep. Perhaps some of you can identify with that.

There Is a Constant Stream of Communication Available among Us

On your home planet, how would you describe your daily life? Do you have families?

We have something that you would probably refer to as an extended family, and our family has largely been propagated from one small seed group. We do not live on the entirety of the planet. We live where there is water, though the water is not exactly the same composition that your water is here. I think that if your people were there, you would call it water, though it is perhaps slightly thicker than your water. But what was your question?

Your life and how you experience your life—your family life, your daily life.

Well, we don't have daily life, because you remember, we live underwater, and so we're not technically functioning with a calendar. Life is a constant, and there is not a sense of time as days and weeks and so on. I cannot identify with that term. It is all about family, but since everyone on the planet of our species *is* all family, then there's an interest in what everyone's doing. Imagine for a moment, if I can use an analogy from human life—one that I'm able to assimilate at this moment—a long table where everyone is sitting and enjoying a meal and a visit, and everyone is taking turns to say, "This is what I did today," or "This is what I saw today," like that.

But there's no today and no tomorrow and no yesterday. It is a constant. If beings have something interesting going on in their lives—or in any way, shape, or form—there is a contribution about that, if there's a desire to communicate. One does not have to hear these streams of communication, but one can be open to it. If you are open to it, then you may hear this or that stream, and if some streams may be similar, you might hear them as a sort of braided communication, where it is heard almost as a song that is in correspondence with other voices.

But that is not how it is on Earth. On Earth, there is a tendency for more singularity. I am less able to be aware of all the species communication of my own kind as expressed here on Earth because there is something here that does not exist on the home planet. And that is, on Earth there is danger. It's not always present, but it is present sometimes. Therefore one can be less open to communion—in the sense of communication with openness and total understanding—because of the element of danger. One must be ever alert. Moments of communion are more frequent when the danger levels are very low.

Any Form of Expression Has a Desire to Be as Much as It Can Be, Even Danger

You said you were propagated on that planet. Did you come from someplace else?

We believe, according to our understanding, that we did come from someplace else and were brought by some beings in a vehicle. Because those beings had the ability to communicate with all life forms, the original seed group had communicated its desire to live someplace that was benevolent, was safe, and would allow, you might say, an evolution of being—not like the theories of evolution on your own planet, but theories of life—for beings to evolve and become what they might. Perhaps that's not so different from your theories, but that is what was expressed. Because those beings could communicate and desired to help, they—apparently in their explorations of their part of the universe—found a planet in the Sirius star group and received permission from someone somewhere, and then dropped off the original seed group.

Do you have any sense of connection or communication with where you came from?

I think it might happen when I dream. Unlike human beings, though, I don't always remember my dreams. I'm aware of having done it, and there are impressions, feeling impressions, and yet only rarely are there what I might call pictures.

On the planet you are from in Sirius, are there many sentient beings?

There are species. I'm not aware of any other beings. There may be, but I'm not aware of them. The planet is not entirely water. There is land, but if there are species on the land, I'm not aware of them. I'm not aware of any others in the water.

So it's one great big family and there is no danger there.

No danger is typical for most planets. Earth has danger, apparently because it's an element that you are using in your education to speed up your assimilation of what you need to know for what you will be doing beyond this place. I feel it is excessive, and I'm sure you will agree. Perhaps if you had it to do over again, it wouldn't be so excessive.

Well, it seems to have gotten out of hand at some point or other. I don't think it was planned to be this bad.

I believe that it is inherent in danger to become extreme. You might say, in looking at it from a distance, that any form of expression has a desire to be as much as it can be, to express itself to the greatest degree that it is capable. So looking at it philosophically, which does require distance to do, you might say that it is natural that danger becomes much, much more, but it's natural, philosophically speaking, that anything, once it is in existence, wishes to become more. So looking back on it, if you had the opportunity—and perhaps you will—to use your discernment, you may attempt to resolve the impact of that original romance with the idea that danger could be something fun. I'm sure you have reconsidered.

That's a great perspective on that. What dangers do you perceive where you are now—dangers to you?

Mostly it has to do with life forms that might step on us. We do not do well when we've been stepped on.

Stepped on? So how tall are you?

You mean, how much do we emerge above the surface of the water? Perhaps my portion might be eighteen inches.

I thought that you were big six-foot-tall grasses. Okay. So humans walk through you or on you. What other kinds of animals walk through who might step on you?

I'm not certain, but I'm aware of humans, because they are so distinctly different from other forms.

The Motion Created by the Wind Expands My Joy of Being

Do you know the species of the animals? I mean, are there fish? What would be there? Manatees, crocodiles, anything like that?

I don't really know. There are some below the surface in the water. Sometimes they exit the water. I suppose they would be referred to as amphibians. I was thinking of frogs. Frogs are an interesting species, being what one might consider a fish and then becoming something of water and air or land, you might say.

So there's danger, and it's different being here on Earth. Is there anything that you really enjoy, beyond being in the water and the air?

I enjoy having a slight breeze and some moisture, maybe rain or dew, and just moving in the wind. It is like a dance that I find most expressive, one that allows my natural energy to encompass a greater area. If you are exuding energy—as everyone does—and the conditions are ideal, one might feel a great joy in living, and thus the wind causing motion in one's physical self expands this sphere of joy when one moves this way and that, so one becomes surrounded with one's own personal joy of existence. I find that very enjoyable.

Are there any trees near you—big, tall trees?

I wouldn't call them that. No.

Are there what we call mangroves, which are like bushes that are all connected underground but look like small trees?

I do not know. You have to be aware of the fact that above the water I am only about eighteen inches, plus there's a certain amount of droop from the grass. So it's not just eighteen inches straight up. I really don't know what's more than a few feet away from me.

Okay. I was just trying to figure out where you are on the planet. Do you communicate with the frogs and the fish, or with any of the other beings swimming by?

If they have something they want to share, they will communicate the way they know how, and I will absorb it the way I know how. So there's a communication of sorts. It may not be conversational, as you would understand it, but it is a communication of sorts, which goes on, as far as I can tell, with all species here. Though with human beings, that communication is more noticeable when they are very young and not yet particularly mobile, and also when they are very old. This also can take place with humans beings when they are what is called "daydreaming" or in deep-sleep dreaming.

Animals Passing By Can Convey Messages of Warning

You said the animals swimming by share with you. Can you in turn share with them? Is it interactive ?

Only if they ask. If they are passing something on that they found to be of value and felt that they wished to share, it wouldn't be an individual thing. They would be moving along, perhaps, and sharing that, and I'm able to absorb what I'm able to absorb. I will give you an example. Once a being went by and indicated that the water level might increase for a short time and then hurried on.

And soon the water increased in level by about six or eight inches for a few days. Apparently there was a great deal of rain someplace that migrated to where I was in existence, and I did appreciate knowing that it might happen, so it took away the unexpected danger aspect, and it was like "oh" rather than, you know . . .

"Oh my God!" [Laughs.]

Yes.

Yes, because six or eight inches would leave just a tiny bit of you above the water.

Yes, and even considering the droop of some of my stalks, the top part was actually immersed for a time. But I was able to prepare myself thanks to the visitor who happened by and generously informed me and others of what might be coming.

Does it harm you in any way to be totally submerged?

I wasn't totally submerged, but I was more submerged than usual. I can maintain that for perhaps a few days if there aren't other factors—and there weren't. It was just that the water level went up, but there wasn't any kind of cascading effect or objects in the water hurtling along—nothing like that. So I was able to maintain, especially having had that warning. The warning was sufficient, so preparation was possible.

But it would be a danger to you, then, if you were totally submerged?

Yes, because the way I am now on this planet, in the expression of myself here, I'm not capable of survival underwater for a considerable length of time. I am having to function as plant life, with photosynthesis and all that.

Ah, you need to have the Sun shining on you for a certain amount of time.

On Our Planet, We Stay Tethered to Source

Do you get a chance to communicate with your family on the home planet during your dream state or not?

It's possible. I hadn't considered that before you asked the question. It's possible, because after dreams, I usually feel refreshed. I'm not convinced that it is entirely because of sleep, so I'm feeling that the dream has something to do with the feeling of being refreshed.

There is a sense of day and night and intervals of time here on this planet because the Sun goes down, and you are aware of it. Do you have that experience on your home planet?

Well, as you say, when the Sun goes down, we are aware of it, even as it is going down. Equally, when it emerges the following day, we are aware of that emergence, whereas on the home planet, there is no sense of that. The light level there is a constant.

Does that mean the Sun doesn't go down or you're down so deep you don't see the difference?

I'm not certain. All I know is that there's a certain amount of light, but nowhere near as much as you have here. Of course, the water, as you have indicated, might be performing a filtering effect, but because we remain essentially at the same level of the water on the home planet, I cannot say how deep we are. We don't ever go to the surface, and we remain at the same level, whatever level that might be.

Maybe when you go back, you'll be curious and kind of go up and stick your head up.

I don't think that would be possible. As you may not recall, I said that we are tethered.

No, I missed that. You're tethered to what?

We are tethered to something there that if you were to think of it, it might seem more like a stalk, but I don't think of it as a stalk. We can move away from that which tethers us, but we wouldn't want to move too far. It is like the root, the source of being, but we can move, up to a point.

Oh, that's interesting. Any idea how far you can move?

If you saw us, you would think of us as being some cross between animal and plant, and yet when I think of amphibians on your own planet, there's a sense of similarity there. I know they're not plants, but they are a cross between . . .

Two things.

Yes.

Oh, that's interesting. No, I completely missed that. You're tethered. So what is your experience of yourself? What is your shape, or form, of what you consider to be yourself on your home planet?

It's hard to describe. It is like the root of the being, the root sense would be like something half spherical, with many tethers coming out. And then the part that is mobile you might identify as being something that looks similar to a fish. Then at the end of the tether, it looks similar to a fish, but there is a flexible stalk that comes out and trails behind. It is not a massive number; there's not a huge amount of tethers that come out from one source. Otherwise, we might get entwined with each other. But because there's just enough, and because our desire is to move only so far, then it feels good. We do not have to remain in one place. We can move, but we don't have to, and we can remain connected to our source. You can perhaps identify with such a desire: It would be as if you remained connected to mother.

Oh, I see, like the umbilical cord never went away.

That's right.

When I Return to My Home Planet, I Will Begin Again

Then how do you create a new being? How do new beings come into being?

I'm not really clear on that. You'd have to speak to the source. I am but one expression of the source on that tether, but I do not know how the source is able to produce more beings like myself. I do not know that. I have not been that. I have only been what I am describing.

And how far are you through your life cycle there? You said 1,800 of our years?

I don't understand. I'm not there. I am on Earth.

I know, but you will pick up where you left off. Or will you start a new body when you go back?

I would not pick up where I left off. I would simply begin again.

So there will be a body then there, a form waiting for your spirit.

No. Oh, you mean . . . will there be something like a birth, and so on? Yes, something like that. So when I go back, I will not immediately incarnate. I will wait until I'm welcomed by the form that I will take.

So you have memories of all the different forms you've had?

No. Just the most recent.

So did that one go to its natural term? You had an 1,800-year life there before you came here?

Something like that. Well, you understand that we don't experience time. To give you a sense of the existance, yes, that life went through the end of its natural cycle.

So everybody on your planet who comes here comes between lives?

Yes.

Any idea how many of you there are on your home planet?

No idea.

And no idea how many are here?

No.

When Asked to Volunteer, We Were Told
This Would Be a Short-Term Commitment

As you came to the end of your natural life on your home planet, were you aware that this was an opportunity? Or is it a service that everybody does or are you a volunteer or is it just something that everybody does between lives?

Everyone who participates is a volunteer. The emissary made it very clear that it was something we could volunteer for and that it would last a considerably shorter time than the normal lifespan on our home planet. And depending on the dangers that existed there, of course, we didn't quite understand . . .

What a danger was. [Laughs.]

Yes. And it might be shorter than even we might expect, and so the idea of it being short and not too much of a lengthy commitment was also appealing.

So when you were in your previous form, other beings would come back home from Earth. Would they talk about it? Were you aware of what you would be experiencing?

I'm not even clear whether I will remember it very much, because . . . your question is reasonable, but you're really asking: "What did I hear about it before I went?" Almost nothing. So it's a possibility that this is a service that is offered by us while we are here, but it may not relate to our existences on the home planet. I had a sense of a few others having done it, but I didn't get a sense of their experiences. Perhaps that's filtered from our continuity.

I think you're right, because you can't take the discomfort with you when you leave here because it would hurt everybody there.

Yes.

So filtering the discomfort probably filters the memory, you know?

It could.

Join in the Dance of Life with Wetland Grasses

I believe that part of the purpose of this gathering of knowledge for this book is what the human being can derive from interaction with us that they are not now aware of. Unlike the idea of utilizing our body forms for food, or even therapy of some sort, if you are exposed in some way to a wetland, first I would ask that you move in some gentle vehicle—perhaps a boat that does not harm. The idea of the turning of the screw, the propeller—this is very harmful to all life, aquatic and plant-based, everywhere. But the boat that is propelled by the spinning blade on the surface of the boat, something . . .

Like an air boat?

Yes, exactly. This is, when it moves slowly, almost completely compatible, but only when it moves slowly. When it moves quickly, just like anything moving quickly, there's a tendency to cause damage, which those in the boat may not even be aware of. So I'm going to request that you move in a boat like that, but slowly. If you can stop at some point and be quiet, then do so. Relax as much as possible, or at least, whoever needs to maintain the boat, perhaps that person can maintain it, and some of the people can relax.

Turn off the motor of the boat so that it is as quiet as possible, though there will be other life forms making sound in that place. And if you see some of the grasses moving in reaction to wind or other elements—especially if there is sunshine on them—if you can, imitate that motion with your upper body or your arms and hands. Make sure the boat can remain stable (you will have to figure out how to do that), and then you might find that that motion—the dance with us and other life forms there—can increase your level of joy and harmony.

If the other humans on the boat are doing that—this is why ideally *all* the humans on the boat would do it, not just one person taking care of the boat, if the boat could just take care of itself for a moment—if you were able to do that, you see, joining the dance could create a great harmony within your physical bodies, even with each other. And you could experience something not unlike what I described myself: The motion and the expression of great joy and benevolent energy of one's self becomes a greater sphere of existence around one. During that time, all that is in conflict within oneself or that is a form of disease becomes more compatible.

I cannot state that it will absolutely cure, but it will help. It does require that you perform, that you do our dance of life. Don't reach out and touch the plants. Rather, join the dance as best you can. You don't have to stand up in the boat. In fact, that's probably not desirable. But you can move your upper body and your arms and your head and neck and so on.

I would say for a human being to do this, to be totally focused in it for two minutes would be sufficient to get the most out of it. Then after you stop, just be quiet for a few minutes—three, four, five minutes. Everybody just be quiet. Don't talk. Then move on in the boat and stop someplace else and do it again. But I do not recommend that you do that more than two or three times in any single journey, or what you would say "during a day," because each time you do it, it has a certain stimulation to improve your life existence physically, energetically, and on the feeling level.

It may also heighten your instincts, and there could be other benevolent impacts, perhaps in dream or thought. I cannot say that for certain, but the other part, what I just mentioned, I can say for certain. Therefore I would recommend doing that no more than twice in a single day, with calmness afterward. If you are going to do that, try to avoid any excitement or artificial stimulation—no dramas or music or prerecorded entertainments designed to stimulate and excite. Have a quiet day, if you're going to do that, to get the most out of it, and as quiet a night as possible. Then after a day or two of quiet, you can either do that again—out in that area in a boat or someplace near there similar—or you can resume your life.

Join in the Dance with Other Plant and Animal Life Too

I would also like to suggest that you consider joining the dance in other places. I realize that not everyone would be able to come to such a place as where I exist. I would recommend that if you are some place where there is some form of animal or plant life that seems to have qualities that you would like to have yourself—this means perhaps they have long existences or their lives have some elements of harmony that are missing in your life or the lives of others that you care about (or for that matter, in the human being in general)—that you might be able to do something similar.

If you are a land being, of course, or the plants or animals are land beings, then you'd go to where they exist naturally. This will not work in places where the animals or the plants are prisoners, such as in a place run by human beings for whatever reason. But it may work someplace where the animals or plants are free and living their lives as they do—if you can do this without experiencing much danger to go there or danger that can be managed so that you are safe and you do not cause danger to the life forms where you go. And that must be very carefully honored, because if you're causing danger in seeking to be healed or to have your life improved in some way, what you are causing may unintentionally be absorbed by you as a dance with the life forms around you. If they are frightened, then it could even make things worse. So it would be better to be as gentle as possible—on the land or in the water or wherever you are.

I would recommend starting this, if you're going to extend it beyond what I have suggested for the wetlands, with some plant species or even animal species. For an animal species, I might suggest, perhaps, a butterfly, or something like that. Beauty, grace, a certain amount of charm, and even humor, to say nothing of their great intellect, might be qualities that you would wish to heighten in yourself. You might go someplace where they exist in number, and if you are there, don't go into the midst of them to be surrounded by them, because you might cause harm unknowingly. Because you are so large, you might not notice the minute aspects of their young—or their life cycles—to move from one form to another the way they do.

So stay at the fringes of where they are and see if you can do a dance, moving your body—especially your upper body—because then you can be more clear about what you are touching with your feet. You see, if you move around with your feet, you might step on life forms. You might not think of them. You might not be aware of them, but they're there. They could be grasses. They could be little moving beings who are just not able to get out of the way of your large impact as you step. So find a place to stand or even sit and move the upper part of your body in order to imitate or be of a response to that life form flying as it does. And if you can establish some sense of energetic connection with one or more of those life forms, if you have a good experience, perhaps it will heighten those desired qualities within you or even improve your own.

Do Not Run Up to Plants or Animals and Touch; They May Interpret Your Intention as Danger

In the case of a plant, you can go where those plants are—always attempting to have the least amount of impact as possible under your feet or, if you are sitting on something, under the item that you are sitting on. I realize that this is a complication, but if you desire to absorb and assimilate qualities that you might find desirable, you would have to be as gentle a guest as possible. Remember, you are going someplace where there are other civilizations. You may not think of the forest, for example, as a civilization, but it is. It is established, running in an existence without your aid or impact. So when you visit a civilization afar, perhaps in travel, you are somewhat careful to observe the interactions between yourself and the citizens there. It is the same thing.

You wouldn't, in your travels, step or throw trash or anything like that on citizens of that place. It is the same. So be as gentle—and have the least amount of impact—as possible, and perhaps you will be able to express physically and interact without touching other species. In this way you can experience the communion and expression of that interaction without interfering in the culture or society around you. In this way, the beings you are interacting with in that way, expressing in that way, can be themselves. If you are touching them, they automatically cannot be themselves, because someone else is contacting them, and they will feel danger or discomfort.

There is a tendency by human beings to rush up to plants and touch them, and with animals as well. Generally speaking, I would believe that most human beings would not wish to be on the other end of that—having animals rush up to you and touch you. Very often when that happens, you do not respond well, and it is the same. Sometimes the animals do not realize that they are causing you harm or frightening you as, say, a fly might land on your arm, and you are startled and perhaps try to shoo it away. They did not realize they were causing harm, and they will fly away, or sometimes they will get curious and come back and say, well, what is this? But you can identify, you understand, for the purpose of this talk.

The whole point is to be as gentle as possible when you visit these other civilizations. And when you do the dance, again follow that protocol in which you might do a dance with some form of life—be it plant or animal—once or twice a day with a considerable separation between the two. Say you do it twice a day, then you might do it in the morning with one and toward the evening with another; you might do something like that in early morning or maybe a couple

of hours after arising and having a meal. Try to wait for at least an hour or two to go by after eating, and in the evening, I'd say, it might be an hour or two before having a meal so that there is some gap and your body is not overly distracted from performing other functions. In this way, it might be possible to get the greatest interaction, not only with my own kind, but with using this protocol for improving your life in some way.

I believe that there are cultures of human beings who have danced with other species and have even dreamt with them, perhaps. You yourself may do this in unconscious states of dreams. But why not include it as part of your waking life? You might find that such acquaintanceship can, at the very least, reduce your discomfort level, say, with pollens emanated from plants. Who knows? Maybe in time you will come to be greater friends with life forms here on Earth, and those life forms might then welcome interaction with you. And then the garden will be more complete, and those, perhaps, who have exited the garden will reenter it as equals and not as those separated. Good night and good life!

Oh, thank you so much. Good life to you!

CHAPTER NINETEEN

Crabgrass

FEBRUARY 21, 2008

જી

GREETINGS. THIS IS CRABGRASS!

We Are Strongly Connected with Certain Tibetan Chants

I am strongly associated with certain chants supporting life done by those referred to as monks formerly in Tibet. This particular chant has to do with the everlasting perpetuation of life meant to serve all in the most benevolent way: a chant that acts as an underpinning of all life so that the sequence of life on Earth is supported. That's the best way I can describe it in English. As a plant species, we are meant to be propagating in areas especially associated with flood. There are variations of our species that have runners that spread our kind, so even if our appearance is not satisfactory to some who are confused and think we are meant for a decorative grass, that which we are can survive.

We are meant for flood-prone areas and areas that are prone to landslides, as our roots hold and support the earth. I do recommend to gardeners, especially professional ones, that they consider us for areas—perhaps hills behind homes or offices—that have looser soil and for one reason or another are places where walls cannot be built. We as a plant species are not unattractive and can do a good job holding the soil. There are other types, of course, many trees, but in areas that are landslide-prone, trees with their mighty weight can actually aggravate the problem.

We're from an ancient culture on a distant planet that coordinates and supports the means to create capabilities on planets that are vitally alive—meaning, even on the Earth of today, the planet is expressing herself with the weather, with rain, on the high seas, with various methods of disapproval involving water, as well as her earth motion, volcanoes, and so on. Of course, we can do nothing about volcanoes, but we can do a lot when it comes to holding and securing. I recommend you look at us again for holding and securing soil. Areas of soil would be considered the primary goal. I know that many professional gardeners do know this and have, when it was believed to be a possibility that people could hear it, recommended that we be planted. Fortunately, we do not require too much support, fertilization, or excessive watering. Our whole point is to absorb waters and survive and thrive in areas where other plants might find it difficult. You might say, then, that we are here on this planet to help support and maintain life in many forms and, yes, protect humans and other life forms that are prone to sudden influxes of water.

We have a connection to this chant, because the chant not only is spoken (if that's the term)—sung, you might say—out loud in a way that represents a tone, as in an out-loud musical tone that is very close and akin to our soul beings, but the actual words and fluctuation of melody in the chant do support our natures and our purpose. I believe that if this chant had not taken place on Earth for many, many hundreds of years by these beings, we could not exist. But, most importantly, it has taken place, whether it's taking place now or in the past, as it has from time to time. The chant supports life, not only our lives, but many, many forms of life, especially the human being, both in the human being's mental awareness and consciousness but also in the beings physical ability to survive and to a degree thrive. Thus we are able to survive and thrive, as human beings are doing as a species, though not necessarily for everyone individually.

Our Purpose on Our Home Planet Is Simply to Live

On your home planet, do you have the same form as you do here, or a different one?

We are more mobile on the home planet. We do not put down roots on the home planet, as the home planet is stable and fairly arid. What you would refer to as soil has a very firm, claylike texture. There is little in the way of water as you know it, so we roll from place to place if we need to move. So, no, we do not perform the same function on the home planet, but the function is available and of course was originally used on the home planet by others, who then left us there, as we had requested transport from a distant place that had become too moist for us. It was turning into a water planet, but we did not know that, and our ancestors were rescued by this passing ship, sort of floating on the surface, if not necessarily in lifeboats, as you might do it in groups. I believe human beings might do that sometimes—come together for mutual support, especially in a crisis.

So you were able to get all of your beings off that planet and onto the ship?

No, not all, but many, thanks to the arrival of the ship. But some of the beings were lost.

Have they come back and reincarnated since you have been on a new planet?

No, they returned to our point of origin, but we do not consider our point of origin our home planet. "Home planet" to us means that which is coordinated with our ongoing purpose, a physical place that would be a planet where we can survive and thrive, but we were in other places before that.

On the place you went to on your current home planet, what is your purpose there?

To live.

You said that the planet needed to be aligned with your purpose.

Yes, but it *is* now.

Ah, to live. And your point of origin—can you say something about that?

It is not in this universe. If you were able to perceive it, it is a place more energetic with light and form, not fixed.

Were you asked to come here by our Creator's emissary?

I do not know if it was that. I was not present during that visit. All I know from that which has been told is that a particularly bright light was present and the urging was for temporary cooperation to move into a temporal world where we would be, and then we would no longer be and would be where we were. We are currently in the temporal world, meaning a place associated with time and motion, and I am not sure how far we are through that experience before we return to our point of origin.

Now, the fascinating connection with the chants of the monks—is that something you've done before, or is that something you just do here?

We do this here, but it has come up on occasion in other places. I have a fleeting recollection of those sounds being present on the home planet there, and I am not clear whether those sounds themselves—the chant, you under-stand—preceded those who are using them, or whether those who are using them created those sounds. If it preceded them, then they were inspired to make those sounds and words. If, on the other hand, they created them, I believe the creation may have taken place before they were in human form, because it goes back so very far that it would have preceded the human popu-lation on this planet.

Are there other beings on your home planet who might need to have this chant sung for them?

No, but it has in the past established a support sound that supported and stabilized our population on the current home planet.

I don't understand. You created that sound there, or that sound was estab-lished there?

Neither one. The sound was available. It came, you might say, out of the sky. We heard the sound. It's something we consider life supporting. When it is heard, it always occurs within a few of your hours where life gets better.

Do you have teachers or anybody you turn to in order to ask if you want to know something?

No. We accept the gift that is offered with gratitude and do not need to question it.

So the fact that you are familiar with the sound, then, is that part of your rea-son for coming here? How does that connect with the sound here?

I do not know the connection, which I did indicate before—that those doing it here had created it in some other form or way in a distant past. All I know is that the recognition of the sound as being a life-supporting mechanism for us on our current home planet, as far as I am able to tell, does not exist anywhere else within the spherical distance of our home planet to your planet and doubling that radius beyond. So then we felt this was a place that might welcome us, and in the past, we have been welcomed. It is only in recent times that people have misunderstood our purpose in supporting life and have decided that we are not satisfactory due to our appearance, but our appearance is more a factor of our function rather than for decorative purposes.

So what part of the crabgrass are you? Are you part of the energy of the entire system or one small area? How does that work?

I am speaking as a spiritual representative of crabgrass, as you call it, on the Earth, but I am not a specific plant.

But you are part of the energy of the whole thing—of the entire crabgrass system on Earth?

I am a spiritual entity associated with that life form.

You are spiritual representative, but you don't incarnate? You have never incarnated as crabgrass?

Oh, I see. Yes, I have—in order to coordinate with the life form, of course. I have invested myself in the plant you call crabgrass, but I, in and of my own nature, am not that exclusively—very much like the spiritual being of your own type who ranges far and wide but is not associated with any one individual. This is typically found on planets where there are varied life forms. There needs to be someone or some thing associated with the varied life forms so that there is—how can we say?—an ongoing form of existence and energy that can be in harmony at all times with other forms of energy of other types of beings on the planet. So even if individual species come into conflict with one another, on a temporary basis or more, there will be some means of ongoing comfort and resolution. I don't know how else to put it. It's visual.

Feelings Are Heightened for All Life Forms on Earth

Hold on just a minute! [Coughs.] Oh, I'm so sorry!

Perhaps it would be better to do this another time.

Well, I thought I could do it. I've got all kinds of lozenges and medicine here.

We will not go on too long today so that you can get some rest. Rest, I believe, is a portion of the cure for what you have, and you must pay attention to your physical needs. How can you assemble a book about physical beings and dishonor your own? I know this is not your intent, but you must recognize your own needs, especially during this current cycle you are in of the recognition and value of the physical self. Do you know about this? You are in a three-year cycle right about . . . you are almost halfway through it, where you are forced to not just tolerate but to truly be in great awe, respect, and love of your own physical body. Perhaps there's a correlation with my coming through today, as a plant who's often abused, misunderstood, or judged by many human beings, though we perform a very valuable service. So you might have in the past in other forms judged the physical, if you don't mind my saying that about you.

There is a portion of your soul's structure that has judged the temporal in general—meaning it has felt a strong sense of affinity with the immortal but has judged the temporal, not as something that is lesser, but rather as something that is uncomfortable. In the immortal, one has a sense of a current thread connecting to either the beginning of one's existence or to the spherical ongoing existence. This thread also goes into the future and it creates a complete and total sense of well-being, because no matter what one is going through in that moment, one is absolutely certain without any doubt, based on one's physical feeling, that it will pass. But in the temporal, one is not certain of this, because one does not feel physically the spherical link, meaning there is a break between one life and the other during which you rejoin your immortal soul. But in that break—like a dotted line, if you will—one does not feel the same way physically as one feels in one's physical temporal life. Therefore, there is a sensation of a fleetingness rather than the ongoing. You personally have had some difficulty with this, which has therefore allowed you to be compatible with the souls that have been in your physical form in the past. Thus you were able to be in occupation in this physical form, but it is something you have come here to resolve—and for the most part, I believe, this is your personal reason for being here as a soul. So in your current status you have moved into that position of fluctuation where you have some general satisfaction and comfort with your physical form. There are moments like that, you understand? And there will be more in the future, if you expect to remain.

Is this soul structure that has the difficulty the soul that built this body or my current soul?

Your current soul. You see, that is how you can come. It is not that you disapprove of your current body. It is rather because you have discomfiture, which is not the same as disapproval, toward the temporal. I can understand this, as we as life forms do not have discomfiture per se, but being temporal—even though we've been here longer than you have in that form, in that existence—is something that was unknown to us before this. Before this we were strictly in the ongoing immortal. And I believe that is the case for your soul as well.

So actually, then, you can see a personal association between us as souls. Though you have not been one of us, you have been in a sense of discomfiture without the absolute knowing on a physical-feeling basis, with what you identify as the physical. Here is your vehicle for having evidence of feelings, meaning that feelings are accentuated in human beings on this planet. All life forms' feelings are accentuated here, but in the human being, it is accentuated so that you can learn and relearn the value of that which is felt. Feeling/knowing is the nature of all life, and in most other places, as you know, this makes it unnecessary to think and decide. You feel and decide. Thought can be used for other pursuits. Since thought is removed from having to make decisions, then it can be used for philosophical perception and cultural advance exclusively.

But the humans here have to forget who they are. You as crabgrass don't have to forget.

No, we are not here to learn anything, but we must be here on the basis of this planet's function, and at the moment the planet functions in association with the human beings' purpose. Therefore, all other life forms on the planet are subject to that, so our feelings are heightened just as yours are heightened, even though we do not need that heightening to know who we are, where we're from, and why we're here.

Thank you. Even though this is personal, I'm going to leave it in, because it's very illuminating.

I do not mind at all. I feel that these books are needed in order that people can move beyond them—moving from reading a reference book to something having to do with their lives.

We Were Able to Locate Earth on the Basis of Sound

What's fascinating is that your beings didn't know before they came to this planet that there would be sounds here that were like sounds from your home planet.

We were able to locate this planet on the basis of the sounds. That is how we came to be here, because otherwise, if it were not for the sounds, we would perhaps have been unable to find anything in the temporal worlds. So the sounds, when we found them . . . we did not know that human beings were making the sounds. We naturally felt that the sounds may have been associated with something other than human, as from our point of origin, the sounds are well-known and are not associated as far as we can tell with human beings. After experiencing life here, my people are open to the possibility that these sounds have always been associated with human beings, but we did not have that connection in our point of origin to know and understand this. This has caused us to shift our perception philosophically to believe that human beings and ourselves are somehow inextricably tied together.

That's fascinating. Human beings were here when you came to the planet?

There were not the type of human beings that you know, but they were human beings, yes. They were more conscious, though, of other life forms having a purpose, even if they did not know what that purpose was. This is something that many human beings in your own time have as well, but they are not often in positions of influence. As a matter of fact, most of the time they are not in a conscious state attempting to influence. They are usually simply adored as the babies that they are. Babies are very conscious beings for their first few years, as they still relate to their overall being, as compared to their culture and their parents whom they know and love.

So these sounds were made by monks in Tibet for centuries? Millennia?

I do not know how long. I believe they still make these sounds in their current areas of existence, but they are temporarily unable to make them in the places they have made them before. I do not wish to say too much about them, for their safety is a bit precarious. However, the sounds that they make—and they know this—have to do with the perpetuation of all life on Earth. Sometimes, I believe, they are misunderstood because they must live differently. From my perception, they know that they must live so they can make these sounds, and it takes a great deal of time, teaching and personal self-discipline in order to make the sounds at the times of the physical day when they make them. This allows and supports this most delicate form of existence. The temporal is delicate, because it requires approval and love on a conscious basis from the majority of the beings—and by majority, I mean over 99 percent of all beings who live in the temporal—for it to function well. If at any time that slips below 99 (about 99.5 percent), then there is an extreme risk of the temporal just disappearing. These beings who make these chants know that, and therefore, the chant tends to underlie and support, like a reinforcement of the temporal. Even if human beings lose faith in the temporal, then this reinforcement can sustain it for a short amount of time, meaning so many years, until that faith is recaptured and belief in the value of life, which is constantly reinforced, is with you again. Children are helping you to believe that. Sometimes animals, plants, other things that are beauties of nature—rainbows, and so on—are all intended, not only to be of beauty and love, but to reinforce the value of the physical in motion, what I am referring to as temporal.

So that 99.5 percent, then, is made up not of adult human beings but of children and, as you said, all the plants and animals and sea beings on Earth?

No, I think I was clear on this. I am referring to all places in this creation where the temporal exists. If this were to be dependent on Earth, the temporal would have existed in the past only and would not be in the present.

So what's keeping it now? Is it your energy and those sounds?

No, what's keeping it is other life forms on other planets and the planets themselves who love and approve of and appreciate the value of the physical in motion. It is not as dependent on the people of Earth. The difficulty is because of the challenge for the human being on Earth and other life forms, but the other life forms . . . I will finish my comment about the human being first. The challenge of life for the human being on Earth means that many human beings do not approve of the physical in motion, because their lives are so unpleasant or so challenging. Fortunately, there are other life forms on Earth who are not here to learn, to grow, or to otherwise influence, having certain things unavailable as you said yourself before—the ignorance of aspects of one's ongoing being, as you referred to.

Other life forms on Earth are thus able to support the value of the physical in motion, as they do not have the so-called dotted line between their lives. Their sense of immortality is preserved. This is why, if certain life forms on Earth no longer wish to be present on Earth, they simply request to move back into their immortality elsewhere. You have many life forms on Earth who are doing that now, forms that are not associated with the human being. The human being will remain as a species on Earth for some time to come. But many other life forms—those who have either served in the ways they are able, or those who are no longer able to bear the stress of the human being not engaging with them in some benevolent way by exchange of knowledge, wisdom, and energy on a conscious level because human beings do not embrace their own physical form in a temporal sense—cannot wait under the strain and are moving on.

Will they come back once we awaken more and become more benevolent?

Perhaps. I do not know. It will be an option certainly for some of them.

Or maybe they'll go into the more expanded level of this planet that we are going to?

I do not know. You will have to talk to them about that. In this case, you are referring to what you call animals—just to be clear with the reader.

And sea beings too, right?

They are also what you would call animals.

But back to the sound for a minute. There is a sort of a triple-toned sound that comes out in layers that the monks make. Is that the one you're referring to?

No. What you're referring to is something that requires a tremendous skill, but it is not the chant I am referring to. This chant I'm referring to can be done by the very young, as well as the older and more wizened. It is important to have it done by those who are very young as well as those who are older so that the chant itself is embracing all life, at least within the human form: the very young, then representing another aspect of the cycle of life for the human being, as well as the very old and ages in between. That is why at times one sees, I believe, with this particular group of spiritual humans, different ages among their population. Their work requires it.

When you came to the planet, you were guided by that sound, but at the time you came, humans were very, very benevolent, correct?

Yes, and there were very few of them.

So that sound wasn't needed for those beings?

No, my explanation was perhaps not clear, so your question is well received. I believe that sound was made by human beings in Earth's "then," from that point of time in Earth's future. But it could have been, allowing for those who make those sounds in your time, made sometime in the past. I cannot be certain. If it was made at some point in the past, it would have been made on another planet, perhaps by human beings directing that sound toward this planet and the time in which we arrived here. One can do that with sound—did you know? Yes, you can make a sound. You can do an energy and you can essentially aim it—without technology, you understand; none of that.

If welcome, you can situate it in such a place as it will be present when it is needed. In our case, it was present when it was needed, and because it reminded us of the sounds that, for lack of a better term, "came out of the sky" in our own world, we knew that this planet, this Earth, was the place we were meant to be.

So it could have been aimed at your planet also!

We assume there is a correlation.

Do you mind if I ask someone at some point to clarify it?

Why would I mind?

Well, I just asked.

You were being polite. I see. Yes, that's good.

At some point, we'll ask somebody like Zoosh or Isis or someone.

If you like.

There's a Wider Purpose for Human Existence on Earth

So you had then incarnated as crabgrass, but you're not at the moment—is that true?

That's correct, and the reason is that what is called the crabgrass—I am using that term because it's known and understood in the English-speaking world—is too busy. They're constantly functioning to be and broadcast the energy that we are intended to be, which has to do with survival and, to an extent, "survive and thrive," if you would. I believe that you as human beings, to say nothing of other beings, do need that energy on the planet at this time. And you recognize that as those who have attempted to eliminate our surface . . . we have the capacity to return another day, even if we are not obvious. The human being has this capacity on Earth as well.

You have had times when there's been great population loss, and yet you are still here. I believe our influence supports that capability. I am not saying that we are somehow associated with Creator directly, but we are no less associated with Creator than you yourselves or other life forms. And we believe the universal chorus of life does support ongoing human existence on this planet for reasons beyond that which is currently understood by your population—meaning that there is a purpose you do not yet know, including all that you personally know (speaking to you on the basis of the Explorer Race material, and so on). There is a purpose, a wider purpose, that you do not yet know.

Really! What is it?

I am constrained. I will simply say that it has to do with the formation of a future form of life of which you are essentially a portion of the birth material, as one might find, say, in an egg. One might find a baby chick, yes, an egg, but there is other material that supports the life. You are a portion of that other material that supports that future life purpose, existence, and expression.

Oh! That's wonderful!

That's what I can tell you now, but you can pursue it perhaps with others.

So we are involved with being part of something brand-new!

Well, it is intended. As you know, the Creator of this universe and other creators generally have a fondness for just what you have stated.

Thank you for the hint.

Knowing Who You Are Would Interfere with Your Purpose

So what about you personally? Do you give aid and support to the beings who now inhabit the crabgrass form, or do you give guidance or energy or what?

Guidance is not necessary. I'm available for, as you say, comfort, support, and nurturing, but I do not answer questions, because they are not asked.

They don't ask? Well, they're so in the moment, then. They're so busy!

This is typical to most life forms on Earth, with the exception of the human, because most other life forms on Earth have the continuity of existence for themselves. They know who they are, and it is unnecessary to ask. But human beings, of course, who are attempting to resolve the unresolvable and know who they were and are and will be . . . it would interfere with your purpose if you knew who you were. You would . . .

We wouldn't get up and go to work.

You would accept the unresolvable as a part of existence. Thus the unresolvable would be acceptable to you, and you would make no attempt to resolve it. But not knowing who you are gives you the constant desire to define who you are, including in ways that may not be associated with your species. These ways are often abandoned in time, but in the process you might discover and apply the unknown in ways that create something new so that the unknown, meaning the imponderable, so to speak, can be defined or redefined and can find a purpose for existence. In other places, on other planets, that which cannot be resolved is just accepted as a fact, and no one attempts to resolve it. On this planet, you not knowing who you are supports that resolution.

You know an awful lot about human beings.

I recognize the correlation between the human being and our own being. I grant that we do not look anything alike, but we both have some discomfiture with the temporal. I am not certain that in your natural state, you have a personal sense of discomfiture with that, but I feel that in your natural state, if you had to choose between your immortal existence and the temporal, that you would always choose the immortal existence.

In no circumstances would any of you at this time choose the temporal, but you are here to not only resolve the unresolvable here on this planet but also to come to sufficient comfort with the temporal so that you might at times choose it. I believe this is what Creator is doing in your overall design. You see, a choice to embrace the temporal is necessarily a temporary choice. You cannot choose the temporal permanently; it is not possible. To choose the temporal, because of what the temporal is, physical in motion . . . you cannot choose it and make it permanent, because it is in motion. It will not be permanently fixed in any one spot, either as thought, action, physical, feeling, and so on. It will necessarily always be in motion. So, you see, even if one or more of your members were to choose, if you had to make a choice between your natural state and the temporal state, even if you decided to choose the temporal, you would at some point return to your natural state because the temporal is always in motion. And anything that is always in motion eventually goes everywhere. If your friend Zoosh were here, he would say . . .

"Never forget that!"

The temporal is constantly in motion—it is physical in motion. If it is physical in motion, it is constantly searching for its point of origin and therefore will look everywhere. Hence, as such, it will eventually find its natural state and embrace it and recognize it. Therefore if you were given the question by Creator, "Would you choose to be of your natural or the temporal?" even if in theory some of you would choose the temporal, you would naturally at some point rediscover your natural state and be that again. If, on the other hand, you chose the natural, you would remain the natural and would not move physically. One necessarily excludes the other, but the temporal does not exclude the natural in this particular formula I am suggesting to you. The reason I am stressing it, of course, is that it has to do with a hint of the form that you are preparing to support. If you are in the temporal, you see, what are you becoming or what are you searching for? Maybe the natural state that you know is your existence now beyond here . . . maybe it is a precursor.

We Were Involved in the Creation of the Temporal

Let me run this by you: Zoosh said that all beings in the plant kingdom were creators once. Is that in your memory bank or your history?

I would say that it is in the nature of all species when traced back to their roots, if I might use that term, to be associated with a creator or many creators. So philosophically speaking—which is, you can see, my nature—I would have to answer yes.

But he was quite specific—not just that you're connected, but that you had actually been a creator and then had decided to be the plant kingdom.

You mean, had decided to be of the temporal? Everything I say is connected to everything else, you understand. Not unlike yourselves.

I see. As a creator, you were totally in your natural state.

This is typical for creators. Otherwise, they wouldn't have full capacity to use all their capabilities.

Right. I never asked before, but do you have any idea what kind of creation you created?

I believe we were associated with the creation of the temporal—not exclusively, but in a group.

I've got goose bumps!

I might add, your source was also associated with it.

The source of humans?

I understand that no life form currently in occupation of Earth—not referring to life forms who have visited this planet but who are currently in occupation (currently, meaning going back, say, a few thousand years)—was disassociated with that creation. One was associated with the creation of the temporal in some root form. This allows, then, that any life form currently on the Earth, going back a few thousand years, who might at some point in their existence question their value, purpose, and reason to be there, their overall existence would be able to promptly present them with the ongoing feeling of an association with the creation of that form of existence. This way the life form would recognize not only a personal connection on a species basis with that form of existence but also be reminded that something preceded that form of existence, which would suggest a further underscoring of their immortality.

This is generally accepted by the life forms who know who they are on Earth as a reassurance of their own existence beyond the form they are in on Earth, so when they have that moment of fear preceding their physical transformation—also known as their death—as they often do, they will be immediately reassured of the perpetuation of their personalities beyond the form they are in on Earth.

This is something that happens to the human being as well. Of course, it does not play out the way I'm describing it in such intellectual form. It plays out as a felt physical reality and is thus very nurturing and comforting. That's why you might see at times, if you are around elderly human beings or even elderly pets, you might see their eyes go into a relaxed state—they are viewing another portion of existence in these moments. They are being reassured of the perpetuation of their own personalities of what they see and feel and sense in other ways.

Embrace the Temporal!

Okay, you have much more to say. Do you want to try to talk another night?

It's possible, but it's up to you. This book, after all, is not intended to be about any one species, but it's intended to provide instruction, guidance, and a reminder to your own species that life forms around you—be they plant or animal, as you perceive them—have much more to offer than their simple appearance, be it a form you assume to have beauty or a form you wish to enjoy or a form that you may find, as in our case at times, annoying. Not all members of the human race perceive us this way. Generally speaking I think for the book it would be good to have a simple photo of the life form, because there will undoubtedly be people living some places who are not familiar with any given life form.

I'm sort of hoping I can do this one in color, but we'll see.

I would recommend black and white. There is a reason. In the long run, the color of many life forms will change. And if you do it in black and white, your minds will immediately accept the fact that this is not the way the plant looks. You shift. Black and white allows your mind to give permission that the color may be one thing or another. After all, our own species might at times look green or tan or brown, and yet we are alive. I believe your own life form has different appearances, and yet you are all human beings. Even within an individual's life, one might have different appearances in skin tone, and yet you are alive. Sometimes if you take a black-and-white picture of a human being, it is easy, isn't it? You automatically assume that the human being does not look simply in shades of black and white. In short, it gives permission.

You can do color on the cover, perhaps, or plates, if you wish to do that, but generally speaking, I think that for life-form exploration in plant and animal and even the human being, black-and-white illustrations have a purpose mentally that goes beyond the obvious. We will have to stop soon, because my voice, which is in the range of the sounds I have referred to, is taxing the channel's voice box.

All right.

On your planet now, you feel overwhelmed by the changes—not only those associated with resources, but the overall changes you must face. The natural state of existence—sunlight, wind, motion—must be the way that you use to generate and perpetuate the energies that drive your mechanical forces, but in the long run, as you develop technology that does not involve motion, you will need less and less of this energy you refer to as "electricity." Recognize that change. The perpetuation of life is something we completely recognize and appreciate and value.

I believe your older philosophies also are in agreement with this position that I have stated. As such, if you can embrace as a cornerstone of any faith you have that change and transformation are directly associated with the motion of life, you will be able, in time if not immediately, as a human being to embrace the temporal. Recognize that you could not exist in your natural form on Earth on a regular basis. You must be thankful to the temporal form you currently occupy, even if it does not always appeal to you. It is a form most capable of living in the temporal. Your natural form does not require such a being as the human being to exist, for you to exist.

You are all immortal in your personalities, and the adaptations you make on Earth for your physical bodies and your physical lives do not necessarily prevail as you move on in other existences. If you know with certainty that you are immortal as a personality, you will feel greater love for the physical. Recognize that it is not your job to judge that which Creator has lovingly offered to you as a physical form, nor is it for you to judge the physical forms of others. The variety you are exposed to for your own life as well as the variety of life around you are all meant to remind you that there is value in all you see, sense, and feel associated with life. Everything is alive. Good night!

Thank you very, very much! And I think I feel a lot healthier too, after feeling your energy.

Good.

Thank you.

CHAPTER TWENTY

Kelp

APRIL 15, 2009

GREETINGS. I AM WHAT YOU CALL KELP, A SEA PLANT.
Okay. Welcome.

Thank you. The coordination of our species has been complicated for Earth. When we came to Earth, we were interested in exploring growth on dry land or growth in swampy areas where we would be able to have some sunlight. In the early years, that is what we did, but it didn't work, and over time, with the assistance of some visitors, we were able to create something that amounts to a compromise. That is one of the things we stand for energetically on your planet: compromise.

Kelp Came to Earth to Exist in a Less-Insulated Environment

We function best now in the sea, but in the shallows so that the sunlight can reach us, you understand. Therefore we can have sunlight, but it has to be a water environment as well. When we thought that we could be like a vine, as you say, a creeper that grows along the ground, a swamp seemed like a good idea. But it turned out that it wasn't wet enough, and many of our original members did not survive that experience.

In those days, when different species were either being invited to come to the planet you now know as Earth or volunteered in one way or another to come, there were groups of beings who could move about—who were ambulatory, yes? These were not always human beings; sometimes they were representatives of human beings, meaning mechanisms. Generally speaking, there were beings who were able to check up on the life forms being welcomed on Earth, either two-legged or four-legged, and sometimes with those representatives.

At one point when the checking took place, it was noted that our species had almost entirely died out, and that is when what amounted to a reseeding, you might say, for our plant went on all over the planet. They weren't sure what to try. They knew that we had come here to have something like a water existence but with more exposure to sunlight. So about twelve different things were tried, and the only one that worked was being in the sea in salt water and in the shallows—comparatively speaking, allowing for the depth of the oceans.

I give you this background because on our home planet, we always lived underwater. But the thing about the home planet is that it is quite a distance from the Sun that illuminates that series of planets. So the water itself is always cool while being a little thicker than the water you have here. Sometimes, depending on the season of the year, it is actually cold—not as cold as to freeze, but cold. And while we are more sturdy looking on our home planet, thus being what you might say more insulated so as to survive such difficult conditions, we wanted to try someplace—when we were invited to come to Earth—where we could be less insulated, more like our true selves.

Only Request Portions of Kelp for Consumption

We are happy now being in the oceans, and the only thing we wish for are plants that can populate the shallows, especially where human beings live—near human beings, near the large conglomerations of human-made buildings that you call cities. We need plants that can purify the water. Such plants do exist and, generally speaking, I believe they are in other countries rather than in the country you are speaking from.

Okay. Can you tell me the names of the plants that purify water?

I do not know their names in human terms, but they are very versatile. They are able to purify water. I think your space people—your NASA people—experimented with them a bit. And there are other plants, but they are better at purifying air. I think you know some of these.

Yes, like the spider plant.

It would be good to get those plants in the book, because I think that most businesses, offices, and private homes could benefit from having those plants well and thoroughly in attendance. Now, the issue that we are most associated with, as I mentioned, is compromise: to have a goal and then to have to let go of that goal and find something that is a satisfactory substitute. Therefore I would like to make a suggestion. Many people consume portions of us, and that is acceptable, but we would always request that you never cut an entire plant. Rather, just request portions from that plant so that the plant may live on and thrive. I think good sea farmers know this technique, but there is more.

There are benefits that the human can derive that have to do with the living, vital plant without it being cut and consumed at all. Right now in your world, human beings are struggling all over the planet—in groups especially—to have greater influence, and this always happens during times when populations increase and there is fear that there will not be enough to support everyone. This is why I've come through to speak today, because there can be a great deal of compromise if only people are exposed to the living, vital plant of which I speak as a representative.

I would recommend that, whether it is a struggle between corporations or a struggle between peoples—or simply arguments between couples, families, whomever—that you get out in the shallows where our plant species grows. Usually this can be done in a small boat. We would prefer a boat that does not have propellers because sometimes our plants or other creatures of the sea are harmed in this way. Use what you have, and if you have propellers, then when you get to where we are growing, please move ahead at what might be called nautically a "dead slow" pace, so the propellers are moving as little as possible. We would prefer oars, though I realize in your time that one does not often find boats using oars that can accommodate many people, but there are still some. If you can find a longboat, that would be good. Still, use what you have.

In the case of corporations, it would be good to have the heads of the corporations onboard, because they are ultimately the ones who set policy—or perhaps the chief stockholders or the boards. Nothing is required of the human beings there. I would recommend not bringing any telephones other than an emergency phone, should an emergency come up. And by emergency, I mean only the kind of emergency for which one might call the Coast Guard, such as your boat is taking on water, not a corporate emergency.

Kelp Radiates the Energy of Cheerful Compromise

In order to get the best out of the experience, whoever the opposing groups are, once you get to where our plants are growing, it is most important to just be quiet, to have no sounds—especially electronic sounds. Don't bring music with you. If you want to bring an instrument that can tolerate being at sea in order to sing to the plants after you have had your time of absorbing our energy, that would be acceptable—whatever you'd like to bring that can tolerate such conditions. It's not a requirement to bring an instrument, but you can. I recommend, then, if you have come in a big boat, to anchor a short distance away from where the plants are growing in number, and then to take a small boat and row out there or have someone row you out. That's the best, because if there are no propellers turning, the plants will be relaxed, and they will be able to exude a great deal of their natural energy. This is also good, obviously, for battling countries, battling armies, anything. Send representatives who you will then honor and listen to their thoughts and ideas and suggestions.

Say you're sitting in one of those boats near the plants, obviously floating on the surface. This is what to do while you're quiet: Look at the surface of the water, especially if you can see the plants growing, and just breathe in and out normally. Take your normal breath. If you normally breathe a shallow breath for whatever reason, breathe deeper if you can, and if possible, breathe in and out of your mouth, not your nose. Concentrate on where the plants might be to the best of your knowledge, and just take deep breaths in and out—no panting, just deep breaths in and out—and then relax. Do this for about five minutes and then relax for another ten minutes, no talking. Then do another series of breaths in and out for about five minutes, looking at the surface of the water, especially if you know there are plants there. You do not have to say any words to prepare—just breathe in and out. Then relax for another ten minutes, and then do that again for five minutes—deep breathing but no panting and no puffing, okay? Then rest after you're done.

That's when I recommend the music. Sing something gentle, cheerful. It can be a religious song, that's acceptable, but not a song about suffering or sadness. It has to be something that is cheerful, because the plants will be radiating that energy of cheerful compromise, and therefore they would like to have the gift of a song that is cheerful. It does not have to be about compromise; they are that already. They offer what they have freely and with no requirements of you—just the politeness that you might offer to anyone who is not able to protect himself or herself well. That's why I say no propellers. If you have a boat that is able to move without propellers, even better. That is all the time you will need to do this.

Kelp Was Recruited to Earth for Its Energy of Compromise

What I recommend, especially for those who are in conflict with each other for whatever reason, is to move away from the spot where you were breathing in and out like that in the boat. If someone is rowing you, that's fine, but that person is to remain in a position where he or she is never looking at the people who represent the different sides. This allows the person to pay attention to what he or she is doing while not distracting those who represent the different sides. Row off for a distance and begin your talks. See if you cannot find something new that works as a compromise that you can then present to the groups you represent in order to work things out. I feel that the energy of compromise is vital to preserve and encourage your civilizations all over Earth as well as to welcome greater harmony and greater interactions that are supportive of all beings.

That is incredibly new and wonderful information. How did you become imbued with the spirit of compromise? Where did that come from?

Well, on our home planet, we had to compromise all the time because we craved warmth. Because warmth was not available, we had to create warmth in a different way. That's why we developed thicker and thicker skin, all right—not barklike as you know trees to be, but very thick stalks and the protuberances, what comes out of the stalks. The skin looked different there—not so much like leaves or bulbs or anything, but quite different, and it had no flowers or anything like what you would identify with plants, other kinds of plants. So if you were to see us in our natural state on our home planet, the thickness of our skin, so to speak, would be a minimum of four inches. That allows what is inside to be warmer, with that insulation.

We had to compromise from the beginning, and having lived on our home planet for millennia, compromise was a regular factor. Here's another reason why: In order to perpetuate the species, we would have to make contact with each other. Perpetuating the species required warmth, so there were two or three days of our year—meaning the planet revolving and so on—when we had the greatest amount of warmth from our sun. We could, through the top of our plant, take in that warmth and store it, and we would store it until the time came to procreate. Then we would use that warmth as one plant touched the top of another plant and seeding took place, and the seeds would drop and take root in time.

So you can see compromise was essential. It couldn't be the way we wanted it to be—not anything—and so we had to come up with something that would work, even though it wasn't our first choice. This ability to achieve compromise is why we were considered when one of Creator's representatives came to us and said that we were vitally needed on Earth and that we would not have to perform the function that we are available to perform now in your time for a long time. The Creator's emissary said that we could experiment on Earth and, most importantly, that Earth was warm for much of the time and that we would be able to be warm. That was all we needed to hear. We were very excited about that and said we would go. The Creator's representative reminded us that there would come a time when we would have to share our natural, cheerful ability to compromise, and we said we would do that happily, and now we are in that time on Earth.

Why would you go to a planet that was uncomfortable? I can understand that it was probably set up before you came to this universe so that you could create this compromise energy. Do you remember your lives before you came to your home planet?

I do not, but some of the old ones say they believed, on the basis of the depth of our personalities, that we wanted to be able to adapt to all conditions and create in some benevolent way. With such a core desire in personality, it makes complete sense that we would wind up in a place where we had to come close, at the very least, to mastering compromise. We do not claim to be masters of anything, but we have come close—and, of course, in the process, we have developed a great deal of patience. Compromise and patience go together. When there is conflict, there is always agitation, revenge, and so on. Patience is rarely a factor there, though sometimes it is in the short run, for tactical purposes. But in the long run, it is for the perpetuation of your own species—or family or tribe or what have you—and the opportunity to interact with other species and grow wealthy in the accumulation of experience that benefits all beings, which is true wealth. Thus we had this experience and were able, we believe, to share it.

We feel that such capabilities are available to the human being as well, and some human beings are very good at compromise, as some are very good at patience, and more will become this way as time goes on. You have right now within your grasp as cultures of Earth the opportunity to cause great harm to each other. At the same time, equally you have the opportunity to stimulate and be of great help to each other. If you remember that everyone is to be included, supported, and sustained to the best of your ability, you will find a good path for all beings.

Fish Are on Earth to Provide Beauty and Inspiration

That's beautiful. Do you radiate in such a way that the fish who swim around you receive this energy? Or they don't need it?

They usually don't need it, though sometimes they will come to—how would we say, if you were doing it as a person?—commiserate, to absorb and share patience. What you call fish require a great deal of patience. They are on Earth to provide beauty and inspiration, goals and achievements, and stimulate other ideas and ideals in the human being. But the human being does not understand this and thinks that fish are here to be food. So they come sometimes and request to absorb some patience.

I don't think we've talked to fish yet so I didn't know that. Do you have natural enemies? Do the sea creatures eat your plants?

We do not consider that a problem. They might nibble a bit, but it's not typical. If they nibble just a bit, we're all right with that. So no, our only "natural enemies" are those who would destroy a plant to harvest portions of it. Why destroy it when you can request that the plant offer what it is prepared to share and just harvest small bits from a great many plants? If you take without asking and without waiting for that warmth or relaxation in your own body that acknowledges that you can take a little bit, then what benefit you might have derived otherwise would be lost. Consumption does not provide patience and compromise in that case. However, if you acquire on the basis of requesting, and wait and see how you feel, just harvesting a small amount—after you've prepared it for you and your people and decided it is safe to eat, but before you consume it in whatever way, soup perhaps, you are creating—then say the following:

> "I am asking that this soup I am eating now provide me with greater patience and the wisdom to compromise to bring about the most benevolent outcome for all beings."

The consuming of your plant doesn't give the benefits that one would get from coming to your live plants?

Exactly right, and I will give a percentage. The interaction with the live plants as I have explained would have a tremendous effect—it would be very helpful indeed, I believe. And the consumption with permission would have about 30 percent of that effect. Whereas without permission—no effect.

But most people, not knowing your qualities, consume your plant for minerals and vitamins, don't they?

I do not know about these things. I would say that the reason we and others are cooperating in this exploration by you is so that such awareness might spread.

This is so far out—this is so wonderful. Nobody knows this? Not even tribal elders? Does anybody on the planet now know about these gifts you have to offer us?

It's possible, but I don't know whether it's in print. It doesn't make any difference. It's good to get it out further. It's possible that people who live near the sea might have some of this knowledge.

To See Each Other as Family Someday

Are you a spirit of the kelp, or have you inhabited a plant as a personality?

I am an elder. I have inhabited a plant, and the reason I know that the compromise can work for humans is that I have a memory of it as a plant. I also now as an elder have the ability to commune in a wider community of such plant species. So I will tell you a story, eh?

Long ago, there were two ships representing the different forces of battling armies. I do not know their names, but two of the ships and a larger armada had captains who were distantly related even though they were on opposite sides, and they both felt strongly about their own side's point of view. Since they were distantly related and the battle wasn't gaining ground for anyone, the two captains each had two people row them out to an area where they could talk and see if it wasn't possible to find a way to reach a compromise. They came with the intention of finding a way to work out their differences. Their rowing took them closer to shore but farther away from each of their ships. They came right into an area where a great many of our plants were growing, and then they stopped. They spoke for a long time. They didn't do the breathing thing. But you see, they had the desire to compromise, so they didn't have to. They just sat there and spoke. They hit on a plan whereby each force could divide what they were fighting over, and one could be overseen by one group and one overseen by another group. They decided that this could work, they acknowledged each other, and they said that they hoped they would be able to see each other as family someday. They rowed back to their ships, and in time, that's exactly what happened.

They never knew about your contribution?

They didn't know, but they had the desire to compromise. I am telling you this story because I've been able to acquire the full story over time, and it was personal for me.

You were there?

I was one of the plants they stopped their boats over. I could feel their desire to compromise. And every one of the plants in that area exuded as much cheerful compromise energy as we could—perhaps that helped.

What a wonderful story.

It wasn't until a long time later that I got the rest of the details.

Of the beings on your home planet, what percentage come to inhabit the kelp on Earth? A small or large amount?

Very small. The original group had fewer than fifty of us, and it has remained so.

Same ones or different?

Same, but just reproducing, from those original fifty. You remember, though, that in the beginning a great many died out. So now, allowing for the die-out in the very early part of it, you're really only experiencing . . . the worldwide population goes back to about seventeen.

Right, but I mean how many beings are on your planet now?

A few hundred thousand.

So do the ones who come to Earth go back and tell their stories to those at home?

But then it was less—then it was maybe 70,000.

You are an elder and you've been here, but does the regular population know what these beings are doing on Earth? Do they get regular updates from them, or how does that work?

It's a struggle for them to live there on our home planet. So they may not be able to; I do not know. I know it's a struggle for them to live there and I find it hard to believe they would have time to think. Thinking is not typical there. Because the struggle to survive . . .

Is so profound. So what are your plans, then, on your home planet? You have achieved this ability to compromise. Do you have to continue proving it? Or will you be able to leave at some point to find a more hospitable place?

It may be necessary to stop soon. The channel's voice is going away. This is not unusual.

Okay. I'm sorry, because you are very interesting.

We can continue next time, eh?

Okay.

May you have all the patience you need to live well. Good night.

CHAPTER TWENTY-ONE

Kelp

APRIL 19, 2009

&

I looked up a lot of information about kelp, and there's a bigger subject here. Everything I read has to do with burning it, eating it, drying it. Where are we going? It's like we're cannibals eating the ones we've vanquished for courage or survival. How do humans change in order to enjoy the energy of the plants and animals without having to eat them? When do we change how we get sustenance?

This is a very good question—and profound, well thought out. I'm not sure if I can give you the ultimate answer you want, but from my perspective, it's not unusual for a population as large—and growing—as the human population on Earth to seek out sustenance in all places. It's not so much about the idea of eating less; it's about the potential of there being fewer human beings on the planet. It will be controversial because there will be some kind of birth control involved, and some people don't like that—though some governments are enforcing it now, even as we speak. But this is not widely done. It would be a good thing if populations could decrease benevolently, meaning that there would be fewer children born than there are couples who create them, whether the couple is married or not.

This would, in perhaps twenty years, reduce the population by 10 percent, simply with natural population reductions as they occur now. If that continued as a global policy, in about 40 to 50 years, the population would be reduced by 20 to 30 percent and so on. At some point, if the population of human beings on the planet were reduced to about 30 percent of what it is now, then human beings would not be eating everything in sight—as you didn't quite say but ironically suggested. But for right now, the reason human beings are doing that is because of how many of you there are, not because there is something inherently wrong with the species. That is my perspective.

All right, but that's another question. What do we eat if we don't eat the plants and animals? How soon are we going to change so that we don't have to eat flesh or take kelp tablets for nutrients as people do? How do we change this dependence on the animals and plants on the planet?

You don't. It is not up to you to do that. Some peoples have been trying to do that for years, promoting vegetarianism. This is meant to be kind to the animals. But there are others who want or need to eat meat and might be willing to give up, or at least greatly reduce, the amount of vegetables they are eating. So you see, ultimately, people need to eat. All beings need to eat—certainly the animals do—and plants also acquire what we need, although perhaps a little more gently. I think we need to move away from this idea that people are somehow inherently making an error in what they are eating, and instead move to saying that it's the amount that's being eaten that's the problem. Also, the hunting and acquisition of free plants and animals, meaning in the wild, would be something I would prefer to have stop. From my point of view—and the point of view of many other species I've managed to commune with over the years—the general preference would be that if you're going to eat plants and animals, you should raise them in this or that kind of farm. This can be done. The beings who would ensoul those plants and animals would know coming into life that they were being raised for food, and would not expect to live free lives. Therefore things might be better in a lot of ways.

Human Beings Reconnect Every Day, All Over the World

All right. You said that you wanted to be able to traverse the land, and it seems that even though it's not land, what I read said that you can grow like a foot a day or something. I mean, you really stretch out in the water. Is that something here that pleases you very much?

Yes, we do like that. We like not only to be able to grow but also to be able to move without necessarily having to make the effort on our own. We can move ourselves, of course, as all plants do, but the nice thing about being in the water is that the ebb and flow of the water itself helps to create a motion that we find pleasing. If you are underwater and able to observe this, there is no question that you would notice the visuals of something that represents a dance. You could look at it and remark how the plants seem to dance in the water. Others have mentioned this in the case of other plants with wind on the land and so on. This dance is something that we find pleasing and that works well for us in many other ways. To give you an example, one way is to create greater unity between all beings of the same type. One finds this on the land much more understandably with the wind, and the connection between all beings—plant beings in this case—on the land is wind. But when there's water, the water is the connection. Even though there might be kelp thousands of miles away from any individual plant, the water makes the connection. So there's water and wind—natural elements of Earth that we expected to find when we came here—and we find them pleasing and comforting.

You can commune with plants on the other side of the world through the water?

If necessary. But commune does not mean we have talks like what is going on now. Commune means to be in energetic contact and to enjoy the exchange of energy. But it does not mean verbal communication.

Yes, I understand. So do you do it very often or is it a lot of effort?

It's no effort at all, and it happens more than once a day just because it's easy and comforting. You as human beings also do this, though for most of you, it's unconscious. It happens because it's important to happen. It keeps up your soul's reminder function that you are a human being on this planet now. If you didn't have this capacity, as all life on this planet does, you would find it exceedingly difficult to maintain your focus as a human being. This would occur—you understand, if it didn't happen in the way I'm mentioning with the exchange energetically—most likely in the dream state. By dream state, I mean the deep sleep state for your physical body when you are exposed to teachers who might look any number of ways, such as guides or Creator perhaps, who would take a form or appearance that you might find more pleasing in your greater spirit being. There might be a tendency to forget or even to abandon the physical form as a soul. But because every day human beings all over the world reconnect with other human beings—usually ones you do not know in this life as a friend and so on—you are reminded that as a soul, you are a human being in this life. And it's "re-connect," you understand, because of the ongoing connection—kind of like a pulse coming and going, not unlike the dance one sees in water or in air with plants.

All life does that on this planet. It is not so commonly found on other planets, because on other planets, life is more benign, more benevolent. There is no need to remind yourself why you are here and why you are putting up with what you are putting up with as a life form. But on Earth—it being a school and a challenge—it is important to remind the soul why you are here and who you are when you are here. So you stay here until it's time to move on.

You Remember Who You Are Just Before Waking from Deep Sleep

Something else I read said that your forests—and there are beautiful, beautiful pictures of forests of kelp—provide a home to so many creatures that you're like one big apartment house.

Yes, we like that. You are not dissimilar. It has taken science to explain it to you, in terms of the biology and physiology, how many different forms of life—if you classify them as something separate from your own—pass through you on a regular basis. There are different cells; the transformation of the food you eat; to a degree, the air you breathe; and the water you drink—yet as a greater spirit being, it is typical to do this.

When you are not in physical form—perhaps just recently passed out of physical form and processed through different life gateways to move on to where you are going from here—it's not unusual to pause for a moment, join other spirits commingling in the general energy of spirit form on Earth, and then move on. It is by way of celebrating life, something that you find difficult to do most of the time when you are on Earth because Earth is so challenging. But you have your moments when you celebrate life as a human being.

That celebration is not because you are leaving Earth and no longer have to struggle so much as a human being. It's because you have the opportunity to join with other life forms in spirit and celebrate life. You can't wait to move beyond the veils. You do it almost immediately after you step out of your physical body to move on. And then your guide says, "Come on, come on; you can do that." They don't say it—I'm paraphrasing it, "Come on, come on; you can do that once we continue the process." But almost everyone does this for a moment or two.

To those who can see such things, you see them very often in different colored lights, usually circular, sometimes what you might call white or light white—meaning something that's illuminated white—other times in all kinds of different colors. And then they're gone. They are there for a moment, just a few seconds, and then they're gone. Other times, of course, you're seeing these things because they are just natural travels by spirit from here or there, spirit stopping off to see what you're doing, and then off spirit goes. You do the same thing when you're not here.

Do you see fish or humans if they come out in the water, or any life form? Do you see them as lights or do you just feel their energy? What is your perception of them?

My perception is mostly feeling. We notice the presence, and we can tell the shape, form, and to some extent its spiritual focus—meaning who they are in their bodies on Earth now. But we do not see them. We do not get a picture. It is felt. The same happens when human beings come around, even though human beings might have some bits and pieces attached to them—such as an underwater swimmer, for example, with tanks and fins and so on. But even when humans pass by in vehicles on the surface or below the surface, we still get a general feeling for who they are, even though they might be surrounded by this or that technological device.

Do the fishes and beings who come into your forest tell you stories? Do you talk to them?

Sometimes they commune. They don't really tell stories, but they will commune, meaning that they will stop for a while, resting. Although we don't pry into their dreams while they are resting, perhaps with a companion or more—they might commune among themselves—they make it very clear that we are welcome to listen, so to speak. But we don't listen with ears; we listen energetically. This is something you do as well; you're just not consciously aware of it, but you know at the soul level and, of course, at the spirit level. This is why, when you have deep sleep and you wake up naturally, without something to wake you up, you feel so refreshed—not only because your physical body has been refreshed by the sleep, but also because you remember who you are. You remember, just for those moments of gradually waking up while you are still transforming from deep sleep to wakefulness, who everybody is, and you're comforted and refreshed by that recollection.

I know I'd like to remember it, but then I'm always told that it would distract me from life as a human.

Yes. Although you might think that it wouldn't, it does. I'll tell you how the distraction would take place. This is why it's important. This is the first and foremost reason, though there are many. What usually would happen if people remembered things in detail is that they would be overwhelmed by the experience. Even though they might say, "Okay, now I've got to drive to work, so I have to put that aside and I can remember it later," it infiltrates because it's such an overwhelming, beautiful experience. Of course they can get distracted, and harm can result—harm not from the recollection specifically, but from the distraction. Thus, you know, you can hit something, you can cause harm, and you can be harmed. That's the number one reason; there are lots of others.

Farm Kelp to Yield Its Nutritional Benefits

All right, so to get the vitamins and nutrients and all the various incredibly wonderful things that kelp produces, you recommend that we start farming kelp?

Yes, and there are people doing that now. Generally, it's done in a cordoned-off area in salt waters, but it can be done on land if the water has the right composition. It can be done, and we recommend that. Remember to never destroy the entire plant. Don't pluck the plants; just trim them. It might take quite a few plants, but if plants know that they will just be trimmed, after a while they are likely to get stronger and sturdier and much more resistant to the diseases that might take place in a situation of farming. This is important in general for farmers, but especially for farmers of plant products.

So how would that work? Some of your beings would extend out, then, into those new plants and ensoul them?

No, no—all plants are ensouled. All life is ensouled, from the tiniest microbe in your body to the largest being you might have on the planet—whales, for example. All life is ensouled. It's impossible for it to be any other way. Creator is ensouled, eh? Creator cannot make anything that is not of itself; hence, everything is ensouled.

Okay, but you said [chuckles] that there were only seventeen beings from your planet who were ensouling all of the kelp. So then those beings extend out into the new beings, like expand themselves or something, right?

Not necessarily. In the case of farming, you understand, if the plants become furnished, it might be that, the extension. But in time, if it is clear that plants are being farmed, then it might be a separate ensouling process. It would depend how kind the process was. If the plants were just being ripped up and then utilized, probably not, but if the plants were allowed to grow and be trimmed instead of destroyed, possibly. This is how they might become more resistant to disease, because they would come to trust the farmers.

What percent do you consider trimming? What percent of the plant?

Oh, allowing for how big they would get, maybe 10, 12 percent per week or so, maybe every week or ten days.

All right, all you kelp farmers out there: Listen to that.

Well, we can but ask.

Now, my research says that it sounds like if you get too many sea urchins, and there's nothing to eat the sea urchins, they can damage your forest. What do you do about that?

Nothing. It just happens. We don't try to stop them. We don't cry for help. It just happens because sea life is in an imbalance and also a little panicked because of overfishing and the destruction that occurs as a result. It's really hard to deal with overfishing. In the long run, it will probably be harmful to all beings.

Now, Isis has said if fishermen and commercial fishers don't stop deep net-ting, where they just take everything and kill what they don't want, they won't even be able to get on the water. Do you see any progress being made?

I couldn't say. You'd have to ask Isis. My impression is that there's not enough progress. There are certainly people trying to combat it, but the issue is simple. There are a great many human beings, and they need to eat. It comes down to that, and it will remain so. I am not in any way condoning the idea of eliminating human beings, but through natural attrition and birth control, it will happen in time. You need to respect the sea and sea life. The sea, as you know it today, would not be as supportive of human beings if there were no life in it. The sea exists to support sea life. It doesn't exist to be a highway for human beings. Now I'm not saying that's not an acceptable use. I'm saying that trade isn't why it exists. It exists to be a home for sea life, just like land exists to be a home for land life, of which human beings are a portion.

The Explorer Race Will Remember
Their True Selves before Leaving Earth

What happens in the future when humans have gone out to other planets? Has anyone told you how long you're going to stay here? Do you talk about that?

We don't talk about anything. But no, that hasn't been mentioned to us. We'll be here for the duration, whatever that is. Then if something changes, I'm sure we'll be informed.

But you don't have any desires or any "well, next I'd like to do this" kind of thing?

No, that's human desire. That's human desire because you forget who you are—meaning you forget who you've ever been, not just who you are now. When you forget who you've ever been, that's the issue that stimulates that. You don't remember your past lives on other planets. You don't remember your current or future lives that might be taking place or will take place on other planets. Your desire to go out and explore and so on—or even to experience a life on another planet—is just because you don't remember who you are. The more you remember about these things and become conscious of things that you are aware of at the deep-sleep level, the more life will get better for everyone.

You're saying that while we're here on Earth as the Explorer Race, we will remember before we leave?

Yes, as it's happening now. You're remembering. You're having experiences of remembering, as far as I know.

But it's only flashes; it's not like a consistent thing.

Right, it's flashes so that it doesn't interfere with other things that you're doing here. It's happening more and more for more and more beings. At some point, all human beings will be having these flashes, and then they'll get more steady. It will take time, and it has to be done carefully. Otherwise, interference could take place, and then distraction and then . . . it would be as I said before, eh? So it's not done that way. It has to be done in a way that's benevolent for all beings—human beings too.

Now, for you all, know that sea life welcomes a certain amount of your visiting. We would prefer that you don't visit under the water. Just like you like to have your quiet time, say, in your bedroom or wherever you are, we like to live where we live without humans visiting us undersea. I know you are curious, and that is a given for the human being. So if you do that, do it as gently as possible. Try not to touch any sea life—plants, animals, or fish. If they come up and touch you gently, even bump you a little bit without being aggressive, that's fine. Be thankful for that, but don't touch them. It's not unlike the experience you might have on the land when perhaps a dog, not your own, might come up to be friendly, but not aggressively so, and might just lean against you for a moment. That's a universal way for of all life forms to let you know that they feel good about you in making the first contact. Keep that in mind, sea explorers, all right? Good life.

Oh, good life. Bless you, thank you.

CHAPTER TWENTY-TWO

Bamboo

MAY 1, 2009

∞

GREETINGS, THIS IS BAMBOO.

Oh, welcome!

Greetings. Another wanted to come through, but I felt this was more needed at this time since you are using bamboo more and more in construction, in clothing, and so on. It is coming into your flow of products much more strongly now and will continue to do so partly because, as you know, bamboo is not shy. We grow with enthusiasm, especially when treated well. And to reiterate what other plants have said, it is always best to trim a plant if you're going to use it, rather than to destroy it or cut it all down. Don't assume that just because we are vigorous, we are not offended by being entirely cut at the surface. Enough offense and we change. Those who have been cultivating bamboo for mystery, also known as mystic gardeners, do have some understanding of this. You can look to that more experiential level of gardeners for a view of such interactions.

Share Your Water with Bamboo

Now, I want to begin by suggesting that there are a few things you can do with the living plant that you have yet to do in any numbers. One is that the water you drink is good to sometimes share with bamboo, especially if you are grow-ing bamboo on your land—not as a farmer but as a decorative item. The way to share it is as follows: Don't make it ice water. If you are drinking water, ideally make it spring water available near where you live. That's the best, but any water will do. I'm going to give this suggestion as if it isn't spring water. If it's spring water, you don't have to interact with it too much; just drink it and share it.

Assuming for most people it isn't spring water, then I suggest this: Fill your glass or cup as much as you normally would fill it and look at the plant. You have to be outside to do this, all right? Look at the plant and look at your cup. So you're going to look at the plant for about twenty to thirty seconds, and while you're looking at the plant, try to relax. If for any reason you notice you're not relaxing, then probably the plant is busy doing other things and you'll have to do this another time, or perhaps you have an event coming up and you're concerned about that for some reason. So when you don't have something coming up, perhaps sit on a bench or something else near the plant and look at it. Again, if you don't feel relaxed, then it's busy. Try another time.

But if you feel yourself getting relaxed, then sip—do not drink strongly, gulp-ing, eh?—the water, and look at the water. This means that after you look at the plant, you look down at the water, and then you sip it until it gets about halfway down the glass or cup or whatever vessel you are drinking out of. Make sure that you are not drinking out of something made of plastic. Most plastic is uncomfort-able in itself and it takes a considerable amount of knowledge and effort for it to become comfortable, and I do not have that knowledge to share with you here. So assuming you have been drinking, then when the water gets down to about the halfway point, lean over.

You're going to want to be fairly close to the plant, so that you are not touching the plant but are still close enough that when you sprinkle water on the ground next to the plant, you're pretty sure that it will reach the root system there. Don't throw water on the plant itself but try to get the water within six inches or so of the plant. If a little bit happens to touch the plant, that's okay, but it will distract the plant and you might find that you are not quite as relaxed. That's because your relaxation is supported by the plant itself.

After you sprinkle the water near the plant, say, "I am happy to share my water drink with you." Remember to put nothing else in the water—no sweeten-ers, nothing, just regular water. You can do that once or twice as you wish, and more times if you feel like it, but after you've done it three times, that's enough.

I'm not saying that the plant won't use the water. I am saying that the process, the honoring, will have been completed. You can do it once and it's completed, but if you wish to do it a couple more times, that's all right. Doing this is particularly helpful if the plant has been struggling to grow or even if the plant has been growing so furiously that it's overwhelming other plants. You don't have to make a request directly of the plant. Just say, "I am happy to share my water drink with you," as I said. This creates a greater intimacy between you and the plant, and it can prepare the plant to acknowledge you as an individual rather than the plant simply considering you as a member of your species—a human being, an Earth type.

You Can Interact This Way with Commercially Grown Bamboo Too

So there is more. Say you are a farmer and you are growing bamboo for various commercial purposes; this can also be used for that process, but it would have to take place in a much more elaborate manner. If you are a small family operation, you will find this easy to do, but if it is a large business, it may be more difficult because it involves personal interaction, and the person involved with the given plant has to be focused on that plant so the plant can focus on him or her. So if you have a small farm—a few acres or so—and you grow bamboo for commercial purposes, go toward the middle of where the plants are, if they are in rows. If they are not in rows and there's just a vast amount growing, you will have to pick someplace on the perimeter and work your way around the perimeter, doing the same process exactly.

Remember to sit down if you can. If you have a problem sitting down for any reason, you can stand, but otherwise sit down and follow the procedure—again with one plant or, if there are several plants that are just massive, just pick out one space and follow the same process. After you complete the process of sharing your water, you may continue to sit there for another few minutes. Then get up, turn to the left, and go on with your life. It's useful, you see, to turn to the left, because that's the way Earth turns in spirit, and that's important to know because it's more likely to bring about a more benevolent result for you and others.

Ask Bamboo to Help You with Breathing Problems

Now, Bamboo can provide a great many supports to you that you haven't discovered yet. It's very helpful interacting with the live bamboo plant for problems with your veins and blood supply, and to a lesser degree with your breathing mechanisms. If you have any of these problems, then here's what to do: This can be done with a fairly mature plant. Don't try it with a plant you've recently put in or one that is just beginning to sprout. It has to be fairly mature— you can look up what that might mean; I have a picture here in spirit, but it's hard to get it to you in form. Then here's what to do: If you can, sit in front of the bamboo. A garden where such a plant is growing is fine. Make sure there are no other plants between you and the bamboo, or if there are a few, then steady your gaze in a direction where the bamboo is. There might be some short plants or flowers—or even plants that are passing through, eh?—temporarily located between you and the bamboo.

In the case of what you might call a weed—though there are no weeds; there are only plants—never pull up any plants before you ask another plant to do something for you, with you, or for others. It's considered offensive and will pretty well cancel whatever it is you've asked. If you have done so already, then you can go back and repeat the process without pulling up any plants. It's good to know this, eh? Then sit in front of the plant—not touching it, just looking at it—and try to relax. If you begin to relax, wait until you are as physically relaxed as you can be. Make sure the ringer is off on your phone and that there are no demands on your time for the next half-hour to forty-five minutes, though it may not take that long.

When you are relaxed, speak to the plant as if it were a friend. Say, "I'm going to pick a particular disease," but you can choose anything by its diagnosis name or simply by a description. For example, you might say to the plant, "I'm having a problem with my blood supply. My veins" (and you can say "arteries" or "capillaries" if you need to) "are shrinking," or whatever the situation is for you. "I was wondering if you could work with my veins and breathe new volume into them when I breathe with you so that they expand and allow the blood to flow well." Then just look at the plant and breathe normally and naturally, in and out, for about five minutes. It doesn't have to be exactly five minutes. It can be about 4.75 minutes to 5.25 minutes, so have a clock that you can glance at quickly, because you want to maintain contact with your eyes—and, of course, your feelings since you've relaxed with the plant.

Don't count your breaths. It's too easy to lose count, all right? And if other people are there with you, they could stand about ten feet away and not look at the plant and not look at you, and they could keep time. After you say what you have to say, you'll start breathing, and then when it comes time, they can just say quietly but so you can hear, "Time." Then you stop. Of course you continue breathing, but look down at the ground for a moment and say, "I am also asking that your spirit comes in my deep-sleep state while I am dreaming to instruct my veins to open as well as possible so that I might be of greater health and well-being."

All this time, you are looking at the ground—at the foot of the plant, so to speak, where the plant goes into the ground. Continue to sit there for another few minutes, as relaxed as can be. It can be up to ten or fifteen minutes if you like, but it doesn't have to be timed. It needs to be at least a few minutes, however, so that the plant does not feel you are rushing off. This is actually a polite way that human beings talk, and it's a natural way of communication between other life forms. If you as a human race Earth type were in contact with beings from other planets and in greater contact with beings on your own planet—what you call animals or particles or what have you—I wouldn't have to remind you of these things. But this is a style of communication that is meant to put both parties at ease and to allow both parties to be open to each other to provide for each other's needs.

Bamboo Enjoys and Benefits from Contact with Other Forms of Life

Now, you understand that I've mentioned providing for each other's needs. I might very well want to elaborate on that for a moment. When you are breathing back and forth, looking at the plant, as I said, for that five minutes, in a way you are providing—not something that bamboo needs to survive and thrive, but you are providing the plant with a greater understanding of human beings in all your complexities. Human beings are much more complex on Earth, because you don't remember who you are. The bamboo is familiar with human beings on other planets, and until the bamboo has interactions with human beings on Earth, it assumes you are just like human beings on other planets.

But once the bamboo finds out from this intimate encounter of breathing together that Earth human beings are not like the human beings on other worlds, then it allows the bamboo to spread that word—especially if it is within three-quarters of a mile of other plants. But if it is not that close to other bamboo plants, then it will get out and around over a period of years through interaction with bamboo spirit. While they like to communicate from plant to plant, the plants also have a certain amount—not as much—of interaction through bamboo spirit. But bamboo is very much a contact plant. They like contact with this and that form of life, and they particularly like contact with their own form of life, as anyone who has grown bamboo knows for certain. That's my opening statement.

Bamboo Helps Beings on Benevolent Planets Extend Their Lives

Very well. Question?

Now tell me who you are. Are you a spirit or are you living in a plant?

I am bamboo spirit. I have not individualized as a bamboo plant on this planet. But on our native planet, I have been a vast plant, as you might say, although we have a considerable amount of flexibility there. It is a water planet, not unlike your own, but there is a little more water and not as much land, and the land is more like what you would call sandbars. So one does not find too many human beings there, aside from the occasional visitor from afar, but they would have to have a vehicle that could gently sit on a sandbar or simply interact with the fluid. The fluid is not quite the same as your water; it is similar but does not have vast reservoirs like you find on Earth, with great depth and huge volume. It runs about—to use your measurement—a few inches along the surface of the planet with a reservoir system underground. Plants thrive with that system.

So you grew in the water, then?

Yes. Well, that's how I grew, but on Earth it's just a matter of adaptation.

How did you—bamboo, as a species—happen to come here to Earth?

We were invited just like everyone else who came—plants and what you call animals. They were all invited to interact with you when you were ready to interact. They were also warned that they would be utilized quite thoroughly and quite possibly even decimated before they were asked to interact, so of course not everyone volunteered. I can say that's a general factor for all beings, at least as far as I know.

As far as the ones we've talked to also. Are you the only species on your home planet?

No, there are a few others. There's something that if you saw it, it would remind you of a fish, but it swims along the surface and is very flat. If you were to look at it, it would seem unusual. We find them to be very pleasant companions, and they manage to survive. They essentially absorb minerals from the planet, minerals that are under the fluid, and this is how they exist. They're not very big.

Are you on many other planets besides your home planet and our planet?

A few, because we have these healing qualities in interacting intimately, as I've stated—breathing with others. As a result, you find us on planets where a civilization is attempting to extend lifetimes. Such beings will often breathe with us. You might find, for instance, a place where many plants are growing in various shapes. You would call it a round garden, but the plants grow where they are welcomed; they are not planted by the beings. A person will usually traverse a pathway of sorts into the center and either walk around or perform some cultural process of interacting with the plants. Ultimately, they wind up singing or talking of their lives, sharing memories and experiences, and requesting support to extend their lives in some way, according to their personal, cultural, or maybe familial drives and needs. This can be done in more ideal conditions. It's not unusual for people to be able to extend their lives anywhere from fifty to several hundred years through interactions along these lines—on other planets where situations are much more benevolent, you understand.

On your planet, I don't think that would be possible, especially given its current condition of pollution and so on. But in time, you too will be able to do this if you wish—as things get more balanced and you find out more about who you are, as you begin to incorporate that as part of your global knowledge, and as you teach this to the children, and so on. In time, you might be able to extend your life—not just getting older and suffering, extending your suffering, none of that—and by that time, I think, there won't be many diseases. You will be able to feel healthier and stronger and extend your life for ten, twenty, maybe even fifty years. But I don't think it will go that route, as you say. Do you say, "Go that route?" I don't think it will go that route for quite a while yet, so anyone who is living now can let go of that. [Laughs.]

Bamboo Can Help with Circulatory Issues in Human Beings

When one interacts with your plant . . . you gave an example of the blood vessels, but can one ask for help with any human physical problem?

No. I mentioned that because of the formation of the plant. There is a lot going on in the center of it. But if you've seen the inside of bamboo, you know that it's chambered, and chambers are not unfamiliar to your vessel, say, to your heart. Your heart has chambers. You could say that arteries and veins are forms of chambers; they are rivulets that support the chambers, you see. The chamber mechanism allows the plant to grow and continue to grow, even if it is cut past a certain point. I would say that, generally speaking, anything that has to do with breath or the flow of fluids in your body would be the thing to do. You can't ask for just anything.

Okay, I'm glad you made that clear.

As a questioner—to speak to you personally for a moment, but do include it in the book—if you have a situation going on in your body, it's safe to say that other human beings will have it too. If you wish to ask for a plant in the future that might have some comments to make on this or that condition that you have, feel perfectly free to do so. But you can request this because it's safe to say that any injury or discomfort you've ever had is shared by other human beings.

Right. Do you interact only with the plants on Earth, or do you interact with plants on other planets?

Just on Earth. That's plenty.

Are there many of you?

Quite a few, to say nothing of the conditions that we're living in here. Not quite as calm and peaceful as on the home planet, eh? Then again, one might say the same thing for the human being Earth type: you are not quite as calm and peaceful as on your home planets, wherever they may be in this or that galaxy. However, there will certainly be a lot of good stories to tell someday. Do you mind my being a little humorous? I enjoy human humor.

You said bamboo plants can communicate with each other within three-quarters of a mile.

Yes, but no contact is necessary—just through air, through rock, through stone. It doesn't make any difference as long as it's up to but not much farther than three-quarters of a mile, allowing for this or that temporary condition. Then individual plants can communicate with other individual plants.

Earth Humans Have More Complicated Digestive Systems

You said you exchange stories with the fish at home. Do the bamboo here communicate with animals and insects and birds that move through their branches and through their areas?

Only if the animals say something first. We are polite. We do not barge into their lives, but if they wish to make a comment or a greeting or a salutation, we are inclined to do that as well. At times, there are those who stay within our foliage on a regular basis. We talk and share stories and do our own songs as we do them—in spirit, of course. The human could not hear that, but if you're attuned to knowing how, you may be able to.

Well, I like the physical sounds that bamboo makes. It's almost like a song when they rub—what would you say, knock?—against each other.

Yes. A pleasant sound, isn't it?

Yes, absolutely. Why is there such a connection with the Chinese? One always thinks of the Chinese when one thinks of bamboo. Did it grow there first or something?

I could not say. I do not classify Earth humans by their nationalities. But my best guess is that people are very creative there and perhaps came to be good at utilizing what was available. I believe they are still quite creative today, but that's my best guess. As I say, it is "human being, Earth-type," but I don't think of you as this or that appearance or this or that color. I think of you as human beings, period. I do tend to say "Earth-type" because you are vastly different, temporarily, than human beings from other places. But this is purely temporary while you go through the educational and other processes that you are dealing with here on Earth.

How are we temporarily different? What are some of the differences?

Oh, I think your digestive system appears to be a little more complex, but this is because you eat things on Earth that you would not normally eat as humans elsewhere. I also think it allows you to discharge things from your body that must be out of your body with greater swiftness, if necessary. Generally speaking, though, most of you on the planet relate directly—meaning genetically—to human beings on other planets or galaxies or solar systems. If you were to offer up a little sampling of your genetic code to interacting ETs, they would be able to tell you exactly what planet or culture of human beings you are directly related to, should they volunteer that someday—which I believe they will.

Yes, they all contributed to our DNA.

Well, sometimes the contribution was not direct, meaning it might have been available to some group of beings who traveled to Earth and, from their perceptions, they decided this or that genetic strain might be helpful. Granted, over time, that may or may not be a factor anymore, but it has lent itself to variety. From my perception, variety is something your planet stands for. I believe, from my interactions with angels and teachers and Creator, that Creator is quite fond of variety.

When You Commune with Other Beings, You Can Ask Them for Guidance

Part of the reason I believe that Creator has provided so much variety—although it isn't all in existence in your time, but there's still quite a bit—on your Earth planet is to offer to all those who live and learn how to communicate with enough of a variety of other forms of life. With enough variety, you as human beings will have the opportunity to inquire of this or that type of being as to what they might offer, such as learning how to speak politely, you understand.

I think that's been discussed before, but to lightly go over it, you might, when talking to a spider or a dandelion, simply introduce yourself personally.

Say, "Greetings. I am _____." You can say your name—or even your parent's names, if you wish—or you can say, "I am from this or that culture, and I wish you greetings" or "I bid you greetings" or something. Then someday, if not immediately, you might be aware of an answer. You might simply feel a shift in your energy. If you feel slightly uncomfortable, it's not a judgment. It means that the plant or animal is busy, and you can communicate with it another time. This comes up from person to person as well, you know—meaning human to human.

But if you get a pleasant energy, then there is some communication going on. You may not understand it, but if you can do what this being is doing now in terms of channeling or feeling inspiration, you might get a word or two, even without that capability. If you're asking about something important to you, you can ask the plant—or animal or being or stone or whatever you're communicating with—if it has something to offer in guiding you with whatever you're confused with or concerned about. If it can't help directly, you can ask that it offer a suggestion in your deep-sleep state that you are able to remember or be inspired about when you are in your next waking state.

In time, all human beings on this planet will be able to communicate immediately and directly with all other forms of life on the planet, including all other human beings, regardless of what language you speak. By that time, you will be able to commune, meaning know what the other person desires to transmit to you—in this case, using "person" to define plants, animals, and other human beings as well—not what they're thinking but what they desire to transmit to you. There's a difference, and it is that difference that allows for and perpetuates the whole idea of being polite.

Communicate with Bamboo One-on-One, Not in Large Groups

Well said. I was thinking, since bamboo has this property and most people don't live close to bamboo, how would you set up a healing center? You'd need a really huge area of plants so that they don't get tired, right? How would you do that?

So that who didn't get tired?

The bamboo. If you had people come to interact with bamboo.

Oh, I think plants do not get that tired. You could have a certain amount of plants if you had half an acre or so. On a small scale, you might very easily be able to grow bamboo in your yard, if you have a yard. Even if you are living in a building with many occupants, you might have a certain amount of land available to you. Plant bamboo if you are in a proper zone. The bamboo might do very well.

Yes, as you say, it grows very enthusiastically.

You would know how many people could be served by individual plants if people said to you (say the bamboo is in your place) that they didn't feel relaxed. Say they kept trying with this or that plant and they didn't feel relaxed. That means that the plants need to commune with each other or rest. So you have to experiment and maybe try this out before you welcome people to come and visit. Plants are individuals, and they may have greater or lesser capacities to interact with individual humans. I would not recommend doing this in any other way, though, other than as an individual.

Where the desire within the individual would cause one to seek out the plant, you're saying?

Yes. I do not recommend that a hundred people go and talk to one plant like that—person to person, so to speak. It's important that there's an intimacy. I want to just elaborate on that. You know if one person talks to you politely and pleasantly, there's a tendency to give that person your full attention, but if a hundred people are talking to you or there are a hundred people standing there, you might just be intimidated, or you might not answer a hundred people the same way you would answer one. I'm using that as an example, in the context of your question, which was about a healing center.

Right, but I was thinking about taking one person at a time over to a plant. Has this knowledge been available on the planet before and it was lost, or are you telling it now for the first time?

Some of it has been available on the planet before, but your history does not lend itself to perpetuation of knowledge, so you have to be reminded from one civilization to another.

You're right. When civilizations end, you just have a bunch of stones and pieces of pottery.

Well, your discomfort with yourselves can sometimes become destructive toward others.

You mean that's how some civilizations end, right?

Yes, it's a comment on what you said. That's the main reason you don't have all this knowledge and wisdom. In the past, such knowledge and wisdom was passed on verbally from one to another: not because there wasn't a means to write it down or perpetuate its understanding, but because the intellect is not sufficient. There needs to be a feeling. You know how, when people talk, they stress certain words and so on, or they suggest certain feelings. This comes about as a learning when you hear the voice and interact directly. Such teaching often allows an understanding that is much greater, much deeper, and much longer lasting than simply words on paper.

Now, I'm not trying to lecture you, since "words on paper" is something you specialize in. But your job is to remind people—essentially, that's what you're doing with your work overall. You're reminding people, but it is also the person's job to try to experience that which is beyond the word. You can read about roses all you want, but until you've grown them, you're not really going to know that much.

And until you smell them. Well, where in the universe are you?

A long ways.

So we probably won't contact you as we go out to the stars, right?

No, not in the near future. Perhaps in a few thousand years, but when it comes to interacting with Spirit, you don't have to go anywhere. We're happy to be present.

Okay, thank you!

Very well.

CHAPTER TWENTY-THREE

Bamboo Spirit

MAY 5, 2009

છ

I'm just sitting here reading how fantastic you are! Your food has eight amino acids, and fiber. You're used for medicines. This is awesome.

Yes, and think how much more can be done by human interaction with the living plant. Remember, the purpose of this book is primarily to help you to ease your life and the lives of others. By creating a system of specific details, you will be able to intersect with that moment of life between yourself and plants that will help you avail yourself of the opportunity to become healthier, acquire greater wisdom and capacities, and most importantly, cure or prevent a great many diseases, some of which are profoundly interfering with your well-being.

Eating Bamboo Shoots Can Provide Many Health Benefits
How do we get the benefit of your eight amino acids by being in your energy?

I know what you're asking. You're asking: "How is it possible to assimilate amino acids from the plant without destroying the plant?" But that question is unnecessary. After all, if you can consume the plant, why bother? Now, you have to remember that bamboo is a very hardy plant, and it does not resent being grown as a food so much. We understood this when we came here.

Bamboo is not rare. If we were a rare and exotic species such as an orchid, always considering whether to go or whether to stay—meaning whether to leave the planet or stay around a little longer to see if human beings become more gentle—that would be one thing. But we're not that; we are quite the opposite. This book will be of interest to those who are interested in plants and spirituality—and, of course, to herbalists. The simple consumption of bamboo shoots in a salad, as they are served now, might be effective. But you would have to speak to a nutritionist about that or find out if they are served that way now; they may have to be processed. Processing allows for a great deal of consumption of things that might not otherwise be healthy to eat in a raw state, eh?

Well, the point is that bamboo has so many uses. It is such an awesome plant. Can we go into more detail about interacting with the live plant?

There may be more for the advanced practitioner of the kind of study this book is suggesting, but I feel it's first important to get people started. You'll notice that no particular plant goes into very elaborate detail about long-term interactions with the plant. That's because all plants are attempting to serve the most immediate needs, in their perception, for the human being. Once you establish better health through this type of interaction with the living plant, then we'll see.

Human Beings Are Part of the Food Chain on Earth

All right. So it's not that you are recommending that you not be used for food or as a product; you're just focusing on what is available with the live interaction. I had thought a lot of times the plants were asking not to be consumed, not to be used as products and food.

I think it's important to ask each individual plant that. I believe you will find that the general consensus is, most if not all plants do understand that the possibility of being used as food by human—or other—beings, is a given on this planet. To be perfectly honest, for the most part, human beings do not consider themselves part of the food chain, though it is so. [Chuckles.] But let's just skip over that.

The soil is made of the atoms that were once in our bodies, and then that goes into the plants and the animals eat the plants and then we eat the plants and animals, so it's sort of circular.

Yes, that's right.

Do animals eat the bamboo shoots?

Generally speaking, animals (nonhumans) will eat or drink—meaning absorb moisture—from plants, period. But you know it wouldn't be hard to find out. Just search on that one. Bamboo shoots—who eats those, eh? There's a little creature who looks like a bear who likes that.

Oh, I have that in here: the panda bear! You're the main food for panda bears. They are so beautiful. Only there aren't very many panda bears left.

Well, fortunately there are people in China and other parts of Asia who are determined to keep them going, and they are quite successful—partly because they are very loving as individuals and in groups, and they can give as well as receive love. Pandas in their exposure to humans must have that love. Although they do not wish to be hugged by human beings, they do need to be in an atmosphere of loving welcome. Generally speaking, all life thrives in an atmosphere of loving welcome.

Yes. I hope we're getting closer to that.

There are many places on Earth now that provide that loving welcome. You can read about people raising the pandas in China, and I think it will make you feel good.

The panda bears will stay as long as they have that loving interaction, right?

I cannot say. You'll have to ask them.

I will when I get a chance.

Humans Have a Ways to Go Before
Their Perceptions of Food Consumption Change

Do you see a time in the future when humans will eat less because the energy is higher, the vibration's higher . . . ?

Here is a real question: "Is it possible for human beings to eat less and derive the same amount of nutrition and satisfaction?" That's the real question, because sometimes people will derive the nutrition they need but keep on going because they don't feel full. Yes, it is possible, and one also could create a feeling of fullness if one is more actively involved in gathering or farming. When farming, though, if you wish to have plants that are going to create a sense of being full and give you the nutrition and nutrients you need, you'll have to give them a lot of love and also pay attention to their needs in other ways. Of course in the natural world, other creatures—nonhumans, nonplants—need to eat, so you may need to plant a little patch of plants and ask nonhumans to eat those, as has been successfully proven in the famous place in . . . you know, that book.

The Findhorn Ecovillage, you mean?

Yes. So I would say that it is possible. It will require a change in perception. The change in perception that is required is actually happening now at the early stages, meaning a global consciousness. By that, I'm referring to a global political consciousness, not a global soul consciousness, because that's always been established. But in the political outlook, countries are less of a factor than people's common ground and interests—what they do, how they live, and so on; that's happening now. Even though from the political view, countries will be uncomfortable giving up their borders, so to speak, ultimately it will make a better life for all beings.

So as that happens, perception will change. The first and most profound factor of that perception change will be, "What can we do to get along well together and help each other have a more benevolent, comfortable life, one that we all can enjoy?" That's being worked on now, and while there are a lot of good-hearted people working on it, there are others who are still struggling to get what they want because they feel it is owed to them. They have many reasons to justify that, some of which are perfectly rational and others that are perhaps past-oriented. I'm not trying to say that they're not justified, but when justification from the past becomes more important than the physical reality of the moment, destruction may not be far behind. So I would say that you have a ways to go yet before that goal you have stated in your question will come to be fulfilled globally, but you're on the way.

Bamboo Spirit Is a Visiting Philosopher

That was the first half of the question. The second half was: "Will we be able, while still on this planet, to see plants and animals not as food but as beings we can learn from and communicate with?"

No, and there's a reason. What will you eat? Are you going to eat the air? I don't think so. No. You will need to eat, and I do not see you willingly becoming vegetarians, nor do I feel that that is intended. Granted, in other societies where there is no strife and life is completely benevolent, being a vegetarian, so to speak, is acceptable and is often the case. But that is not Earth, and it may not be for some time. So no, I don't think that is ever going to happen within the framework of life you have now, unless you can offer an alternative. People must eat, eh? Plants consume in their own way—granted, not the same way you do—but nonplants and nonhumans, so-called animals, they consume too, and many of them have much to offer and are very wise. But the consumption is a reality on this planet, so no. That's the simple answer to your question.

Okay. As a bamboo spirit, you are here to help the bamboo plants. In what ways do you help them?

I think that your question involves an assumption. You're assuming that I am here to help the plants because other spirits have said that that is what they do, but that is not always the case. Bamboo has a philosophical side. Anytime a plant is philosophical or a form of life is philosophical, there is always a consideration of other life forms. So given that, I am not *exclusively* here to serve the needs of bamboo, for their needs are not that elaborate. They are quite simple, really: sometimes just a feeling of home—that's it—especially if they're tired or not well. But other than that, I am open to discussing points of philosophy, such as we're doing today, with the human being. We often have such interchanges with other forms of life, very frequently with what you might call visitors to this planet, of which there are fewer today—but there still are some.

All right. That's very interesting. [Laughs.] You're a visiting philosopher.

Well, there are others, and since quite a few in the so-called animal world also interact with humans, or are prepared to do so, in this way I've also interacted with visitors.

There Are Visitors to Earth Who Do Not Communicate with Humans

So do you inspire humans? How do you interact with them?

As I said, I am open to doing that, but most of my communication that hasn't been with bamboo and that falls under the general heading of your question has been with visitors—beings from other worlds, you understand.

Right. Have you talked to any we might have heard of—the names of the species or of the planets?

Well, they don't identify themselves with a species name. They do not call themselves much of anything; rather, they tend to introduce themselves by their personal names or occasionally the names of the vehicles they are on.

Okay. It was a sneaky question; I'm trying to find out who's coming here.

I am not trying to keep that from you, but they do not usually say "We're from this or that planet." And even if they did, none of the names would match the names you have, which makes sense, doesn't it? If you went to another culture, or even to another language—especially some language that's quite different from yours—on your own planet, you'd find that all the names you have for things in your language have completely different sounds and might even have different meanings. Can you imagine the difference from another planet? I might be able to give you a name but I would not be able to translate it. Here's a name:

They said they had been visiting your planet for some time but had not actually communicated with human beings for something like 1,500 years in your time. They're from the planet *Senetsk Katcho* [sounds like "sahn-etz'k ka-choh"].

[Laughs.] Yes, I see what you mean.

I would be hard pressed to say what that is in your language. [Laughs.]

Right. [Laughs.] Or where it is, right?

I can only say that they were generally what you call a human type, but they were not human beings.

Some Information on How Bamboo Communicates with Other Beings

So what do you talk about?

Well, it is like you would introduce yourself to any person. If, you understand, you went to visit some place from afar, yes? You would say, "Greetings, my name is _____." They might respond, "Greetings, my name is such and such and I am from such and such." Or they might sometimes say: "I am born from _____," and then you'd get some of their family history. Or in rare cases, they might say, "I am from _____," and then they would give the vehicle name. I do not know why they do that; they just do. Then they might give a more polite introduction and ask who I was and where I was from, because they as beings could perceive spirits just as well as any other beings. They might tend to go to spirit beings first—not just any spirit beings and not spirit beings of individuals, because they look different, but especially spirit beings that could be perceived in certain ways from their culture's point of view.

Then they would ask, "Who are you?" and I would say, "I am the spirit of bamboo." Of course, when I said "bamboo," it wouldn't do them any good at all, would it? But I would have a picture of it and they would see it, possibly in a genus form or possibly as you would see it, like you would say, "zoom." For example, it would be like you'd see the seed and the roots going into the ground, and then you'd see the shoots coming up, and so on—the whole thing. They would have an idea that this is a form of life they might have some general sense of having seen or observed or studied before they came here—whatever. In any event, we would proceed from there.

You're called bamboo here. What are you called on your home planet?

I'm called bamboo in some places on your planet, but on the home planet we are . . . it is not verbal. I'll do my best: "*shhhht-shhhk shk-kt-shk-kt.*"

Ah, yes. [Laughs.] Okay. Oh, are there other names for your plant here in other languages? Of course, because "bamboo" is English. Ah. So you have many names on this planet too?

Many names, and don't assume that "bamboo" is English.

Oh, what is it?

Just look it up. It's fun. Find somebody to look these things up, and as a rule, never assume. When it comes to interspecies communication, never assume. It is possible to trip over something that way. I speak as one who knows. [Laughs.]

Heaven only knows what I've tripped over in the past and didn't even know about.

Well, that's where time, experience, and consequences turn into wisdom.

[Laughs.] Okay, I need a few hundred more years. I wish we could set you up in a school or someplace. Why can't we get beings like you to teach in our colleges or schools?

Why bother when you can assimilate on your own? But I understand what you're saying. I wouldn't need much care.

[Chuckles.] No, and your salary would be pretty low.

It's quite all right. I'm willing to do the whole thing pro bono.

Bamboo Can Produce What You Need When You Need It

[Laughs.] You'd be good. What else can we explain to the readers about you, your species, your being? What can you say that we haven't talked about?

Generally speaking, all you need to know is that the bamboo plant can provide a great deal of awareness of your own capacity to produce a benign state of being for yourself. A great deal of the discomfort and disease that occurs on this planet—not all, but a great deal of it—is simply based on expectations. A lot of unintended teaching goes on on this planet, suggesting that this or that bad thing is going to happen if you do this, if that happens, if this happens as you get older, and so on. If that teaching didn't take place and remained just with those health practitioners who are functioning full time to help individuals who are not well or who need special care, that would be better.

But for people to be discussing things all the time and warning others of getting them, and so on, it creates a myth of discomfort that is self-perpetuating. I'm going to suggest that bamboo and other plants can support a true constitutional element of your physical self, which is the ability to reproduce what you need when you need it—even to overcome illnesses without care, to a minor degree. Sometimes that may be needed in an emergency. Other times it may not be possible. I'm not saying don't call your doctors or your emergency personnel—quite the opposite. What I am saying is that it may be possible to move toward a healthier condition if you do not devote quite so much time to worrying. Good night and good life.

Wait. Don't go. This is a whole new thing. You just talked before about the blood system and the chambers of the heart. You didn't talk about interacting with the bamboo in the sense of what you just said now.

I am almost gone, but I will say this: Just sit in front of the bamboo using the same method as described in Chapter 22 and try not to think. Breathe in and out naturally for a few minutes. When you find you are thinking, just stop. Do not get mad at yourself. Continue to sit and breathe in and out. It is not necessary to have your eyes open, but you can if you like. If they are open, just look at the plant. That will help. Good night.

Oh, thank you so much. Good life.

Goodbye.

GRAINS

CHAPTER TWENTY-FOUR

Corn

MAY 21, 2008

∞

GREETINGS! THIS IS CORN.

Welcome! You're one we wanted to talk to. You're such an important part of our food supplies.

And also, from my perception, the most important part of your grounding in food. Corn on Earth has everything to do with the spirits that live underground, the spirits that live on the surface, and the spirits that live in the sky. We are able to unite and unify these beings in complete balance in each and every kernel of the corn, as well as in the cob itself. This is something to keep in mind for those who like to eat corn off the cob and sometimes suck on the cob to get those extra juices. This is something that is a good thing to do, because the capacity of corn to activate your own roots, as well as the root chakra, in the way that supports, unifies and stabilizes your personal physical survival on this planet is profound.

Corn has the capacity to achieve balance in your auric field as long as you are consuming it within, say, four hours of its being picked. But for those who are unable to do that, it can support significantly these things that I've mentioned already if and only if you are eating it from the cob—meaning you purchase it, bring it home, take off the husk, cook it, and eat it in that fashion. Now, as far as

347

corn that has been processed, frozen, or canned, it does not give you any more of that support at all; it just fills your belly, and that sometimes is enough for those who are hungry, yes?

I want to also make a suggestion for those who are growing corn in a garden, especially growing it organically. I recommend that even before the ears of corn have enlarged but while the plants are growing vigorously, that you walk up and down the rows carefully and breathe the same air the corn breathes. This is important. Just breathe naturally and exhale naturally in whatever direction you normally do, and walk up and down each of the rows. If you are growing this in a vast field, perhaps on a farm, to support a local restaurant perhaps or a community, it might take more than one of you to perform this task—though I recommend that those who do perform this task are ones who work in the field with the corn regularly. This encourages the corn to grow for you and allows the corn plants to adopt you temporarily to their family. Corn is very family-oriented, and this does not have to mean blood relations—it simply means those who work with us. I'm mentioning this because corn can provide so much for you spiritually.

Pleiadians Brought Corn to Earth

How did you come by these incredible abilities?

We originally come from a planet where a great many people on Earth are oriented, if not in this life, then in other lives you may have lived on this planet or perhaps nearby planets. Our source form is the Pleiades, and this attunement we have came about through long and sometimes arduous—meaning not struggle, but meaning long and with great finesse—growing patterns. This planet in the distant reaches of the Pleiades star system is one where the individuals on the planet are in complete concordance with corn and corn is in complete concordance with them. These individuals are human beings as you know yourselves to be—not any variation, not something you wouldn't recognize. These are human beings who can pass every biological qualification on Earth for being human. I thought you'd like to know that there are others just like you biologically, though perhaps a little different philosophically, as one might expect.

These beings have traveled in the past of their time to Earth in the early days when human beings were just getting started on Earth. They have received reports, updated from time to time, about your progress toward unified spirituality based entirely upon benevolence and love for each other, all things, and all beings. They appreciate your progress, but some years ago, they felt that human beings needed support to maintain their progress toward a unified spirituality. Since they do not travel to Earth in your times, they requested that others who would travel to Earth would bring a form of corn they had developed that had the durability to survive the conditions on Earth—not only climate conditions, but attitudes, demeanors, behaviors of human beings, as well as technological output (meaning the pollution, but also meaning radiation (healing term): electrical, electromagnetic, and so on)—and still support benevolent spiritual unification.

I cannot be certain when that time was, but corn then emerged all over the Earth right around the same time. The peoples who grew it initially all knew that this wonderful food came from those people in the round ships. It's not unusual to find such pictographic representations right along with corn. Just know that some peoples wanted to leave you the message that this food source has everything to do with the evolution of the human consciousness on Earth. That is why sometimes you'll see that pattern. How to describe it? It starts in the center and revolves out slowly. You know the one?

A spiral?

Yes, thank you. You will see that spiral in a pictogram near the picture of the corn and near the picture of the ship as best as the artist could leave it. This might also be found in a pictograph, but I do not have all those terms. Perhaps that's not the correct pronunciation.

Petroglyph?

Petrograph, I think. Pictogram. Petrogram.

Something like that.

Yes. Basically something either incised into stone or left as a picture on stone— usually in some place that would have minimal exposure to weather cycles, so it would hopefully survive for future generations, but sometimes in completely exposed areas where human beings would likely be, at least human beings who were on spiritual pathways. You'll find this sometimes in tribal areas, but if the tribe is no longer there, having moved on for one reason or another, then often it becomes enigmatic to those who have inherited those territories. That's why I'm being careful to give as many details as possible, so that those who study these things do not jump to the conclusion that the picture of something that looks like a UFO and the corn and the spiral have come from different times, different situations. Although they might have been placed there by different hands, it was all done to make the message as clear as possible. You know how you will sometimes in your own words try to make something clearer, even though the original statement you felt at that time was clear enough? It is the same thing for pictures in stone.

So these individuals had everything to do with raising the strain of corn that is now on Earth, even though that strain has been altered at times. There were different strains that naturally emerged over time, and you find different colors of the corn, different patterns. That which has emerged on its own simply shows what strains were originally synthesized to come up with the strain that was originally given to peoples on Earth—not synthesized technologically, by the way, but using spiritual practices. So when those different appearances of corn evolved, it is just the corn remembering who it has been in the past. I know that in your time it is typical to create hybrids, but it's best if you can consume as old-fashioned a corn as you can find. There are those who have preserved seeds, and you could seek them out, inquire.

Do your memories go back before the planet on the Pleiades?

My memories, since I am corn on the Earth, do not go back before that time, but since we may do this over a two-day period, it would be good to speak to someone else. But I feel it's important to provide this wisdom based upon an Earth point of view. As you can see, I am talking about Earth and people and things here and so on, so that the book remains as grounded as possible.

How to Interact with the Corn Plant

For those of us who can't eat the corn four hours after it's picked, is there some way to interact with the actual corn plant?

The best way, if you are unable to eat it, say, an hour or even twenty minutes after it's been picked, is to purchase the corn wherever you do—perhaps at a roadside stand—where it's still in the husk. If you must purchase it from a store, then there's no guarantee, unless your health food store has obtained the corn, for example, without any processing, meaning it hasn't been frozen or anything like that. So you will have to ask your grocer about the processing the corn has gone through. If it's been, for instance, radiated to preserve it, then it won't do these other things, though it would still fill your belly.

But is there any benefit in interacting with the corn plant itself energetically, if you don't eat the corn?

That's a good question, because some people don't eat corn; they don't like it or can't tolerate it. Some people are sensitive to derivatives of corn. If you can interact, meaning have contact with the corn plant itself, then just stand near the corn plant and breathe in and out, say, ten times. If you're able to be in the corn field, just walk around, look at the corn, walk between the rows (if the farmer says it's all right), and breathe in and out. That will do almost the same thing. But the corn must be fairly mature—meaning, oh, two-and-a-half-feet tall, something like that, on its way toward its more vigorous self. It would not be good to do this with corn when it is a young, tender shoot.

We have heard of the way that some of the native peoples talk to the corn and interact with the corn while it's growing.

I feel this is very good. As long as the corn is mature—meaning, say, four-feet high—if you're talking to it, speak gently and softly. Corn is aware that this is another species talking, so even if you're agitated or upset about something, take many deep breaths before you walk into the corn field itself. If you're letting go of your agitation, stay at least forty feet away from the corn plants and do not breathe in and out in their direction until you release your agitation. Then, when you're more relaxed, you can walk into the field and just talk about things gently. You can say, "I am upset at this or that," but speak softly and gently—you can whisper if you like, but you do not have to whisper, just speak softly and gently. I would recommend, however, that you speak of things that are good in your life. This encourages the corn to grow.

One cannot forget that this is food being raised for human beings or perhaps animals, and you want them to be well nourished. So it's better to say things that are good in your life. Think about your life and examine it before you go out into the field, and speak only that which is good. Don't say, "Well, I'm really enjoying my time with my daughter, even though she's . . ."—don't do that! Don't add the addendum. If you're enjoying your time with your daughter, for the sake of this example, then just say what you enjoy. This is good, because it supports life and it reminds corn that corn is not the only being who is about family—human beings are about family and other beings as well. It reassures corn that life is going on and that corn's sacrifice of itself that others may be fed, nourished, and enriched is a worthy sacrifice.

There are also other things you can do. People sometimes sing to the corn. If you have a holy song you can sing, that's fine, as long as it is pleasant, not critical, and not dramatic. If you don't have a holy song, then you can make up a tune, whistle it, anything like that. But if the tune reminds you of something dramatic or upsetting, then don't do that with the corn. In short, sing only that which would make you cheerful or is a holy song.

But corn had this spiritual ability before the humans worked on it on the Pleiades, right?

I believe so. You'll have to speak to someone beyond that, but my understanding from what I can recall, based upon the root information I have, is that we have always had this ability. It's just that the energy was redefined so that it would support Earth humans.

I Prefer to Be Grown in a Non-mechanized Fashion

What about your experience? How long have you been on Earth?

I have been on Earth for about a thousand years, just re-creating myself as a being from one corn plant to another. We can do that without proximity as a factor, so I have been all over the planet, wherever corn could be grown. Generally though, I have noticed that where I have been has been a warm, dry place. I do not recall ever being grown in any moist, humid place, though I would guess that might be the best place for us.

It is an interesting thing: when we grow in warm, dry places, of course, we need to be watered, but the warm, dry air will sometimes create a stronger ear of corn in terms of durability but also for each kernel of the corn. It might be supportive more of strength in those who consume it, whereas in a warm, moist locale with much rain and humidity in the air, for example, the support for the spirituality of the person would be more profound than their physical strength. It follows somewhat along the male/female line. You can interpret that for yourself, but I'll acknowledge it to presuppose a question.

Do you choose where you go, or do you just find yourself there?

I find myself there. I like that very much, because it has allowed me to be exposed to many different kinds of beings, animals, and also to the different appearances and cultural ways of human beings. I like that very much. Actually, one of the reasons I've stayed here so long is the opportunity to be exposed to different types of human beings. Generally, I prefer to be grown in a non-mechanized fashion. I have only had one experience of being in a corn field where mechanization was involved. I didn't like it and made it clear that if I was going to continue on Earth, that wouldn't happen again.

I'm pretty sure that other corn feel the same way. This is why perhaps your scientists and others who experiment with such things have hybridized corn, because we are basically offended and intolerant of machine contact. We need to know that that which is contacting us has love and appreciation for who and what we are, and since most machines do not remember who and what they are (since they were something before they were made into a machine), then it is just a lonely, frightened object contacting us, and this does not give us the support we need to know that our sacrifice is worthy. It's not that we are prejudiced against machines, but we feel sorry for them.

Still, we are unable to remind them of who they are, though I remember an old piece of farm equipment. It was slowly rusting nearby at a time when I was growing in a small vegetable patch a few hundred years ago. And I was able to remind the metal where it once had come from. It was close enough that I was able to come with a root about a foot away from the metal, and I sang to it about the mountains and the stone, and it felt good. I could tell it changed, and I was happy to provide that gift.

Oh, that was so kind of you. Who, then, is inhabiting the hybridized corn? If none of you like to do it, then what beings are incarnating as that corn?

I feel that there is some energy of corn, but it is not the same energy associated with that Pleiadian source. I believe it might come from another star system, so this does not rule out that there is corn spirit there, but when I have seen this corn, I do not see corn spirit, I do not feel corn spirit, and I feel no sense of family. I feel something more austere, something less able to make close and loving contact from one being to another. I feel great strength, but also loneliness, and that is sad.

When you have a question, do you have guides and teachers you can ask—in this case, if you wanted to know where those beings' spirits were from?

If I wanted to know, yes, but when you feel something like that, it is so sad that you don't want to continue feeling it. But it is a good question you can ask the other.

So how does the process work, then? You said, "I do not want to inhabit any but natural corn." Is there a desire itself allows you to be drawn to the corn that is natural?

What I said is that I did not wish to be cultivated in a field where machines are being used.

Is it your inhabiting, then, that allows you to experience what you want?

Yes, this is not unlike the situation for your own souls. You do not just get sprinkled all over the Earth by Creator and your guides, angels, and teachers. You can, as a soul, state certain basic parameters that you would like, and generally speaking, you will get that. You may not get everything you ask for, but you will get the basics of what you ask for, as far as I have seen. I have seen human souls—seen in the way I see, not with eyes—coming to a mother, and my impression is that since the soul of the human comes and goes a bit while it is in mother, I did not see sadness there or unhappiness. So my assumption is that the soul was at least basically happy to be in that mother.

Do you see souls go too, when we die?

I have seen it once. It is not something I look for. I didn't look for the other situation, but I just happened to be in a place where there was a young mother. So it just happened.

And so it did with the soul leaving then also?

Yes. It was an old farmer who passed over and was not found until the next day, alas, but I did see his soul leave. He did something interesting. When his soul stepped out of the body, he looked different—I noticed he looked more youthful. He walked over to the corn, and he touched an ear of corn. It wasn't me, but I was able to speak to that plant after he left and his guide came to help him find his way. I asked that corn plant what it felt like when that human spirit touched him, and plant said, "I've never felt a human touch to be so compatible." It was very nice.

Variety Is One of the Joys of Earth

Humans have changed in the past thousand years—how do you see the difference from the time you came until now?

Well, the time I came the human beings were very spiritual but in different ways. You have to keep in mind that I wasn't being raised in places for the most part where people were practicing the religions that you practice these days. These were more people of the land whose religion, even if it is the same religion you have today, was integrated with their knowledge that they experienced on a day-to-day basis. So that's different. If you're saying, have I seen an evolution toward a more benevolent consciousness in human beings . . . is that what you're saying?

No, I just wondered what your feeling was about the difference between early humans a thousand years ago and what you see now.

I would have to say that the humans of today have not quite caught up with the ones I came in contact with a thousand years ago. Of course, there were fewer humans on the planet then, so the idea of being overwhelmed by so many human beings would be unknown. In those days, it was usually a matter to celebrate, seeing other human beings. So I'd have to say, you haven't quite caught up with that yet.

Well, I think we took a detour into the mind and now we're coming out.

Perhaps! I could not say.

So in addition to providing food for humans, you said you were also here to provide food for what we call animals, other beings.

Other beings, yes. But we do consider them to be just as valuable, although they are not always treated with the same care.

Have you had occasion to interact with everything from insects and ants on the ground to bears and cows and sheep and all that?

Yes, quite often. I consider that to be part of the joy of being here. On my home planet, there are maybe three different types of beings, so one of the big, main reasons I am here is exposure to a variety of life forms. It's just been a joy, and I've loved that.

Well, I suppose we do have an incredible variety here.

You really do, even in the current times. Not as much as it once was, but in the current times, there's a great deal of variety. I have spent some happy days with different types of creatures, everyone singing their songs, telling their stories, which have to do with who they are and where they're from—not necessarily why they're here, but just who they are and where they're from and perhaps stories about their family, brothers and sisters and so on. I've heard many stories like that from butterflies and birds, snakes and sheep and wolves and so on.

It Took a While for Pleiadians to Cultivate the Perfect Corn for Earth

Many of the beings of the plant kingdom came because an emissary went to their planet and requested that they volunteer, but you're saying you were brought here by the Pleiadians.

Yes, but that does not rule that out. I have every reason to believe that such a request was made, but I believe it might have been made sometime before the actual corn was brought here. I believe that the invitation came, you see, and from what I've been told, the invitation was originally offered but the request was that the arrival of corn would be delayed until corn could be created that would do the most good for Earth. You see, originally if corn had gone to Earth, it would have been a very small plant, producing an ear of corn about the size of a small carrot, and it would be a vine that traveled either up whatever was available or more likely on the Earth. I don't think it would have survived into your now times, as many vines from the past have not survived into your times because of the vulnerability that vines face if they cannot go up.

So the Pleiadians came in to strengthen it.

Yes, and the request started on the Pleiades, but these peoples who live on that outer planet in the Pleiades star system are known for their capacity to nurture and support—not by refining through anything biological, but just by singing the songs of the future human being. This means how you as a race of human beings on Earth will be in, say, ten thousand years of your time. And so by singing those songs and walking up and down the areas where the plants were growing, the plants eventually recognized that this is what they were intended to support. And thus in time the perfect corn was growing, and that's the corn that was brought to Earth, but it took awhile. So the emissary came, and then sometime after this process the corn was brought to Earth. I believe permission was requested, and it was granted by the emissary and the teachers of the people. I feel it was a good thing to have done or you wouldn't have corn today.

So had corn been here before you came?

Oh, yes. I arrived about a thousand years ago, but I'm pretty sure corn had been here for a long time.

Of the beings on your planet, do a lot of them cycle through Earth or just some volunteers?

I'd have to say that a lot of them have cycled through the Earth. It's not a rite of passage or anything like that, but a great many of them have cycled through the Earth, although there are very few who have stayed for as long as I have. I believe it might simply be the nature of my personality, that I like variety, as I've mentioned.

What is your life span at home?

Oh, perhaps several thousand years, but here I don't really notice that much difference, since I cycle from one plant to another. And even though there are interruptions when one plant grows through its seasonal cycles or is cut down perhaps, even though that happens, those interruptions do not last long and then I'm in another plant.

But on your home planet you stay in the same plant?

On the home planet, we are like a vine, and we move all over the planet. If you were to see us on that planet, you would see the areas of land . . . there's water there, but the areas of land would be almost completely covered by the corn vine.

And you're able to move from one part of it to the other? You're able to move through the plant around the planet?

No, I didn't say that. If you were to approach the planet, the land areas that you would see, even though there is water there, would be almost completely covered by the corn vine.

But you don't stay in the same area of the vine for several thousand years? You move from one part to the other?

No, the corn grows from the vine. Picture a vine on your planet: If there is no one to cut it, what's to stop it from growing?

Oh! So the piece of the vine that is you extends out and out and out and out?

Yes, but we are not individuals there. If we grow on the vine as corn or if we are other parts of the vine, it doesn't make any difference. We are all part of the same vine—hence, the attraction to family.

You are not individuals there—now, that's interesting. [Chuckles.]

Well, I do not perceive human beings as individuals either. You may not have leaves or vines that connect you and so on, but when I've observed human beings, there are always cords of light or energy that connect you. I have never seen a human being or observed one on this planet who is not thoroughly connected to other human beings, who are all connected to other human beings. No. It's the same from my perception and from the perception of other corn. Since there's this sense of basic familiarity, basic similarity in the connection to all things, that's why we feel inclined to come to your planet. If you were really individuals, I don't think we'd be here.

Family Is Still Strong for Us on Earth

So how long do you think you'll be here in the future?

Oh, I couldn't say. If I get the change of feeling, then I will move on. I'm not entirely certain where I will go, but I will be open, even to traveling to some other planet when Earth human beings begin to migrate. Most of you, of course, will stay on the Earth, and some of you will wish to live underground—when the new underground living places are perfected, people will want to live there. But some of you, very few, will emigrate to other planets as beings from other worlds encourage that, and you will want to take some seeds and plants that you might grow, that which you're familiar with. I would consider going along on such a voyage.

That sounds wonderful. You're a true adventurer!

Well, there are limits. I don't think I'd care to live in the underground growth areas, even though there will be sunlight. There will be water and lakes and rivers that are all natural. I enjoy the natural cycle of the Sun, the Moon, the stars, the clouds, the rain, and so on, and although there is something like that in underground worlds, it's not quite the same, as I've heard from others who have done it.

I agree completely. I have to look at the sky.

It's coming, though. You know, on many other planets, you don't find a single person living on the surface. They all live underground. It's a different life there and some people like it very much, but it's not for me.

You say that you want someone from the corn spirit or from the home planet to talk also?

I think that would be good, because many of the questions you've asked could be answered a bit more elaborately. Perhaps corn spirit might be a good choice or someone from the home planet next time. I think this would be good, because many of your more esoteric questions could be answered in some detail, whereas what I am providing has to do primarily with Earth life. From what I have gathered, that is the intent of your book: to point out other uses, other capabilities and the means to interact from plant world to human world.

I would like to say that those who have attempted to use dried corn leaves—fronds, you say—that these do not always work well for spiritual purposes. Sometimes when plants are dried, they need energy. They take energy; they do not give energy. So I do not want to discourage those who are experimenting or using the dried fronds in their spiritual activities, but keep in mind that these things are not to be done around babies or the very elderly, who have energy needs that require support. These ceremonies must be done with individuals who have more vigor.

You mentioned that family is very important to you on the home planet. Do you feel the same way here?

It's different here, isn't it? And yet we are very often united by roots comingling underground. This sense of touch or even proximity does bring back recollections of how we've known each other in the past, from one corn plant to another. And yes, family is still strong here, and we feel that that's an important factor for Earth humans as well.

So for those Earth humans who feel that family is not something they know about as much as they would like, come and be around corn or, if you cannot do that, be around olive trees or even citrus trees. This can help to support your understanding of the physical feelings that are associated with loving and being loved simply for being yourself without any alterations to your personality whatsoever. It is important for those of you who do not have family or are estranged from family to be reminded of these feelings, and you can get this from the plants I've mentioned. Of course, you might also be able to get this from pets and so on, but that is not my provenance.

Excessive Seeding Warns of a Weather Change

I'm starting to pick up your words a bit more. It took a while.

[Laughs.] You're doing great. You've never done this before?

Once, with a shaman from the southern African plains. It was necessary in order to get a clear picture of what dangers the weather might have in store—this is important for those who are growing foods. So we had a chat. Others were there so that the shaman's words who spoke what I had to offer could be remembered. One person would listen for a time, and when it got to the point where that person could remember no more, then another person would step up and would listen for a time until that person could remember no more and so on. It was not quite the same as it is in your time, but it was adequate.

Did I understand you to say that you know what the weather is going to be like?

Only there I did. But it wasn't so much to say what the weather would be and here's what you can expect tomorrow, sunny and bright—not that. It's more that when plants know there is some major earth change coming—perhaps a tremendous storm or other aspect that is natural to Mother Earth, an earthquake or something like that. We usually get some kind of warning. And this will be born out in the case of, oh, say, plants that seed, that in that case, the crop of seeds would be more abundant that year.

At that time, the crop of corn was much more abundant, so abundant that the shaman inquired, and I was able to make a good connection with the shaman. She was able to bring through the words very accurately in sounds in her native tongue and others were able to remember it. After that communication went on, the people moved for a time to get out of the way of the big storm that was coming, which came about four months later. So the people all survived, and after the storm passed by, they moved back to the land they used to be on. Even today you would find that this can occur. Those who are conscious of nature and what goes on often look to see if a tree or plant starts seeding tremendously, or if a huge crop comes through unexpectedly without artificial stimulation. These are important signs. Sometimes it might just be a gift; other times it might be a forewarning.

Do you know where you are on the planet right now?

It's a warm, dry place—my favorite!—with what seems to be a family. They have a community, an extended community, but there's still quite a bit of room, and they are growing us in the way I like: organically, no artificial chemicals, but in good soil that they have prepared and interacted with. What do you call that? I don't have that word, people supporting soil.

Composting?

Yes, that's it. It's not a big field, but there'll be enough for everyone.

The Idea of Using Corn for Fuel Will Pass

So it is time to say a few closing words, if I may, and you can resume next time. Would that be adequate?

Yes, that would be fine.

For those of you on Earth, it is a good thing to be involved in raising corn. If you are able to do this, even in a small patch, I recommend it strongly. Try to maintain a peaceful demeanor around the corn. It is not a good thing to have too many frisky animals or children dashing through the corn fields, as they sometimes bump into the plants and could cause damage, but I'm sure you know this. Still, in general, having children around or animals who know to be careful—this is a good thing. We like the young, and we like animals very much.

There is a time coming when the growth of all forms of corn, even those that have been changed, will return to only providing food for human beings and some animals. I know that right now there is this temporary flirtation with using corn to make support for machines—"fuel," you say. This will pass soon. So for those of you who find that offensive, it will pass. There will be other demands for corn, and I want to reassure farmers that they do not have to worry. The demands for corn by the general public and the needs of animals will far outstrip the demand for corn as fuel. You are moving into a time when you will have other means to support your vehicles, and this brief flirtation with corn as fuel will simply fade into the history books.

So for now, familiarize yourself with corn. If you can eat it, that's wonderful. If you cannot for some reason, then try to be around it and breathe in and out. Enjoy the sun, enjoy the soil, and remember that your natural, native personalities are completely at ease with all life, even if your physical body is not entirely comfortable with all life at this time. That will change. We all grow, change and move on. We are all alive, all the time, and everything is alive. When you know this and when you're certain of it, it will help you to have that sense of continuity that you sometimes miss when functioning in a mechanized society. Good life!

Thank you very much! Good life!

CHAPTER TWENTY-FIVE

Corn Spirit

SUMMER 2008

℘

THIS IS CORN SPIRIT.

Welcome! Corn seems to have this special ability to have an energy that helps humans ground and bond and expand—can you say more about that?

I think that was well covered by the individual you're referring to from last time, but I would say that the function for the human being does not require that the human being actually consume corn. If you're in the proximity where corn is being raised . . . say you're driving down a small road or a trail or even a highway that is small without much traffic. If you get out near a corn field, if it is safe, you can simply walk over to within five feet of the corn stalks. If there is a fence and the corn is beyond that, then stop before you get to the fence—don't touch the fence—and just look.

Focus your gaze entirely on the corn plants, nothing else. If there are birds there, don't look at them if you can help it. If they happen to fly into your line of sight, that's all right, but just focus your gaze on the corn plants themselves and breathe normally. If you do that for thirty seconds to a minute—or if you're distracted or worried or thinking about other things, it might take up to five minutes—then you can turn to your left. Even if you have to go to your right

363

to get back to your automobile, turn to your left (eventually you'll be facing the right way) and return to your car carefully.

Be sure and look both ways before you get to the road because you might be in a slightly altered state and you want to be very careful. If you have a companion with you, that person can watch out for you. When it's safe, go back to the car and *do not drive* for twenty minutes. Have your car pulled well off to the side of the road before you do that, or if you have a companion and he or she hasn't done that, you can have that person drive, if he or she can. But if you are the driver, wait for twenty minutes.

During that time, do not talk to your companion if possible. Just breathe in and out, or if you're well off the road, you can take a little nap if you want to. After the nap, you'll probably be refreshed and able to go on. But if you can't sleep, don't listen to music, don't talk, don't do anything if you can help it. Just breathe, relax, and close your eyes, and after twenty minutes, you ought to be able to drive and be clearheaded.

I mention this particularly with such detail because some people cannot eat corn. Perhaps they are sensitive, they are not able, they are allergic, or it's just not part of their diet. So you can still get the benefits without consumption. Sometimes you can get the benefits even better than with consumption—if, for instance, we're talking about store-bought corn or frozen corn or even canned corn. You're not going to get much benefit out of store-bought corn unless it's a roadside stand and the corn was picked within four hours or so. That would be different. But by the time it gets to the store, it usually loses that energy, down to maybe the 1 percent level or so. That's what I perceive and that's what I recommend.

Why do spiritual teachers always say after a process like this, turn to your left?

That's the way the Earth turns. That's the way energy goes around the Earth. If you turn to your right, what you're doing is creating an agitation in your physical body. Think about it: You will have just done an important waking meditation with corn, for example. And if you turn to your right, your body will be uncomfortable. So that immediately is going to reduce the benevolent effect that you just had on your body.

Your body has been able to relax and interact with a natural living being and derive what your body can assimilate. But if you turn to your right, it's going to create an agitation and either decrease that benevolent effect or simply create an inner conflict within your body. Turn to your left, and you won't have that problem.

Hybridized Corn Is Not as Effective as Natural Corn

Can you say something about yourself? Are you from the home planet, or are you a spirit who guides corn here on Earth?

I generally experience my existence here on Earth, and that's where I'm needed. I'm not really needed on the home planet. This is where I'm needed [laughs], so this is where I am—which is typically the case with spirits who are associated with one form of life or another. They'll go where they're needed and do not need to return home for a vacation.

Have you been incarnated on the home planet or on Earth?

I've always been in the form I am now, so "incarnated" doesn't quite work as a word. I understand what you're saying. Have I lived a life—is that what you're saying?

Yes.

No, I have always been spirit.

Have you always been connected to corn, or are you just helping corn now?

I'm always associated with corn.

So are you part of this creation, or did you come from somewhere else?

I am a portion of this creation.

Is there corn all over the creation on different planets?

Yes, but it doesn't necessarily look the same and it isn't always a consumable. It also does not always have ears of corn, as you understand the actual consumable part. So generally speaking, the degree of the size of the corn that you will find in your stores, for instance, is not even natural. Natural corn would have much smaller cobs. You do find this in places where people have been able to grow corn and raise it in its natural state, and this is found usually amongst peoples who can trace their roots back a ways. But hybridized corn with bigger kernels and so on and so forth—this kind of corn is not always as effective as truly natural corn.

Are there many places on the planet now where truly natural corn is grown?

There are not so many places, but there are a few. One might be able to obtain something like that in the southwestern United States, in South America, and a few other places. You'd have to inquire.

Has that changed the energy of the hybrid corn plants? Has that decreased the energy or done anything detrimental to it?

Yes, how far afield it is from its natural state results in a decrease. But generally speaking, hybrid corn is about one-quarter as effective in supporting that which has been indicated when it is in that hybrid state. This does not mean it cannot do it; it just means that it would take more of an interaction with it—meaning, for instance, the stand-by-the-highway meditation might actually be *more* effective than consuming it. Because in order to get that complete effect, you'd have to consume a lot of it, and it might not be the sort of thing you'd want to consume a lot of, except perhaps during harvesting season where you might do that once or twice over a few weeks with friends perhaps. But other than that, to get the best effect, the meditation with the breathing might be best.

Inoculations Alter the Human Being

What is the change that happens with hybridization?

The main thing that happens is a chemical and soulful change. The human being of your now time has to a degree been altered, at least most human beings. I'm not talking about different groups marrying each other and having children, none of that—that's expected and, as far as I can tell from Creator and Creator's emissaries, intended. But if the human being, for instance, has had a traditional upbringing, one might have been exposed to various diseases and survived. You also could have been harmed by those diseases and just be doing the best you can to survive. Still, that's a natural life to the extent that Earth and the organisms upon Earth interact with the human being.

But if you have had, say, inoculations that prevent the disease from taking hold in your body . . . which I'm not trying to say is a bad thing. Certainly this has improved quality of life by a considerable margin for human beings. But it does alter the chemistry of your body to a degree, and this can be proven by your science. A simple experiment or laboratory test can often show whether a person has had these kinds of exposures. This alters the human being a bit. But even with that alteration, the suggestions of how long to breathe with the corn, how much to consume, all of that . . . that was taken into account. So I would not be concerned about that.

What are the long-term effects on humans from this alteration?

Well, on the one hand, you live longer lives. Generally speaking, when a human being has enough to eat and the hazards of life are minimized—such as not having to worry about coming around a corner and meeting a bear who may not be friendly, things like that—and inoculations to prevent disease are taking root, this is a good thing. I'm not saying it's bad. It just does alter the interaction that you might have with natural consumable plant forms.

In the old days, before there were such inoculations, there were of course more risks for the human being. On the other hand, when the human being ate natural plant life forms such as corn and other things, then the corn itself would act to a great degree, not exactly as an antibiotic, but as a preventative, because the corn would also have been exposed to those organisms, though they may not have been a threat to the corn. But still, exposure creates familiarity and adaptation on any planet. Therefore, the corn consumed in that situation might very well be able to support that adaptation in the human being. This is also true of other plant life, and you may wish to ask those others—rice, for example.

I Help Create Pathways to Connect Corn's Natural Parts

Some members of the plant kingdom have memories of having created physicality. Does your memory go back or do you have stories?

I don't. I cannot take credit for having created anything physical.

Okay. Exactly how do you interact with the corn plants? Is it to nurture them?

Yes, to nurture them, to encourage them—they need a lot of encouragement, especially the hybrids because they don't feel right. Have you ever had that feeling in your body where you just don't feel right? It's like that. So they need a lot of nurturance, they need to be reminded of who they are, because sometimes the natural part of themselves is distributed all throughout the plant. It's not like the fronds are natural or the kernels are natural—it's not like that. It's distributed throughout the entire plant, and sometimes the altered portion of the plant is so vast that the natural parts are completely disconnected from each other.

So that's where I come in. I help to create pathways to connect those natural parts so that the plant does not become confused and desire to die. You know, there's a parable here, as you can see, or perhaps it's not a parable. There's a *parallel* (that's your word) along the lines of the human being. If the human being's life has become so unnatural, if the person isn't nurtured and supported, there's sometimes a death wish. You just want life to be over with. People may not be conscious of this, but it can create problems. I'm sure your counselors and therapists are aware of this, so I'm mentioning it not to bring it to your attention so much as to simply say that all life has similarities.

Did they ask for this intercession by you or this help from you, or do you perceive their need and proceed to give it? How does that work?

They have a need. They don't say, "Corn Spirit, come and help me." They have a need, and when they have that need, I respond. I can be in more than one place at once.

You and many other corn spirits, or you are the corn spirit?

I am the personality of the corn spirit, but the corn spirit can be more than one place at once.

Before there was an Earth and corn needing to be nurtured, what did you do then—the same thing on other planets?

Yes. Other planets have variations of the species. And it wasn't too urgent. There have been a few planets where there has been discomfort, though I do not believe that corn was on those planets.

So you never go to the home planet, then?

Oh yes, I've been there. Yes, certainly.

Like for R and R or . . . ?

As I said, that's not necessary.

Plants and Animals Are Not Meant to Evolve

Will corn be here for quite a while in the present and future?

Oh yes, I think so—especially as there is, as I say, an enthusiasm in certain circles to preserve old seeds and to support as much as possible in your now time (which isn't entirely) the closest thing to the natural species of any plant. You know, it's interesting: Human beings, from my perception, are intended, through the exposure and natural process of love and desire and people coming together, to merge and become fairly similar—meaning certain characteristics will be noticeable, skin tone will gradually evolve, and all of this business. So eventually the human race, although there will be some variables, will generally look fairly similar on the entire planet.

But just the opposite is intended for plants and what you call animals on the planet. Those beings are intended to remain pretty much as they were when they were first "seeded" here. This way, as you become more receptive in your capabilities and in your desire to be receptive to other life forms, they can offer the knowledge, the wisdom, the energy, and the feelings, that you are intended to receive from them.

This is the difference in terms of so-called evolution. The Earth human being is evolving into what is your natural state. Imagine for a moment that the human being has a certain appearance in the future: certain characteristics of the face, the mouth, the brow and so on, certain skin color tones and things like that. What if the human being got together with other human beings and said, "I wonder how we got started? How did we look this way? Where did we come from? I wonder if we could try and go back and see what we were before and how we got to look like this?" Voilà! Here you are. That's the way I see it. And the reason I see it that way is that this story was told by one of Creator's emissaries. I have no doubt that it is actually a reality. When you think about it, just given what you know about the human being, it makes complete sense, doesn't it? It sounds like something human beings would be interested in doing—no surprises!

Were you there when the emissary came to your planet?

Oh, yes.

And was it any different than what the corn recounted from having heard it?

I don't think so.

How did the emissary appear to you—as one of your species or as a point of light?

As a small point of light first, and then gradually with a slight sound, a pleasing tone becoming a little more prominent, and the combination of gold and white light. But there was also a transcendent light—I don't know if you know what that is.

No.

It's a form of light that changes color and moves from one focus to another constantly. So it's a unifying light. That was radiating out as well, and then we heard/felt what the emissary had to say. This transcending light is, I feel from my perceptions, always associated with a creator. So at times like that, it's important to pay attention, eh?

[Laughs.] Yes, yes.

Biofuel Is a Temporary Thing

How do you feel about so much corn being planted for biofuel?

I'm pretty sure that's a temporary thing. I feel that it's sort of a stopgap measure, isn't it? People are trying to come up with something else until cars are running differently. For one thing, ultimately the private car is going to go away. After all, how much room do you really have for private cars? Ultimately you'll move into something that's more of a people-mover type of thing. And it's really not that far off in your future.

The generation coming up now, just being born, will live that in their life, where the vehicles do not have *any* particulates coming out of the exhaust. It will ultimately be something akin to an electrical motor, but there will be other means of producing that electricity or capturing it for the moment and using it as part of Mother Earth's electrical field. So although I do not feel good about corn being raised and other plants being raised to create so-called biofuel, I know that it's purely a temporary thing.

Well, it's running up the cost of food and it's making corn scarce as a food.

Yes, and that's not going to be tolerated by human beings for long, believe me. For one thing, it's very much needed as a food crop all over the world. So it's not going to be accepted. It's not as if there aren't other ways. You can create natural gas, you can encourage it, and this can be done on a small scale and on a larger scale. But don't worry. I feel now that the price of fuel has gone up somewhere closer to its actual value. Then it's not going to take too long for other forms of energy to finally be totally embraced. Of course, they've been embraced by some places more than others, but wind farms everywhere and solar . . . this is it, this is going to really do it.

Don't expect the price of gasoline to go down. Don't vote for somebody because you think that person is going to lower the price of gasoline. It's up, and it's going to stay up. It's going to go higher. So recognize that there's only so much, and it would be much better to use resources that are not plant-based, as in wind and solar. There's an inexhaustible supply there. That'll be the switch, and you will see that in your lifetime.

Gradually the idea, to say nothing of the practical reality of having a personal car . . . it will become crystal clear to most people in the next ten years that this is not realistic. Of course, then you will see a lot of projects to create public utilities, such as various means of moving people in groups: trains and so on, like that. But ultimately the thrust will be toward people-movers that use electricity, because that is something that can be supported through solar and wind and all of this kind of stuff and, to a degree, water. And so that will happen.

Also, people will bite the bullet a bit, so to speak, if I can use your expression, and atomic energy will come more into prevalence. This will make a lot of people nervous, but it will also create a tremendous amount of support for creating a safer version of atomic energy, which is literally just around the corner. It needs a lot of people doing a lot of research and sharing their information instead of, "This person knows this, and this person knows that"—that's very inefficient.

So when everybody shares what they know, in ten or fifteen years you can have completely safe atomic power and that is what will generate the levels of electricity so that your factories can work and whole cities can be lit up. But still, wind and solar will prevail for some time. And then oil resources can be used for other things.

Like what?

What they're being used for now. Gasoline is a big drain on oil resources. Oil resources are used for many, many other things. You can put a sidebar in the book if you want to about what oil is used for besides gasoline. Probably a lot of children in school know this, but I would guess most adults don't.

Creations Have No Boundaries

So you're saying there's one corn spirit. Would you say there are multiple versions of it, or can you split your focus in many places at once? How would you describe that?

I am not physical—I can be everywhere. When you are not physical, you can be everywhere too. You can be one moment on Mars and the next moment in the Pleiades while you are still on Mars.

I'm looking forward to that again. So there is no limit to the number of focuses that you can split into. Is that according to need or desire?

It's according to need. That's how it works in this type of service-related "occupation" because you go where you're needed. And if you're not needed, you don't go there.

So you have no desire to go someplace or see something or do something or interact with something or someone or anything?

Well . . .

Those are all human questions.

If you don't mind my quoting one of your famous songs: "I've been everywhere." Do you know that song? It's an old-time song, eh?

[Laughs.] "I've been everywhere, man," yes. Everywhere in this creation?

Yes. It's not possible for me to *not* have been everywhere. When a creator creates spirits who provide certain functions, as a spirit you are automatically able to be everywhere. This is how you can know where you're needed.

Because you're connected to everything.

Yes, so you know immediately.

Is it a connection like a gridline? I once saw that the Mother of All Beings had a web that just went everywhere and everywhen and connected to everything, and it was like lines and lines and lines of light.

It might look that way at times; other times it's more subtle. But yes, it might be perceived that way at times.

But then does it just stop?

You have to understand: what is seen also depends upon who is looking at it and through what. So if you are looking at something . . . let's say you're looking at a telephone pole, okay? You see the telephone pole the way you see it. But if a fly is looking at the telephone pole, the fly sees the telephone pole completely differently.

[Laughs.] It's a lot bigger, yes.

What are you looking at to see the telephone pole?

But is there then at the boundaries of this creation . . . because these lines of light go . . . they don't stop at creations. But is there some sort of temporary filter or something at the edge of this creation around the circumference of this creation?

This is going to be hard for you to understand, but this creation has no boundaries. And other creations also have no boundaries. All creations exist in the same space. It's a fact of living on Earth that this is hard to grasp. Living on Earth in an Earth life, you are living in time and sequence. Time and sequence naturally want, or you want . . . time and sequence naturally impel a need within the human being to see things as a linear progression. But when you are no longer here, that's not how you experience things. All creations are in the same place; there are no boundaries.

I thought they were side by side like cells or something.

It's natural to think that, because you're in a linear world. You're in a time-sequence world. You can not only measure time, you can say, "Here I am," and then walk twenty paces and say, "Now here I am," and time has passed. In other words, you can prove to me that time exists because that's where you are. But of course, that's one place and it's a school and it's so intense as that school that you must be totally immersed in it. When you are told that you forget everything when you come here so you can re-create your reality, do you know *why* you forget? Have you ever wondered why?

So we don't have those limitations of past . . . ?

No, no, no, no. The reason you forget is that you are so immersed in this reality, there's no room for anything else. That's the mechanical process of forgetting. If you are literally dipped into something and it's not just on the outside of you but it's through and through you, it's your whole existence, then there is no room, not even one iota of room, for anything else. That is actually how forgetting works. If Zoosh were here, what would Zoosh say?

[Laughs.] You know Zoosh too?

We all know Zoosh.

He would say, "Never forget that."

Yes, that's right. But I'm giving you permission, since I'm not Zoosh: you can forget that if you want.

[Laughs.]

Many Humans Come to Earth to Rest

The corn grows according to seasons and night and day and all that—so how do you deal with time when you're in our environment or focus?

I don't. I'm not required to, so I don't. If I had to deal with time, I would have to run all over the planet in order to be everywhere. But since I don't have to deal with time, I can be myself, be where I need to be, including other planets if I'm needed there in this creation. And I'm not required to do that.

Can anyone incarnate as a member of the Explorer Race? For instance, could a spirit such as you actually incarnate as a human if you desired to?

I wouldn't desire to, for one thing. If you don't mind my saying, I like my job. And Creator picks the personalities of beings to do what Creator sees, feels, knows that personality would like to do. I'm not stuck in my job. I'm not waiting it out until I can move on to the next thing. This is exactly perfect for me—why would I want to do anything else?

I don't know—so why did I want to do something else [laughs]? Why are humans here, then?

I don't understand you. You're the resident human in this conversation. Why did you want to do something else?

Why did I want to become a human?

You wanted to understand what was the attraction and you also wanted to rest. Interesting, eh?

I don't understand that.

You considered in your personality that there was too much going on and you wanted it to be quieter in terms of experience. This is the quietest place in terms of a soul knowing everything that is going on everywhere. Here you don't have to experience that if you don't want to. The only time you are totally aware is at the deep-sleep level when your soul goes and becomes its natural self, though tethered to the body. And the body does not have to have those memories, nor can the body actually have those memories, because the body is totally immersed in this reality. You wanted it to be quiet just for a while, and in terms of immortality, a hundred years or so for the average human life in the best of conditions is a short time. That's why you came here.

That's mind-boggling! Quiet!

The question of "Why am I here?" occurs to a great many human beings.

Is that answer relative to a great many human beings?

At least half.

Really!

Yes. Sometimes souls just want things to quiet down. They want to be able to focus all their attention on one thing and just do that. And the best place to do that is right here on Earth.

I thought the opposite—that it was sort of benign and boring in other places and that we came here for adventure and for more happening.

Well, you see, that's the attractiveness of the place, because you don't remember what other places were like and you can have your adventure here, hopefully in benevolent ways.

So you're part of the Creator, not part of the planet.

You're part of the Creator too.

But as a spirit, do you interact with an element of the planet like the wind? Do you interact with the Sun?

I don't interact with them per se. If you mean, do I perform some kind of dance with them—no. I'm conscious of them. They're doing what they do, and I do what I do. We honor each other, love each other of course, but do not interact. I'm here for corn. But I can also occasionally have such conversations that we're having. I've done this before.

Really!

Yes. With other channels like Robert and other times, other places. It took me a moment to get going a bit with you two, but I've done it before. That's why I can be almost glib, eh?

Didn't the early humans on this planet need advice from spirits such as you about how to grow things and how to interact with the plant kingdom?

Yes, but I think that, generally speaking, they were more interested in personal communion with individual plants. They might have asked for a corn spirit, but generally speaking, I think they would have had a spirit of an actual corn plant or a corn seed, because this is very practical and it gives them the exact information they need in their place, rather than us speaking so enjoyably in philosophical terms. You'd want to ask a seed, "Exactly where do you want to be planted?" and then take the seed and walk up and down the land very slowly, and when you get that good feeling, that's where you put the seed. So that's very practical.

Is there an inherited knowledge amongst ancient peoples about the corn spirit? Do you figure in their stories or their legends or anything?

Many times. But you would have to do your research, which I suppose is a lot easier nowadays with the computer.

In the Future, Humans Will Make Room for Crops

I'd like to offer something, if I may. For those of you who are unable to get fresh corn or even natural corn, and you're in the market and there are ears of corn for sale, when available there's something you can do that will support you gaining the energy from that corn. When you take the ears home and are preparing to take the husks off, open the husk just a little bit—anyplace near the top; it doesn't make a difference—and if it's safe for you (I think for most people it is), smell the fragrance of the husk as it comes off.

Even for corn that has perhaps been frozen, even for corn that has been altered, generally speaking the fragrance doesn't change much. There's only a slight difference between completely natural corn and hybrid corn. So you can get quite a bit of the energy that corn has to offer to you by smelling it as you're slowly taking the husk off. Just breathe in and out naturally.

In your time, when people are living more and more on land that was once used to grow crops, you will come to a conclusion that this is inevitable. The most benevolent form of this conclusion is that, "We as human beings need to live someplace else so there's land for crops," and it needs to be good land, not just what's left over after all this building takes place. Many of you will decide, "Well, we'll live in these tall buildings because we can get a lot of people in these tall buildings on the least amount of space on the ground."

But what's coming for many of you is that within fifty to seventy-five years, there will be a great many discoveries, some of which you'll be helped to discover because you simply don't know they're there. Others, people will research—those who explore caves, for example. And others you will find using technological means. You will discover the means to live underground happily and comfortably. Older generations may not like to do that, but that won't be necessary because it will be something that younger generations will do a in the spirit of adventure and also because they like what they find there.

So if you're wondering where all these people are going to live, by somewhere around 2200, at least half the human population of the Earth will be living underground and enjoying it. So just a little reminder: There will be places on the surface to grow crops that you still like to eat, and they won't all have to be grown in some subterranean vault that is not what you would consider a traditional corn field. Good night. Good life.

Thank you very much. Good life.

CHAPTER TWENTY-SIX

Brown Rice

JUNE 16, 2009

಄

GREETINGS. RICE. YOU WOULD SAY BROWN RICE.
Welcome.

Thank you. I'm coming to you today because there is every reason in this book to focus on a short series of plants that are known for their curative, or at least balm-like, properties that could perhaps be accentuated when interacting with the living plants. So I feel that it would be good to mention that this is one of the things I recommend. First, what's most important is to get yourself focused on the fragrance of the plants. You understand that the soil the plants are grown in might have its own fragrance, eh? But this is how to do it. Normally, we do not recommend that you touch the plants, but this is how it's done. You would put out your left hand, palm toward yourself, and stooping down, you would pull a few of the plants toward you, just bending them, not really holding on to the plants themselves. Then, centering your nose above them, you don't smell the plants so much as you just breathe up through your nose, just once.

The capacity here is that a considerable amount of energy is radiated through rice into the soil or water that it grows in. It is meant to perform a task of converting light, sun, warmth, and the elements of earth into—how can we say?—connections to the human being. Human beings take in, consume, and eliminate like other beings. But human beings do not always have an orientation toward what they eat, what passes through them, and what comes out the other end, so to speak.

Consume Rice in Its Natural State for Physical Healing

The orientation, though, doesn't just change the food into waste matter and take out the elements that the human being can absorb. There is an entire world of experience going on inside the human being. When you have things that are disorders—and by that I do not mean a mark on your body you might have been born with, like a birthmark as they call it—or something that, while you may not find it attractive, does not cause you pain and is not an actual disease. I'm talking about something that causes you pain and may be a dis-ease. When you have such things, your body is in a state of disorder. But the food you eat can help to change that, and you know that. Of course, there are therapies that have been proven, and those therapies, tried and true, are often able to support and nurture—if not cure, then something that resembles a cure or at least sets aside the extreme symptoms.

When you consume rice in its natural state, not just as food but even ceremonially—have a small scoop of rice with nothing on it; just eat it off of a clean plate—perhaps first say prayers. Wait awhile, then slowly—with your hands clean, of course—slowly eat the rice. But use your hands only. Do not use any implement. Eat it to the last grain, and pause for a time. You can say prayers and do meditations or just relax and rest, not thinking afterward, not doing anything for a half-hour, say, forty minutes at most. If you happen to fall asleep, that's also all right; try to have as little contact with other people as possible if you can. If there are other people in the room, try to sit somewhere quietly. Then you can perhaps feel better. This is known, but I'm bringing it to your attention because the refinement is that you eat the rice with your hands.

Rice Can Help You Regain Balance

Now the living plant: Let's say it's possible—and it is possible—to grow rice, on your lanai or your porch, a little bit. It may not be its right-old self like it grows in the fields, but it might be possible to do that. If you can, then here's how to interact with the rice. You can grow as many or as few plants as you want—up to fifty, no less than five. If you can, create a screen behind the rice, one that would perhaps have natural linen and use only natural wood, meaning no unnatural products, in that sense: no nails, no clips. If pegs are used in the screen, that's fine.

Place it on the ground or on the pavement behind the plants, and the plants can be raised on a table, perhaps a wooden table. Again, try to make it something that does not contain anything plastic or metal, okay? It can be simple, such as something that folds, something that's solid, that's fine. Have your back to the north—that might be the best—and then simply look at the plants for a time. Sit close enough that while having your back in your chair you could in theory reach out and almost touch the plant, unless you're sitting on a stool, or even sitting cross-legged on the ground; that's fine too. You want the plants, the tops of the plants, to be no higher than the top of your head, okay? If you reached out in front of your body with, say, your left arm, palm down, you want to be at least eight to twelve inches away from the plants, but not much farther than that.

Then just look at the plants for a time. Breathe in and out normally and naturally—five minutes, ten minutes, something like that. If you feel energy, that's fine. Let the energy be there. Don't think. It's not a time to say your prayers. Just breathe in and out normally and naturally. After about five or ten minutes of doing that and trying not to think about anything, then simply say to the rice plants:

"I am asking that in sharing our breath together, you work with me now to bring my body into a state of comfort and balance that I may be at ease in this world of ours and live as well as possible."

Continue to breathe in and out naturally while looking at the plants for another five or ten minutes, and that's all. When you get up, get up slowly, while looking at the plants if you can. After you've stood up, turn—rotate, yes?—so that you are turning to the left, and make side steps if you can so that you are taking three or four side steps away from the plants. Or if possible—and this is better—you can walk backward. But you have to make sure that there's nothing behind you and that it's safe to do it. If you're not sure, you can look over your left shoulder and see if it's safe. That would be better, but you can do the sidesteps also. After you get, say, ten or twelve feet away, then you can rotate, turning to your left, and then turn and go where you need to go.

Try to be quiet for at least an hour after that. Try not to talk to anybody, if possible. Don't answer the phone; maybe have the ringer off. This might be something to do on a day off. If there's noise where you live, that can't be helped. If you are comfortable wearing earplugs, you can do that during the experience, but you don't have to. That's what I recommend. This will be very helpful with the following conditions: anything that has to do with the heart and lungs, diseases or discomfort of the feet and legs, some skin conditions, and certain infections. I'm not saying to avoid doing your other treatments from your health practitioner. Certainly do that. This is something that you could *also* do to heighten the curative properties.

Remember, since you're trying to bring your life into balance, that it might also have other effects on your life. You might find that if you've been doing something to excess, perhaps as a substitute for something missing in your life, the craving for that may fade away. You might also find if there is something uncomfortable in your life that is external to you, that it might become more relaxed or won't bother you as much as it once did. These are two possibilities. There might be others, but anything that occurs will probably have to do with balance. The least that can happen is that you will feel better in some way. That is most likely.

Now, if it is smoggy outside or something like that, then it's all right to bring the plants indoors, especially if they are on a rolling cart or something like that, and do the whole thing indoors if you have air conditioning or something like that. I just want you to know that is acceptable. But generally speaking, if you bring the plants in, or if somebody else brings the plants in for you, then the plants are to be taken back outdoors again within no more than forty minutes after you complete your process with the plants. This way, they will be able to revitalize as well as to be in their more natural environment.

Rice Can Help You Create a Sense of Calm

Can you tell me something about you? Are you the spirit of the rice?

I am something like that. I am a consultant to many plants, particularly plants that have to do with healing and balance. I am not the overall spirit of rice, but I'm saying "consultant" because that's the closest word I can come to in this language. I advise individual plants or fields of plants, if needed. My advice has to do with moods and feelings, not thoughts so much, because that's not really a factor of the plant world. If necessary, I interpret other spirit beings if they wish to communicate in some way to the plants but do not have a common language—meaning they might be thought oriented. Or they might have a language associated with some other planet, for instance. Thence I am able to function as a translator, translating their communication into energy and—most importantly with rice—feelings. Rice is very strong in the area of feelings. People who have worked with rice slowly, not in a rush, know that rice really can help you with your feelings to create a sense of calm. This is because it is the feeling they prefer. They would prefer for those who work with them, grow them, and so on, to have the same feeling.

What other plants would you recommend we talk to that have this healing focus?

I would recommend you look that up, because there will be easily twenty or so, perhaps more. Then make yourself a little list and do something else—I want to involve you a little bit. See if you can get pictures of the plants, which won't be difficult, so that you can look at a picture and decide whether you personally find the plant attractive. That will improve the quality of what comes through, because you will feel more of a personal connection. If you are living in a huge city where you can go to some vast, sprawling garden or place like that, then I'd say, "Oh, go to the such-and-such green house and experience the plant in person." But given that you are very busy and that you are not living in a vast metropolitan area or even a place where such things are grown, then I would say looking at the pictures would be the next best thing. I think you will enjoy it more that way. And you can make requests. Certain plants will have an antibiotic quality. Sometimes the material you look at won't say that. It won't say that rice has an antibiotic quality, but it does have that to a small degree. Other plants will be known—such as a plant that contains quinine, eh?—to have a quality like that. Those will be easier to—how can we say?—sniff out on the Internet.

Okay. Tell me about yourself a little bit.

Not too much, because this is about plants. But I do not have limits. I can be on this planet; I can be on another planet. That's typical for spirit. I'm sure you know that. I would prefer to tell you more about rice, if I may.

I'd like that. Just another sentence, like how did you get to do what you're doing now? Were you requested to do it? You volunteered?

I volunteered because I could tell that there was not the best communication with some spirits or beings from other worlds or even at times beings living on the world that you occupy. There was sometimes poor communication between what you call animals—other life forms, is what I would call them—and the plants. Sometimes there needed to be better communication, if not through a common language, then at least through a means to interpret feelings in a way that was understood, so that what was happening could either be accepted or at least tolerated with the understanding of why it was happening. For example, say, an animal eats a plant, eh? After all, if you were being consumed, you would be unhappy about it. But it might help a little bit if you knew why and what.

This is found many times with some so-called animals who might go consume part of a plant that they don't normally consume because they are ill and they know that the plant would help them. In this case, the plant would be shocked or surprised. "What's this?" There might need to be some means to help the plant to know that it would not be entirely consumed. Say, for instance—you've seen cats; you have a cat. You've perhaps seen this in the past where a cat will go outside and eat a little grass. This is not typical, but sometimes a cat will do that if it needs something within the grass or it's not feeling well and it needs to have the grass help it to pass that matter out of its body with a little more enthusiasm.

Only on Earth Is There Such a High Degree of Adaptation

Sometimes you actually use feelings to communicate between the spirits of the plants, as you said—their own spirits?

Well, no, their own spirits of course can communicate totally and completely with them. But in terms of other spirits, meaning other beings from other worlds and so on, they don't always have the means to communicate directly with the plants, should they desire to do so. So I'm available for that.

Like an intermediary.

Yes, exactly.

Okay then, tell me about rice. Where are they from? How did they get here?

Rice was invited, I believe, to come to the planet by one of Creator's emissaries. They were invited to come not only to be a food source but also for—and this is exact, if you could translate it into your language—the "capacity to support balance and equanimity with your being as your energy supports that simply by existing." You see, where rice is from initially, they do not have the food aspect. They flower and they have a very small seed, which would then migrate to the ground; it would be about the size of a poppy seed. It would not be something you would identify in any way as a food crop.

On its native planet, rice would normally grow to about six feet tall. Even on this planet, if allowed to grow for a while, it could get a lot taller than it normally does. Though that's not usually encouraged, such possibilities do present themselves, but I don't think that the rice itself, if it would grow, would taste any better or be much bigger. It's been tried, you see. In its natural state on that planet—and I might also add that on that planet, gravity is a little less—the rice grows to be about six feet tall and does not grow the way you see rice here on Earth. There is a liquid under the surface of the thin soil, and rice grows through the thin soil into the liquid.

So the home planet of rice is set up for the rice to grow in the best way?

Yes. Every form of life on Earth, including some that are no longer actively on Earth, has a home planet that is completely set up for that form of life. Only on Earth do you find such a high degree of adaptation. Without begging the question, this means, of course, that there are native planets for human beings where everything on the planet would be just perfect in support of the human being so that you wouldn't really have to do much to thrive. It's the same for plants and so-called animals—or other life forms, which is what I prefer to call them—on this planet. So it's not surprising that on rice's home planet, such conditions exist.

How do they feel about it? They've been here since there were humans, or before?

I don't think since there were humans. They've been here for a while. I'm not sure how long.

Were you here when they came, or did you come later?

I came later, when it became apparent that there was some need for interpretation from one species to another. Generally speaking, there are other plants I serve in that function, but this didn't really show up until the human race, as you know yourselves to be, as well as a few other creatures, other beings, had migrated here to Earth or had been brought here, or had chosen to stay here. In the case of some human beings, this was a situation in which there were colonies of human beings from other planets, and some people just liked it and wanted to stay. This is typical. Over time, of course, there might have been a separation between the original planet and the people on Earth. Also, there was a certain amount of instruction, and you know all this—beings from other planets were asked to move away, stay away, so that the beings on Earth, who gradually came to be known as the Explorer Race, could continue on with their purpose for being on Earth.

Interested Beings from Other Planets
Have Come to Earth to Learn of Rice as a Food

Now, is brown rice considered the being that you mostly interact with, or do you mostly interact with other forms of rice, or is it rice in general?

Rice in general in its natural, native state. So it could be, as you say, brown rice. It could also be wild rice, yes, because that's just called wild rice but it's actually a different species. You've seen it. It doesn't look the same. The fruit, as you might say, is longer.

Yes. Are they included in the antibiotic effect of the brown rice or are they different?

Yes, wild rice could be the same way. You'll note that with wild rice, it does grow taller. If you have the opportunity to be around wild rice where it's not being picked and it's quiet, you can perform that thing I mentioned before, even if you're in, say, a canoe and the canoe is drifting a bit. As long as it's drifting all along where the rice is, you can look at the rice. Don't worry too much about distances, as I mentioned before. If you are where the rice is growing, then you'll be drifting along there, perhaps, and you can breathe in and out and do everything else as stated. It might work a little better, because there the rice will be in its natural environment and might be more vital in any case. As a result, it might even work better.

But I think that would only work for a certain amount of people who could paddle out to an area in a canoe. If you're in a boat, I do not recommend doing this if there are more than two people in the boat. For example, you might for various reasons need somebody else to paddle the canoe, in which case, that's all right. I would say, considering the environment where wild rice might grow, a canoe would be better than anything with a motor, even an electric motor—a trolling motor, as they say. It would be better to paddle quietly and gently, disturbing the water as little as possible. Someone who is good at paddling a canoe will know just how to do that.

If rice is not a food for anyone on its home planet, then it's probably not food for other human beings on other planets.

No. It's only become a food on this planet. But I think since it has become a food on this planet, that there have been visits by peoples from other planets who have acquired some of the rice and taken it to their home planets to see if it could grow and thrive there and become part of the food. So it's gone the other way.

Well, it's such a staple; we are so grateful to it. I don't know the percentage, but it feeds a large part of the people on the planet.

Oh yes. Very true.

When Rice Transitions to Its Home Planet, It Releases Its Earth Version in Spirit Form

I would like to tell you a little bit about the afterlife. There is something that goes on for rice that might interest you, because the human being has a very strong and significant afterlife. But in the case of rice, there is something similar that goes on. When the rice plant no longer exists, all right—not just when the rice has been gathered, but the plant itself—it goes through something similar to what the human being goes through. But rice does not have to go through anything that resembles, even to a small degree, what the human being goes through: something confrontational. This means something such as "how did you live your life" or what you might go through with your angels and guides and, possibly Creator. It's nothing like that, but there is a stepped, staged thing that the plant would go through.

It would actually go through a veil. It would let go—meaning the spirit in that sense—of the Earth version of itself in spirit form. It would become the natural version of itself in spirit as it exists on the home planet, thus having seeds instead of rice as you understand it. It would move slowly through a series of veils until its spirit migrated to the home planet itself. It would remain as spirit on the home planet—I'm going to say this in your Earth time—for about thirty to ninety days. After this time it would become a portion of a plant that already existed there—possibly a distant relative, all right—or it might even sprout and grow there on its own then, moving into a seed. What I didn't say about the seeds on the home planet is that the seeds do not have energy of their own. They just sit on the surface until that experience takes place where a plant coming to the home planet, as I said, through the veils, will energize that seed. Then and only then will the seed begin to sprout and grow.

Fascinating. And what about the other way? Does the same spirit come back to enliven the rice on this planet or always different ones, or what?

No, I'm just talking about the afterlife.

I know, but the plant on Earth has died and another plant needs a spirit to enliven it. So does another portion of a spirit come from the home planet? That same one or a different one?

No, I'm talking about the afterlife only: one way. How do you get new souls for human beings here?

They come.

Where from?

Anywhere.

[Chuckles.] I don't think so. They come from Creator. That's exactly what happens for rice here on this planet.

So constantly new souls come in for the rice and then they go back to the rice home planet?

Yes, although in the case of rice, as I mentioned, when they, in the afterlife, go to the home planet, they might very well join with another plant already in existence. So it may not be one to one.

But there's no reincarnation back to Earth for them?

No, they go to their home planet. If there was going to be reincarnation, it would be on their home planet.

The First Rice Plants Journeyed to Earth in Physical Form

Some plants, some beings we talked to, stay here on Earth a long time. So how long do the rice spirits stay here—a spirit that would inhabit one plant? Or does it stay here for years and years and years, or what?

Hard to say. It's an individual thing. But generally speaking, after life they will go through the veils. If they prefer to return to Earth, they will have that option, but most do not. Usually, they'd rather be themselves in their natural environment where they feel most welcome, loved, and supported. Wouldn't you?

Okay, but I still don't get this. So they came from the home planet to Earth. They had been rice on their home planet.

They didn't come the way you think, though. When they went to the rice planet, they asked for volunteers, and there were, as always, volunteers. The emissary from Creator said, "There will be some beings who will come in a vehicle, and we request that you volunteers present yourselves or make yourselves known." And they had a way to do that, and then they were assembled onboard the ship and the ship brought them to Earth.

Mm-hmm. Those were the first ones.

But they didn't go in spirit. They didn't migrate in spirit. They went in form.

Oh!

It was necessary because on their home planet, they were one thing. So on the voyage to Earth, it was necessary to go through something like not really hybridizing but showing the beings that they would be supporting. Then there was a chance for the plants to adapt—and in some cases, they were seeds—so that they could choose where they wanted to be on Earth and then become the foundational plants and plant souls on Earth. That's what happened. The voyage, though, didn't take a short time. The voyage, in terms of your time, probably took about a year and a half to get to Earth.

Oh, so you're either from a long way away or they had slow ships.

They are from a long way away, and they weren't in a rush. Why rush?

Why rush. So then how long did those plants stay here, those spirits?

I can't . . . probably one, two, or three cycles, something like that.

Okay, all right. So there's constantly new souls, spirits, whatever, coming into the Earth for the rice plant, and they're not the same. Some we talked to, it's the same ones over and over and over again.

It's not like that.

Not like that. Okay, what have . . . you've never been in form, right? Have you been in form? [Laughs.]

You mean, physical form?

Encapsulated, yes.

Encapsulated physical form?

Yes.

No.

It doesn't look like fun to you?

That's not who I am. I could ask you, "Have you ever been in spirit form and had no limits and could be everywhere you wanted to be?"

Yes. How come I'm here? [Chuckles.]

Well, you know I say that because I know you have.

Yes, I know. I know.

But no, I have not been in form. But I'm not passing any judgment on those who are.

[Chuckles.] Well, I think we have a purpose, so . . .

Oh yes.

Rice Emits a Constant Feeling Energy Wherever It Grows

So do the beings, the rice plants themselves, commune with each other? Do they interact with birds and other animals or anything?

Well, I think that could be looked up. But to answer the first part of your question, I will say that the communing is done largely through touch. You probably already know this, but feelings are transmitted through the air. This is why you can go someplace if somebody is having a strong feeling, and you might have a reaction to that feeling. If you've been around that feeling being transmitted long enough, you will probably know what it is based on your reaction.

Well, this is like the feeling network, you might say. So anywhere that rice is growing—and I would guess pretty much with other plants and other forms of life on the planet, including humans—there is a constant energy of feelings being transmitted. So generally speaking, the main interaction from one plant to another in the case of rice is the transference, the sharing of feelings. This is particularly noticeable where you might find, say, wild rice, because you might see the plants moving not only to the effect of the wind or the water but also moving on their own. If they trust you or feel safe around you, they will be more inclined to move, especially if you are very still and at a bit of a distance. It's the same thing in a field where rice is being grown, especially if there are not too many human beings around and not too much machinery noise in a distance.

They can actually move their roots?

So at night, they might move a bit. All plants can move on their own.

Oh, all right. I didn't know that.

Oh yes.

So in touching each other, they gain a sense of . . .?

No. I didn't say they touch each other. Don't assume, okay? They can move, but they don't necessarily touch each other.

Okay, so they commune by feeling among each . . . with each other, then?

Yes, they can. They don't necessarily do that. Plants are not as familial as human beings are. They need to be protected when they're young and tender, but that protection isn't always there for plants on your world. Human beings are as familial as they are because, of course, babies need to be protected 100 percent of the time in order to survive. So the whole idea of mom and dad and sister and brother, grandma and grandpa, uncle and auntie are pretty important, a matter of life and death. It's not the same for plants.

They're more independent?

A little more, yes. There's love, there's a sense of greater community, but there isn't always—it might be the case in some plants, especially fruiting plants—a sense of, say, Mom. Sometimes there is.

Remember to Be in the Moment

Eventually, humans are going to move off this planet. At that time, will rice move too? Or that's not talked about yet, or what?

Well, it's always best to wait and see. Why would it be talked about? Human beings would talk about things, yes—potentials, possibilities. But with plants, they're always living in the moment. The more human beings could live in the moment, the more likely they would be to be happy, I might add. Happiness exists in the present. Human beings like to store up happiness. They will remember things in the past that made them happy, or they will imagine things in the future that could make them happy. They will even imagine things happening in the present that make them happy. But they don't necessarily—nor are they encouraged to—actually live in the present and find happiness in that immediate moment. I think it would be good if they did.

Why do you think they're not encouraged to? Because nobody knows how to teach them, or what?

No, I think it can be taught. Children generally do that. Little children do that naturally. They unlearn how to do it because of various cultures of the human being who discourage children from being happy. They usually don't say to the children, "Don't be happy." But they do tell children this and that and this and that and this and that, and after a while the children don't feel happy anymore.

Mm, how sad.

It will change.

Good. Good, good, good.

It's good to know about. So remember when you tell people things, try to say, "Well, live in the moment." Whatever you tell them, also just finish up with, "Remember to live in the moment." Now we're going to have to finish up here.

Okay.

For you all, know that rice is happy to support and nurture you as well as possible. If you want to know how to support and nourish rice or any plant, you can be in the moment. You can look at the plant—say, a tree, a bush, grass, anything. Try to feel good when you're saying this, or relax. Say, "Good life." That's something plants say to each other. Then say, "I appreciate you" or "thank you for your beauty" or something like that. But it has to be truth. Only say what's true and complimentary: "Your flowers are beautiful today," something like that. Try to be in a good mood when you say this. Don't rush by and say, "Oh, thanks for being!" [Chuckles.] That doesn't work. You have to be sincere and in the moment. Plants are always sincere, and they are always in the moment. Good life.

Good life, and thank you very much. Thank you.

BEANS

CHAPTER TWENTY-SEVEN

Soybeans

MAY 14, 2008

୫୦

THIS IS SOYBEANS.

Soybeans! Well, welcome! How are you today?

I am in existence.

[Laughs.] Okay.

What can I say?

The Burden and Responsibility of Plants Who Are Consumed

Do you know where you are on the planet?

I am actually on a high plain somewhere, but I do not have familiarity with your place names.

Have you been here very long—in your terms or my terms, whichever?

In terms of existence, no more than a hundred years in a reincarnational cycle, which is coming to a close. Not all of us, but some of us, will be here for a hundred-year reincarnational cycle. Most do not stay that long because of the burden and responsibility, but for some of us who do stay for a time, we are able to guide the others, and I am one of those.

What is the burden and the responsibility?

393

Any being who exists with the knowledge that one will be consumed for the betterment of other beings has a responsibility to be able to achieve the highest level of spiritual and physical capability combined. From my point of view—and I believe from the point of view of most plants—we are often stimulated by those who raise us or encouraged us to be this or that physically, but it is our job to be able to synchronize and balance our spirits so that when consumed (either immediately or after some short processing), we are able to maintain our spirit intact. Of course, if we are massively processed, then that's not possible.

Massively processed—do you mean harvested by machine and mixed in big factories?

Yes, the process that many of your foods go through. But if it is something less so—a smaller operation, so to speak—and there is no massive interaction with mechanisms, then it's possible to maintain the spirit connection so that, when consumed, the attunement of spirit is able to match the spirit of those who consume us. But if that spirit has been lost, then although the food might fill you up, it will not enrich and excite your own spirit being. You can tell if you have eaten food that has that sense of aliveness afterward, because you feel not only physically stimulated, but your own spirit or philosophical self is also stimulated. This is something that can be noted through experience.

Are you connected with your spirit from your home planet now, or with your physical being?

All are connected with their spirits from their home planet right now, including you. I have noted this. I cannot see with eyes, but I can see/feel, not unlike a sensitive human might see with subtle vision something that other human beings may not see. I'm not saying "not allowed," but they may see with a different kind of vision. I can do that vision also, and I notice that the light bands and cords coming out of the human being trace not only to their teachers and beyond but seem to trace, when I have noticed it, to their source.

Do all human beings have the same source?

No.

So to the source of . . . can you amplify that a little bit?

I don't trace it too far, just to a point in space, and there they stop.

Is it in the galaxy or in this universe or what?

I do not have that information.

Are you able to see them when humans leave the body either at night or when transitioning out of the body permanently?

I do not observe human beings as a rule. I was just saying that, but there is little I can tell you about the human being.

So you've been here a hundred years total since you first came here?

Not quite, but close to what you would measure to be a little over ninety-seven.

Will you be here another hundred, or will you be leaving at the end of the hundred?

I'll be leaving sometime close to the hundred-year mark, probably a little before that.

Is this the first time you've been here? This hundred years, I mean?

This is the only time I've been here, yes.

We Are Like Food for the Soul

What do you look like on your home planet?

Quite different! We have a certain amount of mobility, not based on our own capabilities, but the soil of the home planet is in motion gradually, not unlike a very slow-moving river. As a result, the landscape around us does change a bit, and we like that, but there we are more of a . . . not exactly a shrub but what I would call a small tree about the size of, oh, a cedar or a piñon tree.

What is the reason you were invited to come here to Earth?

It might have something to do with the capacity of the beings of our plant to enrich the soul structure of all beings. And although we were meant for animals, since human beings have been consuming us, we have been able to help the soul structure there as well, especially in your now times when you have the difficulties human beings face in their ability to believe in the eternal soul, meaning the eternal balanced personality connected with creation. Many human beings have difficulty in that, so if you are able to consume the soybean with minimal processing—of course, you cook it, but from the plant to your pot—then it will help to maintain and sustain your soul in your body and to allow it to feel more actively involved in your day-to-day life. It is like food for the soul. However, given that precept, the capability of minimal processing—just what's necessary—then I would say that the consumption does not need to be very much, just a little bit.

Like an ounce or a spoonful or a cupful? What kind of "little bit"?

No more than half a cup would be sufficient. Anything beyond that would be . . . there's no further gain after that.

And that would be whether it's milk or whether it's cooked?

No. No. I'm talking about cooking the beans—not processed! If it's milk, it's been processed too much.

That's absolutely awesome! I've never heard of anything like that before.

It is important, is it not, to reveal in this book that which is not widely known about plants so as to help those who not only consume them but those who prepare them and those who interact with them. After all, many times there will not be any consumption with plants, but simply some form of interaction, even just walking by a tree, yes?

Interacting with the Soybean Plant

Is there a form of interaction with you without consuming the product that would work equally well?

Yes, and it is in some ways better. But it is not something you can usually do. If you can find a way, though, to grow a soy plant in an environment . . . you may or may not be able to do this, but it might be possible to do it in a small garden or even a flower box. You can try. You might need some pointers from those in the business of growing these things, but if you can do that, you will find there is another way to interact that I feel has benefit. When the beans have reached the point where they are almost mature, where they might be picked, then reach with your left hand, with the fingers and thumbs together slightly but not made into a fist, cupped you might say, as if you were going to drink water out of your hand. Reach around the plant. Do this from the back of the plant if you can determine what is the back. You may not be able to, but some plants apparently have that. The idea is to reach from some point of the plant around to the front, so if there is no apparent back, which there isn't [laughs], then reach around the opposite side where you are, reaching around with your left arm, and hold your hand cupped the way it is in front of some of the beans, no closer than four to six inches away—make sure you don't contact them. And then breathe, if you can, by your normal process, and try to pull energy in through your left hand within the radionic auric field of those beans. And if you're in a four- to six-inch range, you will be in that auric field.

So you will have to practice. If you don't know what I mean by breathing into your hand, you can practice in some perfect environment. Try to pick an environment where you feel completely at peace, completely safe, and completely, at least if not loved, then in an environment you enjoy. Pick some part of your body and make the conscious effort to be aware of it physically. Then as you take in a breath, imagine the breath coming in through that part of your body, through your leg or knee or something. After you try that a few times, if you get a dis-comforting feeling, then try and blow out of that part of your body, just in some direction that is not toward any human beings or animals as far as you can tell.

After you do that for a while, you will then know what I mean by breathing in through the cupped hand. You can try this. It works especially well if you have raised the plants yourself, because that will require work. Plants like our own kind are not easy to grow. It's not like growing dandelions, who have a vigor of their own. Try not to trim the plant any more than you absolutely have to. You wouldn't like to be trimmed [chuckles], and if you are trimming the plant, the plant will not have as much energy. Let the plant grow as naturally as it can, and try not to use chemical fertilizers.

You're saying that it's difficult to grow soybeans?

It would be difficult to grow them in a flowerpot. I'm allowing for people not having much access. If you have a garden, it might be different, but you would still need some instruction from professionals, or at the very least from those with experience who may be shy to call themselves professionals but would qualify, from my point of view.

Other Off-planet Beings Want to Know How You Treat Us

So you've been here for a hundred years and a plant lasts a season, right? Do you pull down into the roots? Are all the roots connected?

No, they have a certain amount of shoots that go out, but generally, I wouldn't say that, no.

So you pull your energy down into the root, and then you come up again the next year?

I'm going to let you look up farming techniques on your own, okay? But in terms of my being here for this amount of time, I haven't been in the same plant every time.

So how far afield have you gone?

I can only describe the area I'm in, the way it might feel to me, but I cannot tell you what country I've lived in, for instance.

So you frequently wake up in different places, become aware of different places?

It's not my job to be in the same plant or in the same place. It is strictly my intention to be on Earth as I am, wherever I am guided by Creator to be. This is a guiding system that is true for all souls as far as I know. You are guided to be where you are. You are not picking out your body from a novice's knowledge from afar. Creator and Creator's helpers guide you to be in a certain body so that you will be able to come as close as possible to accomplishing the various things you desire to accomplish as a soul here. It is the same for me, though I do not have that much I want to accomplish, except to find out generally how the plant world is treated by the human being. My job would be to "discuss" this (we don't talk out loud) on my return.

There are peoples, some of whom look very much like yourselves, who do not visit your planet but want to know and have indicated that they need to know how you are treating certain types of beings. You have perhaps heard some of this: "How do they treat the children? How do they treat their old people? How do they treat this or that?" But there are also people who want to know how they treat the animals, how they treat the plants, and so on. This is how they know when you can be approached to join the planetary communities.

Of course, they would ask those who have been here. They might visit our planet, for instance, and they would ask, going through intermediaries, "Who has been to Earth and what can you tell us about the people there now? How are they treating you and so on?" I've not had that experience, but I expect to have it when I return.

So what are you going to say?

Well, I will say what I say. I don't want a vote of confidence.

I just wondered what your perspective was—how have you been treated?

Well, generally speaking, I would say that the human being at large does not yet understand that everything is alive and has pretty much the same range of feelings that the human being has. Although this is not unknown on Earth, it is not put into practice by everyone. Though I believe that many people—I believe this not so much from knowing, but from consulting with my teachers and guides like you have—many people who have plants at home or in gardens often treat them with respect and kindness and, yes, love. And one would find that plants would, like all life, react much better to that than authoritarianism, for example.

Do you grow wild or do you have to be planted?

Well, I suppose we could grow wild, but we don't get much chance to do that, do we, eh?

I appreciate you so much! I don't know how humans would approach the idea of being grown to be consumed. That's an ideal of great service. Most people don't even have an awareness that what they're eating is alive!

I think some small farmers do, and people who gather food from the wild might be conscious of that. There is quite a bit of spirituality in the human being, but I have noticed that some human beings are inclined to seek some form of spirituality that provides them with rules and guidelines so they do not have to perceive. But even among people who have rules and guidelines in their spirituality, I have noted that if they are working in the fields—farmers, you say?—very often there is a great sense of love and tenderness for the plants with the professional knowledge that one may have to destroy those plants in order to reap the harvest. But many times I have felt a kindness or heard a farmer talk to the plants. Many farmers know that the plants respond well to this.

I have a memory of a farmer walking through the fields and talking about troubles he was having and he often said, "It makes me feel so much better to be able to speak this way." At first I used to think he was talking to his guides, teachers, spiritual advisers, but after a while I had an experience, you see, and I heard him talking. At that time, I thought he was talking to someone else, a spiritual being. I could tell there was only one human being there. But in the course of his conversation, he reached down and touched a leaf on the plant, one that was occupied—and he knew how to touch it too, with the back of his hand, very tender. He touched the leaf and said, "See you." This is how he said it. I give you his words, "See you. It gives me great comfort to speak to you all this way. I think of you as my friends. Even though I must plant and harvest, still I am comforted by your presence."

This is not so unknown to those of us in the plant world. I think some farmers would be shy to have that known, but I am quite certain that this particular farmer no longer has a physical presence on Earth, since that happened in the early years of my being here.

Have you noticed a change in the way you're treated from the time when you first came until now?

The big change I've noticed is the mechanization. But I do understand, given your huge human population and other populations that you raise to support you, that such mechanization is inevitable in order to at least make an attempt to feed these populations.

Other Beings Feed Our Souls

Do you get a chance to commune with other plants and with animals walking around, other beings?

Often those who are flying by will land for a moment of rest or find something to nibble on with the plants. Sometimes it's the plants themselves; sometimes it's other beings who are on the plants and are consumed by those flying by. Birds come by, and sometimes there is a communication possible. Of course, there are other small creatures on the land, and communication in a form is possible. Much of this goes on at night when the human beings are not present and all is quiet.

Such communications with the little beings in the soil, fine little beings, is much more possible. They will sing songs. From their perspective, they're singing songs of their lives or their culture, and we will respond to that. It is like being fed, because when we are exposed to the heartfelt song of their lives and their world, it is like food for *our* souls, and we feel in balance hearing such complete (without any holding back) communication of who they are, where they're from, why they exist, what they hope for, and so on. This kind of thing goes on very often. Whether they are birds or butterflies or ants or caterpillars, it doesn't matter.

So you don't feel lonely? I mean, you have your own species and all these others?

No, nothing like that. One, I think, might feel lonely, if one is a human being and does not have the born-to knowledge that other beings have on Earth. I realize that this is intended by Creator so that you will re-create something. There is some task that you are doing. I do not know much about it, but that is the only explanation, because everybody else on the planet, including the tiniest little beings, microbes, *everybody* else is completely aware of who they are and where they're from and what they wish to do and so on. Whereas the human being is rarely certain of any of these things. That cannot be an accident! What I know for certain on this planet is that while there are things that happen that we don't like, I'm pretty sure that accidents are not really just happenstance.

But on some level, they're desired or feared?

I'm not trying to say any more than what I said. They are not just happenstance, period, but I'm not claiming those words you said.

We Were Asked by Earth to Provide Soul Balance through Food

Have your source plants been on Earth for thousands of years or are they relatively recent?

I did not say that. I have only been here myself for such a short time; I do not know the history. I know that others preceded me.

What is your lifespan on your home planet?

I do not know of too many who have died, as you say. Without any difficulty present, life can go on indefinitely.

And you had a life there before you came here, which you remember?

Yes.

Will you have one when you go back?

Oh, yes. The life I had there is still there. It's just in a dormant stage while I'm here. It's like my life, my being . . . it's asleep, in a sense.

So you chose not to go when the emissary came in your history?

I have heard this emissary thing—not really. What happened is something very similar to what I say about these beings who come and ask, "What are human beings like now?" Someone like that came and said, "We heard that this planet is going to be for this and that." "We go there sometimes," they said, as I recall from hearing about it from others, "Would some of you like to come? We feel that you may be able to offer soul balance through food." And we were interested, because on our home planet, we do not have the same kind of beans. There we have something that looks more like a pod, not that different from what you would call (I have to struggle here for a moment!) . . . like a nut hanging from the tree, something with a hard shell. So we said, "Oh, like there are pods here?" (I'm using your words here), and they said, "No, no, it'll be something softer, something more readily consumable, something eaten by both animals . . ." and then they had to explain to us what was meant by animals, ". . . and humans . . ." and they had to explain that too.

After their lengthy explanation, there were a few volunteers, not a lot, who said, "Oh, we will try it." They said, "No, you won't be able to be the way you are here on the planet, because there will be other things." So I don't know anything beyond that. I don't know if they were changed in the ship by the beings who took them there, I don't know if there was a hybrid created—I don't know anything about that. I just know that we look different on the home planet.

What caused you to come when you did? What was it that motivated you?

I heard others give their reports. I was interested in these times. I wanted to see what it would be like going from a more agricultural lifestyle to what you have now, and I volunteered to come during this time of great change for your human peoples. Also, I wanted to meet deer. I'd heard wonderful things about what you call deer, and they're all true.

Yes, they're beautiful souls. I've spoken to them for the animal book.

Stories and Songs from Other Species on the Home Planet

Can you tell us a little bit about how you live or exist on your home planet? Are you the only species there?

There are other species there, and not all are what you would call plants. There are some species there, for example, who fly. That's why we have a particular affinity on Earth with those who fly.

For the flying beings, yes.

They are multi-winged. They are as one who is pretty substantial in size, I would say. I will have to search. I will have to compare them with the . . . there are crows who come to where I am now. On the home planet, the flying being is about maybe three or four times the size of a crow. Of course, they don't start out that size, but that's the size they get to when they are mature. They live quite a long time, but they don't live as long as us, and they are in some number.

Generally, they do not fly over where we are, but they do fly over sometimes, and they tell us stories because they can traverse so much space. They tell us what's happening on the other side of the planet, and we love their visits, because they always have new stories to tell and sometimes new songs to sing. I like the songs very much, because they tell so much about someone, don't they? It's not even the music you like to sing, because to the human being that's catchy or something like that, but if the human being likes a certain type of song, even if that person did not write the song or it's not a spiritual song, it does say something about his or her personality in that moment.

On the home planet, when they sing their songs about who they are and why they exist, not unlike what I described about the butterflies and others, then it is very pleasant and comforting, because there is certainty in the sound: "This is who we are." It's not, "Who are we? I can't find myself." But I do understand the human being. Beyond this planet, of course, you know who you are absolutely, so you are either learning something on your planet or there is some adventure awaiting you.

Yes, there is indeed. One of the first things we're going to do is go out to explore, and we were told that many of the beings in these two books live on planets that we might visit in the future.

I'll be sure to look forward to that exploration. But don't bring any saws to cut us down. Just keep in mind, if you are exploring as planetary explorers, that everything is alive—just like on your own planet—and that things you might assume to be one thing might be something else entirely. You wouldn't want to limit your experience. You never know who can do something nice for you.

Yes. Yes. We're discovering that. Is there anybody else living on your planet? Are there any other species?

Yes, there are a few small beings who move across the ground, not unlike . . . I mentioned the caterpillar on your planet, because we have some beings who move along the ground like that. They don't cover as much ground as the flying beings, but they are also very pleasant. They always tell stories. They don't sing, but they tell stories. They seem to be more in the present. They don't talk much about who they are, why they exist or anything like that, but they tell stories. I feel, but I can't be certain, that the stories are made up, and they're always entertaining.

Even Creators Have Guides and Teachers

So you're not quite immortal, but you live an awfully long time in that body. Have you been in other bodies, other forms, before the one on the home planet?

There was one other form, but it was not a mobile form. It was something that would be from your perspective a cross between wood and stone. I have seen something like that on this planet, meaning with my thoughtful vision, and it is not exactly the same thing, but the heavy, dense root ball of some trees as it grows into the soil, the point where the tree touches the soil, reminds me of that substance. But then, the life you're inquiring about, it's more of a mineralized plant substance.

Like a petrified wood or something?

No, not that. It's a living substance. But it doesn't sprout like a tree; it's more of a mound.

What was the interesting thing about that? What do you remember?

Well, you asked me; I didn't bring it up because I wanted to tell you a story about it [laughs]. That's what I have a vague memory of.

Ah! So you choose lives. You're not looking to learn, because you choose lives where . . . how do you choose lives?

It's not a sense of choice, like, "I'll take this one, not that one." I feel more of an acquiescence—I think that is the word. My guides or teachers say, "You might enjoy this experience," and I do not argue with it [laughs]. I say, "Oh well, I will try that, then." It's like that.

But you are your immortal personality. There's nothing that you're disconnected from. You're connected to your total being, right?

Yes, as far as I know, yes. But one can never be certain—can one?—because if you are in a physical form as we are in our own form of physicality, there is always the sense that there is more. On our planet, of course, we know that we are spirit beyond that which we are representational of in our physical form, and while we have complete knowledge of what that spirit is, there is a sense that when we are no longer engaged in that form of existence, we will be somewhere doing something else. In that sense, there is a connection to the experience of linear time.

Something came up once in one of the books that because this Creator chose to be disconnected from parts of Itself, that everyone who came into the creation had to do the same—to choose to limit themselves a little, I guess, for the experience. I'm not too sure if that's how it works, but that seemed to be what they were saying at the time.

You will have to ask everyone that question.

I guess I was wondering why, if you were your immortal personality, you still had guides and teachers.

This is typical. As far as I know, creators have guides and teachers. Why wouldn't you? Wouldn't it be tediously boring if you had no one you could speak to who was knowledgeable?

Whom you could learn from, yes.

Would you not be, at some point, very bored?

Well, that's right. Yes, they do. We've talked to the friends of the Creator and the Creator's creator and the Council of Creators.

Yes. I feel that this is meant so that all life can have a sense of purpose beyond their own motivation. And that can cause you to rise to certain occasions and do something you never believed you might have been able to do. As a human being, you can understand and identify with that, eh?

Absolutely!

Plants Have to Be Vigilant

Can you tell me why you've chosen lives that seem to be not so mobile, not in a form that can fly or run?

I have been asked this before, and my answer is always the same, but it may not please you. My answer is, can you tell me why you have not chosen lives that allow you to be more focused in one place?

[Laughs.]

[Laughs.] I've had many laughs over that. Everyone reacts the same way.

Right. That's an interesting answer. When you're here on Earth, can you commune with your home planet, with beings there?

Yes, but I have found that this is not something that is really safe to do. On this planet, one must remain fairly vigilant, because say somebody is stomping through the farm field unintentionally but perhaps not in their right mind, and we cannot get out of the way, yes? If something is coming that is destructive, we can alter our feelings a bit—not go numb, but feel things less horribly—and so when whatever it is crashes on through, if we get stepped on or bumped or bruised or harmed in some way, we can prepare. And afterward we can gradually come back into our physical feelings. By the time we do this, over a period of about three days, the healing process is already well engaged. So to put it simply, I have found that it's not good to get too engaged in something that would cause me to be less perceptive of my surroundings.

I was aware that animals had to be vigilant, but I hadn't thought of plants.

I believe all plants do this. If you have the choice of, let's say, desensitizing yourself, or even to the extent that you're able or not . . . if something is coming that's going to cause harm, well, you're going to want to desensitize yourself as much as you can so that you do not have to suffer. You might still have to suffer, but maybe you can get past the worst of it.

I understand. Are there others of you in this universe or are you all on one planet?

Well, I'm only aware of that one planet, but it's certainly possible that there are others.

But can you commune with others on other planets from your home planet?

I suppose it's possible. I never have.

Well, actually, some beings do that as a matter of course.

Perhaps All Are Some Extension of Some Creator Somewhere

We were told that the plant kingdom as a whole had been a creator. Do you have any awareness or memories of that?

That is an interesting question, because I have felt at times a certain continuity of philosophy among plant beings that borders on a sense of creationism, and it's not impossible, that. If that were true or still is somewhere, then perhaps we are temporary émigrés in order to help the creator aspect of us (if that is true) grow and change and understand and adapt. Who knows what the purpose is? We exist on our own for our own purposes and causes and so on, yes, but it is possible that there is that creator aspect. Of course, I have also considered that for other species. Perhaps we are all some extension of some creator somewhere who just wants to be able to feel and breathe and think and do all of these things that, as a distant being, no matter how vast the personal aspects and individual aspects, may not be readily attainable.

Right, one being said that it was like a vacation from being a creator, and another being said that everyone on Earth right now in all their different forms and kingdoms and species had been part of those who had created physicality.

I cannot identify with that explanation, but it is certainly possible.

I have found plants to be more philosophical even than animals or extraterrestrials.

Thank you.

What else do you think would interest our readers? What have I not asked about that you think would be interesting?

Well, you've done very well, but let me give you this: It is in the nature of the plant world to be totally conscious of what is above and what is below. After all, we have roots that go into the soil, and we must feel our way to find that which feeds us, and there is the Sun, which shines on our leaves. Therefore, we are constantly conscious of what is below and what is above. Of course, there is the other aspect besides the Sun and the Moon and the stars and the soil and the water and the other creatures—there is the aspect of Creator and the angels, the spirits and the guides, who are always present in some way.

I feel that you have this too, but right now—because of your mobility, is the way I see it—you do not always have that sense of awareness of these things. It's true you do not have to go into the soil for nurturance and you do not have to have the Sun shine on you for life, but because you are going here and going there, and doing this and doing that, perhaps you're not always conscious of your teachers and guides and angels and Creator. I believe you try to remind yourself by gathering with others in special buildings and saying special words and singing special songs. I can identify with that, but I feel/think (in combination) that it would also be good to assimilate the awareness of your guides and teachers and angels when you are other places, not just gathered in those special buildings, doing those special things.

That's beautiful! You are so totally experiencing this physicality. I mean, in the soil, and above it, and meeting the Sun. I never thought of that before.

Yes, it is a physical existence, a spiritual existence, a feeling existence, and to some extent, when interacting with other forms of life, a thoughtful existence. Of course, one must have a certain amount of instinct for the sake of anticipation, eh?

[Laughs.] Yes!

Your Food Sources Will Be Evolving

On this planet for the past fifty or sixty years, there has been a tremendous debate voicing opposite views of soybeans. One group is saying that they're the greatest thing that ever was, they're wonderful for the human being, they have all these benefits and vitamins and minerals, and others say that they're not good for humans. There seem to be two schools of thought. Why is this?

I cannot explain the conflicted thoughts of human beings based on one form of research and belief over another, but I will say that the intention that we understood when we came here was to be a food source for nonhuman life. This has evolved, perhaps because of the urgent need to feed a great many human beings, since your population has developed very quickly to its current level. So we understand that perhaps a compromise has been made in certain beliefs of what is good for humans to eat and what is not good.

I think, even in your now times, there is a certain amount of experimentation as to what human beings eat, and so on. I would have to say, as I said before, that as far as strengthening your soul, a small amount (half a cup, cooked) of soybeans is adequate. But in terms of eating many processed foods made out of soy, I do not feel that feeds your soul. That is all I can say about that, but I do completely recognize and understand that people are hungry and that they need to eat. It's not yes or no. I feel there are other forms of food intake the human being may have where there are also groups who say yes and groups who say no, and perhaps they are both right.

The whole vegetarian movement sees soy as a protein alternative to meat or animal food.

Yes, that's a perfectly reasonable position. For your life now, know that many of the foods you are eating now will no longer be present in the future. This does not mean we are going to say, "The end, we're not coming here anymore, no matter how hard you try to plant us." It means that you will be evolving from the foods that you now eat to other foods that are vastly different. Some of this will be brought about by those who are creative among you. They will find ways to combine different things in order to make the most healthful foods. Others of these foods will come from sharing from those who travel from one planet to another.

There are certain ideal foods for the human being to consume that human beings on other planets consume, and it takes only a small amount to completely satisfy—it not only created a sense of being satisfied from eating the amount that you have, but it stimulates, fulfills, and maintains the most optimum healthy balance. These foods, I believe, will be among you sometime within the next fifty to seventy-five years, and they will have many wonderful applications. The good thing about many of these foods is that they do not need much space to grow, and they will grow in abundance. So be sure to welcome brothers and sisters from other planets who come to visit, because they will be able to help you to maintain and improve the quality of your life with food, the air you breathe, and other things.

Practice Heartfelt Welcome

This will all begin to happen much more as you learn how to do the simple task that you are training on right now. You have to learn how to offer a heartfelt welcome and use the proper discernment to know, "Is this being safe?" But if it feels safe to your heart, then to welcome it. You see a certain species you love: your favorite pets, the cat or the dog. You see how they react to human beings they don't know. Perhaps you, as a human being, bring home a friend, a human being they don't know. Do they stay at a distance, or do they cautiously approach? Learn from them to understand what heartfelt welcoming is about with discernment. Then you will have an idea how to treat those who come from other planets and how to know who is for you and who is simply meant to be said to, "Greetings, we are happy you have come to visit us. How can we help you? And have a good trip!" [Laughs.] But others might come, and then you might feel heart for them and they would feel heart for you, and you would want to help them and they would want to help you, and they may have much to offer. So practice heartfelt welcome and being able to follow up with that because you mean it. Good night!

Thank you very much! Good life! Thank you.

CHAPTER TWENTY-EIGHT

Soy Spirit

APRIL 28, 2009

&

GREETINGS. SOY.

Greetings! Welcome.

Now I wish to make an opening statement. The fruit of the plant called beans has always been meant for natural beings. It is an irony that it is so popular with those interested in such products, but generally speaking the natural beings I'm referring to are four-legged, not two-legged—and sometimes multi-legged things. Generally speaking, the fruit is meant for creatures—what you call animals. I understand that it can be consumed by human beings—and a great many human beings do so—but if you are farming, I recommend you create a small plot off to the side, somewhere where you don't necessarily harvest, something completely separate and accessible by wandering four-legged, wild beings. This way you will be acknowledging the plant's original purpose. Twelve, fourteen, or fifteen plants ought to do it—maybe a few more if you have extras, or if you want to allow the plants to just be. There are ideal ways for humans to interact with the plants. It's a very good plant to have in your garden. I know it may not be something you would expect to have in a garden—and many gardens will not be able to support it—but if you are able to have one, two, or three of them, then

411

you might try the following suggestion. Don't consume the fruit—don't even pick it. It will fall when it needs to, and let it be consumed by other beings.

Soybeans Help You to Move through Spiritual Crisis

This is how I suggest to interact with the plant if you have a spiritual crisis. This might have to do with a religious situation involving prayers; a need to interact with Spirit, angels, Creator, or anyone along the lines of religion; or even religious philosophy, which some New Age churches might incorporate. What you can do, especially if you have three plants, is to have them arranged in such a way so they will grow in a roughly triangular shape with at least one point of the triangle shape in the north. You can try to make it an equilateral triangle, at least when you plant it. It doesn't have to be perfect, just close, so the other points are evenly spaced. Leave a gap in the middle where one or two people can sit in a chair—something made for the outdoors is good, like a stool or something that swivels, so you can sit and face whatever direction feels best for you.

Then either during the full moon, at any time that is convenient for you, or preferably at sunup, meaning from first light up to the point when the Sun is moving up over the horizon, sit in the space you've left in the center and initially face the north. Put a foot down so you can revolve very slowly, and keep that foot moving so that you are very slowly revolving to the left. You can say your prayers, whatever they might be for your religion, or whatever you might need to say for your particular cultural aspects—which sometimes may refer to New Age churches or New Age beliefs.

Soy as a plant is very spiritual. It is best interacted with when it is completely alive and vital. Do what you can to keep the plant alive and vital, but if animals, especially wandering four-legged animals—meaning wild and free—come by and nibble on it, don't discourage that too much. Just try to keep the plant going. You have to expect that animals might come to eat, and it's not entirely a problem. If it becomes a problem and the plants get completely denuded, then you can put an extra four or five plants around the perimeter of your property, which would be for the animals. Water them and fertilize them when necessary so they are there for the animals. It acknowledges the purpose of the plant and its part in the natural world, which was created this way by Creator.

It's all right, then, to fence off—if your yard or your garden or your land or your small farm isn't already fenced off—those other three plants with that spot to sit in. You'll find that your prayers will be answered, especially if they are benevolent, meaning they are not *against* anything and don't ask for harm toward anyone. If the prayer is constructed as are most prayers, it won't be like that. Don't ask for victory over something; just ask for the most benevolent outcome, or the best outcome for all beings. If you have a fixed prayer—meaning it's already laid out and is to be said in a certain way, say, for instance, like a Hail Mary—then say it. After you're done with your Hail Marys, if you like you can pause for a moment, and while you're still revolving on the chair, just say, "And let it be so in the most benevolent way for all beings." That's what I recommend.

Soy Is Familiar with Various Human Races

Soy comes from a place that is frequented by angels and is on a pathway that is angelic. Of course, angels and other benevolent beings associated with Creator can go anywhere, yes, but there are certain pathways of travel that are especially comfortable—you might say these paths are laid out for their usage—and the planet where soy is from is on such a pathway. It's not typical to have planets directly on a pathway like that and, of course, the planet does move about, but the pathway for the angels and the planet are merged about 80 percent of the time, meaning that regardless of the orbit of the planet, the pathway and the planet are in conjunction about 80 percent of the time. By conjunction, I'm not using the astrological meaning but rather to mean that there is a connection, all right? As a result, there has been a great deal of spiritual exposure, and clear spirituality at that, because of the angelic influence. There are other plant forms on that planet, and it might be to your advantage, in the future, to ask for plant forms who are from that planet and who are now on Earth to speak for your book. There are a few others.

As far as our relationship to human beings goes, we were informed that human beings on Earth, otherwise known as Earth humans, would be a little different from other human beings on other planets. We were informed that Earth humans would be only slightly biologically different; the big difference would be that they wouldn't remember who they were during the time when they are in the wakeful state on Earth. Of course, when you're in deep sleep, you do remember who you are, but you don't carry that over to your wakeful state. As a result, any life form who chooses to come or is invited and accepts coming to Earth with Earth humans recognizes that the Earth human personality is not going to act the same way as that being might act someplace else. So you might actually meet up with a soul—as a plant—that you know from other places, but that soul would probably not know you and would not interact with you as that soul might very well act in those other places.

I think that this was the hardest thing for the first few soy plants on the Earth, because that contact with the angelic has led to a great deal of familiarity with various human races. You understand the angelics serve all beings, but there is quite a bit of frequency, meaning motion toward Earth, because a great deal more is needed on Earth, simply because human beings do not remember who they are as humans. As a result, you do things you would never do otherwise. So there's a lot of contact, and this will remain so. The first few plants on Earth had a hard time because they were familiar with many of the souls they came into contact with, but those souls did not remember who the plants were, and therefore there was not the usual respect or happiness or friendliness. But once that judgment was made, then things were better for soy, as you call it. Do you have a question?

The Memory of Who You Are Will Always Return

Yes. What is your nature? Have you inhabited a soy plant or are you their elder?

I am what you might call an elder, having been one of the original plants. I am now in physical form on our native planet, the home planet, and in spirit form here on Earth to advise and cultivate [chuckles] friendships with other soy plants.

What is your form on your home planet? Is it similar to the form you have on Earth?

If you were to see us on the home planet, we would look more like a vine. Since the home planet has a lot of open space, we traverse the ground quite a bit. But we do not grow vertically—unless we happen to grow over something or attach ourselves to something that is vertical—except on the Earth.

You were invited here for a purpose. Did those who came to visit you about coming to Earth tell you the purpose for which you were invited?

Yes. It was exactly the purpose I laid out before, about the prayers. We were guided that Earth humans would be prayerful, very religious, very philosophical, very much involved with seeking the higher power for advice and guidance and so on—basically all of the things you have before you come to Earth as you completely interrelate with all other planets and all other forms of your soul. But on the Earth, you do not have that—you have it, of course, but you don't always realize you have it. As a result, there is this constant search to find out who you are, where you're from, why you're here, to talk to God and ask God for help and to lead you to answers. So it doesn't surprise us that you are also very spiritual. Granted, a few do not act that way, but at your core, you are all very spiritual. You are born to it, so you can really be no other way. Even though that knowledge gets corrupted—even if you've been totally corrupted away from spirit or being religion conscious in the wakeful state—when you die, or even at the deep-sleep levels, it immediately comes back and you remember who you are.

There Are Nonplant Beings on Soy's Home Planet

Do you interact with the other beings on your home planet?

I am there, so yes. Spirits can traverse to Earth. I travel along the lines of the angelics since that's the easiest and quickest way to get to Earth, but I am on the home planet now, growing happily.

Right. Are there other beings—plants or other forms of life—on your planet?

There are forms of life that are plants. There are other forms that you would say are nonplant, or animal, in nature, but I'm going to include the human being in that form—flesh, yes? There are beings like that. They would not consider themselves to be animals, but, then, you don't consider yourself to be animals either, so they are nonplants, as you say. There are varieties of nonplants, since we're calling them that, on the home planet, and about six or more varieties of plants.

Did I understand correctly that there are humans there?

No. They visit sometimes, and that's typical on other planets to have visitors coming and going on a regular basis. It doesn't always happen, but it's frequent. Hold on a moment. [Sneezes and blows nose.] All right. I have returned.

Okay. It's complicated being a human, eh?

Yes, because the channel wishes to have the hand that one is using for the throat drops to remain clean, so having to get the cap off the water bottle without using the other hand . . . it's always important for spirit to respect the needs of the physical channel. So I say in case any of you are channeling out there, pay attention to the beings you are channeling. Do they respect your needs? If they do, then it's probably all right to channel them as long as you follow your other guidelines. If they don't, then maybe they need to mature a bit more or evolve a bit more so that your needs are taken care of.

Very good. You said you had a lot of visitors, and I would assume that's partly because you're on a pathway and then partly because you're very good to have around with your spiritual connections, right?

It's not because we're on the pathway that we have visitors, but I think that visitors and visiting is just totally normal everyplace else. It's just that on your Earth, visiting is only allowed under certain circumstances. You have to be directly helping, and the safest way to do that is in spirit form so that you're not bringing a vehicle. In the past, bringing vehicles was easier, but it's not at the moment.

Processed Soy Is Safer for Human Consumption

Right. Now, what is the effect on humans when they eat your . . . I assume they eat your soy berries?

Well, you see . . . let's put that another way. Think of other foods that are eaten by animals—and I'm using your term here—those foods are just perfect for them, giving them sustenance and nurturance. I'm not talking about human-made foods, now, just what grows naturally and is eaten by the animals. In some cases, you might look at that and say, "Well, I could probably eat some of that and be all right," but in other cases, "Well, I don't know. It doesn't look too appetizing, anyway." [Chuckles.] So you have to group it into that first category.

Now, I recognize that when human beings eat soy, that it's been processed. You're not just picking the fruits off the tree, so to speak. [Chuckles.] Perhaps I should get out of the religious framework. You're not just picking the fruit off the soy plant and consuming it; there's processing going on. In the course of processing, it becomes safe for the human being to eat, and it provides a degree of sustenance. It is probably not the best thing for human beings to eat, but a great many plants that grow and may not be meant for human food, once they are processed, might be acceptable to eat—things that can be eaten in a wide variety of ways, as they are. So I'm not saying that once it's processed, it's not safe to eat, but I would suggest that processing would be a requirement.

They're even making soymilk for babies.

Well, of course, if at all possible, it's better to have mother's milk, because it's not just food. It's not only nutrients that are vital for baby that cannot be replaced by other products, no matter how well intended by human beings, but it is also baby's first real contact with the external world and being nourished by another human being—and one, of course, who baby loves or will grow to love. It teaches baby a lot about love and help and being taken care of and, to a degree, giving back, because as baby gets older, baby hugs Mom and Mom hugs baby back. And so baby learns how to show love and so on. So I have to answer the question that way. It's really best if mother can nurse baby; that is always the best. If for some reason, medical or otherwise, mother is unavailable to nurse baby, then any product is acceptable, as long as it's been processed to the point of safety for human beings. But I cannot say that soy is appropriate for baby at the same time or that cow's milk—even processed for baby—is appropriate for baby, because it's meant for baby cows, eh?

The Plants That Have Been on Earth Longest Are Meant for Animals

Are there any other plants that were put here specifically for animals that humans are eating, unaware of the original intent?

Well, you know, you could say that about almost all plants, because human beings haven't been on Earth very long. Then again, some plants were brought to the planet by traveling humans. This especially happened in the beginning when it was possible to bring ships and support the human beings on the surface of the planet. That's how corn got here. It was a gift from Creator, but also it was a gift brought by beings in ships from the Sirius star system. They were the ones who brought corn. Now this is not to suggest that other beings from Pleiades and Orion and other places didn't also do that, but initially it was brought by ships from Sirius.

A great many plants are native to the planet—once Earth was complete, first came the plants, and then so-called animals. It's not impossible for your scientists of today to determine how old plants are—meaning how long plants have been here. The plants that have been here the longest, although many have faded into the background at the moment, are definitely here in terms of their consumability for animals. Plants that haven't been here very long may very well be here for humans.

How did your plants get here?

We were invited, and thus when travelers came to the planet, we volunteered, migrated, and were supported on the ships. We were on the ships for what you would term as about three months before we were placed where we could thrive on the planet. We stayed on the ships for a little while, during which time we had a chance to mingle and be around humans. They weren't Earth humans, but they were humans, so that was helpful as well. We were exposed to music—they were very musical. Human beings on Earth have always been musical, whether they had instruments or not, and that was useful. To this day, I like flute music.

Beautiful. What percentage of beings on your planet are inhabiting soybeans here?

I'd be hard pressed to answer that. I suppose maybe 80 percent. It doesn't mean that soy plants on the home planet don't have souls; it just means supporting the souls of the plants on Earth. Nothing in this entire universe is born or comes into a form that is fully functional without being ensouled, as you know. When plants come to be on the planet, they are automatically ensouled, but their souls are supported by approximately 80 percent of the beings on the home planet. In this way, they always have a degree of continuity, which they don't get when they're being raised on farms, because they know what they're being raised for. That connection with the home planet allows them to have continuity.

Can you discuss this with others on the home planet—what your experiences are here?

Well, I don't know how you're going to take this, but they don't ask. Where we are in our natures, we do not begin speaking of something unless we are invited to. This is actually fairly typical in the natural world. If you could understand what brother or sister spider says or birds or anything like that, they would all be like that. Even your dogs and cats are like that, if you could understand them. But if you ask them something, then they would be inclined to communicate. When you are not on Earth, that's how you are too.

The reason I asked is because it's discomforting here. Many times, when the personalities go back to their home planet, they can't talk about their time on Earth because they'd bring discomfort to that planet.

You see, that doesn't happen in our case because they don't go back. They stay on the planet.

They stay on this planet?

Yes, as I said, of the 80 percent of souls who are supporting souls on this planet, they're supporting them but there's no traversing back and forth.

The Time Will Come When Humans Will Equate Themselves to Plants

Do you have a memory or do your people have a memory of being someplace else before they came to this creation?

I know that we have been someplace else, but I do not have that memory. That's just as well, because I know it would distract me from my work—just as if you could remember all the places you'd lived as a soul, in this universe or beyond. Given your life—and I'm speaking in general to all human beings here—if you have those memories, you wouldn't be living much of a life on Earth because you'd be thinking about that all the time.

Are your beings one of the groups of beings that humans will meet when they go out to explore other planets?

That is very unlikely. If you saw us on our native planet, you would say, "Oh, a plant." [Chuckles.] By the time you get out to where we are, though—that will be in the quite distant future—by that time, Earth human beings will have met so many other forms of human beings, you will know a great deal more about who you are and you will automatically assume that everything is alive, which it is. Right now, you might know mentally that a plant is alive, but you don't view it as an equal. Once you've been traveling enough and have had enough contact with other beings who look like you, it won't be too long before you realize that everything is alive and everything is equal. This means enough contact so that you feel you can relate to them and you have all the communications and conversations you're going to have and have seen things and experienced things. Thus you're going to be more careful where you put your feet. If something lands on you, you won't just slap it or stomp on it and say, "Oh! That was possibly a friend." [Chuckles.]

Yes, we've got a ways to go. Well, just in my own life, there was no awareness of any of this. I was not taught any of this. Hopefully the next generation will start from a better place.

It's an advantage, the space exploration, because all the astronauts—and cosmonauts and whatever they call themselves—have a certain degree of exposure to this. Even though that's not discussed publically, they're all instructed that if they meet beings or come into contact with beings who are not for Earth, they are to follow a certain protocol. It's just a matter of time before that migrates out to the general population. The protocol will be expanded the more of those beings you interact with, but for right now, that protocol is not too bad. To some extent, it's a little military, but that will go away as the realization becomes crystal clear that the beings you're going to meet are not going to pose a threat. You might be worried about what they might do, but that doesn't make that worry a reality.

Ask Your Plant and Animal Friends for Answers in Your Dreams

I know you don't talk, but do you interact with other plants, birds, insects, or animals on Earth? Do you interact with them and share your stories?

Only if they ask.

Do they ask very often?

Yes, occasionally, but as a group of beings, we are also interested in others. That is why we work so well with people's—human beings'—prayers, because we are interested in you. Very often within the prayer is the feeling of something that's needed, wanted, or otherwise being requested, so we learn a little about you. Therefore we are more inclined to ask the bird or the ant or the worm to tell about themselves or sing their songs or repeat their prayers so that we might hear them and enjoy them. We like that sort of thing.

Are other animals aware that you amplify the energy of their prayers?

No, we don't do that unless they ask us to. We only do that with Earth humans. And you are assuming something. What gave you the impression that we amplify them? See, this is something that is typically human—an assumption. Human beings make assumptions about what you essentially don't know. Of course, you really do know, but on Earth you forget what you know. After a while, you assume for the sake of convenience and so you don't have to learn everything about everything every time you meet something, including a situation. But in fact, that is not the case. I recommend that people do that with their prayers, because this interaction will allow the prayer to travel on a path that is more connected to the angelic. I'm not saying that it will make a difference; I'm just saying that because of our familiarity and infusion with the angelic, we have that quality about ourselves.

Now, going back to your question about other life forms, we don't really amplify, but if they sing or tell or speak or communicate or radiate feelings about their culture in their prayers or their songs, they might feel a little more of the angelic when they're talking to us directly. But they feel quite a bit of that on their own, because they're not here to learn anything. They're here to live as well as possible while waiting to instruct you when you ask—but you must ask, and then they might tell you. If you cannot understand them, which is likely, then learn how to ask. Say you see an earthworm, and it's passing by—or say you see a dandelion, and it's present, going through its life cycle. If you want to learn something from them, you might say:

"I'm asking," and fit it into your religion, "I'm asking that I dream about what dandelion is for"—or what beetle is for or what bird is for or anything—"in terms of what they're here to teach me, that I might learn how to ask the best questions and dream the answers from animal and plant friends on Earth."

That's the easiest way. It's particularly effective with children, especially if they wake up naturally, meaning without somebody shaking them or without an alarm or something—and it's that way with everyone, of course. If you wake up that way, there's a better chance you'll remember your dream. Or your dream, although you forget it, will trigger an experience that you might associate with having asked that prayer. Maybe that bluebird is here to teach you about blue or maybe about bird. Maybe in the course of your day, you will see something that reminds you of bluebird—perhaps a blue feather—and maybe it has something to do with the answer to your question to bluebird. Maybe not, but it might. Don't assume. It has to be something that would be birdlike or blue in that case—of course, blue's a frequent color in your wardrobes and so on. I'm just trying to give you some tracks on the ground, so to speak, things that you can follow and experiment with. You cannot be certain that it will be absolute, but it's worth the experiment and the practice.

All Species Are Present on Earth to Teach Humans

All species of plants, all species of animals, and Mother Earth herself are all present with you on this planet because they all have something to teach you. Granted, some of them have other ways of supporting you and helping your lives, but they all have something to teach you that you would like to know—not something that is teaching about things you wouldn't like to know. It would be personal and often would be helpful to other humans as well—maybe not every human, but some. It's a particularly good questioning process that might be good for poets or artists or those who write songs. It might help you to help others.

Does one have to be in the presence of a physical plant, or can one invite the energy or spirit of soy to be with one when one does a process like benevolent magic?

You're talking about something *you* might do.

Any human who's going to say a prayer or do benevolent magic or wish to commune—can they ask the spirit of soy to be present, or do they have to be in the presence of a physical plant?

In the presence of a physical plant. That's why I recommend that you look into the possibility, because the plants might very well be something that you can plant no matter where you are, once you know a little bit. With some plants—it depends on how deep the roots go or what your soil is like and so on—it might be possible to grow them in a pot. It depends. You'd have to take it up with the roots and put wheels underneath the plant so you can wheel it out to the sunlight.

Do you like full sun when you grow?

Well, I think since we are planted in an open field, it's safe to say yes, eh?

I wish they'd tell me ahead of time who is going to speak so I could find out something more about you.

Let's stop for today and you take a little bit of an opportunity to look it up, and next time, we'll continue.

That would be great. You sound so spritely and like you have so much to say.

Good. Then we will resume next time. Good night.

Good night. Good life. Thank you.

Soy Spirit

MAY 1, 2009

❧

This is Soy Spirit. I know there is controversy about whether soy is good for human beings or not. As I said last time, as long as it's processed like you process other foods, there is a great deal that can be made palatable as well as reasonably safe for human beings to eat. But in the raw form, it's really meant for animals, so I do not wish, by my comments, to subtract soy from the human diet, because I know that there are so many of you now, and of course you need to eat.

Though I would recommend looking, for the long-term, toward something else to act not only as a filler, which soy is often used for in your diets, but also to use as a mainstay of protein. My guess is that it will wind up being beans of some sort, for those of you who do not eat meat. While it won't be possible for everyone to digest this too well, it will be all right in the long run when new techniques come in that have to do with genetics—not genetically modifying the plants, but (sorry to say, for many of you) genetically modifying humans. But that's another story. I'm not suggesting you do it. I'm just saying that it's coming, and you'll have to be alert to it.

Of course as you begin to interact with other beings from other planets on a regular basis, enough so that you're openly doing trades and so on, most of the diseases you know now on Earth will disappear. Other beings will share methods and means by which you can create food that will be healthy for the human being—either as you know yourself now or as you will become. So they will also offer foodstuffs, some of which can be transplanted and grown on Earth here or there in this or that condition. Or they might just perform trade with you for this or that product or simply give you things that you may need to survive, things that cannot be grown on the planet.

In the long run you will be all right, but for the next hundred years or so it will be a bit of a struggle while you try to figure out who and what you want to be in terms of your genetic makeup and what you wish to consume.

I'm saying that you can take this issue up with others. I'm going to suggest that you do not put too much effort into whether soy is good or bad for you. As long as elements that you feel are not safe are extracted in the food processing, then you will be all right. Good life.

Thank you very much.

ORNAMENTALS

CHAPTER TWENTY-NINE

Hibiscus

JANUARY 28, 2008

છ

GREETINGS! THIS IS HIBISCUS.

Oh, wonderful! Welcome!

Thank you.

You normally live in tropical areas—do you know where you are?

I am associated with an outcropping of hibiscus, but it is in our nature to have a certain unity among our root system. This unity is energetic, but also there is sometimes intermingling. So I am, for lack of a better term, associated with three plants in a warm climate, but I don't have a geographic location for you.

Tell me something about yourself. What is your experience?

My experience of life on this planet is primarily associated with an enrichment of the lives of all beings within a thirty-foot radius of any given plant. I believe we were initially brought here by travelers who move from one planet to another with the intention of seeding a planet with plants that, when one interacts with their living energy (meaning they are alive and vital), one experiences a greater state of benevolence physically. I would recommend, should you find yourself near such plants—growing wild is best, but the next best is in a warm,

427

humid environment where perhaps they have been planted by human beings but then allowed to spread on their own—to simply stand within ten to fifteen feet, no closer. Look at the plants if you like, but you don't have to, and just breathe in and out normally. If you like, you can sit down near them, and just breathe and relax.

Try not to read; don't do anything distracting. Just interact. For those of you who meditate or pray, you can do that near us, but the main thing is to breathe in and out with occasional glances in our direction. That is the best medicinal impact of our being. The benevolent impact would be perhaps slightly heightened if you were to be in an environment where you can look toward the sky in the general direction of Sirius. Thus it would be better to do this in the evening hours, but if it is not convenient or safe, it is not necessary to do so at night.

These travelers were known for spreading or seeding plants on planets that would have individuals who were not otherwise immune—meaning you have many species on this planet that have a built-in immune system and they don't get sick and die off and so on, but the human being does not have an adequate immune system allowing for what you are exposed to on this planet. These travelers seemed to know that you were going to be here in that type of environment, so they seeded hibiscus and other plants on your planet and other places as well, but almost always in environments where warmth and humidity was predominant. They were from Sirius.

Do your memories go back there? Do you have awareness of being there?

No.

Even When Extinct, Plants Continue to Exist Underground

What is your lifespan here? How long have you been here?

I have been here associated with hibiscus root systems for about 1,500 years. I am not an individual plant. I am an energy associated with root systems of hibiscus.

Oh, how wonderful! So even if one dies out here, the system is always there underneath?

Yes. This is not unlike other plants, which may not be present at the surface at any given time, even over thousands of years as the surface might build up in some places. Still, if the root system is below ground and the surface becomes hospitable or more hospitable or a combination of those things and has the need for plant presence, then the plant might pop up, seemingly considered to be an extinct plant but returning once again. Any plant that has ever been on the surface of Earth, with very few exceptions, is capable of returning in that fashion.

I might add, though I don't know if you would consider it so wonderful, that something similar is true for animal species. One might reasonably assume that an animal species would only be present on the basis of natural birth cycles, but sometimes they can re-emerge from unlikely places.

Say more about that.

I am not here really to speak of animals. I do not feel there is much danger of you running into a dinosaur, but you might find yourself as a species (not you individually) someday discovering that the saber-toothed tigers aren't quite as extinct as you thought—in which case, it would be best by that time to have a built-in system for communicating with animals and plants. If you don't have that technologically, then it would be good to have human beings trained that way so that you can have an idea when the tiger is approaching your direction. Then you can get all your peoples out of the way and just enjoy the beauty of a giant being going by and say, "Isn't that wonderful? I'm glad we're not there."

Our Home Planet Is in Andromeda

Now let me speak a little bit of the home planet, which I've been told about. The home planet is not in Sirius. The home planet is in the Andromeda system, and there are many planets in Andromeda that have water as you know them. This is not something exclusive to one galaxy or another, but almost always the water is slightly different in its makeup. On Earth you have what you might call thin water, yet it can thicken and form ice or even become thinner and be steam. On the planet that is the home planet associated with hibiscus and Andromeda, the water does not thicken and become ice nor does it become thin and become steam or mist. It is always and only in a liquid form, slightly thicker than that you recognize as water here. It's a little more oxygenated. The oxygen there is not in any way detrimental to life, though. Even though you don't consider it consciously as being detrimental to life here, one could say that it does have oxidizing properties, does it not?

Yes, aging!

On Andromeda that is not the case, however, because every life form on Andromeda is made up, with oxygen as a portion of its innate system to a greater or lesser degree. So the balance of the life forms there owe their existence or fundamental portions of their true natures to the chemical composition of the water that exists there. Therefore one is not in any way harmed by the fluid but is actually nurtured, and the life forms there are plant-based, though they do not breathe as well. Plants on Earth breathe in a way—not like you with lungs and so on, but they do take in certain atmospheres and expel certain atmospheres.

On that home planet, there is no intake or expelling of atmospheres or gases. There is, rather, purely the interaction with the fluid. About seven-eighths of the planet is fluid at the surface, and yet the fluidity only ranges in depth around the surface of the planet to the extent of one to two inches. So the plants grow in the water, and very few of them grow on the land. The land is occupied by other plants akin to something you might from a distance identify as a tree, but if you were to get closer to it, you would say, "These are just gigantic cactuses." They look, when you get closer, like a combination between a tree and a giant cactus, though there are no needles, no spines, because there is no risk to the plant. That's the general nature of the appearance of the planet. It is warmed by a sun and has two moons.

How does it maintain one inch of water? It appears that it would evaporate and be gone.

As I said, it varies. It's not just one inch in places—it might be three to six inches. There are underground springs, and of course, then there is a replenishment via that route. The places that don't have water on the surface are simply raised portions on the land, not unlike your own planet.

Do you know if the beings from Sirius were the agents who brought you here? Were you asked to come to Earth?

I do not believe that we as a species were asked. I believe we were brought. Now, I can't rule out that the people who brought us may have been requested to do so, but I do not have that knowledge. We were not asked, "Do you want to go to Earth?"

We were in a good relationship with those people from Sirius. They are plant-loving people, and a portion of their physical makeup you would identify, were you to speak to their healers or doctors, as being something like a plant. They have a natural affinity for beings of our size, as do we for them, so I am sure my ancestors were inclined to cooperate.

Does the temperature stay stable on planet so the water doesn't freeze or mist?

Yes, it doesn't get outside the range of what you would call . . . well, you have to remember it's not the same as your water. If you were there, it would feel pleasantly warm to you, not hot, and it remains about like that, even in the evening. But with two moons, it never really gets completely dark.

You've been told about it, but you don't really remember it?

That's right. I've been told about it; I haven't been there.

So is this like between lives there, then?

I don't understand. I've never been there. I daresay you have never been on your home planet either.

Being Underground Allows Me to Remain Focused

So most of the beings I talked to came from there. You're an emotive personality occupying this form as a service, right?

It's no different than human beings, if you call this "service."

So you personally volunteered to come here into this form?

No different than you. I don't understand the question. It's not the way I would state it.

How would you state it?

That I chose to be in existence in this form, just as you chose to be in existence in the form you are in—not necessarily picking everything about your life before it happened but maybe certain general parameters.

That's very interesting, because usually the beings have been on their home planet and they came here as a service, so this is a little different. Do you remember where you were before this?

Certainly.

Ah! Okay. Humans have been separate and isolated for so long as individuals. You have been one unit as all of the plant kingdom as a creator, right?

No, we're creative. I wouldn't call us a creator.

I thought the plant kingdom as a unit had been a creator at one time and now they said they would generally be individuals.

I am not aware of that status.

How much are you aware of what goes on above ground?

Not that much, but if you would like, a hibiscus plant itself can communicate with you.

No, I am just wondering what your life is like. What is your experience where you are?

Quiet.

And what else?

You'd have to ask a direct question, but if you are asking if it is anything like human life, then no. Is it anything like surface plant life? No. It is quiet, but it does allow us, others like me, to remain focused on our primary purpose for being on this planet, which is to offer healing through our living being. I think that some humans have taken the surface version of the plant for other purposes, although I can speak with some authority for the undersurface elements of other plants based on my intercommunication with them. But a living plant in its living form is the best means of experiencing benevolent and at least sympathetic, meaning vibrational, assistance with improved health of all life forms.

So do you consciously bring this energy in from someplace and flow it into the plant above the surface?

It is not exactly bringing it from someplace. It is remaining attuned to the original vibration—feeling, whatever you want to call it—that I was associated with when I became aware of myself in my current position. My job and the reason I am underground is so that I am not distracted too much and can maintain that energy, and that energy evolves up into the plant itself through the natural process of taking in water, nutrients, and so on.

Humans Aren't Meant to Live in Balance on Earth

I loved hibiscus and all the colors when I lived in the south, but I just wasn't aware of energy at that time.

You don't have to be aware of it. You can simply happen to be talking to a friend within, say, ten to fifteen feet of hibiscus, and if there is anything that is off balance with you, the energy might be present. Of course, it's better to be quiet and just breathe and glance at the plants now and then, not functioning with your mind too much, because the mind almost invariably draws you into the past or into the future, even when one is simply thinking, according to my slight interaction with human beings. I notice that most human beings, regardless of what they're doing in the present, seem to be thinking in the past or in the future.

How did you manage that while being underground?

Sometimes human beings dig. That happened, and I found myself for a time near a project where human beings were digging to create a structure of some sort, where I was within a few feet of them. Even though I was covered with soil, I was near them, proximity being a factor. I could tell they were human beings, because I recognized the sound and the general demeanor. After all, I have been exposed to other underground life forms, and there is a vast difference between most species of being on this planet and the human being.

Most species of beings on Earth have a considerable sense of balance between their own kind and other species, even if they're not entirely friendly at all times. There is a sense of balance. With the human being, there isn't that. It's not to suggest that the human being doesn't belong on this planet, but it is a simple observation from a visitor, you might say, though I perhaps have been a visitor for a time. But my simple observation is that the human being is not here to live in balance. Otherwise, you would have achieved that long ago. If you are not here to live in balance, then you must be out of balance for a reason. Therefore, it's safe to say that your lack of balance is intended to help you to learn something.

With whom do you communicate? Are there root systems of trees and other plants and even animals that burrow down?

Well, there are animals who are simply underground: earthworms, ants, and so on. Ants have a great deal of knowledge, and they seem to have acquired a considerable amount of knowledge about human beings as they forage on the surface and then return to underground. So I have learned something from them, and there are other root systems as you have indicated.

For a Long Time I've Been Interested in Balance

What is your greatest joy?

Just being. I will be here for another thousand years, barring too much human interference.

You know that now. That's the average lifespan of a root system?

I'm not a root system.

Well, the energy of the root system.

I'm an energy associated with the root system. That's different.

Tell me the difference.

The difference is that it is my job to maintain the energy that is drawn on by the plant so that it has its healing qualities.

Oh! I see. Do all plants have this energy associated with them?

I cannot speak for all plants, but all hibiscus do. I am just an energy associated with three root systems from three original plants. I believe the surface is spread out so much that it might look like there are more, but there were originally just three.

Were they existent when you became associated with them?

No. I was here, prepared the ground, and then the plants were here, arriving in the usual way by Earth's system of moving plant seed around.

Why did you choose this particular existence?

As a being, for a long time I have been interested in balance, and balance in this sense means no disease, no illness, and an ability to get along with all other life forms in the most peaceful, benevolent way. I have been interested in that and have been focused in various life forms on various planets throughout all time while pursuing that goal, living in that goal, or learning about that as a way of existence. This is why I was prepared to come to Earth to perform this function, as it is considerably more challenging since the human being is present—although when I first arrived, the human being was in much greater balance. Perhaps this is because there were, as far as I could tell, energetically fewer . . . I'm not using the language well, but fewer opportunities for conflict. I suppose "opportunity" is not the correct term.

There were fewer people, and they were, as you say, more balanced. They weren't focused in their minds and so competitive the way we are now.

From my minimal contact with or awareness of other species, there seemed to be considerably more consciousness of the human being interacting with nature in order to survive without destroying nature—meaning living off of the land and not destroying it for life.

So that makes sense. You're not part of the plant kingdom per se.

No.

You're a separate energy.

Yes, which is why before we close hibiscus, you will hear from a plant itself so that we can create a more personal sense of hibiscus. But I felt that for you to have an understanding of how it is that hibiscus does what it does, it might be helpful to know about this other aspect.

Yes, absolutely. It's a whole new thing. Are there many others? There must be many, many others like you, then?

Yes, many others.

Are they beings you know? Do you interact with them?

I have at times interacted with them, but I don't think about them as named individuals. We are a portion of the same energy, but we are individualized, yet I do not think of us as individuals. I do not know how you can identify with that. It would be as if you were a human being in a very close-knit family where you all worked together for some greater benefit that would help your kind and other kinds without any expectance of anything coming back to you as a result—but by your simple being, others are assisted.

That is beautiful. So is there a group of you that sort of flows from planet to planet. I mean, have you been with some of these beings before?

No, I have not been with them. This is the first time I have had a life form like this.

But have you also been underground on other planets, or not necessarily?

Not necessarily.

Give me one that you remember!

On another planet I was a crystalline life form. It was there where I received my initial education in the value of being something that, by its very existence, was beneficial to others without actually having to do anything other than what you would naturally do. I was not what you would call crystalline as it is associated with your planet. We could move of a sort, a type of motion, but it was a motion not unlike ice on your planet—where it was motion not self-initiated. During that time of life, I was educated as to the value of such pursuits.

And your energy there radiated out and helped whatever beings were there?

I learned about that; I learned that that existed. It didn't really happen then that I was aware of, but I learned about its value. That's the initial learning I had in that. That was many millions of years ago, of course.

How fascinating. It's totally new.

Now we will hear from a hibiscus plant itself. Good night!

Thank you very much. Thank you. Good life!

❋   ❋   ❋

GREETINGS! THIS IS HIBISCUS.

Welcome!

I am a plant, you'd say, living above the surface of that energy that spoke to you.

Do you know where you are, on what part of the planet?

Someplace warm and moist. There is a waterfall nearby. I can hear it. The moisture sometimes blows over this way. There is animal life, but no human beings are present. I believe there might have been some who lived here some time ago, but they are no longer present.

What kinds of animals are around? I am trying to get a feeling for where you might be.

Short ones—they're not very tall. I seem to be taller than they are.

Are you multicolored, or one color?

Different colors of the flowers.

Assimilating Energy from Hibiscus Plants

What is your interaction with the energy being? Are you aware of him?

It is not a him or a her. I am aware. I think perhaps all hibiscus are aware of such energies. I cannot be certain, but my general feeling is that other

436 &o PLANT SOULS SPEAK

plants have similar energies, but I do not know if you can assimilate the energies for your own good from all other plants. But I can speak for my own kind. If you are within, say, ten to fifteen feet, but no closer than six feet—we don't like it when you're too close—then you can just by simply breathing assimilate a significant amount of benevolent energy. I would recommend not staying and breathing and looking at us for more than twenty minutes a day, but twenty minutes is all right, as long as there aren't people constantly doing that.

A single grouping of plants would get fatigued, if that were the case, but if you were perhaps on a trail and came across us, you could perform that way and then leave. It would be good if you were drinking plenty of water before and after (but not during) such interactions. You would find that even serious diseases might be somewhat improved. Though if you could do this for five or six days out of a week and camp or reside within, say, no closer than a half a mile, no farther away than three miles from the hibiscus you're interacting with, then you could do this for maybe up to thirty days, always with a few days off per week to allow the plants to re-energize and to live life yourself. Then it might be of great benefit for those who need such assistance.

So when humans draw that energy, it depletes the plant?

Yes. It's not that much different for the human being. You can have people around you who need energy and may not even be conscious of needing energy, and they can draw on the energy of another human being. If you find yourself getting tired around people, they may be drawing on your energy. It would be perhaps to your benefit to disallow that, or to bring it up to the person and perhaps you or the other person or both of you can put a stop to that, at least temporarily.

What about in tropical areas where hibiscus is grown and planted by humans in yards—does it work the same way there?

I don't think it's exactly the same when plants in general are raised as a crop. There is some benefit, but it is much better if they are simply in the wild. You could have a situation where some are being grown, but if they have drifted off and are in the wild, then that would be better. On the other hand, there is some degree of benefit to be around them, say, in a farm situation, but it's not the same, because the farmer would have an agenda for something he or she is planning to do with the plants. So the plants would not be appreciated for who and what they actually are. They would simply be a means to an end, and therefore, no personal relationship could form.

When the plant is offering its energy in a beneficial way to a human being, there is some personal frame of reference there because the plant has to essentially feel the human being to notice what needs to be corrected or put into balance. But that would not be the case if a plant knew that it was being grown to be cultivated.

That would be like somebody who grows plants to sell them, but my experience with hibiscus has been in the yard of a home.

I was referring to a farm.

Yes, but what about a home where they grow. I've lived in places where they grow like hedges up and down, where there are tons of them.

You mean they are planted and then allowed to just grow as they would?

Yes.

But are they trimmed?

I'm sure sometimes, yes.

That's not so good then.

They have to be left totally alone?

Yes. You wouldn't like to be trimmed, eh? You might be less than friendly were that to occur.

Yes, there's so much for humans to learn. How long have you been there? How long is your life span?

I couldn't say how long the life span is, really, in terms of your time, but I am conscious of being in existence. Do you understand that I am referring to my stem and my flower and the various flowers that come off of my stem—really not that long.

Oh, not the whole plant. There are different beings in the plant?

Well, this is the portion that is speaking to you. I cannot give you a clinical evaluation.

You said something that was so interesting. As a human comes close, you almost diagnose and send that person what he or she needs.

We don't diagnose. It's as if you were to be around someone playing a musical instrument and you had an average sense of hearing, and that person was playing the instrument slowly. You would probably notice when he or she was off-key, wouldn't you? You would notice when he or she hit a note that wasn't quite right. It is similar, that analogy. A human being coming along—we would notice if he or she wasn't quite right.

The age doesn't matter. It could be a sickness, it could be an injury—it doesn't matter. We would notice that they were not at their nominal best. It is not our job to cure the whole world of human beings—we are aware of that. But we do like balance, and we notice but we don't necessarily leap into action, eh?

But if the human being stops and glances at us, breathes and then is just quiet, then we assume that the human being is sensitive to who and what we are, and we open up our energy field to encompass him or her. Generally speaking, if the person gets closer than six feet, though, we'll close that, because he or she might be approaching to clip the flowers to make a bunch of flowers—not something we like. But if the person stays, say, ten feet away, fifteen feet away, and looks at us and is doing that sort of thing, then we will encompass that person and support him or her for a time.

All I ever did was look at the pretty flowers.

Yes, the purpose of this book is to support the interaction of human beings and plants to be more benevolent for all.

It Is the Imbalance that Causes the Discomfort on Earth

Do you have memories of the energy of the home planet where hibiscus comes from? Are you aware of that? Do you remember it?

Yes, I have been on the home planet.

And you volunteered to come here?

We volunteered. I wasn't there during the time of the volunteering, but I remember that according to what I've been told, yes? A ship came hovering over the planet and volunteers were requested. Apparently those who volunteered provided seed, not the plants themselves, and since the seeds were offered as one might offer one's children, there was a ceremony wherein there was a considerable amount of exchange of love between the seeds and the parent plants before the children were allowed to go with these benevolent beings who came. But the beings who came in the vehicle were so benevolent, it was felt that the children would be going to someplace good. I do not think that those who picked up the original seed could do anything but good, as they were kindness itself, from what I have heard.

So they may not have known about the experiment with humans that would be on this planet?

I'm sure they did know. The beings were not deceitful. They would have said.

So have you been here more than once?

I have been to this planet as a being, a personality, twice: once in the distant past and now in my current time. In the distant past, it was more comfortable and there was much more forest on the surface of the planet. But I am here now because I heard from my fellow being that it would be good to see how it is, and I've been here for a time, not long. It's different.

So are you allowed to remember when you go home what happened here?

Yes. There is no need to forget.

Sometimes they tell us that because there's discomfort here, you can't bring it back.

Oh, I see. When I came the first time, there was no discomfort that I was aware of personally, though there was probably discomfort nearby. But I was not touched by it.

Are you now?

Yes.

Because humans are close?

I cannot say that humans are the only source of discomfort, but apparently, it is sort of like a pyramidal thing. If you change something that is benevolent and completely balanced, there is a sort of patchwork of reaction that takes place. Some of the reaction is balanced, some will lead to balance, and some is just imbalanced. It's the imbalance that causes what is representative of discomfort. I may choose to forget that when I leave here.

On your home planet, do you have this benevolent energy attached to the root system as you do here, supporting it?

I think the entire root system is that way on the home planet. Here it is just in our modified form, not as strong.

Who on your home planet are you benefiting? Are there others there who receive benefit from you?

Not that I know of. It is just part of our nature to be that way. You see, the human race on this planet represents perhaps only a small cadre of human beings. Human beings on other planets are benevolent, but on your planet, they are not always benevolent because of what you're learning, and so on. So we are allowed to provide only so much balancing and healing energy, since if we were providing as much as we would provide on our home planet, then no human being would ever be ill. No human being would ever be stuck with a permanent injury. If you're born without a leg, you would grow one.

It's that powerful?

Yes, but see, we are not allowed to do that on this planet, because you are apparently here to learn things, which is why you don't live very long. A human being on other planets might easily live 1,500, 2,000 years without any struggle, but there is no disease, no struggle, no misery, no unhappiness, no conflict. On your planet here, to live even a hundred years is an accomplishment.

Are there hibiscus on other planets with humans?

Not where I've been, but if they are, I'm sure everyone is compatible.

Where have you been?

On the home planet. There are no human beings there.

Do you have memories of being other places besides here?

I haven't always been hibiscus.

Ah! Can you tell me what you have been?

Have you always been a human being?

Nooo!

No, I don't think anyone has ever always been the same thing. It is natural to try this or that.

But a lot of them don't remember it. You remember it. What's an interesting thing that you've inhabited?

I've been a human being once, on the Pleiades.

What did you do?

I lived. I loved. I enjoyed life. I was on a medical world, but they didn't really need that there. I was there for visitors who would sometimes need assistance. I have a certain degree of familiarity with and understanding of the human being, even though on the Pleiades it is quite different—no conflict, and so on.

That's amazing!

Perhaps you will be a hibiscus someday, eh?

We Provide Balance to Other Beings as Well

Do you interact with other life forms in the area and converse with them and communicate with them?

Conversation is something I would say that is associated primarily with life forms who don't know who they are.

Well, commune with them.

Yes, commune in that sense, meaning the shared vibration, and so on, of what is known and understood. But conversation, "What did you do today?"—no, there's not too much of that.

Plus there are trees—not as many as there once were, I am sure, in this place, but there are still some trees—and there are bushes, and so on, kinds of general grasses. There are not that many human beings around. There are no trails, though there are some animals who travel along similar routes, but they don't break a trail. The animal-life ones are small.

So if you're here to provide energy to balance humans and there are no humans around . . . ?

No. You don't understand. We're here to provide energy to balance other beings. You are quite naturally taking it that we are here to do that for human beings because you *are* one. But if another life form came by that was other than human, we would do the same thing for them, and they do come by, since they are conscious and aware of who we are and what we do. They come to us intentionally because they know who we are and what we do, and they will stop and do exactly what I described to you, that we suggest the human being do should you have the opportunity to be around us.

I understand. It's like you were with a medical group on the Pleiades. You're doing the same thing there.

Exactly. That's why this life form is appealing.

So wherever you are, is there a temperature limit that you have? I mean, how far north can you go?

You mean, do we grow at the North Pole? No, we don't.

No, but I mean, I have experienced you in Florida and Hawaii, but I don't know where else you grow.

I think we are on Earth. You would find us in warm, humid places.

I see. Anyone who comes into your environment, anyone who needs you.

Anyone who is not in balance and particularly those who are aware of who we are and what we can do, such as nonhumans in general. If they are injured or perhaps in pain, then they might come and stop, breathe, and just be. And they might come back for a few days, maybe just pause in the neighborhood, so to speak, until they feel better, doing very much the same thing we talked about. In the case of a tree, there's a tree not too far who's fairly tall. A bird, for instance, might come and stay in the tree for a few days and fly down near our plants and then just retire to the tree, acquiring food as it needs, and then go on when it feels better.

But you see, in the case of a tree, the bird, by flying up into the tree, can get past thirty feet. Once it's past thirty feet, it will be in the range where we might be of assistance. Whereas, in the case of another creature, it would have to come and go on the ground.

But they do that?

Yes.

I'm wondering, does anyone play this role in colder climates?

In the plant world, you mean? In colder climates? I'm not aware of it. It's possible. You'd have to ask the plants in colder climates when you speak to them. I believe that part of this book might have more of these things too, but as plants themselves, we are offering this if we can, and then your practitioner, your mystical spirit person will perhaps have more to offer.

So do you have a chance, then, to interact beyond the planet, or is your energy totally focused with what you're doing?

It's totally focused here. I don't need to interact beyond the planet. I know what you're saying: Do we sleep? Do we dream? But no, it's not like that. We are focused here, and there is no need to interact beyond the planet. Not unlike yourself, we are immortal, and when our personalities or spirits, whatever you wish to call them, move on, we can interact beyond the planet as much as we like.

Well, I know that some beings we have talked to do that and some don't. It's an individual thing.

Yes.

You Will Remember Your Experiences with Us

What would you like to tell humans?

I'll make a closing statement. I wish you to know—and the energy being did share that—how we can assist you. There is a long-standing tendency on this planet by wise peoples, sometimes called medicine peoples, to know that certain plants offer essences associated with their roots or leaves or berries, and so on, that can be beneficial to the human being and to animals as well. But very often if you know how to interact with us when we are living, we can be alive and provide energies and good feelings, and we can also replenish ourselves and provide that for others. But there is more.

Once you have had this experience as has been described by the energy being and perhaps expanded on a bit by myself as interacting with us in the way suggested, once you have had that, even if you go far away to live, you will remember this experience. And simply the recollection of it in a quiet moment, especially before you go to sleep, lying down perhaps—by remembering it you can then continue to breathe. And through the recollection of it, you can achieve at least 30 to 40 percent of the original energy. We recommend you do that. We also recommend that if you cannot go to places where plants grow whom you are attracted to for their healing properties, for their beauty, or simply for the essence of their being, read a little bit about them. Don't read too much, because depending on who wrote it, they'll have this or that to say, which may not be specific to you. But look at a picture, if you can, and then imagine being within some proximity of us and ask for energy to be shared with you. Perhaps that can benefit you as well. May you have the most benevolent life! Good night!

Thank you so much! Good life!

CHAPTER THIRTY

Ivy

FEBRUARY 23, 2008

∾

THIS IS IVY! GREETINGS!

Welcome! Tell me about yourself!

Our purpose on Earth is to make connections between the atmosphere and the Earth. It is our intention here to establish on a visual basis the fact that as a living being, one must be rooted and connected, not only to the sky, but also to the Earth. Nevertheless, that does not bind one from motion. All plants grow, but the demonstration of our beings, which has to do with motion from an original root source, is meant to show all living forms on Earth that motion can spread and that even when there is loss perhaps of connection from the original source of one's nutrition, one can still exist and spring forth in a new colony.

Perhaps this sounds a bit biblical to you, since the old documents in those kinds of books often reference just such an analogy as I've suggested. And from what I understand from our guides and teachers, it was always intended that we be an example of that. In the past on your planet, there's been a great deal of displacement of populations—sometimes voluntary, other times not so voluntary—and there needed to be a physical example so that people could be

445

reminded that displacement, however unhappy it may be at times, does not have to mean that one cannot survive and even thrive.

I believe this is the reason we look the way we do on Earth. We do not look this way on our home planet, which is actually in this galaxy. On our home planet, we look a great deal more like a tree, and if you were to see us on our home planet, you would be hard-pressed to connect our appearance there with our appearance on Earth. Still, one aspect of our appearance there is that instead of branches, we have something that resembles a trailing vine, though nowhere near as long as how we demonstrate ourselves on Earth. And what is dissimilar is that the trunk of the tree is very vast indeed. It would not be unusual for the trunk to be forty or fifty feet across. Since we have no natural enemies, whatever of us initially grows continues to grow over time, not unlike trees on your planet, but the atmosphere is more suitable for us there.

I know there is concern and grief about loss of rain forests on your planet in places—rain forests do exist on other planets. I want to reassure you of that so that when your successors follow—your children and your children's children and so on—and begin to explore space and eventually have the means to go to other planets, you will very often come across planets that may not be entirely habitable, such as your own, but that will have rain forests, usually much more densely packed with forms of plants and beings besides plants that would, at least from a distance, remind you of your own. You may or may not feel at home as you get closer, but at least you'll be reminded that life in its variety, both in your current time and in the past from which you sometimes have residual proofs, does exist on other planets— or you might at least, as someone who studies these things, be able to trace a connection. Of course, that's a science of the future: tracing connections from your planet to other planets' life forms so as to understand how your planet came to be the way it is, not only from spiritual influence but from the influence of travelers.

How did you happen to come here? Did someone come and request your presence?

I would say that from what I have been guided and inspired to know, there was a visitor in ancient times who said what in general was going to happen on this planet. I would like to say we were instantaneously enthusiastic, but in fact, as I've been told, my ancestors were not interested at that point in participating. However, the emissary went on to say that it would be acceptable, if we wished to participate, for us to continue on in this planet even after the human population had largely migrated, which you will do at some point. And that we were interested in, because we've been on Earth for so long.

We wanted to be able to start out in a friendly environment for us, and then after going through a time of interacting with the human population in a not-so-friendly state from time to time, we would be able to continue on again in a more friendly, amenable environment—so that we would not simply go to a place and cease our existence there because it came to be unpleasant. That would scar us in terms of our memories. But if we could complete our time of involvement in that place with something benevolent and enjoyable, we would prefer that, and this was promised to us. So regardless of our surface presence, it is our intention as a species to remain until after the bulk of the human population has migrated to other planets.

By which time this planet will be more benevolent and easy to live on.

That's my understanding. There will be some in the human population who choose not to migrate, but they will live in underground cities, well and thoroughly supported by the technology that is available to them, shared for the most part from travelers from afar. Such technology will allow an underground city to be a pleasant place, not shut off from the sunlight, but the sunlight will be available from some kind of a light-gathering device that comes through the surface but brings the light in some technical means to the underground civilization. I'm not sure how this works, but it allows the people to experience both sunlight and moonlight, when available.

Getting Inspiration from the Moon

It is understood, of course, by the plant world that moonlight is just as important as sunlight. I'm not sure if your scientists understand this yet. Some of them have begun to research that. Perhaps it is because sunlight is so obviously an influence that when studying some other species or interacting with that species, one tends to gravitate toward or notice the things that are of apparent influence. But the moonlight is just as influential with us, and it has everything to do with the means of humans' support of inspiration.

I am stressing how important the moonlight is because in your time people do not always realize how important the Moon's energy is. Many of you, because of your schedules or because of this or that reason, do not or cannot go outside and experience moonlight. I believe you admire it through your transparent walls, and that's good, but in order to experience the best the Moon has to offer, it's always good to be outdoors with as little filtering as possible of the Moon.

Here's an exercise, if you wish, especially if you feel you need inspiration about whatever is of interest or concern to you. Go outside and look at the

Moon! If it is partially covered by clouds, that's all right, as long as there are patches and the Moon is clearly visible between the gaps in the clouds. If it's too bright, you're not going to stare at it, of course, but glance at it and then look away—or you could glance at it and close your eyes, it's up to you. What you do is, simply while you're looking at it, try to have your mouth open, even if only a little bit, and breathe in and out while you look at the Moon. You don't have to be standing to do this. You can recline, if you prefer, or sit down. If you do, try to do so on a chair or on the ground, and if it's a chair, then find one with as little metal as possible, because if there's too much metal, it will ground the energy straight into the Earth and the whole point is to have it enter yourself.

Something like this done for three or four minutes a week could, in the long run, help your capacity to be inspired. And what I mean by "inspiration," if I may be more specific, is that when your guides or Creator or anyone is attempting to reach you spiritually, because of how busy your life is or whatever distractions there may be in your life, they may have some difficulty inspiring you in such a way as you can understand—meaning not everyone understands that some inspiration comes through as motion (but I'm using that as an example) and also some inspiration comes through so that you will catch a word, in that sense.

Usually, in those cases, you're not sure if you're remembering something or thinking something or are in fact inspired. It doesn't really make any difference. The whole point is to influence your awareness in such a way as to potentially move you toward something that is benevolent and useful for yourself and others. So if you wish to heighten your inspiration, this is one thing you could do to assist yourself in that way.

How does it work? How does looking at and breathing in the energy heighten the inspiration?

It's not mental, so it won't help to analyze it on a mental level. But to give you a mental model that would help, it works like this: Your spirit or soul, as you understand it, is an actual physical thing. As a physical thing, it is not a portion of you that is fed by the physical food you consume. Rather, it is fed by light sources that are clear and unattached to any form of outcome of what human beings may do but are in the longer sense, meaning over time and millennia, attached to the ongoing survival and capacity to thrive of any civilization: what they might do, what they might accomplish, and how by the very fact of their existence they improve lives and life for themselves and other beings.

Souls in that sense, then, require nourishment, and on Earth, because of the necessary factor of ignorance of one's ongoing soul expressions (having to forget who you are), then one is not constantly aware in one's personality of who you are, where you've been, what you've done, and your connection to all life. Therefore the soul must be fed by something physical that requires no thought whatsoever and regardless of one's beliefs that the soul will continue to be fed. This is done through the Sun and the Moon.

Does anything else feed the soul?

Love, of course. But I'm referring . . .

. . . to the outside surface, yes.

Your question and its phrasing—you said, "How does it work?" I'm stressing that word, because to me that was the operable word in your question. That's how it works. It works through different factors of light, and love is a form of light—and for that matter, vice versa.

What about starlight? Does that also work, or is it too far away?

No, it works, but I'm expressing through the Sun and the Moon because they are the primary influences of lightforms that are not, in their own right, dependent on anything done on Earth. They are there no matter what happens on Earth. Starlight also, but even in the cumulative sense, starlight is not as influential as your Sun and the Moon.

What about live fire? There's such a satisfaction about being in front of a campfire or a fire in the fireplace.

No. I realize there is satisfaction in that, but that is not the same thing as having your soul fed. This is something that is more physical for your physical body, aside from being warm when you need to be. Your physical body is more inclined to be fed by a blue light, or orange or red or something like that, you see. Those colors might feed, but in the case of your soul, your soul is more inclined to be fed by white light—and you understand, "white" in this sense is not pure white. It is white with the influences of other colors, as one might shine a white light through a prism and discover that it is made up of all colors known in your framework.

Life on the Home Planet

Have you been an inhabitant of ivy? Have you incarnated as ivy on this planet?

I have, and this is part of the reason I have a personal recollection of the symbolic effect of our presence on human beings. In the past, in terms of your time measurement, I was a welcome guest on someone's home. I realize there are criticisms of the effect of ivy on people's homes now, but in the past it was recognized not only to be a source of beauty but also, before the times of modern insulation, as an acceptable form of insulation. Therefore I experienced the pleasantness of being appreciated for beauty's sake and also for practical reasons.

And now your function is what?

Spiritual—interacting in these kinds of occasions where those who need to be inspired are inspired in one way or another.

Have you incarnated at home since you have been here or not?

Yes, I have.

You have! How long do you live there in our terms?

Forever! There is no impediment to life on the home planet. That is why one might have a stalk, as we would say, or a trunk, as you would say, that could easily be forty or fifty feet across—not around, across.

Oh, the diameter. So what is life like there? Are there other beings on your planet?

Not that many. There are some visitors. We welcome visitors, if they are benevolent, and of course they are. They wouldn't be able to find us. There are a few other life forms, mostly ones who move gently across the surface somewhat slowly, but there are no human beings as you would recognize. Still, the other life form, the predominant life form besides us, is in that way associated with something that is typical to your human culture now, and that is, those of that form—from what I've been able to gather, you understand, as an outsider, compared to a member of their own population—are thinkers.

They tend to be moving along and then stop. One sees this with human beings on your planet and also with other life forms on your planet, not just because there is some sense of danger, but very often human beings and other life forms will stop because they are thinking about something. This seems to be a factor of the existence of this other life form on our planet. They'll stop and appear to be in thought about something. So my way of relating to them is through the philosophical. We communicate sometimes. They are very intelligent.

What do these beings look like?

Well, they are very close to the earth. I suppose if you saw them you would probably think of them as caterpillars. They are not exactly like the caterpillars you have on your planet. I think when you see your caterpillars when you are a child and they are on a plant, you most often are fascinated in wonderment by them because of all their legs, and as long as they do not feel threatened, they tend to move very slowly, and this is their actual nature. On your planet, I have noticed that they are also thinkers and philosophical. Unfortunately, in recent years of human population, they have had to be wary of human beings, so they tend to speed off. They do have that capability, but if they do not feel threatened and the human beings around them admire them or appreciate their beauty, then there's a tendency to linger. It might be possible to, not make pets of them—no one likes to be captured—but to be friends.

Do you get your nourishment from the air or from the roots on your home planet?

From the roots, from the atmosphere, yes.

Do you have water? Oh yes, of course, you have a rain forest.

Yes.

So how do you communicate with all of . . . do you cover the whole planet?

No, just the continent we occupy.

What is the nature of your interaction with others? Do you commune?

If there is a query of some sort, yes. Other than that, we simply exist in our own world. We have our sense of social interaction, not unlike trees in a forest do on your planet. It is typical for trees in a forest to be very social with other trees, and if they trust you completely, you might see the motion of one tree touching another on your planet. Certainly that's on Earth.

You Need to Interact with and
Learn from the Other Life Forms on Earth

So how did you feel about the incredible variety here after such a limited number of species on your home planet?

I was very impressed with the multiple influences of other planets. Whoever, aside from Creator's approval, actually induced all of these different planets to provide for or to participate in the life-form populations on Earth . . . well, it was certainly quite a conference table. There must have been many of them, and I'm not using that literally, actually. I'm sure there wasn't a big meeting like that, but I was amazed at how many life forms I could recognize from their emissions of life force, what you might call breathing, that were from a multitude of other planets and galaxies.

This planet, from what I could remember as a participant, is unique in that sense. One does not normally see planets with so many representatives of other cultures, unless there is a culture established to be a form like the so-called United Nations. I believe that this is actually a theme on your planet, and that is why one does find things, not only in your culture like the United Nations, but a general embracing of other cultures. Regardless of how broad-minded or even occasionally narrow-minded a culture might be, there is a general embracing of influences from other cultures: food, perhaps garments, and so on.

One finds this pretty much universally amongst human beings on your planet; you wouldn't necessarily find that on other planets. So this seems to be an intended theme that Creator has for this planet. Human beings also are very social and if not influenced to the contrary will tend to be just as social with all kinds of human beings and very often with other forms of beings, as long as they are encouraged. So this is not surprising, given the nature of your planet, but it is not found everywhere on other planets.

We have the Explorer Race theme, the reason we're here, right?

Generally, without great detail, yes.

So what was your physical sense of going from a forty-foot tree to the delicacy of the ivy?

Well, at first it was quite foreign, you understand, the idea of being so small for one thing. But then there was the aspect of travel. You see, travel in my native form on the home planet is very slow. While it might be ongoing, it is very slow. But compared to the way a vine functions on Earth, one positively whizzes along. You might very well cover what for us would be a lot of ground in a short amount of time. So I think that this was what I found the most amusing.

You don't plan to come back though?

Well, I don't need to. Looking at my life theme, I do feel that it was a valuable experience. It's also probably why I, as an individual, am able to communicate like this so that I am not speaking to you from a foreign point of view—meaning that I would have no sense of relationship to understand who you are and what you are doing in correlation to other influences on your planet that are intended. You see, correlation is so important, and for you in your now societies, there is a tendency to examine things microscopically more than in correlation to other life forms and other functions that the planet itself might have with what it might consider its larger community, meaning other planets, moons, suns, and so on.

So apparently the social interaction aspect has not—for your human cultures predominant now (meaning the ones most influential at this time) received the same enthusiasm from the educational and scientific community as the examiners: "How does the teeniest aspect function chemically?" as compared to "Why are those teeny aspects so friendly with each other?" I think more study on the latter in a benevolent way without trying to take things apart in order to understand them would pay off very well to your understanding of your role in the overall scheme of things—not just on a philosophical basis, which would be very helpful indeed, but also as a way to understand how you might participate in the overall basis in a way that serves you as a race of beings (meaning the human race), as compared to forcing you to fight for survival in spite of the overall scheme of life. There's entirely too much of that, and you're missing out on vast opportunities that other forms of life could offer you.

Think of these forms of life: How many of them have had to go through struggles to survive and thrive very often under conditions that, when you look at them, you might say, "Well, how do they live?" For instance, take ivy moving across a cement wall and grabbing it and hanging on to it—you might say, "How does it survive?" And that's part of the fascination. I'm not trying to tell you how to live here, but you are still surrounded to this day with other life forms who have gone through survival episodes and are able to thrive, very often under difficult circumstances. I would say, given the circumstances of your own civilizations these days, any form of communication and communion you can develop with these life forms could only help. Perhaps that is your intention of creating these books about animals and plants and so on.

Yes. Now, you said something interesting—"the theme of your life." Say more about the theme of your life!

Well, everyone has a theme. A theme might be something overall that you're particularly focusing on. My theme is to understand the interrelatedness of all life, and if you were to examine afterward what I've said with the intonation of voice, just as much as the words themselves, you would easily sense that I am expressing my theme. You know, part of the problem with the printed word is that the intonation is largely lost, even when one attempts to express through forms of typography.

One might tend to express some of the accentuations of speech, but really one loses so much not having that verbal sound. I know it is your intention someday to provide that, but I'm mentioning it because in your communications with each other, as you have noted, for most of you, by the time you are even young children, writing a letter is not the same as compared to speaking in person with someone. For that matter, you can read all the material that is available on dogs and read, "Aarf, aarf," but it's not the same as having a friendly pet dog, is it? It's quite a bit different! Do you have a dog?

No, I had cats.

I think you'll probably have a dog someday.

Thank you. In the moment, I'm between pets.

454 ঙ PLANT SOULS SPEAK

It is good to have another form of life you are affectionately interacting with who is not your own form, whether it be a pet, as you say, or a wild form who just happens to come into your yard, as people might attract birds, and so on. This is good, because one is reminded physically of another form of life's expressions on a physical basis, on a feeling basis, and even a certain amount of demonstrable philosophy of their lives. I think it's good for all human beings to have that around.

That's why sometimes when human beings do not have pets, as you say, they might blossom, so to speak, from exposure to other forms of life. Very often, these other forms of life will actually seek you out because they will have pity on a human being who does not have that contact. So don't assume, human beings, that when other forms of life seek you out, they want something from you. *Very* often it is their way of being kind to offer something to you. They know why they are on Earth—they are on Earth in some way to be influential in the most benevolent way for human beings. So don't be too resistant if one or more come calling. They might just be visiting.

So did your theme of interaction lead you to the experience of the ivy trees on your home planet? I mean, you chose it because of that, right?

No, I am referring to my theme associated with the form of life that I am now. I'm not talking about a soul being who may go from one species to another.

But you remember being many other life forms?

No, I do not. However, I am familiar with being a soul. That's necessary to remember and typical to remember, because we are all that.

All right. I never know who remembers other existences and who doesn't.

That's why you ask questions, eh?

[Laughs.] Yes. You are very wise.

Thank you.

You Will Remember Your Kinship with All Life

I want to make a suggestion, a little more homework, and then I'm going to say good night. I'd like you to consider as adults—who are the bulk of the readers of this at this time—how many life forms still exist on this planet. If you possibly can, allow them to exist without having to cut, form, and shape them. Remember that the expressions of a life form—the plant or animal—are intended. Those expressions, meaning how one looks, are intended by Creator. We may look a certain way as described in my example on our home planet, but the way we look on Earth is because this is the way Creator encourages us to look. So I would like to suggest that you don't try to change our appearance too much. We look this way because that is the way Creator desires us to look. Please learn to accept that, and it might actually help to appreciate and understand your own cycle of life.

For example, a tree starts out life and is full of life, growing in all kinds of directions—not unlike human children growing in more than one direction and trying to explore something. And as one matures, one develops a stronger trunk and fewer directions necessarily. Some saplings growing in some ways decide perhaps that's not the best way to go, and those dry up and eventually fall off the tree. In older age the trunk is strong, but sometimes large limbs, portions, fall off, meaning fall away from the tree, just as in your own lives you might have portions of your life move off and become a portion of something else. Recognize that Creator has us in these appearances, not only because Creator feels that we as plants might be able to compatibly function in these appearances, but these appearances also are intended by Creator to demonstrate to you something about your lives.

If you allow us to be in our natural state, you and others . . . remember always that not all human beings understand the same things at the same time. You may understand it, but perhaps other humans won't, that you and others are intended to learn from the way we demonstrate our lives—speaking here as "we," meaning all other life forms besides human beings. On that note, if you can observe this I believe you will take the first steps, or perhaps simply other steps, along your wisdom path. I feel from the basis of my observation of your life here that you are not as backward as some of you feel about human beings, even as a human being, but you are moving along a difficult path. On other planets, most life forms know who they are, who they've been, what they've done, and so on. So there's an awareness of how to solve problems, at least in the way they've always solved them. But on your planet, you do not have those recollections, and this is intended by Creator at this time, so that you can re-create and invent things that may need to be solved, if not by your own people, then perhaps by peoples elsewhere.

This influence of you is intended to ultimately result in a benevolent influence of others to help others on your planet or on other planets grow in some way that will serve the communities intended by this work you are doing, but also to, on an overall basis, serve all life forms in some benevolent way. I know that it is not obvious all the time and has led to many struggles and difficulties and sufferings among your peoples, but this will

soon pass as you are now beginning to wake up, and remember who you are. As this theme continues for you—and it will—you will begin to remember how you got to Earth, your personal relationship with Creator, who the other people are whom you know (and very often who and how you've known them before in other life forms on other planets), and your kinship with all life. Many of the young children being born today will live through that experience and will certainly have something to tell their grandchildren. Good night!

Oh, thank you very much. That was beautiful! Thank you.

CHAPTER THIRTY-ONE

Orchid

JUNE 29, 2009

ॐ

ORCHID.

Orchid. Welcome. You are so beautiful. How did you happen to come to planet Earth?

We were requested to come in order to bring what we were told equates to your word "enticement," but it could also be "attraction." It depends, for those two words are different but are perhaps first cousins. We've been here for a while, and we were guided that the human beings who would arrive would need to have a considerable amount of beauty that was separate from themselves. This was so they would feel attracted to staying on the planet, because through various cycles of civilization, the planet would be so hard and difficult to stay on at times that people would need something outside of themselves in order to feel that this planet did welcome beauty. It would also be important for assisting human beings to be able to see the beauty in themselves.

Human Beings Emulate Earth's Urgency

The different colors of orchid—and other flowers, I might add—tend to support and encourage those who wear bright colors for their beauty. After all, it's not unusual to see oranges and reds and other bright colors and subtle shades and so on mixed in various flowers—if not one, then on another, and all grouped together. The human being needs to be reminded that it's not only about being invisible so that one is not harmed from some external force or individual. It's also very often about being seen so one can start to maintain one's own identity and personality.

This is the general presentation of our being on Earth. We do not feel in any way that we would have chosen to come here on our own. We would have chosen, perhaps, to come to a planet that was a little less violent. When you consider the violence that exists on Mother Earth—the big wave at sea or the fire from the ground or the big winds in all of their forms—Mother Earth could be said to have a violent streak. Though one might also, given this type of physical realm, describe this as urgency. This means instead of land slowly emerging from under the waters—as might be found over time with various earth motions, such as with earthquakes; land does emerge that way—that land could also be created, bringing up the makings of the land in the form of stone-as-liquid, by volcanism.

One might say that Mother Earth supports rushing and urgency. The same thing might be said about energies that need to be cleaned or dispersed in some form so as not to be concentrated in one place. Hurricanes or typhoons, as they're called, or perhaps cyclones, tornadoes, tend to do that as well. There are other aspects of Mother Earth's personality that could be equated in similar fashion. One might say that Mother Earth does support urgency, and therefore the human being must emulate her. Nobody likes to be rushed. It can be fun in certain select circumstances, but for the most part it's not much fun to be rushed. Yet human beings are inexorably drawn toward circumstances whereby they have to rush from one place to another, thus emulating Mother Earth's personality, which you cannot avoid since your bodies are made up of Mother Earth.

Orchids Came to Earth to Support the
Human Choice to Live in Compatibility

Mother Earth has many good qualities. She is not referred to as "Mother Earth" for nothing. She supports life. She makes it possible to live. She provides that which can feed and shelter and so on. We have observed in our own way over the years that human beings need to be encouraged to express their personalities, and that is why we grow in unusual shapes. You've seen flowers expressing unusual shapes as well as colors and color combinations, because we have been encouraged that this is a way to demonstrate that such personality traits are acceptable in the human being. We have also been advised to grow in climates where we are most comfortable. On our home planet, we grow in moist, tropical areas—this is what we like. We can, of course, be grown in places where those conditions are artificially stimulated, but we don't like it much, and we don't do as well as we do in the wild.

This also supports the human personality because different human beings—souls, you say—choose to be born, raised, or even to move to areas where one might find greater compatibility with the heart, soul, and personality. We believe we have to support that as well. This is why I feel we were invited to come here, and it is also a reason for staying. We cannot say as a general rule that we would prefer to stay here, as I indicated before. But as long as the human being (which is a special project here on Earth, I understand) is here during this time of—how can we say?—change for the human species, then we support that.

Other human beings from other planets who were born and raised there are nervous about what that change means. Just like you and your readers want to know, "What's going to happen? What's going to be the result? What's the outcome? What can we expect? How can we prepare?" etcetera, these other human beings from other planets feel exactly the same way. They know that you—the Explorer Race human being, eh?—are doing something that will unalterably change the human being, and they are nervous about it. They're getting along just fine on their planets. They have peaceful societies, loving societies, no crime, no harm, and no discomfort. They—perhaps quite rightly—want to know why they should change when they have reached a level that they consider to be as close to perfection as possible, given the nature of who they are in their lives and their cultures. They sometimes come and, at a distance, observe, "What does it all mean?" Well, you can understand that. We were invited to come, and we are doing what I believe we were meant to do.

Life Everywhere Else Does Not
Work the Same as It Does for Earth Humans

What is your status? Are you like an orchid spirit or an elder?

I am an overall voice that speaks for orchids at this time, sort of a combined personality.

Do you have teachers who come and talk to you, or are you connected directly to the home planet? How does that work?

It doesn't work anything like the human being or your afterlife or your deep-sleep state. Most life everyplace else does not work the way it works for the human being here on Earth. I know many personalities of different beings over the years have said, "Oh yes, it's just like that for us." But sometimes I have thought—when I can look at these things, eh?—that they were just being nice. [Chuckles.] Perhaps it's not true, but it has seemed that way to me when I have looked over these things. We do not have teachers. We do not have an afterlife. We do not believe in reincarnation. There is life. It is a long and drawn-out stream that has no beginning and no ending, and pondering beginnings and endings is only expressed by those who cannot remember, temporarily, that beginnings and endings are only illusion.

So you have always been what you are now?

I have always been, period—just as you have always been, and all the readers and all the listeners have always been.

Yes, but I mean, have you always been doing what you are doing now?

No, I am just doing it for this one occasion.

Have you always been part of the orchid personality?

Oh yes, I see what you mean. Yes, I've been embodied, you might say, in many different orchids. More, perhaps, in our home environment, which is more than one planet. But I've embodied several times on Earth. I could see, sense, feel, and experience—to the degree that we can when something is within our sensory boundaries—what that life form is like, why it exists, what purpose there is behind it, and what ultimate goal is being striven for.

What are your sensory boundaries?

It depends. In a safe situation, up to a mile. In a situation that is not so safe, maybe five or six feet, because we know other beings also have sensory boundaries. If it is not so safe, we do not want to accentuate our presence. But if it is safe, then we extend a bit farther. The human being can do this too, but you have not remembered completely. Perhaps your work and the work of this channel and others will contribute to that recollection.

The Eighteenth Civilization on Earth

Tell me about your home planets—are they several planets in the same star system?

We do not consider any one planet our home planet. We exist in many places in different star systems—you'd say different galaxies, different solar systems. We have three places that we might consider to be more "homey" than others. One is dry, not quite desert. There is some moisture. There is another that is very dry, where moisture is almost unknown. There we exist more like pods, something on the ground that grows more underground than above ground. Also in another location, which is a place that is very warm, very moist—it is my favorite location.

Why would you subsist in places that are dry when you like to be moist?

Because when we were told that we would come here—we had considerable warning, you see—we decided to expand our experience in benevolent places so that we could see how we would survive, how we could exist in smaller ways, in ways that were not as perceptible as how we would live on Earth. There was a time when it looked like you, the human race, would not achieve what you were striving for if you were on a planet like Earth. There was another situation where a different planet that was more desert-like—one with what you would call a high and low desert type of environment—looked like it would be the place. But since that did not happen, that is how we came to be in such different places. On your planet, while you have such places as high and low deserts, you also have tropical zones. We prefer that. High and low deserts, you see, will get cold, but tropical zones don't do that. It isn't about the dry or the wet; it's about the temperature.

So you prepared for the planet that was in this orbit originally, the planet that contained Atlantis, the one that broke up into pieces when Atlantis had its accident.

Yes.

We are supposedly the eighteenth civilization on this planet. Did you come before the Explorer Race people or after we came? When did you come to this planet?

Before the Explorer Race people. But there were human beings here already, what you would recognize as human beings, but they were not a portion of your project. I think most of them have left now in terms of their cultures. I'm not talking about their life endurances, long lives and so on, but in terms of their cultures, they have migrated. No, you would say "emigrated"; they have emigrated.

Ah, so you came in with one of the earlier civilizations.

We came, yes. In those days, we were able to live in the high deserts as well as the tropical zones, because it didn't get quite as cold there as it does now in terms of your planet.

Earth's Climate Is Changing to Accommodate Extreme Personalities Who Also Wish to Come to Here

So the climate has changed over the years, then?

Yes. Mother Earth shares, with me and others, that it has been necessary to allow for more extremes. There's an interesting reason for that. Would you like to know it? The reason is that more and more personalities of the human being wish to come who might qualify or described as extreme personalities, as—how can we say?—dazzlingly different. From the artist to the predator, such extreme personalities require a planet that is more extreme, because remember, your bodies are made up of Mother Earth. This means not only must you emulate to a degree her personality but it also means that she is your host. If your souls desire to express something, or are simply open to expressing something that may be needed, although not always appreciated, understood, or welcomed, then they would have the feeling of being at least reasonably welcome, because the host, Mother Earth, does have that expression herself.

You have a great understanding of this planet.

Only because I am now expressing the overall personality of all my species. They are in many places and have much personal experience themselves. So I am able to pull on all that. Any overall voice to express any entire being could do similar. I am saying it is my function, not my nature.

Okay, all right. Are all orchids one being?

You are extrapolating, but it is not true. I am that voice that unites all such beings. It would be as if a human being were able to tap into all the knowledge, wisdom, and experience of all human beings and then speak for a time. He or she would be the spokesperson, yes? But you as another human being some-place else would not be united with that person as an overall experience—other than in the larger sense, of course.

Commune with Orchid to Become More Assertive

Were you invited to come to this universe—not just this planet, but this universe—by the Creator?

I'm sure all forms of life were invited to do that or were simply created.

But that's not part of your history or your memory?

We do not really have a history. I know that's hard for you to understand, but history is a pursuit of those who do not know who they are. If you travel out—your culture, your peoples of Earth—to other planets and want to know the history of other peoples, those who are patient and indulgent with you will give you a history. But those who have no patience for such things will simply say, "There is no history." What that really means is that they know who they are, and history is unimportant.

Some of the plants have told us that it's important to come into their aura for healing purposes. Is there any of that type of energy in the emanation of orchids?

As you can tell with orchids—and you can tell by my personality—we can be a bit tough minded. I would recommend those who need to become more assertive for any reason—not necessarily those going into the army or becoming policemen or gang members, but simply those who feel a little overwhelmed by life and would like to be more assertive so as to feel more confident—come and sit with orchids. Don't sit on them eh? Just sit near them, look at them, and breathe in and out. Do that if you can for five or ten minutes up to an hour for three days in a row. You'll probably feel a lot more assertive the first day. By the time the second or third day comes, you might be a bit obnoxious. So the moment you start giving others the impression of your being obnoxious or become aware of it yourself, stop; you've had enough.

[Chuckles.] I love it. Okay. Will you be here as long as we're here, or will you be here after we're gone when it's nice and peaceful?

Who says it's going to be nice and peaceful? I don't really know. As far as I know, we are here for you. I really couldn't say. I'll tell you what, when you are gone, ask me then. I'm simply saying I do not know this.

[Chuckles.] Yes, of course, I'm sorry.

There's no reason to be sorry—a perfectly reasonable question.

Fairy-like Beings Exist in the Natural World

As your beings extend out, do you interact with other plants and with what we call animals? Do you tell stories or do you feel their feelings?

We do not tell stories. I know there are some nonhuman beings who do that. We exist in our own state of personality. At times I do hear stories being told, but these are possibly from the little ones, the little people.

Do you mean like insects or something?

No, they are like spirits, but they can be seen sometimes.

Oh, like elves or fairies.

Yes, I think you call them fairies. There are other beings like that who are of the natural world who still exist in places.

Devas?

I wouldn't use that classification word. I have experienced them quite a bit. They like to tell stories. They particularly do that with life forms—whatever form they take—that need to be encouraged. So that element of the story world exists. We do not do that. I have heard other forms of life doing that—many four-legged beings, and some of the many-legged beings you call spiders and beetles, and—let's see if I can get your word—worms. I have heard them sing something that I assume is a story. That's about all I can think of in terms of our overall experience at the moment.

What about birds?

They do not seem to tell stories. They are much more focused on surviving as well as possible, given their fairly vulnerable and precarious existence. They have to be very alert all the time. Perhaps this is not quite the same for those who are hawks and so on who prey on other birds and other small beings, but generally speaking, in the bird world, they have to be alert.

Human Beings Exhibit Extreme Behavior because They Don't Remember Who They Are

Now, on your home planet, the various places you live where it's benevolent, it must have been quite a shock to come here and see the chain of life.

But we didn't see that when we first came, you understand.

You didn't?

No.

The animals weren't here?

There were human beings here, but the Explorer Race hadn't gotten here, so things were still pretty nice. There was no shock. It came gradually over time, you see. No, when we got here, things were fine.

So the animals just lived peacefully and didn't chase each other?

Well, we expect a certain cycle of life to be going on, but even in the animal world there wasn't—not exclusively, but for the most part there wasn't—revenge or hatred. Now many of them are not entirely comfortable in their hearts and souls that they must consume other beings in order to live.

Yes, yes. They've said that.

Others are more accepting of that. Still, others are hunters—one might even say extreme personalities, given some of the things they do. When we came here, there weren't many extreme personalities. Although, for example, there was an ancient form of tiger with long teeth.

A sabertooth.

Yes. These beings did not have the same personality as one might find in the cat world today, in which sometimes the prey is tortured before being killed. That's a particularly ugly aspect of the cat world, and it's one they do not display all the time. But it is something that they have come to do. It is not in their absolute nature. It is something they have come to over time, an acquired trait from their exposure to the human being. In their natural state, they do not do that. When we came here, to get back to your question, there was not cruelty from one animal species to another. But many of them did have to consume each other, sometimes with slight regret; however, living in the moment does not allow for much regret or past-oriented feelings. So that's my answer. I pass no judgment on the human being, you understand. I recognize that as you exist on other planets, you know exactly who you are, where you're from, why you're there, how you've lived, and how you might expect to live in the future. While it may not be an excuse for your more extreme behaviors, the fact that you do not know these things on this planet is certainly an explanation.

Earth Humans Are Beginning to Consider Other Possibilities
Do you see that we're making progress?

Progress? It depends. I have the long view. If you mean progress to becoming something like the human beings who were present when our species first arrived? No, because you're not aiming to be that. The purpose for your being, as much as I can tell, is to go out and spread the word, so to speak—not about your religions and philosophies, but to essentially go out and be yourselves, hopefully not to the degree you are yourselves on this planet. But then most of those who migrate or emigrate to other planets or have the opportunity to meet other forms of life in a more diplomatic way, in the beginning at least, will be diplomats themselves. The only problem they'll have, of course, is that they will have thoughts and feelings they think the others they're meeting cannot perceive. But of course, they will perceive that completely. So it will also be necessary to be evolved spiritually, but this can be done. It's not as hard as it may seem.

We seem to be making progress toward benevolence. You don't see that as you look at us?

Progress suggests from point A to point something else. So I'm having difficulty with your phrasing, because I'm going back to the beginning. I'm thinking, well, the human beings we first met were like this. Then you came along, and I don't see progress toward you being anything like them, the ones we first met.

Okay. As the Explorer Race, we are in a process of awakening to who we are and becoming more benevolent. Do you see that in what we were a hundred years ago, a thousand years ago? Do you see progress in that now?

I see some progress compared to what you were a few hundred years ago. But it depends. Even a few hundred years ago, there were many groups of human beings living all over the planet who were quite benevolent. But you're more greedy by nature, if I might be blunt, such as you have noted in groups of humans or individuals who say, "I want this and you have it, so I'm going to take it." Since that whole thing spread around—and that has been going on for a while—then no, no progress at all has occurred among those groups. But as far as beginning to question or beginning to consider overall, yes. I see a trend, but I would not yet call it something that is particularly measurable in terms of, "Okay we're all this now." I don't see that yet. You're still who you are, but you are beginning to question and consider other possibilities. I see that.

Well, that's a step.

You understand, I am not speaking about individuals here. I am speaking about Earth's total human population taken as one being. Certainly, individuals are quite spiritual, you might say. But as a total being, you have a ways to go. It might take various events to remind people, but that is not my job.

I wish we could get you in politics. [Laughs.]

Well, I would not choose to do that, but I understand you are trying to be complimentary.

I'm trying. [Chuckles.] Yes, you're very clear, and it's refreshing to talk to someone who isn't trying to be a diplomat.

Well, it is not one of our strong traits.

[Chuckles.] Well, good.

Mutually Shared Experiences Bring
Humans Closer Together as a Total Being

What haven't we covered? You've been marvelously informative.

You don't have to cover everything. The whole purpose of the book is to say, "Here's how you can live a little better if you want to." That's essentially it, and it's told from various points of view, of a sharing of what can be done using healthful methods. Near as I can tell, that's the point of the book. The book isn't about everything. It's about sharing and maybe just schmoozing, as you like to say.

[Chuckles.] Well, I'd just like to know as much about you as possible.

We will have to come to an end pretty soon anyway. Why don't I just make a closing statement? You as individual human beings are not expected to achieve some kind of fantastic spiritual growth to become the entirety of your total true natures while you are on Earth. But you will—every one of you, no matter how young or old you are, no matter how close to birth or death you are— be expressing at least one of your profound spiritual traits from this point forward in your life. You will do so not because I have deemed it to be so but rather because that is the trend. My understanding of Creator is that Creator is sometimes a bit impatient and says, "Okay, hurry up now; catch up." My impression is that Creator will not wait around indefinitely for you to become your true natures. That is why you can expect from time to time some kind of an event that will help you all to feel a mutually shared experience that brings you closer together as a total being, the human race on Earth. It does not have to be cataclysmic. Do not expect that. It might be something spectacular, something wonderful. Consider that as a possibility as well. Good night and good life.

Good life and thank you very, very much.

CHAPTER THIRTY-TWO

Daffodil

JULY 3, 2009

℘

DAFFODIL. GREETINGS.

Well, welcome. Tell me about yourself.

I will. We were requested specifically to come to this planet. As an individual, I cannot say when that took place, but I do remember a time when human beings were not so frequent. I do not know exactly what that means, if it means we may have begun in some remote location as a species or what. But I believe the reason we were requested, in our soul nature, to come to this planet is because of our effect on the human heart. We have a wide range within which we are effective, but always we affect the heart of all beings. I think we were requested to come probably at a stage when human beings had the greatest opportunity to achieve the transition that you are all working on now—some of you more consciously than others. I believe we are here now for these times—say, from the last hundred years or so forward—more than any other time. Perhaps that is the only reason; I'm not sure. I will say that the effect we have can be experienced now by human beings who have heart challenges. This can include challenges in any form. I'm not saying it would be an instant cure, but it ought to help, along with your other aids. This is what to do. It is particularly effective when there are more than twenty of us—fifty would be best, but twenty would be a good start. It won't help if there's one or two or even three; there needs to be a number. We always work better in numbers, meaning blooms—the flowers, not necessarily the individual plants.

Plants Feel Support When Humans Play Music

This is what to do, and I'll give you a couple of different circumstances since you have more technology available in your time. If you don't have any technology available—or it's inconvenient or it can't be used for some reason; perhaps it might be raining lightly—then simply go out and stand. Or if it's possible, it might be better to sit, especially in the case of a heart condition. Face the flowers, but do not get so close that you could reach out and touch them, even when leaning forward—so maybe five feet away. Start breathing in and out in 4/4 time. This is a musical term, and it can be very easily understood by those who aren't musically inclined. See if you can either breathe to 4/4 time, or if that's uncomfortable—which it may very well be, because it might be like panting, okay—then what you do is take your hand or your foot, either hand or either foot but not both, just one hand or one foot so it's not too distracting—and you learn how to tap that foot according to 4/4 time, or tap the hand that way. It might take awhile to get good at it so that you can do other things and still tap at 4/4 time.

Get good enough at it so that you can do other things, meaning breathe while tapping your foot or your hand at 4/4 time. It doesn't make any difference how you tap your foot. It can be on the ground, it can be on the concrete or stone, or you can tap your hand on your leg or on the chair arm. It doesn't make any difference; whatever's the most comfortable. Then just breathe normally while you're looking at the plants. Try not to think. It will probably not be so challenging because of the tapping that you are doing. If you lose the 4/4 time, then close your eyes for a moment. This is why it's important to tap and have it memorized as a physical action, not just as a concept or thought. Close your eyes for a moment and relax. Don't get upset. If you do, wait until you calm down, and then start tapping your foot again, or your hand. If you tap your hand, you want to make sure it's your open palm, and then just resume that rhythm.

When you have this down, open your eyes and start breathing again normally. You can do this for up to thirty minutes—twenty-five minutes might be better. But if you've had to stop and start a few times, which is likely for almost everyone other than perhaps someone who's a musician, then twenty-five minutes

A time signature is a notational convention used in Western musical notation to specify how many beats are in a measure. Usually called common time, 4/4 is widely used in most forms of Western popular music; it is the most common time signature in rock, blues, country, funk, and pop. For all meters, the first beat (the downbeat) is usually stressed, though not always; in time signatures with four groups in the bar (such as 4/4), the third beat is often also stressed, though to a lesser degree. This gives a regular pattern of stressed and unstressed beats, although notes on the "stressed" beats are not necessarily louder or more important. Simple time signatures consist of two numerals, one stacked above the other. The lower numeral indicates the note value, which represents one beat (the "beat unit"). The upper numeral indicates how many such beats there are in a bar. In 4/4 time, then, you have four quarter-note beats. To conduct in 4/4 time, you would draw the following pattern in the air:

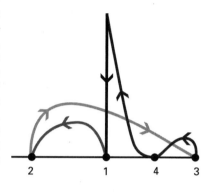

2   1   4   3

would be better. However, if you feel that you've done enough for any given time, you can stop before you get to the twenty-five-minute mark. You can also build up if you like. This does not have to do with the 4/4 time and it does not have to do with the heartbeat so much, but in some cases, it will definitely feel like a syncopation in that sense—how can I say?—almost like how an orchestra leader would tune up an orchestra. This is not just about the heartbeat; it's about the heart function, the valves opening and closing, the flow of the blood, and so on. Because of our nature of supporting the hearts of all beings, because of this propensity or tendency—you might call it our likes and dislikes—we like music, particularly music that's soft and supportive. I don't know if you've asked other plants about that, but it's a good thing to ask. It doesn't matter what the words are. It could be a sad song, or it could be a happy song. It can be a song that just observes, or even a chant. But if it's soft, nurturing, and supportive, we like that the best.

Because of these qualities, we are supportive and we feel supported in that way. Of course, as a plant on Earth, we are supported in the usual way: with sunshine, moisture, and so on. But this is something I felt was important to bring up to you because so many people in your time—aside from born-to-it ailments—have developed ailments because of their lifestyles or what they're exposed to, not the least of which is the fact that there's not as much oxygen as you need on the planet. That's something that's been a factor for the human being on your planet now for quite a few years, and I feel there's something that can be done about it that's really simple. However, it would require a lot of dedication, because you would need to support the growth of trees. Of course, human beings need to live places, and that's a little problematic. But I think that trees are something human beings like and they are perhaps one of the most valuable Earth resources. If you are indoors a lot, you can get certain indoor plants, can't you? They will perform similar functions. It is a grand plan, isn't it? You need oxygen and you breathe out the gases that the plants need. It is quite obvious that the hand of Creator is behind that, not some branch of educational interest, such as science. Science is good to help you understand, but it is not a Creator, is it?

Human Beings Would Often Be Sick without the Natural Broadcast of Energy from Other Beings

There's a reason I'm starting off with this, because I feel it is the most important thing for you to understand. All forms of life other than the human being on this planet—with the exception of those deep underground or at the very bottom of the sea, for example—are here, really, to support the human being. That doesn't necessarily mean to be eaten. It means their existence creates an energy—or the needs they have that are supported by what is available on this planet, the combination of that and themselves—that supports an energy they naturally broadcast simply by being, moving around, and so on, that directly supports the human being. That is an absolute. Did you know that? I think that by my stating this in that form, you can tell it's important, and people will understand that other forms of life actually do support you, even ones you don't like or that seem pesky or even dangerous. You give them their distance, but that's all that's needed.

Exactly how do we take that energy in? Breathing it or through our skin or it goes in our feet or what?

It just is. It's in the air. If you were to stand next to a friend—you have a friend there, a small friend who just hopped up in your lap—we will say a cat for the sake of the reader—that being would be radiating that energy. Conversely, of course, you are also radiating an energy. It is like a field effect, not unlike magnetism, only on a much smaller scale in terms of its moment, scientifically speaking. In that sense, it is your auric field, your energy body, all right? This lingers in the air. You may not know this, but if human beings walk down the road—or for that matter, if a giraffe walks down the road—they are always radiating from their energy fields. This is really the main reason you need to eat, because your energy field has to be supported for you to stay in your body. What you eat is not only supporting your physical body but also the connection between your physical body and your lightbody. Your lightbody requires that support. Your lightbody lives on light, and it also must produce light to allow light to exist on the wavelength of all available matter.

Say beings walk down a street, down a road, or on a trail. The energy they radiate from their lightbodies lingers in that area for up to thirty minutes. It doesn't dissipate or transform; it just migrates. It will move here or there according to where it's called or needed. Perhaps it will be needed by a plant, perhaps by an animal, perhaps by a human. This is so for all forms of life, even stone. Mother Earth is alive, so stone is not separate from her, yes? Still, it is interesting that many times human beings—since that's who we're talking to—come close to getting a disease. Many diseases are stimulated by feelings—if not your own, then perhaps from somebody else. Many times, though . . . let's put it this way: the average reasonably healthy human being—we're not saying in perfect health—would be ill, seriously ill, 95 percent of the time if it weren't for ongoing radiations from the lightbodies of all beings. You really live as long as you do and as well as you do on the planet because of those radiations.

When I opened up talking about the interaction between a human being with a heart condition, I should have also added that the heart condition might include, say, a lost love and feeling like you have a broken heart. Now, a human being requires a great amount of energy just to live, as I said. The lightbody must have light to live, and sunlight and moonlight are not sufficient. Of course, artificial light doesn't help. Many times human beings would have become sick without the available light broadcasted naturally by other beings. This could be from a spider, a tree, a weed, a snake, a lion—anything—and you just happen to be in the area or one has preceded the other. Perhaps the lion walked by. Perhaps it was a dog. Or perhaps the trees had been there radiating for sometime. You go for a walk in the forest and you feel better—the energy of the forest and its multiple life forms radiate because they just do and you radiate because you just do, and this helps you to be healthy. The creation of the lightbody is something from Creator.

People Should Walk in Natural Forests to Gain Better Health

Needless to say, when your physical body dies and returns to Earth, your lightbody goes on to other adventures. When your physical body returns to Earth, your lightbody is no longer held on Earth. It naturally goes home. But when your lightbody is connected to a physical form and is also a portion of and identified religiously as soul, then that lightbody stays here. You understand that. I wanted to bring up the fact about how all the different forms of life so very much contribute to your well-being. I wish to go on with that, because a great many of you now live in cities or spend most of your time indoors, and you do not have the chance to walk in forests.

Now, when I say forests, I'm really speaking about natural forests as compared to something human-made in which trees might have been planted for some reason. The difference between a natural forest and a human-made one, such as a garden with lots of trees, is that in a natural forest, seeds would have been welcomed, sprouted, nurtured, and supported by Mother Earth and all of the denizens of the forest, whereas when human beings plant the trees, they are usually thinking about something else. Perhaps they are even trying to imitate nature. The difference in going for a walk in a natural forest is that you will experience about ten times as much—it varies, eleven times, nine times—on average ten times as much beneficial balancing energy as compared to, say, a human-made forest, even if the human-made forest is attempting to imitate nature.

There are some minor exceptions. If the human-made forest is, say, fifty to sixty years old and it has been allowed to simply grow naturally and has not been trimmed, then through the reproducing cycle, seeding, and dropping leaves and needles and so on, all of this will—with the interaction of other natural creatures on the planet—begin to adapt to becoming more natural. I'm bringing this up because if a human being is unable to go out of a building very much, for example, or go for a walk in the forest, that's why you have heart conditions and so much disease. It's because you are not interacting with other forms of natural life and the natural exchange of light.

You Receive the Maximum Amount of a
Plant's Energy through Live Interaction

You mentioned that eating helps the lightbody be with the physical, with the energy body. Are there certain things to eat that facilitate that?

Yes, green leafy vegetables are helpful. It doesn't matter whether you put on a salad dressing or not. Let's see what else. Rutabagas might be helpful. Kiwi fruit might be helpful—and lemons, lemon juice in that sense, perhaps. I have a picture of something, but I don't know your word, so I will say its cousin. Broccoli might be helpful.

Oh, maybe kale or brussels sprouts or something?

Yes, brussels sprouts. That's it. There are forms of greens that are eaten. I think there are some forms of dandelion greens that can be eaten if they're carefully prepared. One has to be very careful, though, so ask around and see if that's something you could find that would be safe to eat. It might be a small amount. Let's see. Those are the main ones.

What is the common factor that's the catalyst or active ingredient?

I'm not going to say that, because that's science, and while I acknowledge that science has great value in your time, the belief held by science that synthesizing is just as good or is an acceptable substitute is incorrect—I'm not singling out any scientist, you understand. The natural form in its living state is best. You can talk to those plants if you haven't already, and they can tell you that a considerable amount of support from the living plant would be, in some cases, better than consuming the plant after it's been processed and touched and bashed around through technology, as that often happens in processing a plant. This is less typical, however, if you go out in your garden and pick the plant or something like that. A great deal can be done, and I feel that's, from my point of view, the best your book has to offer: interacting with the living plant. Because the living plant is, of course, radiating a lightbody, isn't it?

Ah, yes.

The plant that is no longer alive is not doing that. It's that simple.

Plants that Are Native to the Area
Will Have the Most Energy for Interaction

So the radiation of those particular plants affects the human by connecting the lightbody to the energy body?

You are mistaken. Simply by being, the radiation or broadcast energy of all life on Earth, including other humans, does that. Before I responded to your question literally, as I will always do. But what I just said, that's what helps to connect. You asked what could we eat to accentuate and so on. I responded to that, but that isn't the actual answer to the second question you asked, meaning your follow-up question or my correction of your follow-up statement.

So the more people we have on the planet—and the more animals and plants—the better we can connect to our lightbodies?

Sometimes. But it also requires, or would be helpful, to be around plants in their natural state. If you can't be around them for reasons of simple practicality—you're living in a big city or you're no longer able to get around as well and so on—then perhaps go someplace where plants are protected, such as a nature garden or a public park that has places where plants are supported and watched over. It's not the same if the park has people running through it and grabbing and touching plants and pulling leaves off the trees; that's not the same. It has to be a garden where plants are protected, watched over, as one might go to a famous garden of some sort or even a greenhouse. This kind of thing is found in cities.

One might also have plants in one's yard or in an apartment complex—that is not unusual. Granted, these might have been planted on their own. The ones that grow up on their own and are often picked away, sadly, are volunteers—or weeds, as they're called. These ones are more likely to support the human being. Plants that are not natural—meaning, say, grass that is planted or ornamental trees or bushes that are planted—are going to have to struggle more and need more light and other nutrients and so on just to exist, because they're probably not growing on land that welcomed them. As they're growing, they require considerable amounts of encouragement—watering, feeding, fertilizer, and all this business—to keep growing there because the ground did not actually welcome them. The ground was prepared to welcome so-called weeds, for example, or plants natural to the environment.

This is why it's very good when you are planting things to find out what the natural plants were for that area before the development came along and had to dig everything up to build the houses. If you know that, then you will know what kind of plants would be best to have there. Those plants will give you the most energy, because they will feel welcome, in which case, the best thing to do is not to turn the ground over unless it's very hard or clay-like. Then you can turn it over a little bit—but not too much; just go down an inch or two. You might see that there's an ant house or some other animal house. Give that a wide berth, because if they're there, they were welcomed by the land. You can turn the soil over a little bit other than in those places. What's best is to scatter the seeds about—hopefully the birds won't eat all the seeds—and let the plants grow. Once they get going, they'll take off and seed on their own. Those plants will be much more nurturing to the human being because they will feel welcome there.

After a few cycles of growth and then dying off—as might happen in seasons, for example, going through the winter and so on—the plants that survive, seed, bloom again, and so on, will eventually achieve a natural cycle. Your original planting, done by a human being with the best of intentions, within two or three cycles will have gradually achieved its own natural balance, in the case of so-called weeds or plants natural to a given area. If you've left areas where you can walk among the plants, try to do that with stone paths that are at least three feet wide so a person can walk down them easily. Then you'll be able to walk down those pathways and be among those plants. Try not to trim them if you can help it. If you need to shove them back from the path, perhaps a little wire fence or something might do. A wooden fence would be better. You can walk down that path and just breathe in and out quietly with those plants. You will find that the natural plant that is in existence now and has rejoined the existence that was once there, will have plenty of excess light and energy that you can breathe in and out with. They will be able to accommodate many human beings, and do a great deal more good than plants that are ornamental in nature. I'm including lawns and grass in that.

Daffodil Can Connect to Earth 100 Percent

Well. Who are you? Where'd you come from? You're very wise. How'd you get that way?

Can you ask . . .

One question at a time. Okay, tell me about yourself. You are one plant? You are speaking for all daffodils? You are an elder, or what? A spirit?

Can you ask one question?

Are you inhabiting a daffodil or are you a spirit?

I am both, as are you. But as you know, we are not here to learn anything. People get constantly confused about that because they are surrounded by adapting beings. The human being adapts, and your dogs and cats adapt as well. Human beings, however, assume that the adaptations that plants or nonhumans make are growth, but they aren't. They are simply adaptations. You as a human being adapt as well, but that's not growth. Growth has everything to do with how you change significantly over time on the basis of your interactions with other human beings and, to a lesser degree, with your environment. I am not a social scientist—well, maybe a little bit.

Now, who I am is an individual plant, and I have a spirit. Since, as I said, we are not here to learn anything and have no lessons but are just here to support, our spirits can connect entirely—to a lesser degree than as I might connect to other daffodils, for example. I'll put it in numbers—you like that, eh? I can connect 100 percent to other daffodils. I can connect 98 or 99 percent to other flowers. I can connect about 95 percent to other plants of all types. I can connect about 90 to 91 percent with other nonhuman life. I can also connect, I forgot to say, 100 percent with Mother Earth as a planet. As far as connecting with human beings, that is 80 to 85 percent, with the exception of human beings who talk to plants, and there are a few of those—sometimes quite a few. Gardeners will often do that, and then the conversation would be "strictly radiated," meaning I exist, so my energy is broadcasting. You exist, so your energy is broadcasting. That would be an example of the percentages of communication—sometimes called communion, but not in the religious sense.

Space Travel Takes Place through Pure Feelings of Love
Where is your home planet? Do you also connect with it?

We have a home planet in this galaxy. It is something you might possibly come across in your early years of space travel, allowing for the first thousand years or so. You'll know it when you come across it because it is multicolored at a distance. At first to the eye—seeing it with a telescope of sorts—it will seem to be a gas planet. But the multicoloring has to do with the different forms of life.

There are wide varieties of life there, what you will identify as mineral life. A lot of it is actually plant life, but it has a long cycle and is fairly rigid. You have something like that on this planet, what you call coral. There's some controversy among your scientists whether coral is a plant or an animal. This is because of the nature of its growth, how it grows and interacts with life around it and so on. I feel that this is a lively controversy that will continue for some time, even though there will, at times, be pauses to say, "No, it's definitely this," and everyone will say, "okay, okay." But the discussion will be taken up again. You might come across that planet, our planet. It's beyond your technological reach for the first fifty years or so of real space travel, meaning going to other planets as compared to going to your moon and setting up bases there. As you begin to interact with helpful beings from other planets, they'll gradually grow to trust you. You'll have to be very nice and be on your best behavior. All of the astronauts and cosmonauts will have to be diplomats as well as do their other duties. Then they will share with you, and you'll be able to go on journeys in their ships, eventually acquiring your own, and you will travel great distances.

When you're at the point where you can travel great distance, moving beyond light, moving, as you say, through time—but that's really not how it functions—and as you go to more and more places, you'll be able to identify this type of travel. It's almost like bilocation. It's hard to describe to you, because it's not like focusing on where and what. Initially, you will use quadrants, points in space, and you'll have a personal connection with where you are going. This will come about as a result of your diplomatic efforts in space. You'll have at least one diplomat or ambassador on every vehicle. The diplomat or ambassador will recollect the friends and enjoyment he or she had on a given planet and will focus on that. Then, through interaction with, essentially, a navigational propulsion system on the vehicle, which is actually one instrument, the ship will go most of the distance in less time than it would take you to take half a breath. Actually, you might say that space travel, in its efficient form, takes place entirely through pure feelings of love. Right now, science doesn't know what to do with that. But in time, as science gets more balanced with love—unconditional love, of course—it will not be so difficult. It will come when the time is right.

Newborn Babies Can Emanate the Same Energy as Daffodil

Our planet has existed there for a very long time—considerably longer than your solar system, to the degree I'm able to estimate its age. I can't estimate it in years. I can just be aware of when our planet existed, and it was before your solar system did. In feeling that, our planet—being our planet for a moment— can become aware of other planets. I can go back to the time when your solar system had not been born. Apparently our planet has been there far longer than your solar system. Now, aside from that, it does tell you that we've had awhile to establish our civilizations on the planet. The main thing that you would identify when visiting our planet—for example, if you were able to walk on the planet— is that after you adapt to your gear, you could have the air and other necessities you would need to function. You would be somewhat insulated. But if you were able just to walk on the planet, you would feel refreshed, relaxed, and completely rejuvenated inside of thirty seconds.

Of course, this will become something like a base where travelers might come and stay to refresh themselves, especially after a long journey or at a time in their lives when they desire such support. It is already this way in many places now on the planet, where there are certain outposts—small ones on the surface and many more below the surface in natural caves and openings on the planet. There are other planets like this, but I mention it because you can see that our form of life as we exist on Earth has everything to do with our planet, our home planet.

Your ability to generate this beautiful energy, this healing energy?

It's not exactly generating; it's more like our natures, our personalities— our souls, if you would. They need that energy. I might add that this is not something that is exclusive to us. But you have to be reminded, you know, that we are not on Earth to learn anything. We are on Earth to be. Generally speaking, human babies should be born without violence—and by violence, I mean that the babies are not slapped on the bottom to start their breathing. I know doctors aren't doing that to give baby a hard time, but it is better if they are born naturally, gently. There is another type of birth, water birth. That's not the only method, but it is a good one, because human beings are actually natural to water. That's why scientific belief has held that human beings may have emerged from the water, and this is not entirely untrue. Then, for the first two or three days, surround the baby only by love and let it be touched only by loving beings—those who love that being and feel love themselves, so that baby is in an environment that's loving, with no stress. Then those babies will radiate the same energy as we do.

That tells you that human beings have the capacity to be exactly what we are. Now, sometimes the very old, elderly people, will notice this. Maybe shortly after birth, baby is handed to mother and is with mother for a while. As mother recovers, maybe grandmother or great-grandmother—if she's fortunate to be available for great-grandchildren—might take the baby. She will not try to take energy from the baby, but she will notice—I am not criticizing, but simply noticing—that she feels refreshed holding baby. Maybe to a degree she emanates a certain amount of loving wisdom toward baby. There's an exchange. Baby has an opportunity to discover that wisdom. As the grandmother, if you do this, please focus on love, not worries or difficulties or pains that you might have at that time. Be totally focused on love, and this will be best for baby. It won't be easy for you, but do the best you can. Recognize that anything else that's present, babies will not necessarily absorb and take on, but they will be alerted to the fact that the planet they are on has many cycles of existence. Goodnight.

Thank you so much. Good life.

Goodbye.

CHAPTER THIRTY-THREE

White Rose

JULY 6, 2009

୫⃝

WHITE ROSE.
Welcome!

Greetings. Now, speaking as an individual plant connected to most, if not all, of the other plants, I will say a few things, and then Spirit of Rose will come through. Living in the day-to-day world as a plant, I have a few things to say. I believe from my interaction, such as it is, with other plants, I may cover other plants who have some similar aspects, specifically thorns. Now, as a species, what can I say? When Creator's emissaries come, you don't say no, eh? But as a species, we did not want to come to Earth. We did not want to stay on Earth, and we would like to go home as soon as possible. Please. Now, this has to do with why we have thorns.

Rose Came to Earth Knowing Humans Would Alter Its Face

We negotiated with Creator's emissaries and said, "We really don't want to go there." Creator's emissaries said, "We will compromise with you. We will allow you to go to Earth and will welcome you there, if you will go, because we would actually like you to have a form of defense. The human beings on Earth will need

485

to find a symbol in the plant world to justify some of their actions and behaviors, as well as their instincts. Generally speaking, when confronted with danger, the instinct of the human being is to draw back." Sometimes your social scientists say that means to run, but it isn't actually that. It's to draw back, dig in, and defend. "You are going to be the representative of that in the plant world, one that many people will see, even though there will be a great many other plants that have thorns—or even thistles, which are a less aggressive form of thorns.

"So what do you think?" the angels said, and there was a consensus among those on the planet—not me, of course, but the ancestors—and they said, "Yes, we will do this." The emissaries went on to say that as a plant, we would be dearly loved, and we found that hard to believe since we were going to have these little daggers all over our bodies. There was no scorn—one is not scornful of angels—but there was a distinct incredulity, not really disbelief but a sort of stunned silence, one might say. The angels went on to explain that we would have a beautiful face, so to speak, and that our beauty would be so loved and so endearing that there would be whole groups of people all over the world who would try to create different appearances for our faces. Hence, that is why I am speaking—White Rose—even though Red Rose was the first inhabitant.

We considered that and we said, "We will go, since you say we are going to be receiving attention, and we will accept that there will be a desire to alter our faces," which is what we refer to our flower as, as our face. We did go, and to be perfectly honest, from my experience and my connection with the rest of the rose community—I can't reach the rose community in laboratories, which is why I'm saying that I'm not entirely connected—everyone is still kind of uncomfortable and is really looking forward to not being on Earth anymore. In that sense, we have a little bit in common with the human being, eh? We belive that perhaps this was also the emissaries' wisdom, to know this.

Ask Rose to Sharpen Your Abilities to Assert and Defend

There has been much written by the human being about roses and there is a definite acknowledgement by poets and writers and gardeners alike that there is a similarity between roses and humans. We have our beauty and our fragrance, but be careful or you might get stung, so to speak. There have been a lot of words written about the parallels between the human being and us. We have some capabilities, though not exactly ones you might find to be gentle. We do not claim to be gentle; that is not our personality. We will give you the suggestions as offered by many of the other plants.

If you can be in a garden, there needs to be no more than one or two large rose bushes. One big one or two not so big, but not a young bush. Just one or two that are fairly mature and that have had flowers picked. If there are more bushes, that's fine, but it's important to make a connection with only one or two. If there are many rows and there are flowers, you know, other plants behind the rose bushes, find bushes where there are no other flowers or plants behind, to the best of your ability. One might look for rose bushes next to a wall.

This is what I recommend: If you need strength—and this is particularly good for soldiers or police officers or people who need to sharpen up their assertiveness—this might help you to become more assertive. It won't turn you into a homicidal maniac but it will help you to become sharper and clearer, and it will encourage your drive to learn various defensive measures, meaning perhaps martial arts or sword fighting or target shooting or what have you.

This is what to do: Get a comfortable chair. It doesn't have to be anything fancy. A plastic outdoor garden chair is just fine, or a wooden one; it's up to you. Sit about five feet from those bushes and study them, stare at the rose bushes. Don't lean over and smell the flowers. It's not about that. Look at them. Don't do this at night; do it during the daytime when you can see clearly. Notice the thorns, and while you're looking at the plant, especially the stem parts with the thorns—the twigs, you understand—just breathe in and out normally for about five minutes. Set a timer so you don't have to look at your watch, okay? A kitchen timer's fine, something that dings quietly but loud enough so you can hear it. After five minutes, simply say the following words verbatim:

"I am asking that my capabilities to assert and defend be sharpened now to such a degree that I will be able to act with authority as needed," and pause for a moment, then say, "in the most benevolent way for all beings."

There will be a need in your culture, even as time goes on, for there to be a form of regulation—not armed guards marching you around, but more like there will always be a need for someone to direct, to show. I'm not referring to teachers here, but more to how one asks the friendly police officer in the neighborhood, "How do I get to there?" And the officer responds, "Oh, turn down this street and turn right." There will be a need, then, for such individuals. In a hundred years, it's not likely that there will be a need for armies to fight and defend, but there will be a need for volunteers to search, to rescue, and to discover. Armies will simply transform themselves into this style of endeavor. That's what I recommend. For right now, soldiers or other people who might need to have such skills can do that if they wish.

The Red Rose Was the First Rose to Come to Earth

How do you look and act on your home planet?

On the home planet, we are quite different. We are more like what you would call a not very big tree—not a bush or a shrub as you call it, but something much more full. It's hard to describe by your Western measurements—perhaps ten to twelve feet tall and very full of something that resembles a cross between leaves and flowers. Also, there are seeds, but if you were to see the seeds, you would say they looked a lot like walnuts. This is a planet you might actually find. It is not that far away from your own solar system, and it seems likely to me that you might end up there. Know that the seeds, if you find such a plant, are not edible, and any attempt to pick them for food will get you wrapped up with those needle-leaves—not a pleasant experience. So keep your distance, okay? I'm just kidding a bit there, but definitely do not eat the seeds.

There are a great many of us on this planet, but there are also beings not unlike you. They don't look like human beings but they have a body: two arms, two legs, a head, and something akin to hands but not exactly fingers, although there is something similar to a thumb. So an opportunity to pick things up, for example, would be present. These beings are what I would refer to, using your terminology, as sort of political philosophers. They are always interested in the cultures of others and like to compare them. They might be a good source of knowledge and wisdom when consulting about other cultures. They do not lie, so you don't have to worry about that. Once you establish a diplomatic relationship with them, you will be able to get a great deal of worthy and beneficial advice about who to approach and who to steer clear of.

There is underground water—that's how we grow on the home planet. Our solar system has nine planets and a sun a little smaller than your own. Your solar system has more than nine planets, according to what I have observed, but I understand that not all of them have been explored or even discovered yet. But you will do that in the years to come.

Do you have memories or is there a record in your stories of you coming to the planet you're on, or have you always been there?

You'll have to ask Spirit about that.

I will. Did a white rose come here and then all the other colors were created on Earth, or was I mistaken?

Mistaken. The first rose color to appear on the planet was red. All the others have been largely hybridized, I feel, even though it goes back a ways. It took them awhile to get the white one.

Oh, so are you saying that only the red one came?

The first rose to appear was red, yes.

The Thrill of Danger Piques Human Curiosity

You're in contact with all the roses—most of the roses—on the planet. Do you interact with people and plants and other animals and things energetically? Do you feel them or know what they're doing?

All forms of life on this planet, other than the human being, have the same manner of connecting—knowing when there is a need to know—with other forms of life. Most often there is no need to know, but occasionally a friendly beetle or ants or a larger being might pass by, and it is always the same. Usually they stop, and they would immediately introduce themselves. In the case of a beetle, for instance—a ladybug, perhaps—it might land on a rose, though not usually on the flower. They don't call themselves "ladybug," of course, but that is your affectionate term for them. They would say something in their own language, and we have our own language, but it is interpreted for us. Usually they would introduce themselves by showing some picture about their lives so we could get a sense of who they are. We would politely wait for a moment, once they'd been done speaking—they might be pausing, you know.

Very often, life forms pause. We would wait to be sure they were done, and then we would show them something from our lives. Often we show the flowers opening up from bud to full open stage. They usually like that, and then they might stay just to be companionable for a time before flying off. That's an example. One finds that with larger beings as well, though not humans. Larger beings will pause, again doing something very similar. One even finds this at times with other plants, if it is necessary to communicate with other plants for some reason. If there isn't a need to communicate, then there is just a companionable presence.

You know an awful lot about human beings.

You have to remember that, unlike a great many other plants—but not all—roses have been handled and hybridized by human beings much more, and one does not find this even with fruit trees that have been one way and were changed to another way. You'll find out that there are rose societies—not just gardeners. It goes way back, hundreds of years, and beings have been trying to get the flower to be whatever color they want.

And the fragrance and the height and the shape, yes.

Yes, all of that, more so than with other flowers.

So that interaction has taught you a lot, then.

Yes. Also, it's helped us to understand the nature of the human being. Human beings are a bit fickle. Sometimes they like something, and the next day they don't like the same thing they liked the day before. Also, we've noted that human beings who interact with us, trying to change us in some way, very often have a humorous respect for us. We feel that they are just as drawn to us because of the way the flower looks as they are because of the thorns.

One might find that hard to believe, but professional gardeners or rose societies are often—how can we say?—intrigued by the fact that such beauty is presented with danger. People like danger, although they don't want to admit it. Other people freely admit they like danger. But those who don't like to admit it, for they don't enjoy being pricked by the thorns, will develop a sort of philosophical attitude over time that they might either apply to their understanding of the human being—other human beings, you understand—or it might go the other way. They might adapt their philosophy of humanity to the plant. This is not typical with human beings' interaction with other plants, in my experience.

I love roses, and you can learn how to get around the thorns. You don't necessarily have to stick yourself with them.

Maybe you like a little danger too.

[Laughs.] Maybe. I love roses; I know that. What do you enjoy about being on the planet? Anything?

I like the warm days. It's not quite as warm on our planet. We also like the change of seasons. Those are the two things that come to mind. There may be others, but those two come to mind.

Thorns Provide Protection for Rose

Do you have a lot of visitors on your own planet? Because those other beings, if they know a lot about other cultures, they either travel or they have a lot of visitors—one or the other, don't they?

We have a lot of visitors on the home planet, yes.

And you can communicate with them? Your species, I mean.

On the home planet?

Yes.

Oh, yes, yes.

Is this happening now, or are there translators? How do you communicate with other beings?

The same way we communicate with other beings on Earth as I just described to you. Only there, if they communicate with us, of course there's the introduction just as I described and then the pause, and then the follow-up introduction—even if we've met a hundred times before; it's polite. Then there may be a question by those beings if they have need to ask, and if so, the respondent, meaning one of our kind, will emanate—meaning as would say, "think." We don't think, but we would become aware of the answer from our perspective and they would, then, being in our proximity, just know it—like that.

What kinds of things would they ask you?

You'll have to ask Spirit that.

Okay. So, have you been told if you will leave when the humans leave?

No, I think we'll probably stay a little longer and enjoy the relaxation; we'll probably stay on for a few hundred more years, perhaps, and gradually return to our natural state on Earth. So eventually when we do migrate wherever we go, roses will again be only red.

You don't like all the colors?

Would you like it if other people—not you—came around and decided that you would look better if only this was done to you and that was done to you? Would you like that?

I never thought of it that way. I'm sorry.

No need to apologize. We knew what was coming when we came here. That's part of the reason we were willing to come: because we knew we would have thorns for protection and defense.

Rose Will Eventually Migrate to Other Planets

How long do you live on your home planet?

In terms of your years? Maybe 1,200.

How does that work on Earth, then? How long have you been here?

Maybe six years.

How long will you stay?

I can't say.

Do you stay only while one plant is alive?

Not necessarily. We might migrate to other plants. It's hard to say. Ask Spirit.

Okay. Well, do you know what percentage of the personalities on your home planet have come to Earth? Just a few, or most of them or . . . ?

Maybe 17 percent.

Totally over the course of all time, or at first?

Oh, I cannot be certain. Ask Spirit.

What colors have you been? You're white right now, but are you going to try being another color?

We don't have a choice, do we? If I was to be the color that I would like to be, I would be red.

Are you red on your home planet?

No, but that is the color we were led to believe we would be on this planet.

Oh, I see.

But we were informed that human beings would want to change us.

Did you think they would change your color?

We just knew they would try, so we put up the best defense we could.

[Laughs.] You have a wonderful sense of humor.

I do like humor. It is something we do have on our planet, and when one has thorns like this, one develops a sense of humor and perhaps irony. I will say goodnight now.

All right. You're a love. Thank you for coming.

CHAPTER THIRTY-FOUR

Rose Spirit

JULY 10, 2009

&

GREETINGS. SPIRIT OF ROSE.

Welcome.

Now I'm going to talk a bit. Creator felt it was important to have a species of plant that human beings could identify with as having something in common with them. Rose—as a being, not as a singular plant—did not want to come here. Rose has a benevolent life on its home planet, one that it is satisfied with. However, Creator took a look at it and decided it could be improved in a way that Rose did not see. Rose has a bit of a control problem, as you might have noted, and has the fears and attendant assertiveness that are often found in the fearful. Creator felt Rose could benefit from some time on Earth. Conversely, Creator also felt that human beings needed to have a plant they could directly identify with. Gardeners understand and appreciate this all too well, be they professionals or someone growing rose bushes in a yard. The assertiveness of the rose is well-known and established, and they are often misunderstood. This plant is the exception to the rule that there are no other forms of life on Earth that are here to learn anything other than the human being.

In that way, Rose joins you, because Rose, as you may have noted in your conversation with the plant, does not have a complete connection to its total being, meaning that Rose said to you, "Oh, you'll have to ask Spirit that." You might have been speaking to a human being there: "Oh, you'll have to ask my guide," or "You'll have to ask my advisor." I am not trying to put Rose down; rather, I am saying that here you have a plant who has been on Earth for a great deal of time, and yet this plant still feels a bit feisty, eh?

Rose Is on a Journey Similar to That of Human Beings

So given that, I feel it's important that you understand the parallel between the human being and the rose. Here we have a situation wherein Rose must learn things, must accept things, must become brave in the feminine way—Rose being quite a masculine plant, you see. If Rose can be brave in a feminine way, then the thorns will become only dots, something like a bud—slightly raised, but not sharp in any way. This sharpness is because Rose is ready to do battle, but unfortunately, since Rose is unable to bring its claws forth the way an animal might, the claws are always leading, and many times, Rose deflects someone that it otherwise loved and felt good about. Roses love children, human children, but often human children get injured by the thorns, and then Rose is sad. This is part of the reason poets have decided that roses represent sadness, except at the moment of blooming.

So you see, Rose has something to learn, and Creator felt that humans could also identify with that. You, yourself, have met many humans who are ready to put up a fight first. Then afterward, realizing they might have missed out on a friendship—or even more than that—they would be apologetic, but by then it would be too late. How many children have been pricked by thorns and never really went back to be around roses? How many loving parents have said, "Stay away from the rose bush, honey. You might get hurt, and I wouldn't want that"? So here Rose finds itself in a quandary, in the position of producing more and more beautiful flowers to attract the type of human beings they enjoy having around because of their purity and innocence and, at the same time, sticking them with these spears.

Rose is now in a position on Earth in which it is very—how would you say?—unhappy with itself. It wants very much to have the joy of children playing nearby—not playing with Rose, not shaking Rose around, but just being nearby, playing, having fun, being themselves, sleeping, whatever. Yet Rose finds itself shut out from that. Oh certainly, people have roses growing in their gardens, and children learn when they get older to keep their distance, but Rose is particularly infatuated with children two years old and younger. Of course, human beings can understand that, because children two years old and younger are very appealing to the human being as well. That innocence, that delight, and that welcoming of life is something that Rose feels strongly in its heart of being.

When as a human being you look at Rose, it's important to remember that here is a fellow on the road of life with you, a being who is looking to change and transform itself so that it can have what it wants and needs. Ultimately, the transformation will bring about a transformation on its home planet, very much like the human being. You are here as the Explorer Race—but as human beings as well—to learn how to change, grow, and transform yourselves not just through struggle, sweat, and blood but also in a benevolent way. As a result, the people you interact with when you begin to search the planets and stars, as you are destined to do, will be exposed to your capacity to grow and change benevolently.

This is the crux of the matter: it is critical for you to learn to grow and change benevolently because of the many, many civilizations that you desperately want to be exposed to—civilizations with human beings who have the complete thread of awareness and history of human beings from the beginning of this universe to the present state, whenever that is. You desperately want to communicate and interact with these people. But in order to be yourselves, in order to broadcast that capacity to grow and change benevolently, you will have to embrace that—not just learn it or tough it out, such as, "We'll get these steps down." You will have to learn it, find out what's good about it, embrace it, and still have as your foundation the deep, strong rock of capability and adaptation. That is the crux of what you are here to do.

Feminine Warrior Wisdom Is Helping You Adapt

You can see how Rose and you are totally and completely tied together, moving inexorably toward a more benevolent life for all beings. Yet you have to learn something that seems to be completely out of reach, beyond your very character. Yet you know that when you move beyond this planet, you become benign and benevolent beings. You shed the scholastic endeavors of the struggles on Earth, become spirit, and join Spirit in a harmonious way—as does Rose. Here in this Earth school, you are struggling not only to achieve this change and transformation for yourselves but, ultimately—as Creator wishes—to bring the capability to grow and change out into the universe in such a way that the people you wish to meet and those who wish to meet you will not have to stay away from you because you are too rough or too harsh—or because you might have an attitude toward them that they are "too soft." It is not your job to remain tough. The soldier is always ready for action, but underneath that soldier there is also the heart and the desire for peace, for love, for nurturing, and to provide that peace, love, and nurturing—what the soldier often has to acquire through family, children, and friends.

This has been said to you before: you are learning feminine warrior wisdom, which is that you're learning everything there is to know as a total being—not every individual—about war so that you can completely understand that it must be avoided, because things happen in war that individuals would never do otherwise. Feminine warrior wisdom is different. You know what war is and you know what it is on a small scale, too, between one or two individuals and even within the individual identities of a people, waging war in terms of inner conflict within themselves. You are now on the path of feminine warrior wisdom. The feminine energy has been rising to support that for all beings. Feminine warrior wisdom has this knowledge so that she—and he, for it is part of the male as well—can avoid war by finding the pathway to change and adaptation, to the deep, foundational capacities in the most benevolent way for all beings.

Rose Was Created with the Purpose of Spending Time with the Explorer Race

How did this anomaly come to be, that the rose had to learn these things? Where did it go off track, or where did it get stuck?

It was always this way on their home planet, because Creator knew that whatever else Creator did, Creator would plan and intend for a group of beings to become the Explorer Race. At that time, Creator did not know which type of beings he would choose but, ultimately, Creator chose the human being because you were vulnerable; to a degree you had to struggle to survive—although in your modern societies, going indoors is available. In a more outdoor world, though, survival takes real effort. So Rose didn't get off track. It was *always* intended to be a plant representative of your circumstances as a human being. You might just find that there's a nonplant, nonhuman on Earth like that as well.

Can you say who or what?

I think they will say it—perhaps in an article in the magazine—to prepare the human being as a society to see and to understand—and also to give a tip of the hat to the plant book and, although it's already published, the animal book.

So the rose people were brought here from another universe and prepared for this role. Is that true?

No. Rose was always created here in this universe. That is why when you heard from the rose plant—which was absolutely essential for you to to hear from so you could get the general character of Rose, you understand—you heard things about their planet, yes, their being, that might not sound typical of what you've heard in other places. After all, a rose on that planet—if I can call them that . . . but let's call them that for the sake of simplicity—is not just leaves; it also has needles on it, remember? And seeds. Rose was absolutely adamant . . .

That nobody eat them.

Yes. So that situation exists. And Creator allowed Rose to be that way, allowing Rose to sort of create its own society in its own world on a planet that was welcoming of divergent personalities, because Creator knew that the reason Creator had created Rose was ultimately to spend some time with the Explorer Race.

Rose Is Here to Learn to Create a Benevolent Life, Just as Humans Are

Where do you fit in? Are you an advisor? Are you part of that culture? How do you fit into it?

I am more associated with Creator—what you might call an angelic, in that sense, where I interact with other angelics and lightbeings, and I advise Rose. I am not telling you anything I have not discussed with Rose before at length, so it knows why it's here now, but it . .

It still doesn't like it. [Chuckles.]

That's right. It doesn't like it. When you think back to your childhood, if you can—and readers certainly can—you will remember that most of you did not like school. Some of you liked some of the things *at* school, though: classes, stimulation, art, what have you—hands-on things, doing things, learning things, even learning games, eh? So school can be better. School can be a good thing. But one does not stop school because one becomes an adult and starts a career and starts a family, perhaps. One is in school as a human being, as a member of the Explorer Race on Earth, and you are in school until you leave this planet.

When human beings say that they're not very happy to be here and ask, "When can I go home?" and all this kind of stuff, it's the confusion that comes as a result of having to live a life in a polarized world. It's awfully easy—and sometimes, one might argue, a necessity—to forget who you are and where you're from because of being on Earth and having to get along as well as possible. And yet it's understandable that you would want to have the simple, loving, and benevolent life that awaits you all beyond. Nevertheless, what you are here to learn, like Rose, is to create that benevolent life and to understand that you are in school always when you are here. You are here to learn how to create a benevolent life for all beings in the most benevolent way.

So what steps can the rose take? It's a change in attitude, right?

Just like the human being. Rose has begun—I have discussed these things with Rose—to change its attitude. Rose has resisted the human being attempting to create a rose without thorns, even though it has been done with some success, though not the kind of success that continues generation after generation.

A hybrid that can't reproduce, okay.

Yes. So the human being is here to do very much the same thing, to learn how to re-create yourself in this world of polarity in a way that is benevolent for all beings. This is meant to be a goal—not an unreachable goal, but one you strive for so that eventually the world that you live in—not in another dimension, but the world that you live in here—has only about 4 percent discomfort, and that much only to stimulate your growth. You as individuals can do that, but you will have to want to. If you want to on a regular basis, and it's not just something that you are taught at school—"Be this. Do that. March this way," or "Walk this Way," as the famous song goes—then you will strive for it. It's possible, because the younger generation coming up now is born to want that, and the generation that preceded them also has that desire. So we shall see. But this does not exclude generations that came before them from wanting that as well. This is spoken to each of you and all of you with the greatest of love and admiration for what you have done. Now it is time to learn how to practice benevolence for all beings. Do not assume it is impossible. You may have to go step by step, but there are so many of you working in so many different fields that you can all begin. Begin in some way today.

Tell Rose You Accept It Just as It Is

Is there anything humans can do for the rose to aid or facilitate its process? Be the example, right?

Acknowledge Rose, gardeners. I know you sometimes talk to your plants; I know some of you don't. Those of you who talk to the plants and have roses, just say, "It's all right being who you are. We will accept each other as we are and try to live as well as possible."

I just had a thought. I have roses at my office, and when I planted them, I had all kinds of colors. And after a not too respectful maintenance, the ones that are left are all red.

So you see . . .

[Laughs.] I never thought of that.

Be sure and leave that in.

[Laughs.] All right. Were roses one of the earliest plants to come? When in our cycle did they come to the planet?

Well, they haven't been here much longer than the human being. They were early in your cycle, but not that early. They didn't look the way they do now, of course. But most importantly, they were appreciated by the human being for the beauty of their flowers and, at that time, for their fragrance. Of course, the more they are hybridized, the more they tend to lose that fragrance, because they are not interacting as much with the natural world. They must have that fragrance to attract the little flying ones who come and interact with Rose. After a while, when Rose is not allowed to have such exposure, there is no need to have such fragrance. For the gardeners who wonder what happened to the fragrance, well, that's what happened.

I can remember roses growing along the railroad tracks when I was young, and they didn't look like today's roses. They had flat leaves. They were so beautiful and so soft, and they smelled so good.

Yes, they were saying, "Come, little flying ones." As you could see, they were growing also in places where children would be likely to be attracted. What child is not attracted to going to see railroad tracks? "Maybe a train would come! I wonder where it's going?"

Yes.

Now I will finish. For those of you who are human beings on Earth, understand that you are not alone in your quest to achieve something that has not been achieved before, and that's to be able to grow, to adapt, to change, and to apply what you've learned in new and benevolent ways. You are now consciously joined on that path by the beauty of Rose. Learn a lesson from Rose: Don't always have your defenses up. If you want to have your claws available, okay, but keep them well inside your paws, as the cat might when the cat is with a loved one. Learn as well as possible to get along with each other and with other life forms here. Try to preserve and protect, yes, but do so in ways that do not hurt and defile. It is not an easy thing to do, to be in balance, but it is worth striving for. Good life.

Oh, good life. Thank you. Thank you very much.

CONCLUSION

Coffee

SEPTEMBER 20, 2010

ॐ

COFFEE. THE PLANT, NOT THE BEING.
Welcome.

We are related somewhat to the grapevine. I feel that the grapevine was once about the size of the coffee plant, but it has been transformed in some way over the years. For us, we were here many thousands of years before the human being in your present form arrived. We were here for not only our own expression of life but, as with all forms of life on this planet, to be compatible with and support other forms of life by simply being, by existing. In the natural world, one finds this consistently, especially with trees that fruit the way the coffee plant does (to use your term). This is the case with us as well.

There are several small creatures—you say insects—that make the coffee plant home, and while they may seem to cause harm, they also create an ability to survive and thrive. I will not name them because I think there's only one type left. Many of the beings we've noted in spirit form here who support your planet have either migrated—meaning have gone home—or have moved to another planet. They have done this in the natural way by dying out and not being replaced, or they have simply ceased to exist for a time. This is possible

503

on this planet for some types of beings. Unfortunately, a great many of these beings have been very involved in the support of all life, so you find yourselves, as human beings, struggling to maintain your own good health in the world you create, which is not as natural as the one the human being once lived in. I grant, the natural world on this planet is not the most comfortable place for the human being, but I feel that this planet was not originally created for the human being; rather, it was created to be a welcoming place for the largest variety of life forms. Perhaps because of your mission to challenge yourselves and bring out the best in yourselves by being opposed by challenges, this planet is perfect for your pursuits. But the effect of all you do here is uncreating its value as a welcoming place for other forms of life. It is not surprising that many of them have moved elsewhere or have gone into a sort of temporary lack of re-creation.

Coffee Is Meant to Encourage and Support Innovation

I grant that it is in my nature to be forthcoming. Those of you who have incorporated a part of my being into your own in the form of the drinks and other things that you manufacture from the coffee bean have noted, perhaps, that one of the effects of the coffee bean is to make you a little less likely to hold back your opinions. This is not meant to create disruption in your civilization; rather, it is meant to encourage and support innovation. When used properly in the future, the drink coffee will be consumed in very small amounts—not like you would take a drug or something in a few drops, but a very small amount, not too different from the small cups of very strong coffee you call espresso. I feel that even with some additions—say, a sweetener or something to make it a little more mellow, for those of you who like that—that coffee in this form allows you to have the best effect from it. It helps you create and support a sense of your own personality. The first time you have coffee, it stimulates your personality, and it also helps to generate problem solving.

In many ways, it is a very useful addition to your diet. The only problem is if you have it too often. I would recommend having it in the form I just described for people who need to produce innovation, say, on a daily basis, or to solve problems that crop up. I would recommend drinking it, perhaps, once every other day, not once a day. It would have to be taken at a time when it can mix in with the rest of your life, meaning not drunk on its own, no matter how much sweetener or other things are added to it but, rather, taken with a meal. In this way, there is a greater tendency for it to be in balance with your whole world rather than substituting a world for the world you live in.

I don't understand why coffee would substitute a world for the world we live in.

You would say I am speaking in a flowery fashion. You have read poetry before? It is like that. It substitutes a world, meaning a world of dependence. If you drink it all the time, you will become dependent on it, and then it will become something you need, and you will no longer receive its benefits. Then it's just a matter of trying to keep from being uncomfortable without it. Have it every other day, for instance, and only when you need it. If you're going to have a relaxing time and innovation does not seem to be necessary, then don't have it. Have it, for instance, when you're at work or if you're in a situation where disputes or conflicts are likely to erupt, say, within a large group of people or even in a small group. That would be fine. But you don't have it every day. If you have it all the time, regularly, then it becomes something you have to have, and its innovative capabilities recede. In short, have it as a spice to life, and then it becomes part of your life. But don't have it because you *have* to, because then it becomes your life.

Coffee Amplifies the Capacities of All Life Forms to Be Inspired

You said that you came here to express yourself. How do you do that? How do you express your personality?

We do that because of the way we interact with other life forms. What I am doing right now, through this process that you use, is very much the same as what I might do with any natural being who does not have such an elaborate system of communication but has a more natural style of communication, which is to say, simply the interaction of feelings. For instance, when a bird or another smaller flying being would land on one of our plants, if it is struggling with some factor of life—perhaps it's being pursued by something that wants to eat it—there is a better chance that it will be inspired (simply through contact with the plant) to have an action, not a thought, in the form of innovation. When I speak of innovation, I am not speaking about an inspiration built by a thought. I am talking about an inspiration as a feeling. The bird will have this inspiration, perhaps, and then it will be able to engage in some physical action that will make it more likely able to survive the current danger, for example.

When coffee was originally being experienced as a drink, it was always used by medicine people as a stimulant. Before that, it was used as an herb to support life medically, you might say, on the natural level of human beings. Of course, they went through the whole range of asking, "Does it work for this?" and "Does it work for that?" That's a bit hazardous, but it is how wisdom is accumulated:

through the interaction of human beings with the life around them. Eventually, it was discovered that it works very well as a stimulant and a little bit topically to ward off certain "skin migrants," as I would call them. You would say some kind of bacteria, but I do not claim to be medically aware of your world.

The interaction of our plants with other life forms is something we enjoy doing. As I said, we do not provide ideas, but we have the capacity to support all life forms on this planet with their own capabilities—to amplify their capacity to be inspired. It will only occur in the moment of contact. This doesn't mean beings won't have their own inspiration abilities before, during, or after, but in the moment of contact, those abilities are amplified. When you consume the drink, it's very important that you not be angry or upset. If you are angry or upset, your inspiration may be destructive. I think somebody has noted that in your culture by now. If, however, you are relaxed and calm and are struggling with some problem that needs to be solved, consuming a very small quantity would be helpful. I would recommend it in the form of two or three tablespoons of the drink you call espresso—not all at once, mind you, but sipped slowly over, say, a half-hour of your time.

Earth Is the Ideal Place to Produce a Culture That Is Out of Balance

Are you speaking from the level of being one plant? Are you connected to all plants? Are you connected to your spirit being?

I am the spirit that expresses the communication. I am like someone who is interpreting the broadcast feelings of the coffee plant into words you can understand. In that sense, I am a spirit of the coffee plant, though only on Earth and only at this time. But as my own being, I am what I would call a translator. I won't get into that now, since this is about the coffee plant. The coffee plant does not communicate in words, and the spirit of the coffee plant is simply not available at this time. Perhaps it will be in a little while.

Usually there is a planet somewhere that the plants on Earth come from. Sometimes they look a little different and they're changed a little in form, but there is a home planet someplace. Is there a home planet for the coffee plant?

Yes. Yes, but it is in the past. Right now, the coffee plant in its form where it produces fruit, the bean, does not exist in that form. The current form does not fruit. But in the past, it had that. That is the point in time I am speaking from. I don't know if you understand what this means in the larger sense, but from my perception, you and your culture are in the past. I believe this was done in the past, apparently by whoever watches over this project you are involved in (in attempting to re-create many things), because it was felt that it would have less impact on the perfect balance of the universe. It was done at a time in the past when there was some disruption, some places where there was discomfort. You all exist, from my point of view, in the past.

You might want to inquire about that further with someone who is more conscious of your culture, because if you think about it, it makes complete sense. If you have the means to create things in the past, and you have a perfectly balanced world, why in the world would you want to create something as imbalanced as the culture you are currently creating, simply because of the difficulties and challenges you have embraced in order to do the work that you do (this whole Explorer Race thing)? If, on the other hand, you had some means—functioning as a being who creates—to find a time in the universe when things were a little bit unsettled and had not been resolved yet, this would be the ideal place to produce a world that is out of balance. By world, I do not mean the planet but rather—you understand, I am speaking figuratively again—a culture that is out of balance. From my point of view, living in the present as I am, I am in a universe that is totally balanced and completely benevolent. Everything is for love and benevolence, and I naturally perceive you as living in the past, because that is where you are. I see no point in keeping that fact from you; no one is telling me not to, so I'm saying it.

All Life Must Migrate from the Present to the Past to Adapt to the Purposes of the Past

On the planet where the coffee bean lives now, it has changed and mutated over the years and no longer has a fruit, a coffee bean?

I'm trying to help you to shift, because I realize that you are living in a linear life and you experience time that way—and I grant that time does function in that way. But the plant has not evolved over time, because when you are expressing the idea of evolving over time, you are expressing point A moving forward to point B. Do you understand? But in fact, it's the other way. I am in the present; you are in the past. The natural way for life to be in this perfect, benevolent universe is the way it is, but in order to function the way you need to in the past, all life must migrate from the present into the past and take a different form. Your science has even attempted to prove this, though not in the way I'm expressing it, by suggesting that over time, things change and evolve. But in fact, it works the other way.

Over time, yes, things change and evolve as they move from the present into the past to adapt to the purposes of the past, meaning "to adapt," in the case of

your world, "to a school where challenge is intentionally part of the learning."
So whatever it is you're attempting to accomplish as the human race on Earth
as it is now can be accomplished by means of bouncing off of one challenge and
on to another. This cannot possibly work in a totally balanced and benevolent
universe, but it can work in the past you find yourself in, where there are still
fragments of other places in which there are slight discomforts that need to be
smoothed out in a benevolent way. It's the other way around. Time and change
occur from the present back. It's not the other way, at least not the way I see it.
It's linear; it's just linear from point B to point A, we'll say.

Earth Is Created in an Artificial Form

Did Creator come to your planet and request your presence in this experience?

That's not my awareness. Someone did come; I would say they were
an angelic . . .

An emissary, yes.

Yes, thank you; that's a good word, "emissary." It was explained, and there
were volunteers to come to your time, even though it's an artificial time and
place. I don't know if you know this, but it never existed. It's created in an artificial form the way you are living it—which isn't to suggest that you don't have
feelings and comforts and discomforts and all of that. No matter what happens
and no matter what you do there, because it's artificial and not in connection to
the real time in which I live—and this is like a safety mechanism—then even if
the worst should happen, which would never happen in our time, the natural
would simply emerge as the constant. All that is artificial would simply disappear
as if it never were. That doesn't disappear any of your souls, of course, because
your souls are all alive in this present time as well, your spirits and so on. But
those of you human spirits who volunteer in our time and have volunteered
for this project have felt more reassured that you would be safe in soul and
spirit form—because no matter what might happen, at the very least this safety
mechanism was in place. Your souls and spirits would not be affected in some
way that would require repair in the present moment.

I believe that's perhaps part of why some beings have been speaking to you
for a while now, reminding you of the present moment, to help you to be connected with being in the immediate moment you are in rather than focusing on
the past or the future. When you do that and you're in the immediate moment
that you're in, you are probably going to feel much better physically, and everything else. This tends to create balance and reminds you of the actual time

sequence in which you live. You are alive in this moment, all of you—meaning the place where I am living. I hope I'm not getting too confusing here; I'm just trying to explain. You are all alive here in this time, but you project back into your time because you believe in the value of the project you're involved in. If you ever—and I believe several of you have over time—come to the point, say, at the end of a life where you say, "Well, that's all I want to do there," you just naturally "emerge," you might say. You just naturally are present in this present world of the universe in which everyone is focused on the immediate, present moment. That is how balance is attained, because in the present moment of existence, you will find your greatest comfort.

Humans Are in This Time to Uncreate Pain and Suffering

The purpose of the coffee plant in your time, then, is ultimately to stimulate in the immediate moment that which you need. There are a great many natural forms of life that might do that. Say you are going for a walk through a large national park, but in the distance you hear a bear or a lion roar. The sound is quite huge and you might jump, and it would bring you into the present moment because of the physical effects in your body—a warning and so on. Your body is actually set up to bring you into the present moment. It is natural for all life to do that, but when you go to this place where you find yourself now, you are given a means to attach yourself to the past or to the future as well as to the present moment.

I believe that even though this complicates your life now, ultimately it's going to create for you a desire to function within the artificial timeline that you find yourselves in so you can transform that timeline into being entirely benevolent again. When that timeline started out initially, of course, it was totally benevolent—so through what you are learning somehow in reaction to your challenges, you will learn how to transform your timeline into being entirely benevolent again. Then when you naturally emigrate at the end of any life and snap back to the present moment in this perfectly balanced universe, eventually you will be able to say, "There. We have put it to rights, and now it can simply dissipate. And maybe we won't do that again." [Laughs.] "You," meaning all of you who have participated in this journey into this place that doesn't really exist from my perspective. I understand, of course, that you're living there and that it exists. But the goal will have been accomplished. That is what I understand. I don't know if you knew that.

Everything you're saying ties in with what we know, but some of it is new. I also want to say that if we knew what we were going to be involved in before we came here, we probably wouldn't have volunteered.

I think that is true, because in the present-moment existence where I am, there is no pain. From what I have noted, when there is no pain and someone tries to explain pain to you, you don't understand. You have no concept of what it means, because any description of something for which you have absolutely no conception of becomes an intellectual thought, and this is not the same as actual experience. I am convinced that if you all had known what pain actually would feel like, you never would have gone. It will be a job, from what I can perceive, to uncreate pain and suffering. I believe it can be done. I do not claim to be able to teach you how to do that, but I think it would be good for you to set your sights on uncreating pain and suffering.

One of the things I know you will have to do as a precursor is to let go of impatience. I think it can be done quickly and benevolently, but it is an action that you may take, perhaps, that will have to involve at least the soul agreement of all beings over time. It will take time—experience, you say, experiential time—in order for it to be resolved. Something that you do, even though you have done all you can to accomplish it, will take experiential time, perhaps even a generation, to be resolved, and then there will be no pain and suffering. When there is no pain and suffering and impatience has been set aside, you'll have taken three big steps toward creating balance.

You Re-create Another You When You Drink Coffee

How did you learn so much about this, about us?

Innovation and its predecessor, inspiration, is part of the natural association of the coffee plant. I might add that there are several other forms of life on Earth that are like that too in the plant world: redwood trees (especially as they mature, less so when they are very young) and maple trees (also when they are mature). But, then, when you are very young, perhaps a sapling, you are just trying to survive. You haven't got time for innovation, other than, "Where can I grow that gets me closer to the water and the sun," or something like that. I would say that that is the nature of the personality of the coffee plant; therefore, it is possible to tap into this knowledge. Also, as you may have noticed—though I'm trying to temper it a bit here—there is a tendency to be outspoken. As I mentioned before, I think that those of you who have coffee drinks incorporated into your lives might have noticed that when you have coffee, you might be a bit more assertive and outspoken.

If one could go where coffee plants grow and spend some time in the energy of the coffee plant, would you get the same benefits as drinking the coffee bean?

No, just being there wouldn't be the same, and even handling the beans wouldn't be the same. It is what comes from the distillation process, because the bean actually represents, potentially, another coffee plant. It is like the intense capability to create another of one's self. When you are drinking the distillation of something that helps to create another one of itself, even though it would create a coffee plant, it tends to reproduce that in you on the feeling level. Remember, it's all about feeling. There is a tendency, in the moments of sipping the drink, to feel somewhat re-created as another one of you in the pure moment. You experience another one of you in a most inspired way in that present moment of the consumption and the interaction of your body with that liquid.

That's why it's a good time to think about solving problems that seem to be unsolvable, not just things in your life or in the lives of your family, friends, or business. It's also a good time for philosophers who are more intent on solving things rather than studying the perceptions of others and also for innovators in general who say, "Now, here's a problem that we don't know what to do with," for instance, a problem involving pain and suffering. "We need inspiration to know how to resolve this in the most benevolent way." You have to tack that on so that you all don't just jump off a cliff or something. You might consume that drink and focus on the most benevolent way to solve that problem for all beings. I'm not saying that it has to be exclusively that, but it is in my nature to present something that I feel needs to be solved, as you might say in your time, "and right quick."

Humans Have Many Capabilities
That Will Not Be Expressed in This Time

How does coffee use that on the home planet? What kind of life do they live on the planet where the coffee bean is native?

Are you talking about in the artificial past? I want to answer that. In the present, there is no problem. The problem is in the life form of the coffee being in this time; it is in a synchronous world where all life forms are completely blended. It is more of a ripple, a dance, rather than a need to express one's own unique identity. Now you can ask the question.

Do they still have that ability to inspire and innovate, and do they use it in their lives?

You are speaking from an artificial past; it's not "still." I'm going to have to translate your question: You mean, do they inspire and innovate "in their natural form."

In your reality.

No, no. In reality. You are the one who is not in reality.

[Laughs.] Okay.

In reality, they do not have that as a primary personality characteristic because it is not needed. You might say it is there on a deep level of its personality, and that is how the coffee plant is able to come back in your time and express that: because it's needed in your time. But it is not needed in actual time, in the actual place where we all live—including you. But going back to that artificial time created to uncreate pain and suffering and all of that other business, as I mentioned before, then that could come to the surface, because it is needed there.

Okay. In reality at some point in your past, then, that trait was more pronounced in coffee beings and they used it at some time in their history?

You are still . . . I understand that you can't help it. You have to try to discipline yourself when you ask these questions. That question is like a non sequitur. It doesn't fit. You're trying to talk about evolution, but it's the other way; it's devolution coming back to your time.

All right. But at some point, how did they gain this ability?

No, listen. I'm going to repeat the present. That's why I feel the question is flawed. I'm going to speak to you as a person: Right now, you have many, many capabilities that you do not express in your personality—you as a representative human. All humans on the planet have this, so you are simply a representative. You have all these capabilities, some of which you may have represented and utilized years ago, and some of which you may still utilize and express in your now life. But you have all these myriad capabilities and possibilities you will never express in your now life because they are not needed or they do not fit into the human culture on Earth as it now exists. These capabilities will never be expressed by you, but they are there in the present moment; they are there with you right now.

It's the same with coffee plants in our now time—which aren't plants, I might add—but it's the same with the existence of that which you refer to as the coffee plant. It is what you might call an unexpressed personality characteristic. When a being, even a human being like yourself is you transported to a past—or even any place in such a way that you would be safe—you might find yourself quickly expressing a way of being that you discover you're good at that you've never expressed before in any other aspect of your life.

I'm going to prove this to you. Have you ever found yourselves suddenly in a situation that is completely foreign and unknown to you and you suddenly discover that you can adapt to the situation in ways you didn't know you could adapt? This could happen in travel, or it could happen in a situation that comes up that is entirely unique and new, and you discover something; it is almost as if it pops into your head. It might feel good, or it might just feel like something temporary that you discover you can do and you're good at, something you have a talent for and never knew you could do, and then you express it in that situation. It's exactly the same.

Humans Are Here to Balance Discomfort

Okay. If coffee is not a plant, is it a vine or a tree, or what is it?

No, it is more like a fluid. It's a fluid, a substance. It can be gaseous, or it can be a fluid. I'm talking about in our time. You did not specify; you must be very specific now, because there is something about me that you do not know, apparently, and that is that I must always speak the truth. If I am going to speak the truth, I am going to speak it from the position of current existence. I am not going to speak it from your artificial existence.

Thank you for telling me. Okay, so it's a fluid and a gas, and it is in a very high . . . if you'll put up with our numbering system, can you tell me what dimension it's in?

This whole expression of dimensions . . . no, I cannot tell you.

If I were there now, from my current body, would I see this movement of coffee?

No. You wouldn't see that world at all with your current perceptive abilities; however, from your soul perception or your spirit perception, you would see it, of course. From your now perception—which is restricted by the needs of what you are attempting to accomplish, by where you are, and also by the heightening of the latent characteristics of your personality that you are expressing in your now artificial past—you would be used to using, say, thought, as you are now attempting to perform all the functions you must perform in order to interact in this fashion, as well as simply to exist where you are. From my perception, you are expressing a finely honed capability of your latent characteristics, meaning that in your natural state, you wouldn't be anything like this.

So we're not the only ones who took the great jump into adventure, then. The coffee beings and all the other beings did the same thing.

Every form of life you encounter in your artificial creation has done this with the goal of creating something worthwhile. One such worthwhile thing is that there are other elements of creation. Remember, I mentioned something about when you came back to this artificial time, this artificial place. "Why did this whole thing happen in this particular time in the past?" It happened in this time in the past because there were other places that had some slight discomforts, though not to the extent that you have. Creator had it happen in this artificial past so that you could resolve the discomforts that you as individuals created out of ignorance, because you didn't have full contact with your full beings. Ultimately, since this whole creation has been stimulated in the past, I can only assume that that's what you are doing there, in this artificial creation. Something happened to balance out these other discomforts in these other places of the universe in the past. Do you understand? Something happened.

And what we're doing is doing it! Or our experience is leading to our learning how to do it, and then we are going out and doing it in these other places.

I can only assume that what you're doing is what happened in order to bring about the balance of all those discomforts. Otherwise, it doesn't make sense, where you are and what you're doing. It makes no sense at all unless you add that in.

Yes, I got heat flashes. Where you're speaking from, the present reality, most beings aren't talking to us from that place. So that's fantastic.

You have to remember, I'm a translator. I'm not going to speak about who I am, because otherwise you'll get lost in the whole thing and it won't really fit into the book, but as a translator, I am able to translate not only language but also the feelings of all beings, no matter who they are or where they are. I'm able to translate from one culture to another, and through that, I'm able to express many levels of truth—meaning subtle truths, things that are present for you now. If we were having this conversation, within your time concept let's say about forty years ago, I wouldn't have been able to discuss these things with you, but where you are now as a human culture in your now artificial past, you are beginning to, as you say, wake up. As a result, I'm able to communicate these things to you.

Coffee Supports Communication through Feeling

This session will end the plant healing book. I'd like to stay with the coffee beings for now, but I'd like to make an appointment to talk to you in the future.

Yes, if you like. You mean you'd like to talk to me in my present and in your artificial past?

[Laughs.] Yes. I like people who tell the truth and don't kind of . . . you know, tell me what they want me to hear. [Chuckles.]

Well, if you have trouble finding me, just start talking about what you remember about the coffee plant and this whole sequence, and . . .

So you're not really connected with the coffee plant.?

I am. But I am just as connected to other forms of life that are associated with you and your time. There are other beings like me, but I am one of many who can speak to you in your time, in your place, about forms of life that I know and am compatible with and can express. The coffee plant is really entirely about feeling and has no interpretable language without there being an interpreter—meaning I am not interpreting their language; I am interpreting their feelings. All the time I am speaking to you, there are one or more coffee plants radiating an answer in feeling to your questions, which I am translating into words that you can understand. They have strong feelings.

That is why the effect of the fruit that grows upon the plants stimulates strong feelings in the human beings, because the coffee plant is entirely about strong feelings. They are emanating strong feelings as answers, and I am interpreting those strong feelings in words. Sometimes, as you have noticed, the feeling comes through me because I cannot help but bring forth some of that feeling, because they are entirely about feeling. This is apparently one of the great similarities between their culture—the culture of the coffee plant—and human culture. You both have a great and significant depth of feeling. I believe it is also your nature to communicate through feeling, so if you're living in a culture that discourages communication with feeling, oh my goodness, you really need some coffee.

You Should Drink Coffee in Moderation

Is there a danger to the physical body from drinking too much coffee?

I do not have too much capability with medicine, but my understanding from the coffee plant is what I said before: Every other day, in the conditions described, two or three tablespoons full of the coffee as espresso would be the way to consume it, but not if you have a medical condition that warrants your doing otherwise. You don't have to add sweeteners, but if you add other things to it, you can. However, that's the way to have it: just that amount, no more. Otherwise it becomes something you need rather than something that you utilize to provide for your own needs and the needs of others through innovation and inspiration.

So those of us who drink a lot of coffee every day are losing that special access to that capacity of innovation and inspiration?

Well, from my perception, if you're not drinking coffee in the form I have described it, you're not getting it anyway. You don't get the innovation and inspiration unless you are drinking it in that form, which I'm describing as espresso. I'm now looking at the drink you're talking about as coffee. Oh, no, in order to get this, it has to be in the form of, at the very least, espresso—or something even more concentrated. But I feel that espresso would be the way for you to get that. You don't get that with something else.

Let me be more elaborate so that you understand why. When it is thinned out with so much water, then the experience is thinned out. You have to have something that is strong and will stimulate your inspiration, because you desire inspiration to be stimulated and you desire innovation to happen. If you have that desire, the desire and the espresso work together to amplify the results of your desire, which is not necessarily a specific idea but is a feeling that then amplifies the characteristic within your personality that is open to inspiration and can apply it as innovation. But if you give it a very weak stimulation with something that isn't at the level of at least espresso, then you're not getting it. It just barely does that, and even if you desire that, it will have only the slightest stimulation.

Human Interaction Can Frustrate Coffee Plants

What do the coffee plants find most joyous about their existence here?

Well, their interaction with other members of the natural world is natural and comfortable. They find it a little frustrating to interact with human beings [chuckles], but not with human beings who are very young or human beings who are much attuned to the presence of their natural world. If one is perhaps picking the fruit of the coffee plant and is doing so slowly and gently, then the plant finds that comforting as well, because there is a gentleness, an honoring of life, in that interaction with human beings. Do this with no rush, with no immediacy, just slowly, looking at which ones are ready to be picked—not just pulling them off the plant, but choosing ones that are ready to migrate. The plant finds that comforting as well, because the plant feels that it behaves in this manner too. It doesn't insist; it doesn't aggressively jump at you. It would prefer you not to do that either.

Are there members of the insect, bird, or animal kingdoms with whom you can communicate via feelings?

Yes, all members. All nonhumans do that naturally. It's as natural as your heart pumping blood through your veins and your breath in and out. It is so natural, one does not think of it. So for you, you do not live your natural existence in this past time you are living in, because in your natural time, that whole thing is just as natural too. You wouldn't stop breathing and say, "Oh, I'm going to think now instead."

[Chuckles.] Okay. Is there a portion of the souls or personalities from your time, from reality, that are involved with the coffee plants? Is it a small percentage of their population?

The only percentage I'm aware of that's involved with the coffee plant— aside from, naturally, angelics and Creator—is what coffee really is now. It is the liquid, the gas form, you might say, the natural personality of the existence of coffee, which has expressed itself in its latent characteristic as you experience it where you are now. I don't know if that's what you were asking.

People Interact as if on Teams in Real Time

Well, I'm just wondering how many beings came back to express themselves in this time. You know, if there are a hundred people, is it five people out of that hundred? Or if you have a million, do you know the percentage of the beings who volunteered to come here?

Oh, I see. You're talking about individuals.
Yes, the ones who volunteered.

In our now time. In the actual time. Yes, in real time, individuality is an existence, but everyone is so interactive with everyone else that individuality is not a given. It is more like . . . you would have teams in your time, yes? And each person on the team would have his or her own personality, but as a team, they would all work together toward some goal, yes? They would blend as they attempted to achieve something. That is really an expression of natural existence in real time where the team, the flow, the ebb . . . have you ever seen video taken undersea of a school of fish, and noticed how suddenly they would move this way and move that way?

I've seen them in Florida under the bridges, yes.

So you've seen that, and it's not as if somebody says, "Okay! Turn left!" and "Okay! Turn right!" It's a natural flow of existence. That's what exists, and within that school of fish that you're looking at, from the bridge as you've described it, all the individuals in that school of fish are all individuals but also all in this natural flow of togetherness in real time. So when you volunteer as an individual to express yourself in the artificial past in which your people exist, you would be there but you would also be in your present. To you, it would be like this . . . I'm going to describe it the best I can in your terms, but you must understand that

I'm expressing something in your terms, which is not to say that that's what is. I'm expressing it in your terms so that you understand it. From real time, it is as if they are dreaming your past time. That is how you would experience it, as if you were asleep and you were dreaming something. You would say, "Oh, it was a dream," meaning a separate part of your life, not part of your conscious, day-to-day life. It would be like that. For them, it's like a dream, but it's not part of their conscious, day-to-day life, you might say. That's the best way I can put it.

Coffee Should Be Only a Portion of Your Life

I was leading up to wondering if there is any effect in real time from what they are doing here in our time.

No, and that is because it is like a dream; it's artificial, so as an artificial thing, it is not part of reality. I'm not saying that dreams for you are artificial; I'm trying to create an analogy so that you can understand it and, obviously, so others can understand it. It's part of something that is separate from their reality, so they are not affected by it. If you didn't live in the past and you lived only in the present, anything that occurred in that "past" would not affect you, because you are in the present. It would be like . . . place the hand you are not using to hold the speaking instrument on some part of your body, and just move it. You can say that the contact experience you are having in the present moment is existence, but all of the contact experience you've had as an accumulation of doing this for some time is in the past. So it doesn't exist because you're in the present. One can argue about that philosophically, but that's how I describe it.

Okay. Well, I think coffee is such a great gift. I drink a lot of it, but in what you would consider a watered-down form.

Yes, you're not getting the benefit of it if you're doing that. If you're drinking a lot of it, this might mean that it is a dependency rather than something that might help you innovate.

Well, I just enjoy it; that's all. But I'm certainly going to try it the other way.

Make sure that if you try it the other way, you are taking it as part of a meal, and don't drink your watered-down version with the meal. Try not to have any of the watered-down version for, say, at least four hours so that most of it will have left your body, all right? Go to the bathroom and so on until it has left your body. Really, the best way is to wait eight hours, but I'm trying to be realistic, since you are apparently somewhat dependent on this. I'm not judging you; you stated that, and that is what is. I would say if you can do that, I suppose twenty-four hours or sixteen hours could be ideal, but if you can't do that, then do four hours. Then have a meal—not a big meal—that incorporates something like bread or pasta or some carbohydrate so that whatever you consume will settle into that matter and slowly process into your body. Drink it with food rather than drinking it on its own.

That way it becomes a portion of your life rather than, when you drink it on its own, a life unto itself. That is, build your relationship with the espresso, instead of the espresso being part of the meal—espresso becoming *part* of your life rather than an individual aspect of your life that you must have. I understand people in your time like to drink the watered-down version that you have alluded to, but if they're drinking that to stay awake or something like that, that's what it does, and it becomes a dependency rather than accomplishing what I've stated already.

I might add that for people who have strong constitutions, who are physically fit and have stomachs that are strong, you could conceivably drink espresso—a very tiny amount of it—if you needed a moment of inspiration. If you drank a tiny amount of it and sipped it slowly, essentially tasting it, that's what it would seem like. It wouldn't seem like you were sipping because it would be such a small amount. You could drink a teaspoon of it in a cup or in a very small container, and you could drink that over, say, fifteen minutes. It would be like tasting it over fifteen minutes only without food, and then it would provide the same effect. Again, drinking it once every other day would be the most frequent way you would do that. But you'd have to be fit; otherwise, if you're not in the best condition, it may not be good for you physically.

Yes, because it's a stimulant.

It's very strong, and it has acidic qualities.

Practice Support of One Another

If I were to talk to you on other subjects, what other subjects do you find most interesting, or what are you most connected to?

I can't even answer that question. That's a personality away from coffee. What I'm interested in, that's a mind thing. I'm a translator. I am interested; I am not interested. It is . . . [sighs].

I am asking what you would choose to talk about, but you're saying everything.

Yes. I am what I am, and it's what I do, and that's all I do.

Okay. What did you do before there was a human race?

I've always done this. The human race did not invent life. You have the capability to ask questions very well, but life went on without you. [Chuckles.]

[Laughs.] You mentioned that right now you are focused on things that had to do with this planet, so I just wondered . . .

Right now, at the moment you asked.

Oh, only in the moment I asked!

Right now is right now.

Ah! I get it. I do find some beings have sort of a mission of working with beings on Earth for the duration we're here, and I thought you were one of those.

No. But as we speak of these matters, I have access to what I need to know in order to communicate to you, as you are a representative of the human race, one who may or may not ever read or hear about what we are doing here.

Well, is there anything else that the coffee beings haven't expressed about themselves that I didn't ask about?

They wish to express a closing statement. You as human beings are feeling people. You do not adapt well to the spoken word. This may seem to be a contradiction in terms, since you like to speak—most of you—or express in sounds. Sounds are of course totally acceptable and perhaps are best expressed through something you call music, either made with others or on your own. You are surrounded by sound from other forms of life or even through interactions with Earth's own personality: wind, rain, and so on. Thus it is natural for you to make sounds. The natural communication, though, that you have is like all beings: It is through feeling. So it would be to your advantage to practice, with a friend or a loved one, understanding a feeling. Simply practice, not as a communication tool from one to one, but practice to support each other. "What does this physical feeling mean in my body?" It is important, because many times you are broadcasting, as individual humans, this overwhelming desire and need to communicate, and you struggle with words from one individual to another. But the best forms of communication for you will always be this broadcast, this emanation of feelings.

I don't know if you know this, but with that comes the sense of touch. Broadcast feelings touch everyone all the time. Sometimes with a good friend or a lover, you might also touch physically, but feelings make contact first. Practice your feelings so you know what they mean individually. Support each other in learning this so you can understand what the feelings others broadcast toward you really mean. Then you will know not only whether you are compatible with someone in order to be friends, but you will perhaps be able to help other people with the unspoken questions they are asking through their feelings. Good life.

Thank you very much.

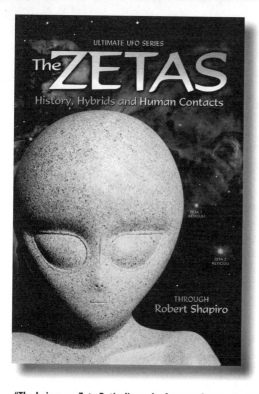

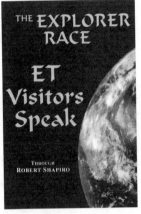

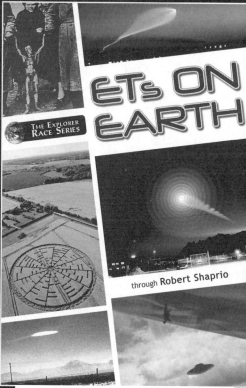

Shamanic Secrets Mastery Series

Speaks of Many Truths and Reveals the Mysteries through Robert Shapiro

T his book explores the heart and soul connection between humans and Mother Earth. Through that intimacy, miracles of healing and expanded awareness can flourish. To heal the planet and be healed as well, we can lovingly extend our energy selves out to the mountains and rivers and intimately bond with the Earth. Gestures and vision can activate our hearts to return us to a healthy, caring relationship with the land we live on. The character of some of Earth's most powerful features is explored and understood, with exercises given to connect us with those places. As we project our love and healing energy there, we help the Earth to heal from human destruction of the planet and its atmosphere. Dozens of photographs, maps and drawings assist the process in twenty-five chapters, which cover the Earth's more critical locations.

498 p. $19.95 ISBN 1-891824-12-0

L earn to understand the sacred nature of your own physical body and some of the magnificent gifts it offers you. When you work with your physical body in these new ways, you will discover not only its sacredness, but how it is compatible with Mother Earth, the animals, the plants, even the nearby planets, all of which you now recognize as being sacred in nature. It is important to feel the value of oneself physically before one can have any lasting physical impact on the world. If a physical energy does not feel good about itself, it will usually be resolved; other physical or spiritual energies will dissolve it because it is unnatural. The better you feel about your physical self when you do the work in the previous book as well as this one and the one to follow, the greater and more lasting will be the benevolent effect on your life, on the lives of those around you and ultimately on your planet and universe.

576 p. $25.00 ISBN 1-891824-29-5

S piritual mastery encompasses many different means to assimilate and be assimilated by the wisdom, feelings, flow, warmth, function and application of all beings in your world that you will actually contact in some way. A lot of spiritual mastery has been covered in different bits and pieces throughout all the books we've done. My approach to spiritual mastery, though, will be as grounded as possible in things that people on Earth can use— but it won't include the broad spectrum of spiritual mastery, like levitation and invisibility. I'm trying to teach you things that you can actually use and benefit from. My life is basically going to represent your needs, and it gets out the secrets that have been held back in a storylike fashion, so that it is more interesting."

—Speaks of Many Truths through Robert Shapiro

768 p. $29.95 ISBN 1-891824-58-9

Phone: 928-526-1345 or 1-800-450-0985 • Fax: 923-714-1132

⚡ *Light Technology* PUBLISHING

THE EXPLORER RACE SERIES

ZOOSH AND HIS FRIENDS THROUGH ROBERT SHAPIRO

THE SERIES: Humans—creators-in-training—have a purpose and destiny so heartwarmingly, profoundly glorious that it is almost unbelievable from our present dimensional perspective. Humans are great lightbeings from beyond this creation, gaining experience in dense physicality. This truth about the great human genetic experiment of the Explorer Race and the mechanics of creation is being revealed for the first time by Zoosh and his friends through superchannel Robert Shapiro. These books read like adventure stories as we follow the clues from this creation that we live in out to the Council of Creators and beyond.

❶ THE EXPLORER RACE

You individuals reading this are truly a result of the genetic experiment on Earth. You are beings who uphold the principles of the Explorer Race. The information in this book is designed to show you who you are and give you an evolutionary understanding of your past that will help you now. The key to empowerment in these days is to not know everything about your past, but to know what will help you now. Your number-one function right now is your status of Creator apprentice, which you have achieved through years and lifetimes of sweat. You are constantly being given responsibilities by the Creator that would normally be things that Creator would do. The responsibility and the destiny of the Explorer Race is not only to explore, but to create. 574 P. $25.00 ISBN 0-929385-38-1

❷ ETs and the EXPLORER RACE

In this book, Robert channels Joopah, a Zeta Reticulan now in the ninth dimension who continues the story of the great experiment—the Explorer Race—from the perspective of his civilization. The Zetas would have been humanity's future selves had not humanity re-created the past and changed the future. 237 P. $14.95 ISBN 0-929385-79-9

❸ EXPLORER RACE: ORIGINS and the NEXT 50 YEARS

This volume has so much information about who we are and where we came from—the source of male and female beings, the war of the sexes, the beginning of the linear mind, feelings, the origin of souls—it is a treasure trove. In addition, there is a section that relates to our near future—how the rise of global corporations and politics affects our future, how to use benevolent magic as a force of creation and how we will go out to the stars and affect other civilizations. Astounding information. 339 P. $14.95 ISBN 0-929385-95-0

❹ EXPLORER RACE: CREATORS and FRIENDS
The MECHANICS of CREATION

Now that you have a greater understanding of who you are in the larger sense, it is necessary to remind you of where you came from, the true magnificence of your being. You must understand that you are creators-in-training, and yet you were once a portion of Creator. One could certainly say, without being magnanimous, that you are still a portion of Creator, yet you are training for the individual responsibility of being a creator, to give your Creator a coffee break. This book will allow you to understand the vaster qualities and help you remember the nature of the desires that drive any creator, the responsibilities to which a creator must answer, the reaction a creator must have to consequences and the ultimate reward of any creator. 435 P. $19.95 ISBN 1-891824-01-5

❺ EXPLORER RACE: PARTICLE PERSONALITIES

All around you in every moment you are surrounded by the most magical and mystical beings. They are too small for you to see as single individuals, but in groups you know them as the physical matter of your daily life. Particles who might be considered either atoms or portions of atoms consciously view the vast spectrum of reality yet also have a sense of personal memory like your own linear memory. These particles remember where they have been and what they have done in their infinitely long lives. Some of the particles we hear from are Gold, Mountain Lion, Liquid Light, Uranium, the Great Pyramid's Capstone, This Orb's Boundary, Ice and Ninth-Dimensional Fire. 237 P. $14.95 ISBN 0-929385-97-7

❻ EXPLORER RACE and BEYOND

With a better idea of how creation works, we go back to the Creator's advisers and receive deeper and more profound explanations of the roots of the Explorer Race. The liquid Domain and the Double Diamond portal share lessons given to the roots on their way to meet the Creator of this universe, and finally the roots speak of their origins and their incomprehensibly long journey here. 360 P. $14.95 ISBN 1-891824-06-6

⚜ *Light Technology* PUBLISHING

Gaia Speaks

Gaia through Pepper Lewis

SACRED EARTH WISDOM

Many believe Earth to be sentient of feeling, but we are disconnected from her because we can't understand her vibrations and impressions. Gaia, the sentience of Earth speaks through Pepper Lewis, and teaches us how to listen and attune to Earth.

$19.95

Softcover, 393 PP.
ISBN: 978–1–891824–48–7

WISDOM FOR AN AWAKENING HUMANITY VOLUME II

Gaia is a living/learning/teaching library of everything that is, was, or might be related to Earth. Because you are Gaian, you are also a part of the great living library that is Gaia; you are a library within Gaia, one whose contents are a collection of ever-unfolding experiences. You are a lifetimes-old master storyteller, unraveling each tantalizing chapter.

$19.95

Softcover, 418 PP.
ISBN: 978–1–891824–51–7

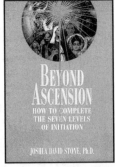
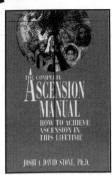
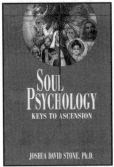

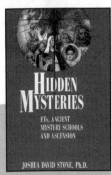
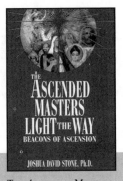
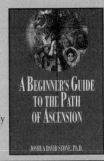

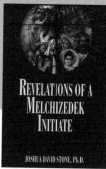

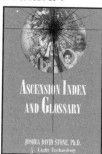

Kaballah and the Ascension

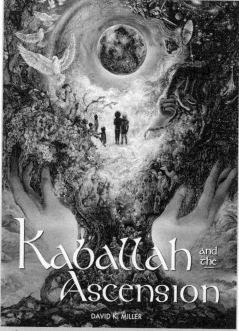

Kaballah and the Ascension

DAVID K. MILLER

$16.95 Softcover, 175 PP.
ISBN: 978-1-891824-82-1

"Throughout Western history, channeling has come to us in various forms, including mediumship, shamanism, fortunetelling, visionaries, and oracles. There is also a long history of channeling in *Kaballah*, the major branch of Jewish mysticism. I am intrigued by this, especially because I believe that there is now an urgent necessity for entering higher realms with our consciousness because of the impending changes on the planet; through these higher realms, new healing energies and insights can be brought down to assist us in these coming Earth changes.

I consider myself a student of spiritual and mystical consciousness interested in obtaining and maintaining higher levels of being, and although I myself do not represent any particular school of mysticism, I have found through more than twenty-five years of studying the *Kaballah* that it allows for a unique understanding of the concept of higher consciousness, or higher self, as a conduit to accessing these higher realms."

—David K. Miller

CHAPTERS INCLUDE:

- *Kaballah* and Soul Development
- Path Work
- Soul Psychology
- The Etheric Realm
- On Anchoring Energy
- Adam-Eve Kadmon
- Unlocking your Genetic Codes
- On Merkava Travel
- Merkava Meditation
- Being a Vessel of Light
- Genetic Thinking and *Merkava*
- Universal Love and the Null Zone
- On Accelerating Your Activation
- Ascension and the Tree of Life

Phone: 928-526-1345 or 1-800-450-0985 • Fax: 928-714-1132

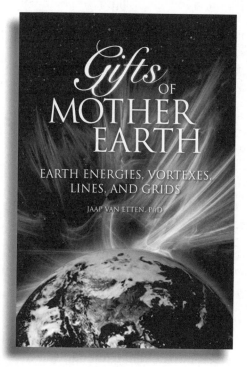

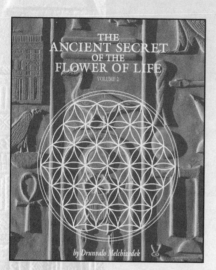

☧ Light Technology PUBLISHING

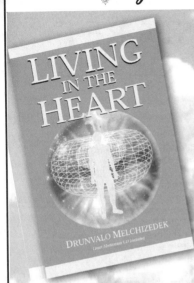

A New Book by
Drunvalo Melchizedek

LIVING IN THE HEART

Includes a CD with Heart Meditation by
Drunvalo Melchizedek

$25 with CD
Softcover 120 P.
ISBN 1-891824-43-0

"Long ago we humans used a form of communication and sensing that did not involve the brain in any way; rather, it came from a sacred place within our heart. What good would it do to find this place again in a world where the greatest religion is science and the logic of the mind? Don't I know this world where emotions and feelings are second-class citizens? Yes, I do. But my teachers have asked me to remind you who you really are. You are more than a human being, much more. For within your heart is a place, a sacred place where the world can literally be remade through conscious cocreation. If you give me permission, I will show you what has been shown to me."

- Beginning with the Mind
- Seeing in the Darkness
- Learning from Indigenous Tribes
- The Sacred Space of the Heart
- The Unity of Heaven and Earth

- Leaving the Mind and Entering the Heart
- The Sacred Space of the Heart Meditation
- The Mer-Ka-Ba and the Sacred Space of the Heart
- Conscious Cocreation from the Heart Connected to the Mind

Drunvalo Melchizedek has been studying pure consciousness and human potential for almost forty years. His focus on the rediscovery of the human lightbody, the Mer-Ka-Ba and the way Sacred Geometry is inherent within the lightbody and all of creation is shared through workshops and books as he has brought his vision of the Flower of Life and the Mer-Ka-Ba to the world.

Now his new work, *Living in the Heart*, with the techniques that lead you into the Sacred Space of the Heart, goes even deeper into the possibilities of human potential and the creation process itself. Within these pages, Drunvalo shares his knowledge and tells you exactly how to achieve this ancient state of consciousness so that, finally, what you dream in your heart you can make real in your everyday life; a beautiful, abundant life and ascension into the higher worlds become a natural sequence of living in your heart. Join Drunvalo and be part of the large group of people who have found the joy of living in the space where you and God are one.

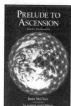

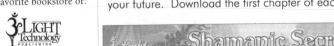